P9-CJK-123

PYTHON PROGRAMMING
AN INTRODUCTION TO COMPUTER SCIENCE

SECOND EDITION

John M. Zelle
Wartburg College

Franklin, Beedle & Associates Inc. ✛ 22462 SW Washington St. ✛ Sherwood, Oregon 97140 ✛ 503/625-4445 ✛ www.fbeedle.com

President and Publisher   Jim Leisy (jimleisy@fbeedle.com)
Production   TomSumner
Associate   Jaron Ayres

Printed in the United States of America

Names of all products herein are used for identification purposes only and are trademarks and/or registered trademarks of their respective owners. Franklin, Beedle & Associates Inc. makes no claim of ownership or corporate association with the products or companies that own them.

©2010 Franklin, Beedle & Associates Incorporated. No part of this book may be reproduced, stored in a retrieval system, transmitted, or transcribed, in any form or by any means—electronic, mechanical, telepathic, photocopying, recording, or otherwise—without prior written permission of the publisher. Requests for permission should be addressed as follows:

Rights and Permissions
Franklin, Beedle & Associates Incorporated
8536 SW St. Helens Drive, Suite D
Wilsonville, Oregon 97070

Library of Congress Cataloging-in-Publication data

Zelle, John M.
  Python programming : an introduction to computer science / John M. Zelle. -- 2nd ed.
     p. cm.
  Includes bibliographical references and index.
    ISBN 978-1-59028-241-0 (alk. paper)
  1. Python (Computer program language) I. Title.
  QA76.73.P98Z98 2010
  005.13'3--dc22
                        2010013947

Contents

Chapter 1   Computers and Programs   1

Chapter 2   Writing Simple Programs   27

Chapter 6   Defining Functions   167

Chapter 7   Decision Structures   201

Chapter 8   Loop Structures and Booleans   233

Chapter 9   Simulation and Design   267

Chapter 10   Defining Classes   297

Chapter 11 Data Collections   339

Chapter 12 Object-Oriented Design   385

Foreword

When the publisher first sent me a draft of this book, I was immediately excited. Disguised as a Python textbook, it is really an introduction to the fine art of programming, using Python merely as the preferred medium for beginners. This is how I have always imagined Python would be most useful in education: not as the only language, but as a first language, just as in art one might start learning to draw using a pencil rather than trying to paint in oil right away.

The author mentions in his preface that Python is near-ideal as a first programming language, without being a "toy language." As the creator of Python I don't want to take full credit for this: Python was derived from ABC, a language designed to teach programming in the early 1980s by Lambert Meertens, Leo Geurts, and others at CWI (National Research Institute for Mathematics and Computer Science) in Amsterdam. If I added anything to their work, it was making Python into a non-toy language, with a broad user base and an extensive collection of standard and third-party application modules.

I have no formal teaching experience, so I may not be qualified to judge its educational effectiveness. Still, as a programmer with nearly 30 years experience, reading through the chapters I am continuously delighted by the book's clear explanations of difficult concepts. I also like the many good excercises and questions which both test understanding and encourage thinking about deeper issues.

Reader of this book, congratulations! You will be well rewarded for studying Python. I promise you'll have fun along the way, and I hope you won't forget your first language once you have become a proficient software developer.

—Guido van Rossum

Preface

This book is designed to be used as a primary textbook in a college-level first course in computing. It takes a fairly traditional approach, emphasizing problem-solving, design, and programming as the core skills of computer science. However, these ideas are illustrated using a non-traditional language, namely Python.

In my teaching experience, I have found that many students have difficulty mastering the basic concepts of computer science and programming. Part of this difficulty can be blamed on the complexity of the languages and tools that are most often used in introductory courses. Consequently, this textbook was written with a single overarching goal: to introduce fundamental computer science concepts as simply as possible without being simplistic. Using Python is central to this goal.

Traditional systems languages such as C++, Ada, and Java evolved to solve problems in large-scale programming, where the primary emphasis is on structure and discipline. They were not designed to make writing small- or medium-scale programs easy. The recent rise in popularity of scripting (sometimes called "agile") languages, such as Python, suggests an alternate approach. Python is very flexible and makes experimentation easy. Solutions to simple problems are simply and elegantly expressed. Python provides a great laboratory for the neophyte programmer.

Python has a number of features that make it a near-perfect choice as a first programming language. The basic structures are simple, clean, and well designed, which allows students to focus on the primary skills of algorithmic thinking and program design without getting bogged down in arcane language details. Concepts learned in Python carry over directly to subsequent study of systems languages such as C++ and Java. But Python is not a "toy language." It is a real-world production language that is freely available for virtually every programming platform and comes standard with its own easy-to-use integrated programming environment. The best part is that Python makes learning to program fun again.

Although I use Python as the language, teaching Python is not the main point of this book. Rather, Python is used to illustrate fundamental principles of design and programming that apply in any language or computing environment. In some places, I have purposely avoided certain Python features and idioms that are not generally found in other languages. There are many good books about Python on the market; this book is intended as an introduction to computing.

Besides using Python, there are other features of this book designed to make it a gentler introduction to computer science. Some of these features include:

- Extensive use of computer graphics. Students love working on programs that include graphics. This book presents a simple-to-use graphics package (provided as a Python module) that allows students both to learn the principles of computer graphics and to practice object-oriented concepts without the complexity inherent in a full-blown graphics library and event-driven programming.

- Interesting examples. The book is packed with complete programming examples to solve real problems.

- Readable prose. The narrative style of the book introduces key computer science concepts in a natural way as an outgrowth of a developing discussion. I have tried to avoid random facts or tangentially related sidebars.

- Flexible spiral coverage. Since the goal of the book is to present concepts simply, each chapter is organized so that students are introduced to new ideas in a gradual way, giving them time to assimilate an increasing level of detail as they progress. Ideas that take more time to master are introduced in early chapters and reinforced in later chapters.

- Just-in-time object coverage. The proper place for the introduction of object-oriented techniques is an ongoing controversy in computer science education. This book is neither strictly "objects early" nor "objects late," but gradually introduces object concepts after a brief initial grounding in the basics of imperative programming. Students learn multiple design techniques, including top-down (functional decomposition), spiral (prototyping), and object-oriented methods. Additionally, the textbook material is flexible enough to accommodate other approaches.

- Extensive end-of-chapter problems. Exercises at the end of every chapter provide ample opportunity for students to both reinforce chapter material and practice new programming skills.

Changes in the Second Edition

The first edition of the textbook has aged gracefully, and the approach it takes remains just as relevant now as when it was first published. Fundamental principles do not change; however, the technology environment does. With the release of Python 3.0, updates to the original material became necessary. This second edition is basically the same as the original textbook, except that it has been updated to use Python 3. Virtually every program example in the book had to be modified for the new Python. Additionally, to accommodate certain changes in Python (notably the removal of the string library), the material has been reordered slightly to cover object terminology before discussing string processing. A beneficial side-effect of this change is an even earlier introduction of computer graphics to pique student interest.

Some new exercises have also been added to this edition, including a few image-processing examples. In general, though, I have tried to preserve as much as possible of the original book with its emphasis on simplicity and readability. In my teaching career, I have seen firsthand how new editions of textbooks tend to add ever more "features" in an attempt to please every potential user. Eventually these once-excellent resources become overly thick, disjointed, and unusable. I hope I have avoided this pitfall.

Coverage Options

In keeping with the goal of simplicity, I have tried to limit inclusion of material that would not be covered in a first course. Still, there is probably more material here than can be covered in a typical one-semester introduction. My classes cover virtually all of the material in the first twelve chapters in order, though not necessarily covering every section in depth. One or two topics from Chapter 13 ("Algorithm Design and Recursion") are generally interspersed at appropriate places during the term.

Recognizing that different instructors prefer to approach topics in other orders, I have tried to keep the material relatively flexible. Chapters 1–4 ("Computers and Programs," "Writing Simple Programs," "Computing with Numbers," "Objects and Graphics") are essential introduction and should probably be covered in order. The initial portions of Chapter 5 ("Sequences: Strings, Lists, and Files") on string processing are also fundamental, but the later topics such as string formatting and file processing can be delayed until needed later on. Chapters 6–8 ("Defining Functions, Descision Structures," and "Loop Structures and Booleans") are designed to stand independently and can be taken in virtually any order. Chapters 9–12 on design approaches are written to be taken in order, but the material in Chapter 11 (Data Collections) could easily be moved earlier, should the instructor want to cover lists (arrays) before various design techniques. Instructors wishing to emphasize object-oriented design need not spend much time on Chapter 9. Chapter 13 contains more advanced material that may be covered at the end or interpersed at various places throughout the course.

Acknowledgments

My approach to CS1 has been influenced over the years by many fine textbooks that I have read and used for classes. Much that I have learned from those books has undoubtedly found its way into these pages. There are a few specific authors whose approaches have been so important that I feel they deserve special mention. A.K. Dewdney has always had a knack for finding simple examples that illustrate complex issues; I have borrowed a few of those and given them new legs in Python. I also owe a debt to wonderful textbooks from both Owen Astrachan and Cay Horstmann. The graphics library I introduce in Chapter 4 was directly inspired by my experience teaching with a similar library designed by Horstmann. I also learned much about teaching computer science from Nell Dale, for whom I was fortunate enough to serve as a TA when I was a graduate student that the University of Texas.

Many people have contributed either directly or indirectly to the production of this book. I am grateful to Dave Reed at Capital Univeristy, who used early versions of the first edition and offered numerous insightful suggestions. Ernie Ackermann test drove this new edition at Mary Washington College. I have also received much help and encouragement from my colleagues at Wartburg College: Lynn Olson, my department chair who offered unflagging support; Josef Breutzmann, who supplied many project ideas; and Terry Letsche, who prepared PowerPoint slides for the first edition. I also want to acknowledge the fine folks at Franklin, Beedle, and Associates, especially Jim Leisy, Tom Sumner, and Jaron Ayres, who turned my pet project into a real textbook.

I want to thank the following individuals who read or commented on the manuscript for the first edition: Rus May, Morehead State University; Carolyn Miller, North Carolina State University; Guido Van Rossum, Google; Jim Sager, California State University, Chico; Christine Shannon, Centre College; Paul Tymann, Rochester Institute of Technology; Suzanne Westbrook, University of Arizona.

A special thanks also goes out to all my students, who have taught me so much about teaching, and to Wartburg College for giving me sabbatical support to work on both editions of the book. Last, but most importantly, I acknowledge my wife, Lib Bingham, who has served as editor, advisor, and morale booster while putting up with me during my writing spells.

—*JMZ*

Chapter 1

Computers and Programs

Objectives

- To understand the respective roles of hardware and software in a computing system.

- To learn what computer scientists study and the techniques that they use.

- To understand the basic design of a modern computer.

- To understand the form and function of computer programming languages.

- To begin using the Python programming language.

- To learn about chaotic models and their implications for computing.

1.1 The Universal Machine

Almost everyone has used a computer at one time or another. Perhaps you have played computer games or used a computer to write a paper or balance your checkbook. Computers are used to predict the weather, design airplanes, make movies, run businesses, perform financial transactions, and control factories.

Have you ever stopped to wonder what exactly a computer is? How can one device perform so many different tasks? These basic questions are the starting point for learning about computers and computer programming.

A modern computer can be defined as "a machine that stores and manipulates information under the control of a changeable program." There are two

1

key elements to this definition. The first is that computers are devices for manipulating information. This means we can put information into a computer, and it can transform the information into new, useful forms, and then output or display the information for our interpretation.

Computers are not the only machines that manipulate information. When you use a simple calculator to add up a column of numbers, you are entering information (the numbers) and the calculator is processing the information to compute a running sum which is then displayed. Another simple example is a gas pump. As you fill your tank, the pump uses certain inputs: the current price of gas per gallon and signals from a sensor that reads the rate of gas flowing into your car. The pump transforms this input into information about how much gas you took and how much money you owe.

We would not consider either the calculator or the gas pump as full-fledged computers, although modern versions of these devices may actually contain embedded computers. They are different from computers in that they are built to perform a single, specific task. This is where the second part of our definition comes into the picture: Computers operate under the control of a changeable program. What exactly does this mean?

A *computer program* is a detailed, step-by-step set of instructions telling a computer exactly what to do. If we change the program, then the computer performs a different sequence of actions, and hence, performs a different task. It is this flexibility that allows your PC to be at one moment a word processor, at the next moment a financial planner, and later on, an arcade game. The machine stays the same, but the program controlling the machine changes.

Every computer is just a machine for *executing* (carrying out) programs. There are many different kinds of computers. You might be familiar with Macintoshes and PCs, but there are literally thousands of other kinds of computers both real and theoretical. One of the remarkable discoveries of computer science is the realization that all of these different computers have the same power; with suitable programming, each computer can basically do all the things that any other computer can do. In this sense, the PC that you might have sitting on your desk is really a universal machine. It can do anything you want it to do, provided you can describe the task to be accomplished in sufficient detail. Now that's a powerful machine!

1.2 Program Power

You have already learned an important lesson of computing: *Software* (programs) rules the *hardware* (the physical machine). It is the software that determines what any computer can do. Without software, computers would just be expensive paperweights. The process of creating software is called *programming*, and that is the main focus of this book.

Computer programming is a challenging activity. Good programming requires an ability to see the big picture while paying attention to minute detail. Not everyone has the talent to become a first-class programmer, just as not everyone has the skills to be a professional athlete. However, virtually anyone *can* learn how to program computers. With some patience and effort on your part, this book will help you to become a programmer.

There are lots of good reasons to learn programming. Programming is a fundamental part of computer science and is, therefore, important to anyone interested in becoming a computer professional. But others can also benefit from the experience. Computers have become a commonplace tool in our society. Understanding the strengths and limitations of this tool requires an understanding of programming. Non-programmers often feel they are slaves of their computers. Programmers, however, are truly in control. If you want to become a more intelligent user of computers, then this book is for you.

Programming can also be loads of fun. It is an intellectually engaging activity that allows people to express themselves through useful and sometimes remarkably beautiful creations. Believe it or not, many people actually write computer programs as a hobby. Programming also develops valuable problem-solving skills, especially the ability to analyze complex systems by reducing them to interactions of understandable subsystems.

As you probably know, programmers are in great demand. More than a few liberal arts majors have turned a couple of computer programming classes into a lucrative career option. Computers are so commonplace in the business world today that the ability to understand and program computers might just give you the edge over your competition, regardless of your occupation.

1.3 What is Computer Science?

You might be surprised to learn that computer science is not the study of computers. A famous computer scientist named Edsger Dijkstra once quipped that computers are to computer science what telescopes are to astronomy. The computer is an important tool in computer science, but it is not itself the object of study. Since a computer can carry out any process that we can describe, the real question is *What processes can we describe?* Put another way, the fundamental question of computer science is simply *What can be computed?* Computer scientists use numerous techniques of investigation to answer this question. The three main ones are *design*, *analysis*, and *experimentation*.

One way to demonstrate that a particular problem can be solved is to actually design a solution. That is, we develop a step-by-step process for achieving the desired result. Computer scientists call this an *algorithm*. That's a fancy word that basically means "recipe." The design of algorithms is one of the most important facets of computer science. In this book you will find techniques for designing and implementing algorithms.

One weakness of design is that it can only answer the question *What is computable?* in the positive. If I can devise an algorithm, then the problem is solvable. However, failing to find an algorithm does not mean that a problem is unsolvable. It may mean that I'm just not smart enough, or I haven't hit upon the right idea yet. This is where analysis comes in.

Analysis is the process of examining algorithms and problems mathematically. Computer scientists have shown that some seemingly simple problems are not solvable by *any* algorithm. Other problems are *intractable*. The algorithms that solve these problems take too long or require too much memory to be of practical value. Analysis of algorithms is an important part of computer science; throughout this book we will touch on some of the fundamental principles. Chapter 13 has examples of unsolvable and intractable problems.

Some problems are too complex or ill-defined to lend themselves to analysis. In such cases, computer scientists rely on experimentation; they actually implement systems and then study the resulting behavior. Even when theoretical analysis is done, experimentation is often needed in order to verify and refine the analysis. For most problems, the bottom line is whether a working, reliable system can be built. Often we require empirical testing of the system to determine that this bottom line has been met. As you begin writing your own programs, you will get plenty of opportunities to observe your solutions in action.

I have defined computer science in terms of designing, analyzing, and evaluating algorithms, and this is certainly the core of the academic discipline. These days, however, computer scientists are involved in far-flung activities, all of which fall under the general umbrella of computing. Some example areas include networking, human-computer interaction, artificial intelligence, compu-

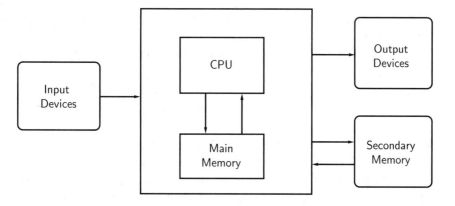

Figure 1.1: Functional view of a computer

tational science (using powerful computers to model scientific data), databases, software engineering, web and multimedia design, management information systems, and computer security. Wherever computing is done, the skills and knowledge of computer science are being applied.

1.4 Hardware Basics

You don't have to know all the details of how a computer works to be a successful programmer, but understanding the underlying principles will help you master the steps we go through to put our programs into action. It's a bit like driving a car. Knowing a little about internal combustion engines helps to explain why you have to do things like fill the gas tank, start the engine, step on the accelerator, etc. You could learn to drive by just memorizing what to do, but a little more knowledge makes the whole process much more understandable. Let's take a moment to "look under the hood" of your computer.

Although different computers can vary significantly in specific details, at a higher level all modern digital computers are remarkably similar. Figure 1.1 shows a functional view of a computer. The *central processing unit* (CPU) is the "brain" of the machine. This is where all the basic operations of the computer are carried out. The CPU can perform simple arithmetic operations like adding two numbers and can also do logical operations like testing to see if two numbers are equal.

The memory stores programs and data. The CPU can only directly access information that is stored in *main memory* (called RAM for *Random Access Mem-*

ory). Main memory is fast, but it is also volatile. That is, when the power is turned off, the information in the memory is lost. Thus, there must also be some secondary memory that provides more permanent storage. In a modern personal computer, this is usually some sort of magnetic medium such as a hard disk (also called a hard drive). Optical media such as CD (compact disc) and DVD (digital versatile disc) and flash memory devices such as USB memory "sticks" are also common.

Humans interact with the computer through input and output devices. You are probably familiar with common devices such as a keyboard, mouse, and monitor (video screen). Information from input devices is processed by the CPU and may be shuffled off to the main or secondary memory. Similarly, when information needs to be displayed, the CPU sends it to one or more output devices.

So what happens when you fire up your favorite game or word processing program? First, the instructions that comprise the program are copied from the (more) permanent secondary memory into the main memory of the computer. Once the instructions are loaded, the CPU starts executing the program.

Technically the CPU follows a process called the *fetch-execute cycle*. The first instruction is retrieved from memory, decoded to figure out what it represents, and the appropriate action carried out. Then the next instruction is fetched, decoded, and executed. The cycle continues, instruction after instruction. This is really all the computer does from the time that you turn it on until you turn it off again: fetch, decode, execute. It doesn't seem very exciting, does it? But the computer can execute this stream of simple instructions with blazing speed, zipping through millions of instructions each second. Put enough simple instructions together in just the right way, and the computer does amazing things.

1.5 Programming Languages

Remember that a program is just a sequence of instructions telling a computer what to do. Obviously, we need to provide those instructions in a language that a computer can understand. It would be nice if we could just tell a computer what to do using our native language, like they do in science fiction movies. ("Computer, how long will it take to reach planet Alphalpha at maximum warp?") Unfortunately, despite the continuing efforts of many top-flight computer scientists (including your author), designing a computer to fully understand human language is still an unsolved problem.

Even if computers could understand us, human languages are not very well suited for describing complex algorithms. Natural language is fraught with ambiguity and imprecision. For example, if I say: "I saw the man in the park with the telescope," did I have the telescope, or did the man? And who was in the park? We understand each other most of the time only because all humans share a vast store of common knowledge and experience. Even then, miscommunication is commonplace.

Computer scientists have gotten around this problem by designing notations for expressing computations in an exact and unambiguous way. These special notations are called *programming languages*. Every structure in a programming language has a precise form (its *syntax*) and a precise meaning (its *semantics*). A programming language is something like a code for writing down the instructions that a computer will follow. In fact, programmers often refer to their programs as *computer code*, and the process of writing an algorithm in a programming language is called *coding*.

Python is one example of a programming language. It is the language that we will use throughout this book.[1] You may have heard of some other languages, such as C++, Java, Perl, Scheme, or BASIC. Although these languages differ in many details, they all share the property of having well-defined, unambiguous syntax and semantics. Languages themselves tend to evolve over time.

All of the languages mentioned above are examples of *high-level* computer languages. Although they are precise, they are designed to be used and understood by humans. Strictly speaking, computer hardware can only understand a very low-level language known as *machine language*.

Suppose we want the computer to add two numbers. The instructions that the CPU actually carries out might be something like this:

```
load the number from memory location 2001 into the CPU
load the number from memory location 2002 into the CPU
add the two numbers in the CPU
store the result into location 2003
```

This seems like a lot of work to add two numbers, doesn't it? Actually, it's even more complicated than this because the instructions and numbers are represented in *binary* notation (as sequences of 0s and 1s).

In a high-level language like Python, the addition of two numbers can be expressed more naturally: c = a + b. That's a lot easier for us to understand,

---

[1]Specifically, the book was written using Python version 3.0. If you have an earlier version of Python installed on your computer, you should upgrade to the latest stable 3.x version to try out the examples.

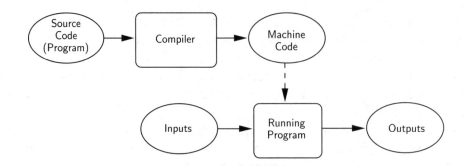

Figure 1.2: Compiling a high-level language

but we need some way to translate the high-level language into the machine language that the computer can execute. There are two ways to do this: a high-level language can either be *compiled* or *interpreted*.

A *compiler* is a complex computer program that takes another program written in a high-level language and translates it into an equivalent program in the machine language of some computer. Figure 1.2 shows a block diagram of the compiling process. The high-level program is called *source code*, and the resulting *machine code* is a program that the computer can directly execute. The dashed line in the diagram represents the execution of the machine code (also known as "running the program").

An *interpreter* is a program that simulates a computer that understands a high-level language. Rather than translating the source program into a machine language equivalent, the interpreter analyzes and executes the source code instruction by instruction as necessary. Figure 1.3 illustrates the process.

The difference between interpreting and compiling is that compiling is a one-shot translation; once a program is compiled, it may be run over and over again without further need for the compiler or the source code. In the interpreted case, the interpreter and the source are needed every time the program runs. Compiled programs tend to be faster, since the translation is done once and for all, but interpreted languages lend themselves to a more flexible programming environment as programs can be developed and run interactively.

The translation process highlights another advantage that high-level languages have over machine language: *portability*. The machine language of a computer is created by the designers of the particular CPU. Each kind of computer has its own machine language. A program for an Intel Core Duo won't run directly on a different CPU. On the other hand, a program written in a high-level language can be run on many different kinds of computers as long as there is a

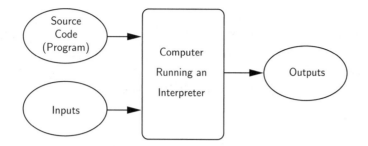

Figure 1.3: Interpreting a high-level language

suitable compiler or interpreter (which is just another program). As a result, I can run the exact same Python program on my laptop and my PDA; even though they have different CPUs, they both sport a Python interpreter.

1.6 The Magic of Python

Now that you have all the technical details, it's time to start having fun with Python. The ultimate goal is to make the computer do our bidding. To this end, we will write programs that control the computational processes inside the machine. You have already seen that there is no magic in this process, but in some ways programming *feels* like magic.

The computational processes inside the computer are like magical spirits that we can harness for our work. Unfortunately, those spirits only understand a very arcane language that we do not know. What we need is a friendly Genie that can direct the spirits to fulfill our wishes. Our Genie is a Python interpreter. We can give instructions to the Python interpreter, and it directs the underlying spirits to carry out our demands. We communicate with the Genie through a special language of spells and incantations (i.e., Python). The best way to start learning about Python is to let our Genie out of the bottle and try some spells.

You can start the Python interpreter in an interactive mode and type in some commands to see what happens. When you first start the interpreter program, you may see something like the following:

```
Python 3.0 (r30:67503, Jan 19 2009, 09:57:10)
[GCC 4.1.3 20070929 (prerelease) (Ubuntu 4.1.2-16ubuntu2)] on linux2
Type "help", "copyright", "credits" or "license" for more information.
>>>
```

The $>>>$ is a Python *prompt* indicating that our Genie (the Python interpreter) is waiting for us to give it a command. In programming languages, a complete command is called a *statement*. An interactive environment for interacting with an interpreter is called a *command shell* or just *shell* for short.

Here is a sample interaction with a Python shell:

```
>>> print("Hello, World!")
Hello, World!
>>> print(2 + 3)
5
>>> print("2 + 3 =", 2 + 3)
2 + 3 = 5
```

Here I have tried out three examples using the Python `print` statement. The first statement asks Python to display the literal phrase `Hello, World!`. Python responds on the next line by printing the phrase. The second `print` statement asks Python to print the sum of 2 and 3. The third `print` combines these two ideas. Python prints the part in quotes `2 + 3 =` followed by the result of adding 2 + 3, which is 5.

This kind of shell interaction is a great way to try out new things in Python. Snippets of interactive sessions are sprinkled throughout this book. When you see the Python prompt $>>>$ in an example, that should tip you off that an interactive session is being illustrated. It's a good idea to fire up your own Python shell and try the examples.

Usually we want to move beyond one-line snippets and execute an entire sequence of statements. Python lets us put a sequence of statements together to create a brand-new command or *function*. Here is an example of creating a new function called `hello`:

```
>>> def hello():
        print("Hello")
        print("Computers are fun!")


>>>
```

The first line tells Python that we are *defining* a new function and we are naming it `hello`. The following lines are indented to show that they are part of the `hello` function. (Note: some shells will print ellipses ["..."] at the beginning of the indented lines). The blank line at the end (obtained by hitting the <Enter> key twice) lets Python know that the definition is finished, and the shell responds with another prompt. Notice that typing the definition did not cause Python to print anything yet. We have told Python what *should* happen when the `hello` function is used as a command; we haven't actually asked Python to perform it yet.

A function is *invoked* (or *called*) by typing its name followed by parentheses. Here's what happens when we use our `hello` command:

```
>>> hello()
Hello
Computers are fun!
>>>
```

Do you see what this does? The two `print` statements from the `hello` function definition are executed in sequence.

You may be wondering about the parentheses in the definition and use of `hello`. Commands can have changeable parts called *parameters* (also called *arguments*) that are placed within the parentheses. Let's look at an example of a customized greeting using a parameter. First the definition:

```
>>> def greet(person):
        print("Hello", person)
        print("How are you?")
```

Now we can use our customized greeting.

```
>>> greet("John")
Hello John
How are you?
>>> greet("Emily")
Hello Emily
How are you?
>>>
```

Can you see what is happening here? When using `greet` we can send different names to customize the result. You might also notice that this looks similar to the `print` statements from before. In Python, `print` is an example of a built-in function. When we call the `print` function, the parameters in the parentheses tell the function what to print.

We will discuss parameters in detail later on. For the time being the important thing to remember is that the parentheses must be included after the function name whenever we want to execute a function. This is true even when no parameters given. For example, you can create a blank line of output using print without any parameters.

```
>>> print()

>>>
```

But if you type just the name of the function, omitting the parentheses, the function will not actually execute. Instead, an interactive Python session will show some output indicating what function that name refers to, as this interaction shows:

```
>>> greet
<function greet at 0x8393aec>
>>> print
<built-in function print>
```

The funny text 0x8393aec is the location (address) in computer memory where the greet function definition happens to be stored. If you are trying this out on your own computer, you will almost certainly see a different address.

One problem with entering functions interactively into a Python shell as we did with the hello and greet examples is that the definitions are lost when we quit the shell. If we want to use them again the next time, we have to type them all over again. Programs are usually created by typing definitions into a separate file called a *module* or *script*. This file is saved on a disk so that it can be used over and over again.

A module file is just a text file, and you can create one using any program for editing text, like a notepad or word processor program (provided you save your program as a "plain text" file). A special type of program known as a *programming environment* simplifies the process. A programming environment is specifically designed to help programmers write programs and includes features such as automatic indenting, color highlighting, and interactive development. The standard Python distribution includes a programming environment called IDLE that you may use for working on the programs in this book.

Let's illustrate the use of a module file by writing and running a complete program. Our program will illustrate a mathematical concept known as chaos. Here is the program as we would type it into IDLE or some other editor and save in a module file:

```
# File: chaos.py
```

```
# A simple program illustrating chaotic behavior.

def main():
    print("This program illustrates a chaotic function")
    x = eval(input("Enter a number between 0 and 1: "))
    for i in range(10):
        x = 3.9 * x * (1 - x)
        print(x)

main()
```

This file should be saved with the name chaos.py. The .py extension indicates that this is a Python module. You can see that this particular example contains lines to define a new function called main. (Programs are often placed in a function called main.) The last line of the file is the command to invoke this function. Don't worry if you don't understand what main actually does; we will discuss it in the next section. The point here is that once we have a program in a module file, we can run it any time we want.

This program can be run in a number of different ways that depend on the actual operating system and programming environment that you are using. If you are using a windowing system, you can run a Python program by clicking (or double-clicking) on the module file's icon. In a command line situation, you might type a command like python chaos.py. If you are using IDLE (or another programming environment) you can run a program by opening it in the editor and then selecting a command like *import*, *run*, or *execute*.

One method that should always work is to start a Python shell and then import the file. Here is how that looks:

```
>>> import chaos
This program illustrates a chaotic function
Enter a number between 0 and 1: .25
0.73125
0.76644140625
0.698135010439
0.82189581879
0.570894019197
0.955398748364
0.166186721954
0.540417912062
```

```
0.9686289303
0.118509010176
>>>
```

Typing the first line import chaos tells the Python interpreter to load the chaos module from the file chaos.py into main memory. Notice that I did not include the .py extension on the import line; Python assumes the module will have a .py extension.

As Python imports the module file, each line executes. It's just as if we had typed them one-by-one at the interactive Python prompt. The def in the module causes Python to create the main function. When Python encounters the last line of the module, the main function is invoked, thus running our program. The running program asks the user to enter a number between 0 and 1 (in this case, I typed ".25") and then prints out a series of 10 numbers.

When you first import a module file in this way, Python creates a companion file with a .pyc extension. In this example, Python creates another file on the disk called chaos.pyc. This is an intermediate file used by the Python interpreter. Technically, Python uses a hybrid compiling/interpreting process. The Python source in the module file is compiled into more primitive instructions called *byte code*. This byte code (the .pyc) file is then interpreted. Having a .pyc file available makes importing a module faster the second time around. However, you may delete the byte code files if you wish to save disk space; Python will automatically recreate them as needed.

A module needs to be imported into a session only once. After the module has been loaded, we can run the program again by asking Python to execute the main command. We do this by using a special dot notation. Typing chaos.main() tells Python to invoke the main function in the chaos module. Continuing with our example, here is how it looks when we rerun the program with .26 as the input:

```
>>> chaos.main()
This program illustrates a chaotic function
Enter a number between 0 and 1: .26
0.75036
0.73054749456
0.767706625733
0.6954993339
0.825942040734
0.560670965721
```

```
0.960644232282
0.147446875935
0.490254549376
0.974629602149
>>>
```

1.7   Inside a Python Program

The output from the chaos program may not look very exciting, but it illustrates a very interesting phenomenon known to physicists and mathematicians. Let's take a look at this program line by line and see what it does. Don't worry about understanding every detail right away; we will be returning to all of these ideas in the next chapter.

The first two lines of the program start with the # character:

```
# File: chaos.py
# A simple program illustrating chaotic behavior.
```

These lines are called *comments*. They are intended for human readers of the program and are ignored by Python. The Python interpreter always skips any text from the pound sign (#) through the end of a line.

The next line of the program begins the definition of a function called main:

```
def main():
```

Strictly speaking, it would not be necessary to create a main function. Since the lines of a module are executed as they are loaded, we could have written our program without this definition. That is, the module could have looked like this:

```
# File: chaos.py
# A simple program illustrating chaotic behavior.

print("This program illustrates a chaotic function")
x = eval(input("Enter a number between 0 and 1: "))
for i in range(10):
    x = 3.9 * x * (1 - x)
    print(x)
```

This version is a bit shorter, but it is customary to place the instructions that comprise a program inside of a function called main. One immediate benefit of this approach was illustrated above; it allows us to run the program by simply invoking chaos.main(). We don't have to restart the Python shell in order to run it again, which would be necessary in the main-less case.

The first line inside of main is really the beginning of our program.

```
print("This program illustrates a chaotic function")
```

This line causes Python to print a message introducing the program when it runs.

Take a look at the next line of the program:

```
x = eval(input("Enter a number between 0 and 1: "))
```

Here x is an example of a *variable*. A variable is used to give a name to a value so that we can refer to it at other points in the program.

The entire line is a statement to get some input from the user. There's quite a bit going on in this line, and we'll discuss the details in the next chapter; for now, you just need to know what it accomplishes. When Python gets to this statement, it displays the quoted message Enter a number between 0 and 1: and then pauses, waiting for the user to type something on the keyboard and press the <Enter> key. The value that the user types in is then stored as the variable x. In the first example shown above, the user entered .25, which becomes the value of x.

The next statement is an example of a *loop*.

```
 for i in range(10):
```

A loop is a device that tells Python to do the same thing over and over again. This particular loop says to do something 10 times. The lines indented underneath the loop heading are the statements that are done 10 times. These form the *body* of the loop.

```
x = 3.9 * x * (1 - x)
print(x)
```

The effect of the loop is exactly the same as if we had written the body of the loop 10 times:

```
x = 3.9 * x * (1 - x)
print(x)
```

```
x = 3.9 * x * (1 - x)
print(x)
x = 3.9 * x * (1 - x)
print(x)
x = 3.9 * x * (1 - x)
print(x)
x = 3.9 * x * (1 - x)
print(x)
x = 3.9 * x * (1 - x)
print(x)
x = 3.9 * x * (1 - x)
print(x)
x = 3.9 * x * (1 - x)
print(x)
x = 3.9 * x * (1 - x)
print(x)
x = 3.9 * x * (1 - x)
print(x)
```

Obviously, using the loop instead saves the programmer a lot of trouble.

But what exactly do these statements do? The first one performs a calculation.

```
x = 3.9 * x * (1 - x)
```

This is called an *assignment* statement. The part on the right side of the = is a mathematical expression. Python uses the * character to indicate multiplication. Recall that the value of x is 0.25 (from the input above). The computed value is $3.9(0.25)(1 - 0.25)$ or 0.73125. Once the value on the right-hand side is computed, it is saved as (or *assigned to*) the variable that appears on the left-hand side of the =, in this case x. The new value of x (0.73125) replaces the old value (0.25).

The second line in the loop body is a type of statement we have encountered before, a print statement.

```
print(x)
```

When Python executes this statement the current value of x is displayed on the screen. So, the first number of output is 0.73125.

Remember the loop executes 10 times. After printing the value of x, the two statements of the loop are executed again.

```
x = 3.9 * x * (1 - x)
print(x)
```

Of course, now x has the value 0.73125, so the formula computes a new value of x as $3.9(0.73125)(1 - 0.73125)$, which is 0.76644140625.

Can you see how the current value of x is used to compute a new value each time around the loop? That's where the numbers in the example run came from. You might try working through the steps of the program yourself for a different input value (say 0.5). Then run the program using Python and see how well you did impersonating a computer.

1.8 Chaos and Computers

I said above that the chaos program illustrates an interesting phenomenon. What could be interesting about a screen full of numbers? If you try out the program for yourself, you'll find that, no matter what number you start with, the results are always similar: the program spits back 10 seemingly random numbers between 0 and 1. As the program runs, the value of x seems to jump around, well, chaotically.

The function computed by this program has the general form: $k(x)(1 - x)$, where k in this case is 3.9. This is called a logistic function. It models certain kinds of unstable electronic circuits and is also sometimes used to predict population under limiting conditions. Repeated application of the logistic function can produce chaos. Although our program has a well-defined underlying behavior, the output seems unpredictable.

An interesting property of chaotic functions is that very small differences in the initial value can lead to large differences in the result as the formula is repeatedly applied. You can see this in the chaos program by entering numbers that differ by only a small amount. Here is the output from a modified program that shows the results for initial values of 0.25 and 0.26 side by side:

```
input    0.25          0.26
-------------------------
        0.731250      0.750360
        0.766441      0.730547
        0.698135      0.767707
        0.821896      0.695499
        0.570894      0.825942
        0.955399      0.560671
```

```
0.166187      0.960644
0.540418      0.147447
0.968629      0.490255
0.118509      0.974630
```

With very similar starting values, the outputs stay similar for a few iterations, but then differ markedly. By about the fifth iteration, there no longer seems to be any relationship between the two models.

These two features of our chaos program, apparent unpredictability and extreme sensitivity to initial values, are the hallmarks of chaotic behavior. Chaos has important implications for computer science. It turns out that many phenomena in the real world that we might like to model and predict with our computers exhibit just this kind of chaotic behavior. You may have heard of the so-called *butterfly effect*. Computer models that are used to simulate and predict weather patterns are so sensitive that the effect of a single butterfly flapping its wings in New Jersey might make the difference of whether or not rain is predicted in Peoria.

It's very possible that even with perfect computer modeling, we might never be able to measure existing weather conditions accurately enough to predict weather more than a few days in advance. The measurements simply can't be precise enough to make the predictions accurate over a longer time frame.

As you can see, this small program has a valuable lesson to teach users of computers. As amazing as computers are, the results that they give us are only as useful as the mathematical models on which the programs are based. Computers can give incorrect results because of errors in programs, but even correct programs may produce erroneous results if the models are wrong or the initial inputs are not accurate enough.

1.9 Chapter Summary

This chapter has introduced computers, computer science, and programming. Here is a summary of some of the key concepts:

- A computer is a universal information-processing machine. It can carry out any process that can be described in sufficient detail. A description of the sequence of steps for solving a particular problem is called an algorithm. Algorithms can be turned into software (programs) that determines what the hardware (physical machine) can and does accomplish. The process of creating software is called programming.

- Computer science is the study of what can be computed. Computer scientists use the techniques of design, analysis, and experimentation. Computer science is the foundation of the broader field of computing which includes areas such as networking, databases, and information management systems, to name a few.

- A basic functional view of a computer system comprises a central processing unit (CPU), main memory, secondary memory, and input and output devices. The CPU is the brain of the computer that performs simple arithmetic and logical operations. Information that the CPU acts on (data and programs) is stored in main memory (RAM). More permanent information is stored on secondary memory devices such as magnetic disks, flash memory, and optical devices. Information is entered into the computer via input devices, and output devices display the results.

- Programs are written using a formal notation known as a programming language. There are many different languages, but all share the property of having a precise syntax (form) and semantics (meaning). Computer hardware only understands a very low-level language known as machine language. Programs are usually written using human-oriented high-level languages such as Python. A high-level language must either be compiled or interpreted in order for the computer to understand it. High-level languages are more portable than machine language.

- Python is an interpreted language. One good way to learn about Python is to use an interactive shell for experimentation.

- A Python program is a sequence of commands (called statements) for the Python interpreter to execute. Python includes statements to do things such as print output to the screen, get input from the user, calculate the value of a mathematical expression, and perform a sequence of statements multiple times (loop).

- A mathematical model is called chaotic if very small changes in the input lead to large changes in the results, making them seem random or unpredictable. The models of many real-world phenomena exhibit chaotic behavior, which places some limits on the power of computing.

1.10 Exercises

Review Questions

True/False

1. Computer science is the study of computers.

2. The CPU is the "brain" of the computer.

3. Secondary memory is also called RAM.

4. All information that a computer is currently working on is stored in main memory.

5. The syntax of a language is its meaning, and semantics is its form.

6. A function definition is a sequence of statements that defines a new command.

7. A programming environment refers to a place where programmers work.

8. A variable is used to give a name to a value so it can be referred to in other places.

9. A loop is used to skip over a section of a program.

10. A chaotic function can't be computed by a computer.

Multiple Choice

1. What is the fundamental question of computer science?
   a) How fast can a computer compute?
   b) What can be computed?
   c) What is the most effective programming language?
   d) How much money can a programmer make?

2. An algorithm is like a
   a) newspaper   b) venus flytrap   c) drum   d) recipe

3. A problem is intractable when
   a) you cannot reverse its solution
   b) it involves tractors

c) it has many solutions

d) it is not practical to solve

4. Which of the following is *not* an example of secondary memory?

   a) RAM   b) hard drive   c) USB flash drive   d) CD-ROM

5. Computer languages designed to be used and understood by humans are

   a) natural languages

   b) high-level computer languages

   c) machine languages

   d) fetch-execute languages

6. A statement is

   a) a translation of machine language

   b) a complete computer command

   c) a precise description of a problem

   d) a section of an algorithm

7. One difference between a compiler and an interpreter is

   a) a compiler is a program

   b) a compiler is used to translate high-level language into machine language

   c) a compiler is no longer needed after a program is translated

   d) a compiler processes source code

8. By convention, the statements of a program are often placed in a function called

   a) import   b) main   c) program   d) IDLE

9. Which of the following is *not* true of comments?

   a) They make a program more efficient

   b) They are intended for human readers

   c) They are ignored by Python

   d) In Python, they begin with a pound sign (#)

10. The items listed in the parentheses of a function definition are called

    a) parentheticals   b) scripts   c) comments   d) parameters

Discussion

1. Compare and contrast the following pairs of concepts from the chapter:

(a) Hardware vs. Software

(b) Algorithm vs. Program

(c) Programming Language vs. Natural Language

(d) High-Level Language vs. Machine Language

(e) Interpreter vs. Compiler

(f) Syntax vs. Semantics

2. List and explain in your own words the role of each of the five basic functional units of a computer depicted in Figure 1.1.

3. Write a detailed algorithm for making a peanut butter and jelly sandwich (or some other everyday activity). You should assume that you are talking to someone who is conceptually able to do the task, but has never actually done it before. For example, you might be telling a young child.

4. As you will learn in a later chapter, many of the numbers stored in a computer are not exact values, but rather close approximations. For example, the value 0.1 might be stored as 0.10000000000000000555. Usually, such small differences are not a problem; however, given what you have learned about chaotic behavior in Chapter 1, you should realize the need for caution in certain situations. Can you think of examples where this might be a problem? Explain.

5. Trace through the chaos program from Section 1.6 by hand using 0.15 as the input value. Show the sequence of output that results.

Programming Exercises

1. Start up an interactive Python session and try typing in each of the following commands. Write down the results you see.

(a) `print("Hello, world!")`

(b) `print("Hello", "world!")`

(c) `print(3)`

(d) `print(3.0)`

(e) `print(2 + 3)`

(f) `print(2.0 + 3.0)`

(g) `print("2" + "3")`

(h) `print("2 + 3 =", 2 + 3)`

(i) `print(2 * 3)`

(j) `print(2 ** 3)`

(k) `print(2 / 3)`

2. Enter and run the `chaos` program from Section 1.6. Try it out with various values of input to see that it functions as described in the chapter.

3. Modify the `chaos` program using 2.0 in place of 3.9 as the multiplier in the logistic function. Your modified line of code should look like this:

```
x = 2.0 * x * (1 - x)
```

Run the program for various input values and compare the results to those obtained from the original program. Write a short paragraph describing any differences that you notice in the behavior of the two versions.

4. Modify the `chaos` program so that it prints out 20 values instead of 10.

5. Modify the `chaos` program so that the number of values to print is determined by the user. You will have to add a line near the top of the program to get another value from the user:

```
n = eval(input("How many numbers should I print? "))
```

Then you will need to change the loop to use n instead of a specific number.

6. The calculation performed in the `chaos` program can be written in a number of ways that are algebraically equivalent. Write a version of the program for each of the following ways of doing the computation. Have your modified programs print out 100 iterations of the function and compare the results when run on the same input.

(a) `3.9 * x * (1 - x)`

(b) `3.9 * (x - x * x)`

(c) `3.9 * x - 3.9 * x * x`

Explain the results of this experiment. Hint: See discussion question number 4, above.

7. (Advanced) Modify the chaos program so that it accepts two inputs and then prints a table with two columns similar to the one shown in Section 1.8. (Note: You will probably not be able to get the columns to line up as nicely as those in the example. Chapter 5 discusses how to print numbers with a fixed number of decimal places.)

Chapter 2

Writing Simple Programs

Objectives

- To know the steps in an orderly software development process.

- To understand programs following the input, process, output (IPO) pattern and be able to modify them in simple ways.

- To understand the rules for forming valid Python identifiers and expressions.

- To be able to understand and write Python statements to output information to the screen, assign values to variables, get information entered from the keyboard, and perform a counted loop.

2.1 The Software Development Process

As you saw in the previous chapter, it is easy to run programs that have already been written. The harder part is actually coming up with a program in the first place. Computers are very literal, and they must be told what to do right down to the last detail. Writing large programs is a daunting challenge. It would be almost impossible without a systematic approach.

The process of creating a program is often broken down into stages according to the information that is produced in each phase. In a nutshell, here's what you should do:

Analyze the Problem Figure out exactly what the problem to be solved is. Try to understand as much as possible about it. Until you really know what the problem is, you cannot begin to solve it.

Determine Specifications Describe exactly what your program will do. At this point, you should not worry about *how* your program will work, but rather about deciding exactly *what* it will accomplish. For simple programs this involves carefully describing what the inputs and outputs of the program will be and how they relate to each other.

Create a Design Formulate the overall structure of the program. This is where the *how* of the program gets worked out. The main task is to design the algorithm(s) that will meet the specifications.

Implement the Design Translate the design into a computer language and put it into the computer. In this book, we will be implementing our algorithms as Python programs.

Test/Debug the Program Try out your program and see if it works as expected. If there are any errors (often called *bugs*), then you should go back and fix them. The process of locating and fixing errors is called *debugging* a program. During the debugging phase, your goal is to find errors, so you should try everything you can think of that might "break" the program. It's good to keep in mind the old maxim: "Nothing is foolproof because fools are too ingenious."

Maintain the Program Continue developing the program in response to the needs of your users. Most programs are never really finished; they keep evolving over years of use.

2.2 Example Program: Temperature Converter

Let's go through the steps of the software development process with a simple real-world example involving a fictional computer science student, Susan Computewell.

Susan is spending a year studying in Germany. She has no problems with language, as she is fluent in many languages (including Python). Her problem is that she has a hard time figuring out the temperature in the morning so that she knows how to dress for the day. Susan listens to the weather report each morning, but the temperatures are given in degrees Celsius, and she is used to Fahrenheit.

Fortunately, Susan has an idea to solve the problem. Being a computer science major, she never goes anywhere without her laptop computer. She thinks it might be possible that a computer program could help her out.

Susan begins with an analysis of her problem. In this case, the problem is pretty clear: the radio announcer gives temperatures in degrees Celsius, but Susan only comprehends temperatures that are in degrees Fahrenheit.

Next, Susan considers the specifications of a program that might help her out. What should the input be? She decides that her program will allow her to type in the temperature in degrees Celsius. And the output? The program will display the temperature converted into degrees Fahrenheit. Now she needs to specify the exact relationship of the output to the input.

Susan does some quick figuring. She knows that 0 degrees Celsius (freezing) is equal to 32 degrees Fahrenheit, and 100 Celsius (boiling) is equal to 212 Fahrenheit. With this information, she computes the ratio of Fahrenheit to Celsius degrees as $\frac{212-32}{100-0} = \frac{180}{100} = \frac{9}{5}$. Using F to represent the Fahrenheit temperature and C for Celsius, the conversion formula will have the form $F = \frac{9}{5}C + k$ for some constant k. Plugging in 0 and 32 for C and F, respectively, Susan immediately sees that $k = 32$. So, the final formula for the relationship is $F = \frac{9}{5}C + 32$. That seems an adequate specification.

Notice that this describes one of many possible programs that could solve this problem. If Susan had background in the field of Artificial Intelligence (AI), she might consider writing a program that would actually listen to the radio announcer to get the current temperature using speech recognition algorithms. For output, she might have the computer control a robot that goes to her closet and picks an appropriate outfit based on the converted temperature. This would be a much more ambitious project, to say the least!

Certainly, the robot program would also solve the problem identified in the problem analysis. The purpose of specification is to decide exactly what this particular program will do to solve a problem. Susan knows better than to just dive in and start writing a program without first having a clear idea of what she is trying to build.

Susan is now ready to design an algorithm for her problem. She immediately realizes that this is a simple algorithm that follows a standard pattern: *Input, Process, Output* (IPO). Her program will prompt the user for some input information (the Celsius temperature), process it to convert to a Fahrenheit temperature, and then output the result by displaying it on the computer screen.

Susan could write her algorithm down in a computer language. However, the precision required to write it out formally tends to stifle the creative process of developing the algorithm. Instead, she writes her algorithm using *pseudocode*. Pseudocode is just precise English that describes what a program does. It is meant to communicate algorithms without all the extra mental overhead of getting the details right in any particular programming language.

Here is Susan's completed algorithm:

```
Input the temperature in degrees Celsius (call it celsius)
Calculate fahrenheit as (9/5)celsius + 32
Output fahrenheit
```

The next step is to translate this design into a Python program. This is straightforward, as each line of the algorithm turns into a corresponding line of Python code.

```
# convert.py
#     A program to convert Celsius temps to Fahrenheit
# by: Susan Computewell

def main():
    celsius = eval(input("What is the Celsius temperature? "))
    fahrenheit = 9/5 * celsius + 32
    print("The temperature is", fahrenheit, "degrees Fahrenheit.")

main()
```

See if you can figure out what each line of this program does. Don't worry if some parts are a bit confusing. They will be discussed in detail in the next section.

After completing her program, Susan tests it to see how well it works. She uses inputs for which she knows the correct answers. Here is the output from two of her tests:

```
What is the Celsius temperature? 0
The temperature is 32.0 degrees Fahrenheit.

What is the Celsius temperature? 100
The temperature is 212.0 degrees Fahrenheit.
```

You can see that Susan used the values of 0 and 100 to test her program. It looks pretty good, and she is satisfied with her solution. She is especially pleased that no debugging seems necessary (which is very unusual).

2.3 Elements of Programs

Now that you know something about the programming process, you are *almost* ready to start writing programs on your own. Before doing that, though, you need a more complete grounding in the fundamentals of Python. The next few sections will discuss technical details that are essential to writing correct programs. This material can seem a bit tedious, but you will have to master these basics before plunging into more interesting waters.

2.3.1 Names

You have already seen that names are an important part of programming. We give names to modules (e.g., convert) and to the functions within modules (e.g., main). Variables are used to give names to values (e.g., celsius and fahrenheit). Technically, all these names are called *identifiers*. Python has some rules about how identifiers are formed. Every identifier must begin with a letter or underscore (the "_" character) which may be followed by any sequence of letters, digits, or underscores. This implies that a single identifier cannot contain any spaces.

According to these rules, all of the following are legal names in Python:

```
x
celsius
spam
spam2
SpamAndEggs
Spam_and_Eggs
```

Identifiers are case-sensitive, so spam, Spam, sPam, and SPAM are all different names to Python. For the most part, programmers are free to choose any name that conforms to these rules. Good programmers always try to choose names that describe the thing being named.

One other important thing to be aware of is that some identifiers are part of Python itself. These names are called *reserved words* or *keywords* and cannot be used as ordinary identifiers. The complete list of Python keywords is shown in Table 2.1.

False	class	finally	is	return
None	continue	for	lambda	try
True	def	from	nonlocal	while
and	del	global	not	with
as	elif	if	or	yield
assert	else	import	pass	
break	except	in	raise	

Table 2.1: Python Keywords

2.3.2   Expressions

Programs manipulate data. So far, we have seen two different kinds of data in our example programs: numbers and text. We'll examine these different data types in great detail in later chapters. For now, you just need to keep in mind that all data has to be stored on the computer in some digital format, and different types of data are stored in different ways.

The fragments of program code that produce or calculate new data values are called *expressions*. The simplest kind of expression is a *literal*. A literal is used to indicate a specific value. In chaos.py you can find the numbers 3.9 and 1. The convert.py program contains 9, 5, and 32. These are all examples of numeric literals, and their meaning is obvious: 32 represents, well, 32 (the number 32).

Our programs also manipulated textual data in some simple ways. Computer scientists refer to textual data as *strings*. You can think of a string as just a sequence of printable characters. A string literal is indicated in Python by enclosing the characters in quotation marks (""). If you go back and look at our example programs, you will find a number of string literals such as: "Hello" and "Enter a number between 0 and 1:   ". These literals produce strings containing the quoted characters. Note that the quotes themselves are not part of the string. They are just the mechanism to tell Python to create a string.

The process of turning an expression into an underlying data type is called *evaluation*. When you type an expression into a Python shell, the shell evaluates the expression and prints out a textual representation of the result. Consider this small interaction:

```
>>> 32
32
>>> "Hello"
'Hello'
>>> "32"
'32'
```

Notice that when the shell shows the value of a string, it puts the sequence of characters in single quotes. This is a way of letting us know that the value is actually text, not a number (or other data type). In the last interaction, we see that the expression "32" produces a string, not a number. In this case, Python is actually storing the characters "3" and "2," not a representation of the number 32. If that's confusing right now, don't worry too much about it; it will become clearer when we discuss these data types in later chapters.

A simple identifier can also be an expression. We use identifiers as variables to give names to values. When an identifier appears as an expression, its value is retrieved to provide a result for the expression. Here is an interaction with the Python interpreter that illustrates the use of variables as expressions:

```
>>> x = 5
>>> x
5
>>> print(x)
5
>>> print(spam)
Traceback (most recent call last):
  File "<stdin>", line 1, in <module>
NameError: name 'spam' is not defined
```

First the variable x is assigned the value 5 (using the numeric literal 5). In the second line of interaction, we are asking Python to evaluate the expression x. In response, the Python shell prints out 5, which is the value that was just assigned to x. Of course, we get the same result when we explicitly ask Python to print x using a print statement. The last interaction shows what happens when we try to use a variable that has not been assigned a value. Python cannot find a value, so it reports a *NameError*. This says that there is no value with that name. The important lesson here is that a variable must always be assigned a value before it can be used in an expression.

More complex and interesting expressions can be constructed by combining simpler expressions with *operators*. For numbers, Python provides the normal set of mathematical operations: addition, subtraction, multiplication, division, and exponentiation. The corresponding Python operators are +, -, *, /, and **. Here are some examples of complex expressions from chaos.py and convert.py:

```
3.9 * x * (1 - x)
9/5 * celsius + 32
```

Spaces are irrelevant within an expression. The last expression could have been written 9/5*celsius+32 and the result would be exactly the same. Usually it's a good idea to place some spaces in expressions to make them easier to read.

Python's mathematical operators obey the same rules of precedence and associativity that you learned in your math classes, including using parentheses to modify the order of evaluation. You should have little trouble constructing complex expressions in your own programs. Do keep in mind that only the round parentheses are allowed in numeric expressions, but you can nest them if necessary to create expressions like this.

```
((x1 - x2) / 2*n) + (spam / k**3)
```

By the way, Python also provides operators for strings. For example, you can "add" strings.

```
>>> "Bat" + "man"
'Batman'
```

This is called *concatenation*. As you can see, the effect is to create a new string that is the result of "gluing" the strings together. You'll see a lot more string operations in Chapter 5.

2.4 Output Statements

Now that you have the basic building blocks, identifier and expression, you are ready for a more complete description of various Python statements. You already know that information can be displayed on screen using Python's built-in function print. So far, we have looked at a few examples, but I have not yet explained the print function in detail. Like all programming languages, Python has a precise set of rules for the syntax (form) and semantics (meaning) of each statement. Computer scientists have developed sophisticated notations called *meta-languages* for describing programming languages. In this book we will rely on a simple template notation to illustrate the syntax of various statements.

Since print is a built-in function, a print statement has the same general form as any other function invocation. We type the function name print followed by parameters listed in parentheses. Here is how the print statement looks using our template notation:

```
print(<expr>, <expr>, ..., <expr>)
print()
```

These two templates show two forms of the print statement. The first indicates that a print statement can consist of the function name print followed by a parenthesized sequence of expressions, which are separated by commas. The angle bracket notation (<>) in the template is used to indicate "slots" that are filled in by other fragments of Python code. The name inside the brackets indicates what is missing; expr stands for an expression. The ellipses ("...") indicate an indefinite series (of expressions, in this case). You don't actually type the dots. The second version of the statement shows that it's also legal to have a print without any expressions to print.

As far as semantics are concerned, a print statement displays information in textual form. Any supplied expressions are evaluated left to right, and the resulting values are displayed on a line of output in a left-to-right fashion. By default, a single blank space character is placed between the displayed values. As an example, this sequence of print statements:

```
print(3+4)
print(3, 4, 3 + 4)
print()
print("The answer is", 3 + 4)
```

produces this output:

```
7
3 4 7

The answer is 7
```

The last statement illustrates how string literal expressions are often used in print statements as a convenient way of labeling output.

Notice that successive `print` statements normally display on separate lines of the screen. A bare `print`(no parameters) produces a blank line of output. Underneath, what's really happening is that the `print` function automatically appends some ending text after all of the supplied expressions are printed. By default, that ending text is a special marker character (denoted as `"\n"`) that signals the end of a line. We can modify that behavior by including an additional parameter that explicitly overrides this default. This is done using a special syntax for named or *keyword* parameters.

A template for the `print` statement including the keyword parameter to specify the ending-text looks like this:

```
print(<expr>, <expr>, ..., <expr>, end="\n")
```

The keyword for the named parameter is `end` and it is given a value using = notation, similar to variable assignment. Notice in the template I have shown its default value, the end-of-line character. This is a standard way of showing what value a keyword parameter will have when it is not explicitly given some other value.

One common use of the `end` parameter in `print` statements is to allow multiple `print`s to build up a single line of output. For example:

```
print("The answer is", end=" ")
print(3 + 4)
```

produces the single line of output:

```
The answer is 7
```

Notice how the output from the first print statement ends with a space (`" "`) rather than an end-of-line. The output from the second statement appears immediately following the space.

2.5 Assignment Statements

One of the most important kinds of statements in Python is the assignment statement. We've already seen a number of these in our previous examples.

2.5.1 Simple Assignment

The basic assignment statement has this form:

```
<variable> = <expr>
```

Here `variable` is an identifier and `expr` is an expression. The semantics of the assignment is that the expression on the right side is evaluated to produce a value, which is then associated with the variable named on the left side.

Here are some of the assignments we've already seen:

```
x = 3.9 * x * (1 - x)
fahrenheit = 9 / 5 * celsius + 32
x = 5
```

A variable can be assigned many times. It always retains the value of the most recent assignment. Here is an interactive Python session that demonstrates the point:

```
>>> myVar = 0
>>> myVar
0
>>> myVar = 7
>>> myVar
7
>>> myVar = myVar + 1
>>> myVar
8
```

The last assignment statement shows how the current value of a variable can be used to update its value. In this case I simply added one to the previous value. The chaos.py program from Chapter 1 did something similar, though a bit more complex. Remember, the values of variables can change; that's why they're called variables.

Sometimes it's helpful to think of a variable as a sort of named storage location in computer memory, a box that we can put a value in. When the variable changes, the old value is erased and a new one written in. Figure 2.1 shows how we might picture the effect of x = x + 1 using this model. This is exactly the way assignment works in some computer languages. It's also a very simple way to view the effect of assignment, and you'll find pictures similar to this throughout the book.

Python assignment statements are actually slightly different from the "variable as a box" model. In Python, values may end up anywhere in memory, and variables are used to refer to them. Assigning a variable is like putting one of

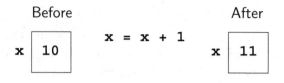

Figure 2.1: Variable as box view of x = x + 1

those little yellow sticky notes on the value and saying, "this is x." Figure 2.2 gives a more accurate picture of the effect of assignment in Python. An arrow is used to show which value a variable refers to. Notice that the old value doesn't get erased by the new one; the variable simply switches to refer to the new value. The effect is like moving the sticky note from one object to another. This is the way assignment actually works in Python, so you'll see some of these sticky-note style pictures sprinkled throughout the book as well.

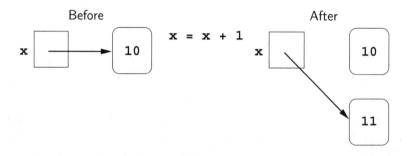

Figure 2.2: Variable as sticky note (Python) view of x = x + 1

By the way, even though the assignment statement doesn't directly cause the old value of a variable to be erased and overwritten, you don't have to worry about computer memory getting filled up with the "discarded" values. When a value is no longer referred to by *any* variable, it is no longer useful. Python will automatically clear these values out of memory so that the space can be used for new values. This is like going through your closet and tossing out anything that doesn't have a sticky note to label it. In fact, this process of automatic memory management is actually called *garbage collection*.

2.5.2 Assigning Input

The purpose of an input statement is to get some information from the user of a
program and store it into a variable. Some programming languages have a special statement to do this. In Python, input is accomplished using an assignment
statement combined with a built-in function called `input`. The exact form of an
input statement depends on what type of data you are trying to get from the
user. For textual input, the statement will look like this:

```
<variable> = input(<prompt>)
```

Here <prompt> is a string expression that is used to prompt the user for input;
the prompt is almost always a string literal (i.e., some text inside of quotation
marks).

When Python encounters a call to `input`, it prints the prompt on the screen.
Python then pauses and waits for the user to type some text and press the
<Enter> key. Whatever the user types is then stored as a string. Consider
this simple interaction:

```
>>> name = input("Enter your name: ")
Enter your name: John Yaya
>>> name
'John Yaya'
```

Executing the `input` statement caused Python to print out the prompt "Enter
your name:" and then the interpreter paused waiting for user input. In this
example, I typed John Yaya. As a result, the string 'John Yaya' is remembered
in the variable `name`. Evaluating `name` gives back the string of characters that I
typed.

When the user input is a number, we need a slightly more complicated form
of input statement:

```
<variable> = eval(input(<prompt>))
```

Here I've added another built-in Python function `eval` that is "wrapped around"
the `input` function. As you might guess, `eval` is short for "evaluate." In this
form, the text typed by the user is evaluated as an expression to produce the
value that is stored into the variable. So, for example, the string "32" becomes
the number 32. If you look back at the example programs so far, you'll see a
couple of examples where we've gotten numbers from the user like this.

```
x = eval(input("Please enter a number between 0 and 1: "))
celsius = eval(input("What is the Celsius temperature? "))
```

The important thing to remember is that you need to `eval` the `input` when you want a number instead of some raw text (a string).

If you are reading the example programs carefully, you probably noticed the blank space inside the quotes at the end of all these prompts. I usually put a space at the end of a prompt so that the input that the user types does not start right next to the prompt. Putting a space in makes the interaction easier to read and understand.

Although our numeric examples specifically prompted the user to enter a number, what the user types in this case is just a numeric literal—a simple Python expression. In fact, any valid expression would be just as acceptable. Consider the following interaction with the Python interpreter:

```
>>> ans = eval(input("Enter an expression: "))
Enter an expression: 3 + 4 * 5
>>> print(ans)
23
>>>
```

Here, when prompted to enter an expression, the user typed "3 + 4 * 5." Python evaluated this expression (via `eval`) and assigned the value to the variable `ans`. When printed, we see that `ans` got the value 23 as expected.

In a sense, the `input-eval` combination is like a delayed expression. The example interaction produced exactly the same result as if we had simply written `ans = 3 + 4 * 5`. The difference is that the expression was supplied by the user at the time the statement was executed instead of being determined when the statement was written by the programmer. Thus, the user can supply formulas for a program to evaluate.

2.5.3   Simultaneous Assignment

There is an alternative form of the assignment statement that allows us to calculate several values all at the same time. It looks like this:

```
<var>, <var>, ..., <var> = <expr>, <expr>, ..., <expr>
```

This is called *simultaneous assignment*. Semantically, this tells Python to evaluate all the expressions on the right-hand side and then assign these values to the corresponding variables named on the left-hand side. Here's an example:

```
sum, diff = x+y, x-y
```

Here sum would get the sum of x and y and diff would get the difference.

This form of assignment seems strange at first, but it can prove remarkably useful. Here's an example: Suppose you have two variables x and y and you want to swap the values. That is, you want the value currently stored in x to be in y and the value that is currently in y to be stored in x. At first, you might think this could be done with two simple assignments.

```
x = y
y = x
```

This doesn't work. We can trace the execution of these statements step-by-step to see why.

Suppose x and y start with the values 2 and 4. Let's examine the logic of the program to see how the variables change. The following sequence uses comments to describe what happens to the variables as these two statements are executed:

```
# variables        x   y
# initial values   2   4
x = y
# now                  4   4
y = x
# final                4   4
```

See how the first statement clobbers the original value of x by assigning to it the value of y? When we then assign x to y in the second step, we just end up with two copies of the original y value.

One way to make the swap work is to introduce an additional variable that temporarily remembers the original value of x.

```
temp = x
x = y
y = temp
```

Let's walk-through this sequence to see how it works.

```
# variables        x   y   temp
# initial values   2   4   no value yet
temp = x
```

```
#                     2   4   2
x = y
#                     4   4   2
y = temp
#                     4   2   2
```

As you can see from the final values of x and y, the swap was successful in this case.

This sort of three-way shuffle is common in other programming languages. In Python, the simultaneous assignment statement offers an elegant alternative. Here is a simpler Python equivalent:

```
x, y = y, x
```

Because the assignment is simultaneous, it avoids wiping out one of the original values.

Simultaneous assignment can also be used to get multiple numbers from the user in a single input. Consider this program for averaging exam scores:

```
# avg2.py
#    A simple program to average two exam scores
#    Illustrates use of multiple input

def main():
    print("This program computes the average of two exam scores.")

    score1, score2 = eval(input("Enter two scores separated by a comma: "))
    average = (score1 + score2) / 2

    print("The average of the scores is:", average)

main()
```

The program prompts for two scores separated by a comma. Suppose the user types 86, 92. The effect of the input statement is then the same as if we had done this assignment:

```
score1, score2 = 86, 92
```

We have gotten a value for each of the variables in one fell swoop. This example used just two values, but it could be generalized to any number of inputs.

Of course, we could have just gotten the input from the user using separate input statements.

```
score1 = eval(input("Enter the first score: "))
score2 = eval(input("Enter the second score: "))
```

In some ways this may be better, as the separate prompts are more informative for the user. In this example the decision as to which approach to take is largely a matter of taste. Sometimes getting multiple values in a single `input` provides a more intuitive user interface, so it's a nice technique to have in your toolkit. Just remember that the multiple values trick will not work for string (non-`eval`ed) input; when the user types a comma it will be just another character in the input string. The comma only becomes a separator when the string is subsequently evaluated.

2.6 Definite Loops

You already know that programmers use loops to execute a sequence of statements multiple times in succession. The simplest kind of loop is called a *definite loop*. This is a loop that will execute a definite number of times. That is, at the point in the program when the loop begins, Python knows how many times to go around (or *iterate*) the body of the loop. For example, the `chaos` program in Chapter 1 used a loop that always executed exactly ten times.

```
for i in range(10):
    x = 3.9 * x * (1 - x)
    print(x)
```

This particular loop pattern is called a *counted loop*, and it is built using a Python `for` statement. Before considering this example in detail, let's take a look at what `for` loops are all about.

A Python `for` loop has this general form:

```
for <var> in <sequence>:
    <body>
```

The body of the loop can be any sequence of Python statements. The extent of the body is indicated by its indentation under the loop heading (the `for <var> in <sequence>:` part).

The variable after the keyword `for` is called the *loop index*. It takes on each successive value in the sequence, and the statements in the body are executed once for each value. Often the sequence portion consists of a *list* of values. Lists are a very important concept in Python, and you will learn more about them in

upcoming chapters. For now, it's enough to know that you can create a simple
list by placing a sequence of expressions in square brackets. Some interactive
examples help to illustrate the point:

```
>>> for i in [0, 1, 2, 3]:
        print(i)


0
1
2
3

>>> for odd in [1, 3, 5, 7, 9]:
        print(odd * odd)


1
9
25
49
81
```

Can you see what is happening in these two examples? The body of the
loop is executed using each successive value in the list. The length of the list
determines the number of times the loop executes. In the first example, the list
contains the four values 0 through 3, and these successive values of i are simply
printed. In the second example, odd takes on the values of the first five odd
natural numbers, and the body of the loop prints the squares of these numbers.

Now, let's go back to the example that began this section (from chaos.py)
Look again at the loop heading:

```
for i in range(10):
```

Comparing this to the template for the for loop shows that the last portion,
range(10), must be some kind of sequence. It turns out that range is a built-
in Python function for generating a sequence of numbers "on the fly." You can
think of a range as a sort of implicit description of a sequence of numbers. To
get a handle on what range actually does, we can ask Python to turn a range
into a plain old list using another built-in function, list:

```
>>> list(range(10))     # turns range(10) into an explicit list
[0, 1, 2, 3, 4, 5, 6, 7, 8, 9]
```

Do you see what is happening here? The expression range(10) produces the sequence of numbers 0 through 9. The loop using range(10) is equivalent to one using a list of those numbers.

```
for i in [0, 1, 2, 3, 4, 5, 6, 7, 8, 9]:
```

In general, range(<expr>) will produce a sequence of numbers that starts with 0 and goes up to, but not does not include, the value of <expr>. If you think about it, you will see that the value of the expression determines the number of items in the resulting sequence. In chaos.py we did not even care what values the loop index variable used (since i was not referred to anywhere in the loop body). We just needed a sequence length of 10 to make the body execute 10 times.

As I mentioned above, this pattern is called a *counted loop*, and it is a very common way to use definite loops. When you want to do something in your program a certain number of times, use a for loop with a suitable range.

```
for <variable> in range(<expr>):
```

The value of the expression determines how many times the loop executes. The name of the index variable doesn't really matter much; programmers often use i or j as the loop index variable for counted loops. Just be sure to use an identifier that you are not using for any other purpose. Otherwise you might accidentally wipe out a value that you will need later.

The interesting and useful thing about loops is the way that they alter the "flow of control" in a program. Usually we think of computers as executing a series of instructions in strict sequence. Introducing a loop causes Python to go back and do some statements over and over again. Statements like the for loop are called *control structures* because they control the execution of other parts of the program.

Some programmers find it helpful to think of control structures in terms of pictures called *flowcharts*. A flowchart is a diagram that uses boxes to represent different parts of a program and arrows between the boxes to show the sequence of events when the program is running. Figure 2.3 depicts the semantics of the for loop as a flowchart.

If you are having trouble understanding the for loop, you might find it useful to study the flowchart. The diamond shaped box in the flowchart represents a decision in the program. When Python gets to the loop heading, it checks to see if there are any (more) items left in the sequence. If the answer is yes, the loop index variable is assigned the next item in the sequence, and then the

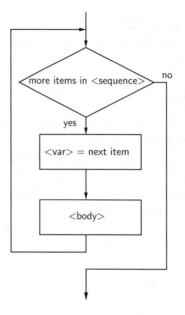

Figure 2.3: Flowchart of a `for` loop

loop body is executed. Once the body is complete, the program goes back to the loop heading and checks for another value in the sequence. The loop quits when there are no more items, and the program moves on to the statements that come after the loop.

2.7 Example Program: Future Value

Let's close the chapter with one more example of the programming process in action. We want to develop a program to determine the future value of an investment. We'll start with an analysis of the problem. You know that money deposited in a bank account earns interest, and this interest accumulates as the years pass. How much will an account be worth ten years from now? Obviously, it depends on how much money we start with (the principal) and how much interest the account earns. Given the principal and the interest rate, a program should be able to calculate the value of the investment ten years into the future.

We continue by developing the exact specifications for the program. Remember, this is a description of what the program will do. What exactly should the inputs be? We need the user to enter the initial amount to invest, the principal. We will also need some indication of how much interest the account earns. This depends both on the interest rate and how often the interest is compounded. One simple way of handling this is to have the user enter an annual percentage rate. Whatever the actual interest rate and compounding frequency, the annual rate tells us how much the investment accrues in one year. If the annual interest is 3%, then a $100 investment will grow to $103 in one year's time. How should the user represent an annual rate of 3%? There are a number of reasonable choices. Let's assume the user supplies a decimal, so the rate would be entered as 0.03.

This leads us to the following specification:

Program Future Value

Inputs

> **principal** The amount of money being invested in dollars.
>
> **apr** The annual percentage rate expressed as a decimal number.

Output The value of the investment 10 years into the future.

Relationship Value after one year is given by $principal(1 + apr)$. This formula needs to be applied 10 times.

Next we design an algorithm for the program. We'll use pseudocode, so that we can formulate our ideas without worrying about all the rules of Python. Given our specification, the algorithm seems straightforward.

```
Print an introduction
Input the amount of the principal (principal)
Input the annual percentage rate (apr)
Repeat 10 times:
    principal = principal * (1 + apr)
Output the value of principal
```

If you know a little bit about financial math (or just some basic algebra), you probably realize that the loop in this design is not strictly necessary; there is a formula for calculating future value in a single step using exponentiation. I have used a loop here both to illustrate another counted loop, and also because this version will lend itself to some modifications that are discussed in the programming exercises at the end of the chapter. In any case, this design illustrates that sometimes an algorithmic approach to a calculation can make the mathematics easier. Knowing how to calculate the interest for just one year allows us to calculate any number of years into the future.

Now that we've thought the problem all the way through in pseudocode, it's time to put our new Python knowledge to work and develop a program. Each line of the algorithm translates into a statement of Python.

Print an introduction (print statement, Section 2.4)
```
print("This program calculates the future value")
print("of a 10-year investment.")
```

Input the amount of the principal (numeric input, Section 2.5.2)
```
principal = eval(input("Enter the initial principal:  "))
```

Input the annual percentage rate (numeric input, Section 2.5.2)
```
apr = eval(input("Enter the annual interest rate:  "))
```

Repeat 10 times: (counted loop, Section 2.6)
```
for i in range(10):
```

Calculate principal = principal * (1 + apr) (simple assignment, Section 2.5.1)
```
    principal = principal * (1 + apr)
```

Output the value of the principal (print statement, Section 2.4)
```
print("The value in 10 years is:", principal)
```

All of the statement types in this program have been discussed in detail in this chapter. If you have any questions, you should go back and review the relevant descriptions. Notice especially the counted loop pattern is used to apply the interest formula 10 times.

That about wraps it up. Here is the completed program:

```
# futval.py
#    A program to compute the value of an investment
#    carried 10 years into the future

def main():
    print("This program calculates the future value")
```

```
print("of a 10-year investment.")

principal = eval(input("Enter the initial principal: "))
apr = eval(input("Enter the annual interest rate: "))

for i in range(10):
    principal = principal * (1 + apr)

print("The value in 10 years is:", principal)
```

`main()`

Notice that I have added a few blank lines to separate the input, processing, and output portions of the program. Strategically placed "white space" can help make your programs more readable.

That's as far as I'm taking this example; I leave the testing and debugging as an exercise for you.

2.8 Chapter Summary

This chapter has covered a lot of ground laying out both the process that is used to develop programs and the details of Python that are necessary to implement simple programs. Here is a quick summary of some of the key points:

- Writing programs requires a systematic approach to problem solving and involves the following steps:

  1. Problem Analysis: Studying the problem to be solved.
  2. Program Specification: Deciding exactly what the program will do.
  3. Design: Writing an algorithm in pseudocode.
  4. Implementation: Translating the design into a programming language.
  5. Testing/Debugging: Finding and fixing errors in the program.
  6. Maintenance: Keeping the program up to date with evolving needs.

- Many simple programs follow the input, process, output (IPO) pattern.

- Programs are composed of statements that are built from identifiers and expressions.

- Identifiers are names; they begin with an underscore or letter which can be followed by a combination of letter, digit, or underscore characters. Identifiers in Python are case sensitive.

- Expressions are the fragments of a program that produce data. An expression can be composed of the following components:

  literals A literal is a representation of a specific value. For example 3 is a literal representing the number three.

  variables A variable is an identifier that stores a value.

  operators Operators are used to combine expressions into more complex expressions. For example, in x + 3 * y the operators + and * are used.

- The Python operators for numbers include the usual arithmetic operations of addition (+), subtraction (-), multiplication (*), division (/), and exponentiation (**).

- The Python output statement `print` displays the values of a series of expressions to the screen.

- In Python, assignment of a value to a variable is done using the equal sign (=). Using assignment, programs can get input from the keyboard. Python also allows simultaneous assignment, which is useful for getting multiple input values with a single prompt.

- Definite loops are loops that execute a known number of times. The Python `for` statement is a definite loop that iterates through a sequence of values. A Python list is often used in a `for` loop to provide a sequence of values for the loop.

- One important use of a `for` statement is in implementing a counted loop, which is a loop designed specifically for the purpose of repeating some portion of the program a specific number of times. A counted loop in Python is created by using the built-in `range` function to produce a suitably sized list of numbers.

2.9 Exercises

Review Questions

True/False

1. The best way to write a program is to immediately type in some code and then debug it until it works.

2. An algorithm can be written without using a programming language.

3. Programs no longer require modification after they are written and debugged.

4. Python identifiers must start with a letter or underscore.

5. Keywords make good variable names.

6. Expressions are built from literals, variables, and operators.

7. In Python, x = x + 1 is a legal statement.

8. Python does not allow the input of multiple values with a single statement.

9. A counted loop is designed to iterate a specific number of times.

10. In a flowchart, diamonds are used to show statements, and rectangles are used for decision points.

Multiple Choice

1. Which of the following is *not* a step in the software development process?
   a) Specification   b) Testing/Debugging
   c) Fee setting   d) Maintenance

2. What is the correct formula for converting Celsius to Fahrenheit?
   a) $F = 9/5(C) + 32$ b) $F = 5/9(C) - 32$
   c) $F = B^2 - 4AC$ d) $F = \frac{212-32}{100-0}$

3. The process of describing exactly *what* a computer program will do to solve a problem is called
   a) design   b) implementation   c) programming   d) specification

4. Which of the following is *not* a legal identifier?
   a) spam   b) spAm   c) 2spam   d) spam4U

5. Which of the following are *not* used in expressions?
   a) variables   b) statements   c) operators   d) literals

6. Fragments of code that produce or calculate new data values are called
   a) identifiers   b) expressions
   c) productive clauses   d) assignment statements

7. Which of the following is *not* a part of the IPO pattern?
   a) Input   b) Program   c) Process   d) Output

8. The template `for <variable> in range(<expr>)` describes
   a) a general for loop   b) an assignment statement
   c) a flowchart   d) a counted loop

9. Which of the following is the most accurate model of assignment in Python?
   a) sticky-note   b) variable-as-box
   c) simultaneous   d) plastic-scale

10. In Python, getting user input is done with a special expression called
    a) `for`   b) `read`   c) simultaneous assignment   d) `input`

Discussion

1. List and describe in your own words the six steps in the software development process.

2. Write out the `chaos.py` program (Section 1.6) and identify the parts of the program as follows:

   - Circle each identifier.

   - Underline each expression.

   - Put a comment at the end of each line indicating the type of statement on that line (output, assignment, input, loop, etc.)

3. Explain the relationships among the concepts: definite loop, `for` loop, and counted loop.

4. Show the output from the following fragments:

(a) `for i in range(5):`
    `    print(i * i)`

(b) `for d in [3,1,4,1,5]:`
    `    print(d, end=" ")`

(c) `for i in range(4):`
    `    print("Hello")`

(d) `for i in range(5):`
    `    print(i, 2**i)`

5. Why is it a good idea to first write out an algorithm in pseudocode rather than jumping immediately to Python code?

6. The Python `print` function supports other keyword parameters besides end. One of these other keyword parameters is sep. What do you think the sep parameter does? Hint: sep is short for separator. Test your idea either by trying it interactively or by consulting the Python documentation.

7. What do you think will happen if the following code is executed?

```
print("start")
for i in range(0):
    print("Hello")
print("end")
```

Look at the flowchart for the `for` statement in the chapter to help you figure this out. Then test your prediction by trying out these lines in a program.

Programming Exercises

1. A user-friendly program should print an introduction that tells the user what the program does. Modify the `convert.py` program (Section 2.2) to print an introduction.

2. Modify the `avg2.py` program (Section 2.5.3) to find the average of three exam scores.

3. Modify the `convert.py` program (Section 2.2) with a loop so that it executes 5 times before quitting (i.e., it converts 5 temperatures in a row).

4. Modify the `convert.py` program (Section 2.2) so that it computes and prints a table of Celsius temperatures and the Fahrenheit equivalents every 10 degrees from 0C to 100C.

5. Modify the `futval.py` program (Section 2.7) so that the number of years for the investment is also a user input. Make sure to change the final message to reflect the correct number of years.

6. Suppose you have an investment plan where you invest a certain fixed amount every year. Modify `futval.py` to compute the total accumulation of your investment. The inputs to the program will be the amount to invest each year, the interest rate, and the number of years for the investment.

7. As an alternative to APR, the interest accrued on an account is often described in terms of a nominal rate and the number of compounding periods. For example, if the interest rate is 3% and the interest is compounded quarterly, the account actually earns 3/4 % interest every 3 months.

   Modify the `futval.py` program to use this method of entering the interest rate. The program should prompt the user for the yearly rate (`rate`) and the number of times that the interest is compounded each year (`periods`). To compute the value in ten years, the program will loop 10 * `periods` times and accrue `rate/period` interest on each iteration.

8. Write a program that converts temperatures from Fahrenheit to Celsius.

9. Write a program that converts distances measured in kilometers to miles. One kilometer is approximately 0.62 miles.

10. Write a program to perform a unit conversion of your own choosing. Make sure that the program prints an introduction that explains what it does.

11. Write an interactive Python calculator program. The program should allow the user to type a mathematical expression, and then print the value of the expression. Include a loop so that the user can perform many calculations (say, up to 100). Note: To quit early, the user can make the program crash by typing a bad expression or simply closing the window that the calculator program is running in. You'll learn better ways of terminating interactive programs in later chapters.

Chapter 3

Computing with Numbers

Objectives

- To understand the concept of data types.

- To be familiar with the basic numeric data types in Python.

- To understand the fundamental principles of how numbers are represented on a computer.

- To be able to use the Python math library.

- To understand the accumulator program pattern.

- To be able to read and write programs that process numerical data.

3.1 Numeric Data Types

When computers were first developed, they were seen primarily as number crunchers, and that is still an important application. As you have seen, problems that involve mathematical formulas are easy to translate into Python programs. In this chapter, we'll take a closer look at programs designed to perform numerical calculations.

The information that is stored and manipulated by computer programs is generically referred to as *data*. Different kinds of data will be stored and manipulated in different ways. Consider this program to calculate the value of loose change:

55

```
# change.py
#    A program to calculate the value of some change in dollars

def main():
    print("Change Counter")
    print()
    print("Please enter the count of each coin type.")
    quarters = eval(input("Quarters: "))
    dimes = eval(input("Dimes: "))
    nickels = eval(input("Nickels: "))
    pennies = eval(input("Pennies: "))
    total = quarters * .25 + dimes * .10 + nickels * .05 + pennies * .01
    print()
    print("The total value of your change is", total)

main()
```

Here is an example of the output:

```
Change Counter

Please enter the count of each coin type.
Quarters: 5
Dimes: 3
Nickels: 4
Pennies: 6

The total value of your change is 1.81
```

This program actually manipulates two different kinds of numbers. The values entered by the user (5, 3, 4, 6) are whole numbers; they don't have any fractional part. The values of the coins (.25, .10, .05, .01) are decimal representations of fractions. Inside the computer, whole numbers and numbers that have fractional components are stored differently. Technically, we say that these are two different *data types*.

The data type of an object determines what values it can have and what operations can be performed on it. Whole numbers are represented using the *integer* data type (*int* for short). Values of type int can be positive or negative whole numbers. Numbers that can have fractional parts are represented as *floating point* (or *float*) values. So how do we tell whether a number is an int or a float? A numeric literal that does not contain a decimal point produces an int value, but a literal that has a decimal point is represented by a float (even if the fractional part is 0).

Python provides a special function called type that tells us the data type (or "class") of any value. Here is an interaction with the Python interpreter showing the difference between int and float literals:

```
>>> type(3)
<class 'int'>
>>> type(3.14)
<class 'float'>
>>> type(3.0)
<class 'float'>
>>> myInt = -32
>>> type(myInt)
<class 'int'>
>>> myFloat = 32.0
>>> type(myFloat)
<class 'float'>
```

You may be wondering why there are two different data types for numbers. One reason has to do with program style. Values that represent counts can't be fractional; we can't have $3\frac{1}{2}$ quarters, for example. Using an int value tells the reader of a program that the value *can't* be a fraction. Another reason has to do with the efficiency of various operations. The underlying algorithms that perform computer arithmetic are simpler, and therefore faster, for ints than the more general algorithms required for float values.

You should be warned that the float type only stores approximations to real numbers. There is a limit to the precision, or accuracy, of the stored values. Since float values are not exact, while ints always are, your general rule of thumb should be: If you don't need fractional values, use an int.

A value's data type determines what operations can be used on it. As we have seen, Python supports the usual mathematical operations on numbers. Table 3.1 summarizes these operations. Actually, this table is somewhat misleading since the two numeric data types have their own operations. For example, I have listed a single addition operation, but keep in mind that when addition is performed on floats, the computer hardware performs a floating point addition, whereas with ints the computer performs an integer addition. Python chooses the appropriate underlying operation (int or float) based on the operands.

Consider the following interaction with Python:

operator	operation
$+$	addition
$-$	subtraction
$*$	multiplication
$/$	float division
$**$	exponentiation
abs()	absolute value
$//$	integer division
%	remainder

Table 3.1: Python built-in numeric operations

```
>>> 3 + 4
7
>>> 3.0 + 4.0
7.0
>>> 3 * 4
12
>>> 3.0 * 4.0
12.0
>>> 4 ** 3
64
>>> 4.0 ** 3
64.0
>>> 4.0 ** 3.0
64.0
>>> abs(5)
5
>>> abs(-3.5)
3.5
>>>
```

For the most part, operations on floats produce floats, and operations on ints produce ints. Most of the time, we don't even worry about what type of operation is being performed; for example, integer addition produces pretty much the same result as floating point addition, and we can rely on Python to do the right thing.

In the case of division, however, things get a bit more interesting. As the table shows, Python (as of version 3.0) provides two different operators for division. The usual symbol / is used for "regular" division and a double slash // is used to indicate integer division. The best way to get a handle on the difference between these two is to try them out.

```
>>> 10 / 3
3.3333333333333335
>>> 10.0 / 3.0
3.3333333333333335
>>> 10 / 5
2.0
>>> 10 // 3
3
>>> 10.0 // 3.0
3.0
>>> 10 % 3
1
>>> 10.0 % 3.0
1.0
```

Notice that the / operator always returns a float. Regular division often produces a fractional result, even though the operands may be ints. Python accommodates this by always returning a floating point number. Are you surprised that the result of 10/3 has a 5 at the very end? Remember, floating point values are always approximations. This value is as close as Python can get when representing $3\frac{1}{3}$ as a floating point number.

To get a division that returns an integer result, you can use the integer division operation //. Integer division always produces an integer. Think of integer division as "gozinta." The expression, 10 / 3 produces 3 because three gozinta (goes into) ten three times (with a remainder of one). While the result of integer division is always an integer, the data type of the result depends on the data type of the operands. A float integer-divided by a float produces a float with a 0 fractional component. The last two interactions demonstrate the remainder operation %. The remainder of integer-dividing 10 by 3 is 1. Notice again that the data type of the result depends on the type of the operands.

Depending on your math background, you may not have used the integer division or remainder operations before. The thing to keep in mind is that these two operations are closely related. Integer division tells you how many times one number goes into another, and the remainder tells you how much is left over. Mathematically you could write the idea like this: $a = (a//b)(b) + (a\%b)$.

As an example application, suppose we calculated the value of our loose change in cents (rather than dollars). If I have 383 cents, then I can find the number of whole dollars by computing $383//100 = 3$, and the remaining change is $383\%100 = 83$. Thus, I must have a total of three dollars and 83 cents in change.

By the way, although Python, as of version 3.0, treats regular division and integer division as two separate operators, many other computer languages (and earlier Python versions) just use / to signify both. When the operands are ints, / means integer division, and when they are floats, it signifies regular division. This is a common source of errors. For example, in our temperature conversion program the formula 9/5 * celsius + 32 would not compute the proper result, since 9/5 would evaluate to 1 using integer division. In these "old-fashioned" languages, you need to be careful to write this expression as 9.0/5.0 * celsius + 32 so that the proper form of division is used, yielding a fractional result.

3.2   Using the Math Library

Besides the operations listed in Table 3.1, Python provides many other useful mathematical functions in a special math *library*. A library is just a module that contains some useful definitions. Our next program illustrates the use of this library to compute the roots of quadratic equations.

A quadratic equation has the form $ax^2 + bx + c = 0$. Such an equation has two solutions for the value of x given by the quadratic formula:

$$x = \frac{-b \pm \sqrt{b^2 - 4ac}}{2a}$$

Let's write a program that can find the solutions to a quadratic equation. The input to the program will be the values of the coefficients a, b, and c. The outputs are the two values given by the quadratic formula. Here's a program that does the job.

```
# quadratic.py
#    A program that computes the real roots of a quadratic equation.
#    Illustrates use of the math library.
#    Note: this program crashes if the equation has no real roots.

import math  # Makes the math library available.
```

```
def main():
    print("This program finds the real solutions to a quadratic")
    print()

    a, b, c = eval(input("Please enter the coefficients (a, b, c): "))

    discRoot = math.sqrt(b * b - 4 * a * c)
    root1 = (-b + discRoot) / (2 * a)
    root2 = (-b - discRoot) / (2 * a)

    print()
    print("The solutions are:", root1, root2 )

main()
```

This program makes use of the square root function sqrt from the math
library module. The line at the top of the program,

```
import math
```

tells Python that we are using the math module. Importing a module makes
whatever is defined in it available to the program. To compute $\sqrt{x}$, we use
math.sqrt(x). You may recall this dot notation from Chapter 1. This tells
Python to use the sqrt function that "lives" in the math module. In the quadratic
program we calculate $\sqrt{b^2 - 4ac}$ with the line

```
discRoot = math.sqrt(b * b - 4 * a * c)
```

Here is how the program looks in action:

```
This program finds the real solutions to a quadratic

Please enter the coefficients (a, b, c): 3, 4, -2

The solutions are: 0.387425886723 -1.72075922006
```

This program is fine as long as the quadratics we try to solve have real solutions. However, some inputs will cause the program to crash. Here's another
example run:

```
This program finds the real solutions to a quadratic

Please enter the coefficients (a, b, c): 1, 2, 3
Traceback (most recent call last):
  File "quadratic.py", line 21, in ?
    main()
  File "quadratic.py", line 14, in main
    discRoot = math.sqrt(b * b - 4 * a * c)
ValueError: math domain error
```

The problem here is that $b^2 - 4ac < 0$, and the sqrt function is unable to compute the square root of a negative number. Python prints a math domain error. This is telling us that negative numbers are not in the domain of the sqrt function. Right now, we don't have the tools to fix this problem, so we will just have to assume that the user gives us solvable equations.

Actually, quadratic.py did not need to use the math library. We could have taken the square root using exponentiation **. (Can you see how?) Using math.sqrt is somewhat more efficient, and it allowed me to illustrate the use of the math library. In general, if your program requires a common mathematical function, the math library is the first place to look. Table 3.2 shows some of the other functions that are available in the math library.

3.3 Accumulating Results: Factorial

Suppose you have a root beer sampler pack containing six different kinds of root beer. Drinking the various flavors in different orders might affect how good they taste. If you wanted to try out every possible ordering, how many different orders would there be? It turns out the answer is a surprisingly large number, 720. Do you know where this number comes from? The value 720 is the *factorial* of 6.

In mathematics, factorial is often denoted with an exclamation (!). The factorial of a whole number n is defined as $n! = n(n-1)(n-2)\ldots(1)$. This happens to be the number of distinct arrangements for n items. Given six items, we compute $6! = (6)(5)(4)(3)(2)(1) = 720$ possible arrangements.

Let's write a program that will compute the factorial of a number entered by the user. The basic outline of our program follows an input, process, output pattern.

```
Input number to take factorial of, n
```

Python	Mathematics	English
pi	π	An approximation of pi.
e	e	An approximation of e.
sqrt(x)	$\sqrt{x}$	The square root of x.
sin(x)	$\sin x$	The sine of x.
cos(x)	$\cos x$	The cosine of x.
tan(x)	$\tan x$	The tangent of x.
asin(x)	$\arcsin x$	The inverse of sine x.
acos(x)	$\arccos x$	The inverse of cosine x.
atan(x)	$\arctan x$	The inverse of tangent x.
log(x)	$\ln x$	The natural (base e) logarithm of x
log10(x)	$\log_{10} x$	The common (base 10) logarithm of x.
exp(x)	e^x	The exponential of x.
ceil(x)	$\lceil x \rceil$	The smallest whole number $>= x$
floor(x)	$\lfloor x \rfloor$	The largest whole number $<= x$

Table 3.2: Some math library functions

```
Compute factorial of n, fact
Output fact
```

Obviously, the tricky part here is in the second step.

How do we actually compute the factorial? Let's try one by hand to get an idea for the process. In computing the factorial of 6, we first multiply $6(5) = 30$. Then we take that result and do another multiplication $30(4) = 120$. This result is multiplied by three $120(3) = 360$. Finally, this result is multiplied by 2 $360(2) = 720$. According to the definition, we then multiply this result by 1, but that won't change the final value of 720.

Now let's try to think about the algorithm more generally. What is actually going on here? We are doing repeated multiplications, and as we go along, we keep track of the running product. This is a very common algorithmic pattern called an *accumulator*. We build up, or accumulate, a final value piece by piece. To accomplish this in a program, we will use an *accumulator variable* and a loop structure. The general pattern looks like this:

```
Initialize the accumulator variable
Loop until final result is reached
     update the value of accumulator variable
```

Realizing this is the pattern that solves the factorial problem, we just need to fill in the details. We will be accumulating the factorial. Let's keep it in a variable called `fact`. Each time through the loop, we need to multiply `fact` by one of the factors $n, (n-1), \ldots, 1$. It looks like we should use a `for` loop that iterates over this sequence of factors. For example, to compute the factorial of 6, we need a loop that works like this:

```
fact = 1
for factor in [6,5,4,3,2,1]:
    fact = fact * factor
```

Take a minute to trace through the execution of this loop and convince yourself that it works. When the loop body first executes, `fact` has the value 1 and `factor` is 6. So, the new value of `fact` is $1 * 6 = 6$. The next time through the loop, `factor` will be 5, and `fact` is updated to $6 * 5 = 30$. The pattern continues for each successive factor until the final result of 720 has been accumulated.

The initial assignment of 1 to `fact` before the loop is essential to get the loop started. Each time through the loop body (including the first), the current value of `fact` is used to compute the next value. The initialization ensures that `fact` has a value on the very first iteration. Whenever you use the accumulator pattern, make sure you include the proper initialization. Forgetting this is a common mistake of beginning programmers.

Of course, there are many other ways we could have written this loop. As you know from math class, multiplication is commutative and associative, so it really doesn't matter what order we do the multiplications in. We could just as easily go the other direction. You might also notice that including 1 in the list of factors is unnecessary, since multiplication by 1 does not change the result. Here is another version that computes the same result:

```
fact = 1
for factor in [2,3,4,5,6]:
    fact = fact * factor
```

Unfortunately, neither of these loops solves the original problem. We have hand-coded the list of factors to compute the factorial of six. What we really want is a program that can compute the factorial of any given input n. We need some way to generate an appropriate sequence of factors from the value of n.

Luckily, this is quite easy to do using the Python `range` function. Recall that `range(n)` produces a sequence of numbers starting with 0 and continuing up to, but not including, n. There are other variations of `range` that can be used to produce different sequences. With two parameters, range(start,n) produces a sequence that starts with the value start and continues up to, but does not include, n. A third version range(start, n, step) is like the two-parameter version, except that it uses step as the increment between numbers. Here are some examples:

```
>>> list(range(10))
[0, 1, 2, 3, 4, 5, 6, 7, 8, 9]

>>> list(range(5,10))
[5, 6, 7, 8, 9]

>>> list(range(5, 10, 3))
[5, 8]
```

Given our input value n we have a couple of different range commands that produce an appropriate list of factors for computing the factorial of n. To generate them from smallest to largest (a la our second loop), we could use range(2,n+1). Notice how I used n+1 as the second parameter, since the range will go up to but not include this value. We need the +1 to make sure that n itself is included as the last factor.

Another possibility is to generate the factors in the other direction (a la our first loop) using the three-parameter version of range and a negative step to cause the counting to go backwards: range(n,1,-1). This one produces a list starting with n and counting down (step -1) to, but not including 1.

Here then is one possible version of the factorial program:

```
# factorial.py
#    Program to compute the factorial of a number
#    Illustrates for loop with an accumulator

def main():
    n = eval(input("Please enter a whole number: "))
    fact = 1
    for factor in range(n,1,-1):
        fact = fact * factor
    print("The factorial of", n, "is", fact)

main()
```

Of course, there are numerous other ways this program could have been written. I have already mentioned changing the order of factors. Another possibility is to initialize fact to n and then use factors starting at $n - 1$ (as long as $n > 0$). You might try out some of these variations and see which one you like best.

3.4 Limitations of Computer Arithmetic

It's sometimes suggested that the reason "!" is used to represent factorial is because the function grows very rapidly. For example, here is what happens if we use our program to find the factorial of 100:

```
Please enter a whole number: 100
The factorial of 100 is 9332621544394415268169923885626670049071596826
43816214685929638952175999932299156089414639761565182862536979208272237
58251185210916864000000000000000000000000000
```

That's a pretty big number!

Although recent versions of Python have no difficulty with this calculation, older versions of Python (and modern versions of other languages such as C++ and Java) would not fare as well. For example, here's what happens in several runs of a similar program written using Java.

```
# run 1
Please enter a whole number: 6
The factorial is: 720

# run 2
Please enter a whole number: 12
The factorial is: 479001600

# run 3
Please enter a whole number: 13
The factorial is: 1932053504
```

This looks pretty good; we know that $6! = 720$. A quick check also confirms that $12! = 479001600$. Unfortunately, it turns out that $13! = 6227020800$. It appears that the Java program has given us an incorrect answer!

What is going on here? So far, I have talked about numeric data types as representations of familiar numbers such as integers and decimals (fractions). It is important to keep in mind, however, that computer representations of numbers (the actual data types) do not always behave exactly like the numbers that they stand for.

Remember back in Chapter 1 you learned that the computer's CPU can perform very basic operations such as adding or multiplying two numbers? It would be more precise to say that the CPU can perform basic operations on the computer's internal representation of numbers. The problem in this Java program is that it is representing whole numbers using the computer's underlying int data type and relying on the computer's addition operation for ints. Unfortunately, these machine ints are not exactly like mathematical integers. There are infinitely many integers, but only a finite range of ints. Inside the computer, ints are stored in a fixed-sized binary representation. To make sense of all this, we need to look at what's going on at the hardware level.

Computer memory is composed of electrical "switches," each of which can be in one of two possible states, basically on or off. Each switch represents a binary digit or *bit* of information. One bit can encode two possibilities, usually represented with the numerals 0 (for off) and 1 (for on). A sequence of bits can be used to represent more possibilities. With two bits, we can represent four things.

bit 2	bit 1
0	0
0	1
1	0
1	1

Three bits allow us to represent eight different values by adding a zero or one to each of the four two-bit patterns.

bit 3	bit 2	bit 1
0	0	0
0	0	1
0	1	0
0	1	1
1	0	0
1	0	1
1	1	0
1	1	1

You can see the pattern here. Each extra bit doubles the number of distinct patterns. In general, n bits can represent 2^n different values.

The number of bits that a particular computer uses to represent an int depends on the design of the CPU. Typical PCs today use 32 or 64 bits. For a 32 bit CPU, that means there are 2^{32} possible values. These values are centered at 0 to represent a range of positive and negative integers. Now $\frac{2^{32}}{2} = 2^{31}$. So, the range of integers that can be represented in a 32 bit int value is -2^{31} to $2^{31} - 1$. The reason for the -1 on the high end is to account for the representation of 0 in the top half of the range.

Given this knowledge, let's try to make sense of what's happening in the Java factorial example. If the Java program is relying on a 32-bit int representation, what's the largest number it can store. Python can give us a quick answer.

```
>>> 2**31-1
2147483647
```

Notice that this value (about 2.1 billion) lies between 12! (about 4.8 million) and 13! (about 6.2 billion). That means the Java program is fine for calculating factorials up to 12, but after that the representation "overflows" and the results are garbage. Now you know exactly why the simple Java program can't compute 13! Of course, that leaves us with another puzzle. Why does the modern Python program seem to work quite well computing with large integers?

At first, you might think that Python uses the float data type to get us around the size limitation of the ints. However, it turns out that floats do not really solve this problem. Here is an example run of a modified factorial program that uses floating point numbers:

```
Please enter a whole number: 30
The factorial of 30 is  2.6525285981219103e+32
```

Although this program runs just fine, after switching to float, we no longer get an exact answer.

A very large (or very small) floating point value is printed out using *exponential*, or *scientific*, notation. The e+32 at the end means that the result is equal to $2.6525285981219103 \times 10^{32}$. You can think of the +32 at the end as a marker that shows where the decimal point should be placed. In this case, it must move 32 places to the right to get the actual value. However, there are only 16 digits to the right of the decimal, so we have "lost" the last 16 digits.

Remember, floats are approximations. Using a float allows us to represent a much larger *range* of values than a 32-bit int, but the amount of *precision* is still fixed. In fact, a computer stores floating point numbers as a pair of fixed-length (binary) integers. One integer represents the string of digits in the value, and the second represents the exponent value that keeps track of where the whole part ends and the fractional part begins.

Fortunately, Python has a better solution for large, exact values. A Python int is not a fixed size, but expands to accommodate whatever value it holds. The only limit is the amount of memory the computer has available to it. When the value is small, Python can just use the computer's underlying int representation and operations. When the value gets larger, Python automatically converts to a representation using more bits. Of course, in order to perform operations on larger numbers, Python has to break down the operations into smaller units that the computer hardware is able to handle. Sort of like the way you might do long division by hand. These operations will not be as efficient (they require more steps), but they allow our Python ints to grow to arbitrary size. And that's what allows our simple factorial program to compute some whopping large results. This is a very cool feature of Python.

3.5 Type Conversions and Rounding

There are situations where a value may need to be converted from one data type into another. You already know that combining an int with an int (usually) produces an int, and combining a float with a float creates another float. But what happens if we write an expression that mixes an int with a float? For example, what should the value of x be after this assignment statement?

```
x = 5.0 * 2
```

If this is floating point multiplication, then the result should be the float value 10.0. If an int multiplication is performed, the result is 10. Before reading ahead for the answer, take a minute to consider how you think Python should handle this situation.

In order to make sense of the expression 5.0 * 2, Python must either change 5.0 to 5 and perform an int operation or convert 2 to 2.0 and perform floating point operation. In general, converting a float to an int is a dangerous step, because some information (the fractional part) will be lost. On the other hand, an int can be safely turned into a float just by adding a fractional part of .0. So, in *mixed-typed expressions*, Python will automatically convert ints to floats and perform floating point operations to produce a float result.

Sometimes we may want to perform a type conversion ourselves. This is called an *explicit* type conversion. Python provides the built-in functions int and float for these occasions. Here are some interactive examples that illustrate their behavior:

```
>>> int(4.5)
4
>>> int(3.9)
3
>>> float(4)
4.0
>>> float(4.5)
4.5
>>> float(int(3.3))
3.0
>>> int(float(3.3))
3
>>> int(float(3))
3
```

As you can see, converting to an int simply discards the fractional part of a float; the value is truncated, not rounded. If you want a rounded result, you could add 0.5 to the value before using int(), assuming the value is positive.

A more general way of rounding off numbers is to use the built-in round function which rounds a number to the nearest whole value.

```
>>> round(3.14)
3
>>> round(3.5)
4
```

Notice that calling round like this results in an int value. So a simple call to round is an alternative way of converting a float to an int.

If you want to round a float into another float value, you can do that by supplying a second parameter that specifies the number of digits you want after the decimal point. Here's a little interaction playing around with the value of pi from the math library:

```
>>> import math
>>> math.pi
```

```
3.1415926535897931
>>> round(math.pi, 2)
3.1400000000000001
>>> round(math.pi,3)
3.1419999999999999
>>> print(round(math.pi, 2))
3.14
>>> print(round(math.pi,3))
3.142
```

Notice that when we round pi to two or three decimal places, we do not get exactly two or three decimal places in the result. Remember, floats are always approximations; we get something that's very close to what we requested. However, the last two interactions show something interesting about the Python print statement. Python is smart enough to know that we probably don't want to see all the digits in something like 3.140000000000001, so it actually prints out the rounded form. That means if you write a program that rounds off a value to two decimal places and you print out the value, you'll end up seeing two decimal places, just like you expect.[1] In Chapter 5, we'll see how to get even finer control over how numbers appear when printed.

3.6 Chapter Summary

This chapter has filled in some important details concerning programs that do numerical computations. Here is a quick summary of some key concepts:

- The way a computer represents a particular kind of information is called a data type. The data type of an object determines what values it can have and what operations it supports.

- Python has several different data types for representing numeric values, including int and float.

- Whole numbers are generally represented using the int data type and fractional values are represented using floats. All of the Python numeric data types support standard, built-in mathematical operations addition (+), subtraction (-), multiplication (*), division (/), integer division (//), remainder (%), exponentiation (**), and absolute value (abs(x)).

---

[1]As of Python 3.1, the interactive interpreter will also show only the shortened result

- Additional mathematical functions are defined in the math library. To use these functions, a program must first import the math library.

- Numerical results are often calculated by computing the sum or product of a sequence of values. The loop accumulator programming pattern is useful for this sort of calculation.

- Both ints and floats are represented on the underlying computer using a fixed-length sequence of bits. This imposes certain limits on these representations. Hardware ints must be in the range $-2^{31} \ldots (2^{31} - 1)$ on a 32 bit machine. Floats have a finite amount of precision and cannot represent most numbers exactly.

- Python's int data type may be used to store whole numbers of arbitrary size. Int values are automatically converted to longer representations when they become too large for underlying hardware int. Calculations involving these long ints are less efficient than those that use only small ints.

- Python automatically converts numbers from one data type to another in certain situations. For example, in a mixed-type expression involving ints and floats, Python first converts the ints into floats and then uses float arithmetic.

- Programs may also explicitly convert one data type into another using the functions float(), int(), and round().

3.7 Exercises

Review Questions

True/False

1. Information that is stored and manipulated by computers is called data.

2. Since floating point numbers are extremely accurate, they should generally be used instead of ints.

3. Operations like addition and subtraction are defined in the math library.

4. The number of possible rearrangements of n items is equal to $n!$.

5. The `sqrt` function computes the squirt of a number.

6. The int data type is identical to the mathematical concept of integer.

7. Computers represent numbers using base 2 representations.

8. A hardware float can represent a larger range of values than a hardware int.

9. A Python int can represent indefinitely large numbers.

10. In Python, 4+5 produces the same result type as 4.0+5.0.

Multiple Choice

1. Which of the following is *not* a Python data type?
   a) int   b) float   c) rational   d) string

2. Which of the following is *not* a built-in operation?
   a) +   b) %   c) abs()   d) sqrt()

3. In order to use functions in the math library, a program must include
   a) a comment   b) a loop   c) an operator   d) an import statement

4. The value of 4! is
   a) 9   b) 24   c) 41   d) 120

5. The most appropriate data type for storing the value of pi is
   a) int   b) float   c) irrational   d) string

6. The number of distinct values that can be represented using 5 bits is
   a) 5   b) 10   c) 32   d) 50

7. In a mixed-type expression involving ints and floats, Python will convert
   a) floats to ints   b) ints to strings   c) floats and ints to strings   d) ints to floats

8. Which of the following is not a Python type-conversion function?
   a) float   b) round   c) int   d) abs

9. The pattern used to compute factorial is
   a) accumulator   b) input, process, output
   c) counted loop   d) plaid

10. In modern Python, an int value that grows larger than the underlying hardware int
    a) causes an overflow   b) converts to float   c) breaks the computer
    d) uses more memory

Discussion

1. Show the result of evaluating each expression. Be sure that the value is in the proper form to indicate its type (int, long int, or float). If the expression is illegal, explain why.

   (a) `4.0 / 10.0 + 3.5 * 2`

   (b) `10 % 4 + 6 / 2`

   (c) `abs(4 - 20 // 3) ** 3`

   (d) `sqrt(4.5 - 5.0) + 7 * 3`

   (e) `3 * 10 // 3 + 10 % 3`

   (f) `3 ** 3`

2. Translate each of the following mathematical expressions into an equivalent Python expression. You may assume that the math library has been imported (via `import math`).

   (a) $(3 + 4)(5)$

   (b) $\frac{n(n-1)}{2}$

   (c) $4\pi r^2$

   (d) $\sqrt{r(\cos a)^2 + r(\sin a)^2}$

   (e) $\frac{y2-y1}{x2-x1}$

3. Show the sequence of numbers that would be generated by each of the following range expressions.

   (a) `range(5)`

   (b) `range(3, 10)`

   (c) `range(4, 13, 3)`

   (d) `range(15, 5, -2)`

   (e) `range(5, 3)`

4. Show the output that would be generated by each of the following program fragments.

   (a) ```
       for i in range(1, 11):
           print(i*i)
       ```

   (b) ```
       for i in [1,3,5,7,9]:
           print(i, ":", i**3)
       print(i)
       ```

   (c) ```
       x = 2
       y = 10
       for j in range(0, y, x):
           print(j, end="")
           print(x + y)
       print("done")
       ```

   (d) ```
       ans = 0
       for i in range(1, 11):
           ans = ans + i*i
           print(i)
       print (ans)
       ```

5. What do you think will happen if you use a negative number as the second
   parameter in the round function? For example, what should be the result
   of round(314.159265, -1). Explain the rationale for your answer. After
   you've written your answer, consult the Python documentation or try out
   some examples to see what Python actually does in this case.

6. What do you think will happen when the operands to the integer division
   or remainder operations are negative? Consider each of the following
   cases and try to predict the result. Then try them out in Python. Hint:
   Recall the magic formula $a = (a//b)(b) + (a\%b)$.

   (a) -10 // 3

   (b) -10 % 3

   (c) 10 // -3

   (d) 10 % -3

   (e) -10 // -3

Programming Exercises

1. Write a program to calculate the volume and surface area of a sphere from its radius, given as input. Here are some formulas that might be useful:

$$V = 4/3\pi r^3$$

$$A = 4\pi r^2$$

2. Write a program that calculates the cost per square inch of a circular pizza, given its diameter and price. The formula for area is $A = \pi r^2$

3. Write a program that determines the molecular weight of a hydrocarbon based on the number of hydrogen, carbon, and oxygen atoms. You should use the following weights:

Atom	Weight (grams / mole)
H	1.0079
C	12.011
O	15.9994

4. Write a program that determines the distance to a lightning strike based on the time elapsed between the flash and the sound of thunder. The speed of sound is approximately 1100 ft/sec and 1 mile is 5280 ft.

5. The Konditorei coffee shop sells coffee at $10.50 a pound plus the cost of shipping. Each order ships for $0.86 per pound + $1.50 fixed cost for overhead. Write a program that calculates the cost of an order.

6. Two points in a plane are specified using the coordinates (x1,y1) and (x2,y2). Write a program that calculates the slope of a line through two (non-vertical) points entered by the user.

$$slope = \frac{y2 - y1}{x2 - x1}$$

7. Write a program that accepts two points (see previous problem) and determines the distance between them.

$$distance = \sqrt{(x2 - x1)^2 + (y2 - y1)^2}$$

8. The Gregorian epact is the number of days between January 1st and the previous new moon. This value is used to figure out the date of Easter. It is calculated by these formulas (using int arithmetic):

$$C = year//100$$

$$epact = (8 + (C//4) - C + ((8C + 13)//25) + 11(year\%19))\%30$$

Write a program that prompts the user for a 4-digit year and then outputs the value of the epact.

9. Write a program to calculate the area of a triangle given the length of its three sides a, b, and c using these formulas:

$$s = \frac{a + b + c}{2}$$

$$A = \sqrt{s(s-a)(s-b)(s-c)}$$

10. Write a program to determine the length of a ladder required to reach a given height when leaned against a house. The height and angle of the ladder are given as inputs. To compute length use

$$length = \frac{height}{\sin angle}$$

Note: The angle must be in radians. Prompt for an angle in degrees and use this formula to convert:

$$radians = \frac{\pi}{180} degrees$$

11. Write a program to find the sum of the first n natural numbers, where the value of n is provided by the user.

12. Write a program to find the sum of the cubes of the first n natural numbers where the value of n is provided by the user.

13. Write a program to sum a series of numbers entered by the user. The program should first prompt the user for how many numbers are to be summed. It should then input each of the numbers and print a total sum.

14. Write a program that finds the average of a series of numbers entered by the user. As in the previous problem, the program will first ask the user how many numbers there are. Note: The average should always be a float, even if the user inputs are all ints.

15. Write a program that approximates the value of π by summing the terms of this series: $4/1 - 4/3 + 4/5 - 4/7 + 4/9 - 4/11 + \ldots$ The program should prompt the user for n, the number of terms to sum, and then output the sum of the first n terms of this series. Have your program subtract the approximation from the value of `math.pi` to see how accurate it is.

16. A Fibonacci sequence is a sequence of numbers where each successive number is the sum of the previous two. The classic Fibonacci sequence begins: 1, 1, 2, 3, 5, 8, 13,.... Write a program that computes the nth Fibonacci number where n is a value input by the user. For example, if $n = 6$, then the result is 8.

17. You have seen that the math library contains a function that computes the square root of numbers. In this exercise, you are to write your own algorithm for computing square roots. One way to solve this problem is to use a guess-and-check approach. You first guess what the square root might be and then see how close your guess is. You can use this information to make another guess and continue guessing until you have found the square root (or a close approximation to it). One particularly good way of making guesses is to use Newton's method. Suppose x is the number we want the root of and guess is the current guessed answer. The guess can be improved by using $\frac{guess + \frac{x}{guess}}{2}$ as the next guess.

Write a program that implements Newton's method. The program should prompt the user for the value to find the square root of (x) and the number of times to improve the guess. Starting with a guess value of x/2, your program should loop the specified number of times applying Newton's method and report the final value of guess. You should also subtract your estimate from the value of `math.sqrt(x)` to show how close it is.

Chapter 4

Objects and Graphics

Objectives

- To understand the concept of objects and how they can be used to simplify programming.

- To become familiar with the various objects available in the graphics library.

- To be able to create objects in programs and call appropriate methods to perform graphical computations.

- To understand the fundamental concepts of computer graphics, especially the role of coordinate systems and coordinate transformations.

- To understand how to work with both mouse- and text-based input in a graphical programming context.

- To be able to write simple interactive graphics programs using the graphics library.

4.1 Overview

So far we have been writing programs that use the built-in Python data types for numbers and strings. We saw that each data type could represent a certain set of values, and each had a set of associated operations. Basically, we viewed the data as passive entities that were manipulated and combined via active operations. This is a traditional way to view computation. To build complex systems, however, it helps to take a richer view of the relationship between data and operations.

Most modern computer programs are built using an *object-oriented* (OO) approach. Object orientation is not easily defined. It encompasses a number of principles for designing and implementing software, principles that we will return to numerous times throughout the course of this book. This chapter provides a basic introduction to object concepts by way of some computer graphics.

Graphical programming is a lot of fun and provides a great vehicle for learning about objects. In the process, you will also learn the principles of computer graphics that underlie many modern computer applications. Most of the applications that you are familiar with probably have a so-called *graphical user interface* (GUI) that provides visual elements like windows, icons (representative pictures), buttons, and menus.

Interactive graphics programming can be very complicated; entire textbooks are devoted to the intricacies of graphics and graphical interfaces. Industrial-strength GUI applications are usually developed using a dedicated graphics programming framework. Python comes with its own standard GUI module called *Tkinter*. As GUI frameworks go, Tkinter is one of the simplest to use, and Python is a great language for developing real-world GUIs. Still, at this point in your programming career, it would be a challenge to learn the intricacies of any GUI framework, and doing so would not contribute much to the main objectives of this chapter, which are to introduce you to objects and the fundamental principles of computer graphics.

To make learning these basic concepts easier, we will use a graphics library (graphics.py) specifically written for use with this textbook. This library is a wrapper around Tkinter that makes it more suitable for beginning programmers. It is freely available as a Python module file[1] and you are welcome to use it as you see fit. Eventually, you may want to study the code for the library itself as a stepping stone to learning how to program directly in Tkinter.

---

[1]See Appendix B for information on how to obtain the graphics library and other supporting materials for this book.

4.2 The Object of Objects

The basic idea of object-oriented development is to view a complex system as the interaction of simpler *objects*. The word *objects* is being used here in a specific technical sense. Part of the challenge of OO programming is figuring out the vocabulary. You can think of an OO object as a sort of active data type that combines both data and operations. To put it simply, objects *know stuff* (they contain data), and they *can do stuff* (they have operations). Objects interact by sending each other messages. A message is simply a request for an object to perform one of its operations.

Consider a simple example. Suppose we want to develop a data processing system for a college or university. We will need to keep track of considerable information. For starters, we must keep records on the students who attend the school. Each student could be represented in the program as an object. A student object would contain certain data such as name, ID number, courses taken, campus address, home address, GPA, etc. Each student object would also be able to respond to certain requests. For example, to send out a mailing, we would need to print an address for each student. This task might be handled by a `printCampusAddress` operation. When a particular student object is sent the `printCampusAddress` message, it prints out its own address. To print out all the addresses, a program would loop through the collection of student objects and send each one in turn the `printCampusAddress` message.

Objects may refer to other objects. In our example, each course in the college might also be represented by an object. Course objects would know things such as who the instructor is, what students are in the course, what the prerequisites are, and when and where the course meets. One example operation might be `addStudent`, which causes a student to be enrolled in the course. The student being enrolled would be represented by the appropriate student object. Instructors would be another kind of object, as well as rooms, and even times. You can see how successive refinement of these ideas could lead to a rather sophisticated model of the information structure of the college.

As a beginning programmer, you're probably not yet ready to tackle a college information system. For now, we'll study objects in the context of some simple graphics programming.

4.3 Simple Graphics Programming

In order to run the graphical programs and examples in this chapter (and the rest of the book), you will need a copy of the file graphics.py that is supplied with the supplemental materials. Using the graphics library is as easy as placing a copy of the graphics.py file in the same folder as your graphics program(s). Alternatively, you can place it in a system directory where other Python libraries are stored so that it can be used from any folder on the system.

The graphics library makes it easy to experiment with graphics interactively and write simple graphics programs. As you do, you will be learning principles of object-oriented programming and computer graphics that can be applied in more sophisticated graphical programming environments. The details of the graphics module will be explored in later sections. Here we'll concentrate on a basic hands-on introduction to whet your appetite.

As usual, the best way to start learning new concepts is to roll up your sleeves and try out some examples. The first step is to import the graphics module. Assuming you have placed graphics.py in an appropriate place, you can import the graphics commands into an interactive Python session.

```
>>> import graphics
```

Next we need to create a place on the screen where the graphics will appear. That place is a *graphics window* or GraphWin, which is provided by the graphics module.

```
>>> win = graphics.GraphWin()
```

Notice the use of dot notation to invoke the GraphWin function that "lives in" the graphics library. This is analogous to when we used math.sqrt(x) to invoke the square root function from the math library module. The GraphWin() function creates a new window on the screen. The window will have the title "Graphics Window." The GraphWin may overlap your Python interpreter window, so you might have to resize or move the Python window to make both fully visible. Figure 4.1 shows an example screen view.

The GraphWin is an object, and we have assigned it to the variable called win. We can now manipulate the window object through this variable. For example, when we are finished with a window, we can destroy it. This is done by issuing the close command.

```
>>> win.close()
```

Figure 4.1: Screen shot with a Python shell and a GraphWin

Typing this command causes the window to vanish from the screen.

Notice that we are again using the dot notation here, but now we are using it with a variable name, not a module name, on the left side of the dot. Recall that win was earlier assigned an object of type GraphWin. One of the things a GraphWin object can do is to close itself. You can think of this command as invoking the close operation that is associated with this particular window. The result is that the window disappears from the screen.

We will be working with quite a few commands from the graphics library, and it gets tedious having to type the graphics. notation every time we use one. Python has an alternative form of import that can help out.

```
from graphics import *
```

The from statement allows you to load specific definitions from a library module. You can either list the names of definitions to be imported or use an asterisk, as shown, to import everything defined in the module. The imported commands become directly available without having to preface them with the module name. After doing this import, we can create a GraphWin more simply.

```
win = GraphWin()
```

All of the rest of the graphics examples will assume that the entire graphics
module has been imported using from.

Let's try our hand at some drawing. A graphics window is actually a collection of tiny points called *pixels* (short for picture elements). By controlling the
color of each pixel, we control what is displayed in the window. By default, a
GraphWin is 200 pixels tall and 200 pixels wide. That means there are 40,000
pixels in the GraphWin. Drawing a picture by assigning a color to each individual pixel would be a daunting challenge. Instead, we will rely on a library of
graphical objects. Each type of object does its own bookkeeping and knows how
to draw itself into a GraphWin.

The simplest object in the graphics module is a Point. In geometry, a point
is a location in space. A point is located by reference to a coordinate system. Our
graphics object Point is similar; it can represent a location in a GraphWin. We
define a point by supplying x and y coordinates (x, y). The x value represents
the horizontal location of the point, and the y value represents the vertical.

Traditionally, graphics programmers locate the point $(0, 0)$ in the upper-left
corner of the window. Thus x values increase from left to right, and y values
increase from top to bottom. In the default 200 x 200 GraphWin, the lower-right
corner has the coordinates $(199, 199)$. Drawing a Point sets the color of the
corresponding pixel in the GraphWin. The default color for drawing is black.

Here is a sample interaction with Python illustrating the use of Points:

```
>>> p = Point(50,60)
>>> p.getX()
50
>>> p.getY()
60
>>> win = GraphWin()
>>> p.draw(win)
>>> p2 = Point(140,100)
>>> p2.draw(win)
```

The first line creates a Point located at $(50, 60)$. After the Point has been created, its coordinate values can be accessed by the operations getX and getY.
A Point is drawn into a window using the draw operation. In this example,
two different point objects (p and p2) are created and drawn into the GraphWin
called win. Figure 4.2 shows the resulting graphical output.

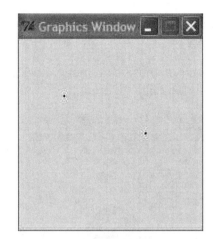

Figure 4.2: Graphics window with two points drawn

In addition to points, the graphics library contains commands for drawing lines, circles, rectangles, ovals, polygons and text. Each of these objects is created and drawn in a similar fashion. Here is a sample interaction to draw various shapes into a GraphWin:

```
>>> #### Open a graphics window
>>> win = GraphWin('Shapes')
>>> #### Draw a red circle centered at point (100,100) with radius 30
>>> center = Point(100,100)
>>> circ = Circle(center, 30)
>>> circ.setFill('red')
>>> circ.draw(win)
>>> #### Put a textual label in the center of the circle
>>> label = Text(center, "Red Circle")
>>> label.draw(win)
>>> #### Draw a square using a Rectangle object
>>> rect = Rectangle(Point(30,30), Point(70,70))
>>> rect.draw(win)
>>> #### Draw a line segment using a Line object
>>> line = Line(Point(20,30), Point(180, 165))
>>> line.draw(win)
>>> #### Draw an oval using the Oval object
```

```
>>> oval = Oval(Point(20,150), Point(180,199))
>>> oval.draw(win)
```

Try to figure out what each of these statements does. If you type them in as
shown, the final result will look like Figure 4.3.

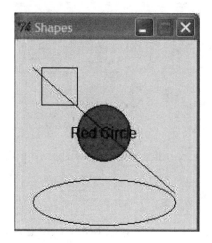

Figure 4.3: Various shapes from the graphics module

4.4   Using Graphical Objects

Some of the examples in the above interactions may look a bit strange to you.
To really understand the graphics module, we need to take an object-oriented
point of view. Remember, objects combine data with operations. Computation
is performed by asking an object to carry out one of its operations. In order to
make use of objects, you need to know how to create them and how to request
operations.

In the interactive examples above, we manipulated several different kinds
of objects: GraphWin, Point, Circle, Oval, Line, Text, and Rectangle. These
are examples of *classes*. Every object is an *instance* of some class, and the class
describes the properties the instance will have.

Borrowing a biological metaphor, when we say that Fido is a dog, we are
actually saying that Fido is a specific individual in the larger class of all dogs. In
OO terminology, Fido is an instance of the dog class. Because Fido is an instance

of this class, we expect certain things. Fido has four legs, a tail, a cold, wet nose and he barks. If Rex is a dog, we expect that he will have similar properties, even though Fido and Rex may differ in specific details such as size or color.

The same ideas hold for our computational objects. We can create two separate instances of `Point`, say p and p2. Each of these points has an x and y value, and they both support the same set of operations like `getX` and `draw`. These properties hold because the objects are `Points`. However, different instances can vary in specific details such as the values of their coordinates.

To create a new instance of a class, we use a special operation called a *constructor*. A call to a constructor is an expression that creates a brand new object. The general form is as follows:

```
<class-name>(<param1>, <param2>, ...)
```

Here `<class-name>` is the name of the class that we want to create a new instance of, e.g., `Circle` or `Point`. The expressions in the parentheses are any parameters that are required to initialize the object. The number and type of the parameters depends on the class. A `Point` requires two numeric values, while a `GraphWin` can be constructed without any parameters. Often, a constructor is used on the right side of an assignment statement, and the resulting object is immediately assigned to a variable on the left side that is then used to manipulate the object.

To take a concrete example, let's look at what happens when we create a graphical point. Here is a constructor statement from the interactive example above.

```
p = Point(50,60)
```

The constructor for the `Point` class requires two parameters giving the x and y coordinates for the new point. These values are stored as *instance variables* inside the object. In this case, Python creates an instance of `Point` having an x value of 50 and a y value of 60. The resulting point is then assigned to the variable p. A conceptual diagram of the result is shown in Figure 4.4. Note that, in this diagram as well as similar ones later on, only the most salient details are shown. `Points` also contain other information such as their color and which window (if any) they are drawn in. Most of this information is set to default values when the `Point` is created.

To perform an operation on an object, we send the object a message. The set of messages that an object responds to are called the *methods* of the object. You can think of methods as functions that live inside the object. A method is invoked using dot-notation.

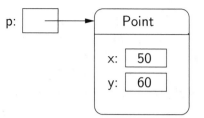

Figure 4.4: Conceptual picture of the result of p = Point(50,60). The variable p refers to a freshly created Point having the given coordinates

```
<object>.<method-name>(<param1>, <param2>, ...)
```

The number and type of the parameters is determined by the method being used. Some methods require no parameters at all. You can find numerous examples of method invocation in the interactive examples above.

As examples of parameterless methods, consider these two expressions:

```
p.getX()
p.getY()
```

The getX and getY methods return the x and y values of a point, respectively. Methods such as these are sometimes called *accessors*, because they allow us to access information from the instance variables of the object.

Other methods change the values of an object's instance variables, hence changing the *state* of the object. All of the graphical objects have a move method. Here is a specification:

move(dx, dy): Moves the object dx units in the x direction and dy units in the y direction.

To move the point p to the right 10 units, we could use this statement.

```
p.move(10,0)
```

This changes the x instance variable of p by adding 10 units. If the point is currently drawn in a GraphWin, move will also take care of erasing the old image and drawing it in its new position. Methods that change the state of an object are sometimes called *mutators*.

The move method must be supplied with two simple numeric parameters indicating the distance to move the object along each dimension. Some methods require parameters that are themselves complex objects. For example, drawing a Circle into a GraphWin involves two objects. Let's examine a sequence of commands that does this.

```
circ = Circle(Point(100,100), 30)
win = GraphWin()
circ.draw(win)
```

The first line creates a Circle with a center located at the Point $(100, 100)$ and a radius of 30. Notice that we used the Point constructor to create a location for the first parameter to the Circle constructor. The second line creates a GraphWin. Do you see what is happening in the third line? This is a request for the Circle object circ to draw itself into the GraphWin object win. The visible effect of this statement is a circle in the GraphWin centered at $(100, 100)$ and having a radius of 30. Behind the scenes, a lot more is happening.

Remember, the draw method lives inside the circ object. Using information about the center and radius of the circle from the instance variables, the draw method issues an appropriate sequence of low-level drawing commands (a sequence of method invocations) to the GraphWin. A conceptual picture of the interactions among the Point, Circle and GraphWin objects is shown in Figure 4.5. Fortunately, we don't usually have to worry about these kinds of details; they're all taken care of by the graphical objects. We just create objects, call the appropriate methods, and let them do the work. That's the power of object-oriented programming.

There is one subtle "gotcha" that you need to keep in mind when using objects. It is possible for two different variables to refer to exactly the same object; changes made to the object through one variable will also be visible to the other. Suppose we are trying to write a sequence of code that draws a smiley face. We want to create two eyes that are 20 units apart. Here is a sequence of code intended to draw the eyes.

```
## Incorrect way to create two circles.
leftEye = Circle(Point(80, 50), 5)
leftEye.setFill('yellow')
leftEye.setOutline('red')
rightEye = leftEye
rightEye.move(20,0)
```

The basic idea is to create the left eye and then copy that into a right eye which is then moved over 20 units.

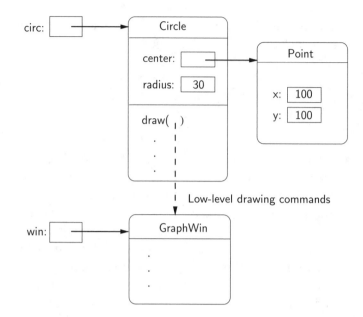

Figure 4.5: Object interactions to draw a circle

This doesn't work. The problem here is that only one `Circle` object is created. The assignment

```
rightEye = leftEye
```

simply makes `rightEye` refer to the very same circle as `leftEye`. Figure 4.6 shows the situation. When the `Circle` is moved in the last line of code, both `rightEye` and `leftEye` refer to it in its new location on the right side. This situation where two variables refer to the same object is called *aliasing*, and it can sometimes produce rather unexpected results.

One solution to this problem would be to create a separate circle for each eye.

```
## A correct way to create two circles.
leftEye = Circle(Point(80, 50), 5)
leftEye.setFill('yellow')
leftEye.setOutline('red')
rightEye = Circle(Point(100, 50), 5)
rightEye.setFill('yellow')
```

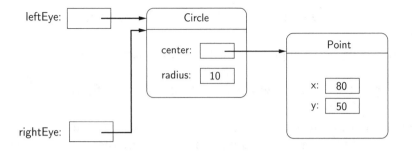

Figure 4.6: Variables leftEye and rightEye are aliases

```
rightEye.setOutline('red')
```

This will certainly work, but it's cumbersome. We had to write duplicated code for the two eyes. That's easy to do using a "cut and paste" approach, but it's not very elegant. If we decide to change the appearance of the eyes, we will have to be sure to make the changes in two places.

The graphics library provides a better solution; all graphical objects support a clone method that makes a copy of the object. Using clone, we can rescue the original approach.

```
## Correct way to create two circles, using clone.
leftEye = Circle(Point(80, 50), 5)
leftEye.setFill('yellow')
leftEye.setOutline('red')
rightEye = leftEye.clone() # rightEye is an exact copy of the left
rightEye.move(20,0)
```

Strategic use of cloning can make some graphics tasks much easier.

4.5 Graphing Future Value

Now that you have some idea of how to use objects from the graphics module, we're ready to try some real graphics programming. One of the most important uses of graphics is providing a visual representation of data. They say a picture is worth a thousand words; it is almost certainly better than a thousand numbers. Just about any program that manipulates numeric data can be improved with a bit of graphical output. Remember the program in Chapter 2 that computed the future value of a ten-year investment? Let's try our hand at creating a graphical summary.

Programming with graphics requires careful planning. You'll probably want pencil and paper handy to draw some diagrams and scratch out calculations as we go along. As usual, we begin by considering the specification of exactly *what* the program will do.

The original program futval.py had two inputs: the amount of money to be invested and the annualized rate of interest. Using these inputs, the program calculated the change in principal year by year for ten years using the formula principal = principal(1+apr). It then printed out the final value of the principal. In the graphical version, the output will be a ten-year bar graph where the height of successive bars represents the value of the principal in successive years.

Let's use a concrete example for illustration. Suppose we invest $2000 at 10% interest. This table shows the growth of the investment over a ten-year period:

Years	Value
0	$2,000.00
1	$2,200.00
2	$2,420.00
3	$2,662.00
4	$2,928.20
5	$3,221.02
6	$3,542.12
7	$3,897.43
8	$4,287.18
9	$4,715.90
10	$5,187.49

Our program will display this information in a bar graph. Figure 4.7 shows the data in graphical form. The graph actually contains eleven bars. The first bar shows the original value of the principal. For reference, let's number these bars according to the number of years of interest accrued, 0–10.

Here is a rough design for the program:

```
Print an introduction
Get value of principal and apr from user
Create a GraphWin
Draw scale labels on left side of window
```

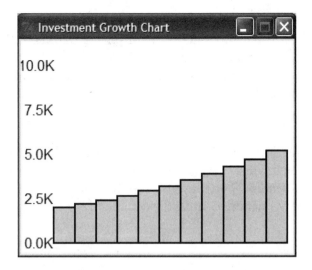

Figure 4.7: Bar graph showing growth of $2,000 at 10% interest

```
Draw bar at position 0 with height corresponding to principal
For successive years 1 through 10
    Calculate principal = principal * (1 + apr)
    Draw a bar for this year having a height corresponding to principal
Wait for user to press Enter.
```

The pause created by the last step is necessary to keep the graphics window displayed so that we can interpret the results. Without such a pause, the program would end and the GraphWin would vanish with it.

While this design gives us the broad brush strokes for our algorithm, there are some very important details that have been glossed over. We must decide exactly how big the graphics window will be and how we will position the objects that appear in this window. For example, what does it mean to draw, say, a bar for year five with height corresponding to $3,221.02?

Let's start with the size of the GraphWin. Recall that the size of a window is given in terms of the number of pixels in each dimension. Computer screens are also measured in terms of pixels. The number of pixels or *resolution* of the screen is determined by the monitor and graphics card in the computer you use. The lowest resolution screen you are likely to encounter on a personal computer these days is a so-called *extended VGA* screen that is 1024x768 pixels.

Most screens are considerably larger. Our default 200x200 pixel window will probably seem a bit small. Let's make the `GraphWin` 320x240; that will make it about 1/8 the size of a small screen.

Given this analysis, we can flesh out a bit of our design. The third line of the design should now read:

```
Create a 320x240 GraphWin titled ''Investment Growth Chart''
```

You may be wondering how this will translate into Python code. You have already seen that the `GraphWin` constructor allows an optional parameter to specify the title of the window. You may also supply width and height parameters to control the size of the window. Thus, the command to create the output window will be:

```
win = GraphWin("Investment Growth Chart", 320, 240)
```

Next we turn to the problem of printing labels along the left edge of our window. To simplify the problem, we will assume the graph is always scaled to a maximum of $10,000 with the five labels "0.0K" to "10.0K" as shown in the example window. The question is how should the labels be drawn? We will need some `Text` objects. When creating `Text`, we specify the anchor point (the point the text is centered on) and the string to use as the label.

The label strings are easy. Our longest label is five characters, and the labels should all line up on the right side of a column, so the shorter strings will be padded on the left with spaces. The placement of the labels is chosen with a bit of calculation and some trial and error. Playing with some interactive examples, it seems that a string of length five looks nicely positioned in the horizontal direction placing the center 20 pixels in from the left edge. This leaves just a bit of white space at the margin.

In the vertical direction, we have just over 200 pixels to work with. A simple scaling would be to have 100 pixels represent $5,000. That means our five labels should be spaced 50 pixels apart. Using 200 pixels for the range 0–10,000 leaves $240 - 200 = 40$ pixels to split between the top and bottom margins. We might want to leave a little more margin at the top to accommodate values that grow beyond $10,000. A little experimentation suggests that putting the " 0.0K" label 10 pixels from the bottom (position 230) seems to look nice.

Elaborating our algorithm to include these details, the single step

```
Draw scale labels on left side of window
```

becomes a sequence of steps

```
Draw label " 0.0K" at (20, 230)
Draw label " 2.5K" at (20, 180)
Draw label " 5.0K" at (20, 130)
Draw label " 7.5K" at (20, 80)
Draw label "10.0K" at (20, 30)
```

The next step in the original design calls for drawing the bar that corresponds to the initial amount of the principal. It is easy to see where the lower-left corner of this bar should be. The value of $0.0 is located vertically at pixel 230, and the labels are *centered* 20 pixels in from the left edge. Adding another 20 pixels gets us to the right edge of the labels. Thus the lower-left corner of the 0th bar should be at location $(40, 230)$.

Now we just need to figure out where the opposite (upper-right) corner of the bar should be so that we can draw an appropriate rectangle. In the vertical direction, the height of the bar is determined by the value of `principal`. In drawing the scale, we determined that 100 pixels is equal to $5,000. This means that we have $100/5000 = 0.02$ pixels to the dollar. This tells us, for example, that a principal of $2,000 should produce a bar of height $2000(.02) = 40$ pixels. In general, the y position of the upper-right corner will be given by $230 - (\text{principal})(0.02)$. (Remember that 230 is the 0 point, and the y coordinates decrease going up).

How wide should the bar be? The window is 320 pixels wide, but 40 pixels are eaten up by the labels on the left. That leaves us with 280 pixels for 11 bars: $280/11 = 25.4545$. Let's just make each bar 25 pixels; that will give us a bit of margin on the right side. So, the right edge of our first bar will be at position $40 + 25 = 65$.

We can now fill in the details for drawing the first bar into our algorithm.

```
Draw a rectangle from (40, 230) to (65, 230 - principal * 0.02)
```

At this point, we have made all the major decisions and calculations required to finish out the problem. All that remains is to percolate these details into the rest of the algorithm. Figure 4.8 shows the general layout of the window with some of the dimensions we have chosen.

Let's figure out where the lower-left corner of each bar is going to be located. We chose a bar width of 25, so the bar for each successive year will start 25 pixels farther right than the previous year. We can use a variable `year` to represent the year number and calculate the x coordinate of the lower-left corner as $(\text{year})(25) + 40$. (The $+40$ leaves space on the left edge for the labels.) Of course, the y coordinate of this point is still 230 (the bottom of the graph).

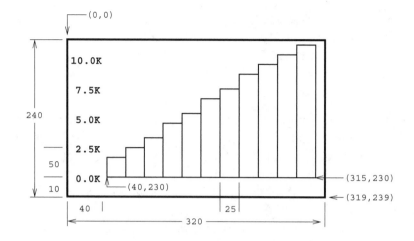

Figure 4.8: Position of elements in future value bar graph

To find the upper-right corner of a bar, we add 25 (the width of the bar) to the x value of the lower-left corner. The y value of the upper-right corner is determined from the (updated) value of principal exactly as we determined it for the first bar. Here is the refined algorithm:

```
for year running from a value of 1 up through 10:
    Calculate principal = principal * (1 + apr)
    Calculate xll = 25 * year + 40
    Calculate height = principal * 0.02
    Draw a rectangle from (xll, 230) to (xll+25, 230 - height)
```

The variable xll stands for x lower-left—the x value of the lower-left corner of the bar.

Putting all of this together produces the detailed algorithm shown below:

```
Print an introduction
Get value of principal and apr from user
Create a 320x240 GraphWin titled ''Investment Growth Chart''
Draw label " 0.0K" at (20, 230)
Draw label " 2.5K" at (20, 180)
Draw label " 5.0K" at (20, 130)
Draw label " 7.5K" at (20, 80)
Draw label "10.0K" at (20, 30)
```

```
Draw a rectangle from (40, 230) to (65, 230 - principal * 0.02)
for year running from a value of 1 up through 10:
    Calculate principal = principal * (1 + apr)
    Calculate xll = 25 * year + 40
    Draw a rectangle from (xll, 230) to (xll+25, 230 - principal * 0.02)
Wait for user to press Enter
```

Whew! That was a lot of work, but we are finally ready to translate this algorithm into actual Python code. The translation is straightforward using objects from the graphics module. Here's the program:

```python
# futval_graph.py

from graphics import *

def main():
    # Introduction
    print("This program plots the growth of a 10-year investment.")

    # Get principal and interest rate
    principal = eval(input("Enter the initial principal: "))
    apr = eval(input("Enter the annualized interest rate: "))

    # Create a graphics window with labels on left edge
    win = GraphWin("Investment Growth Chart", 320, 240)
    win.setBackground("white")
    Text(Point(20, 230), ' 0.0K').draw(win)
    Text(Point(20, 180), ' 2.5K').draw(win)
    Text(Point(20, 130), ' 5.0K').draw(win)
    Text(Point(20, 80), ' 7.5K').draw(win)
    Text(Point(20, 30), '10.0K').draw(win)

    # Draw bar for initial principal
    height = principal * 0.02
    bar = Rectangle(Point(40, 230), Point(65, 230-height))
    bar.setFill("green")
    bar.setWidth(2)
    bar.draw(win)
```

```
# Draw bars for successive years
for year in range(1,11):
    # calculate value for the next year
    principal = principal * (1 + apr)
    # draw bar for this value
    xll = year * 25 + 40
    height = principal * 0.02
    bar = Rectangle(Point(xll, 230), Point(xll+25, 230-height))
    bar.setFill("green")
    bar.setWidth(2)
    bar.draw(win)


input("Press <Enter> to quit")
win.close()
```

```
main()
```

If you study this program carefully, you will see that I added a number of features to spruce it up a bit. All graphical objects support methods for changing color. I have set the background color of the window to white (by default it's gray).

```
win.setBackground("white")
```

I have also changed the color of the bar object. The following line asks the bar to color its interior green (because it's money, you know):

```
bar.setFill("green")
```

You can also change the color of a shape's outline using the setOutline method. In this case, I have chosen to leave the outline the default black so that the bars stand out from each other. To enhance this effect, this code makes the outline wider (two pixels instead of the default one).

```
bar.setWidth(2)
```

You might also have noted the economy of notation in drawing the labels. Since we don't ever change the labels, assigning them to a variable is unnecessary. We can just create a Text object, tell it to draw itself, and be done with it. Here is an example:

```
Text(Point(20,230), ' 0.0K').draw(win)
```

Finally, take a close look at the use of the `year` variable in the loop.

```
for year in range(1,11):
```

The expression `range(1,11)` produces a sequence of ints 1–10. The loop index variable `year` marches through this sequence on successive iterations of the loop. So, the first time through `year` is 1, then 2, then 3, etc., up to 10. The value of `year` is then used to compute the proper position of the lower left corner of each bar.

```
xll = year * 25 + 40
```

I hope you are starting to get the hang of graphics programming. It's a bit strenuous, but very addictive.

4.6 Choosing Coordinates

The lion's share of the work in designing the `futval_graph` program was in determining the precise coordinates where things would be placed on the screen. Most graphics programming problems require some sort of a *coordinate transformation* to change values from a real-world problem into the window coordinates that get mapped onto the computer screen. In our example, the problem domain called for x values representing the year (0–10) and y values representing monetary amounts ($0–$10,000). We had to transform these values to be represented in a 320 x 240 window. It's nice to work through an example or two to see how this transformation happens, but it makes for tedious programming.

Coordinate transformation is an integral and well-studied component of computer graphics. It doesn't take too much mathematical savvy to see that the transformation process always follows the same general pattern. Anything that follows a pattern can be done automatically. In order to save you the trouble of having to explicitly convert back and forth between coordinate systems, the `graphics` module provides a simple mechanism to do it for you. When you create a `GraphWin` you can specify a coordinate system for the window using the `setCoords` method. The method requires four parameters specifying the coordinates of the lower-left and upper-right corners, respectively. You can then use this coordinate system to place graphical objects in the window.

To take a simple example, suppose we just want to divide the window into nine equal squares, tic-tac-toe fashion. This could be done without too much

trouble using the default 200 x 200 window, but it would require a bit of arithmetic. The problem becomes trivial if we first change the coordinates of the
window to run from 0 to 3 in both dimensions.

```
# create a default 200x200 window
win = GraphWin("Tic-Tac-Toe")

# set coordinates to go from (0,0) in the lower left
#      to (3,3) in the upper right.
win.setCoords(0.0, 0.0, 3.0, 3.0)

# Draw vertical lines
Line(Point(1,0), Point(1,3)).draw(win)
Line(Point(2,0), Point(2,3)).draw(win)

# Draw horizontal lines
Line(Point(0,1), Point(3,1)).draw(win)
Line(Point(0,2), Point(3,2)).draw(win)
```

Another benefit of this approach is that the size of the window can be changed
by simply changing the dimensions used when the window is created (e.g. `win`
`= GraphWin("Tic-Tac-Toe", 300, 300)`). Because the same coordinates span
the window (due to `setCoords`) the objects will scale appropriately to the new
window size. Using "raw" window coordinates would require changes in the
definitions of the lines.

We can apply this idea to simplify our graphing future value program. Basically, we want our graphics window to go from 0 through 10 (representing
years) in the x dimension and from 0 to 10,000 (representing dollars) in the y
dimension. We could create just such a window like this:

```
win = GraphWin("Investment Growth Chart", 320, 240)
win.setCoords(0.0, 0.0, 10.0, 10000.0)
```

Then creating a bar for any values of `year` and `principal` would be simple.
Each bar starts at the given year and a baseline of 0 and grows to the next year
and a height equal to `principal`.

```
bar = Rectangle(Point(year, 0), Point(year+1, principal))
```

There is a small problem with this scheme. Can you see what I have forgot-
ten? The eleven bars will fill the entire window; we haven't left any room for

labels or margins around the edges. This is easily fixed by expanding the coordinates of the window slightly. Since our bars start at 0, we can locate the left side labels at -1. We can add a bit of white space around the graph by expanding the coordinates slightly beyond that required for our graph. A little experimentation leads to this window definition:

```
win = GraphWin("Investment Growth Chart", 320, 240)
win.setCoords(-1.75,-200, 11.5, 10400)
```

Here is the program again, using the alternative coordinate system:

```
# futval_graph2.py

from graphics import *

def main():
    # Introduction
    print("This program plots the growth of a 10-year investment.")

    # Get principal and interest rate
    principal = eval(input("Enter the initial principal: "))
    apr = eval(input("Enter the annualized interest rate: "))

    # Create a graphics window with labels on left edge
    win = GraphWin("Investment Growth Chart", 320, 240)
    win.setBackground("white")
    win.setCoords(-1.75,-200, 11.5, 10400)
    Text(Point(-1, 0), ' 0.0K').draw(win)
    Text(Point(-1, 2500), ' 2.5K').draw(win)
    Text(Point(-1, 5000), ' 5.0K').draw(win)
    Text(Point(-1, 7500), ' 7.5k').draw(win)
    Text(Point(-1, 10000), '10.0K').draw(win)

    # Draw bar for initial principal
    bar = Rectangle(Point(0, 0), Point(1, principal))
    bar.setFill("green")
    bar.setWidth(2)
    bar.draw(win)

    # Draw a bar for each subsequent year
```

```
    for year in range(1, 11):
        principal = principal * (1 + apr)
        bar = Rectangle(Point(year, 0), Point(year+1, principal))
        bar.setFill("green")
        bar.setWidth(2)
        bar.draw(win)

    input("Press <Enter> to quit.")
    win.close()

main()
```

Notice how the cumbersome coordinate calculations have been eliminated. This version also makes it easy to change the size of the GraphWin. Changing the window size to 640 x 480 produces a larger, but correctly drawn bar graph. In the original program, all of the calculations would have to be redone to accommodate the new scaling factors in the larger window.

Obviously, the second version of our program is much easier to develop and understand. When you are doing graphics programming, give some consideration to choosing a coordinate system that will make your task as simple as possible.

4.7 Interactive Graphics

Graphical interfaces can be used for input as well as output. In a GUI environment, users typically interact with their applications by clicking on buttons, choosing items from menus, and typing information into on-screen text boxes. These applications use a technique called *event-driven* programming. Basically, the program draws a set of interface elements (often called *widgets*) on the screen, and then waits for the user to do something.

When the user moves the mouse, clicks a button, or types a key on the keyboard, this generates an *event*. Basically, an event is an object that encapsulates data about what just happened. The event object is then sent off to an appropriate part of the program to be processed. For example, a click on a button might produce a *button event*. This event would be passed to the button-handling code, which would then perform the appropriate action corresponding to that button.

Event-driven programming can be tricky for novice programmers, since it's hard to figure out "who's in charge" at any given moment. The graphics module hides the underlying event-handling mechanisms and provides two simple ways of getting user input in a `GraphWin`.

4.7.1 Getting Mouse Clicks

We can get graphical information from the user via the `getMouse` method of the `GraphWin` class. When `getMouse` is invoked on a `GraphWin`, the program pauses and waits for the user to click the mouse somewhere in the graphics window. The spot where the user clicks is returned to the program as a `Point`. Here is a bit of code that reports the coordinates of ten successive mouse clicks:

```
# click.py
from graphics import *

def main():
    win = GraphWin("Click Me!")
    for i in range(10):
        p = win.getMouse()
        print("You clicked at:", p.getX(), p.getY())

main()
```

The value returned by `getMouse()` is a ready-made `Point`. We can use it like any other point using accessors such as `getX` and `getY` or other methods such as `draw` and `move`.

Here is an example of an interactive program that allows the user to draw a triangle by clicking on three points in a graphics window. This example is completely graphical, making use of `Text` objects as prompts. No interaction with a Python text window is required. If you are programming in a Microsoft Windows environment, you can name this program using a `.pyw` extension. Then when the program is run, it will not even display the Python shell window.

```
# triangle.pyw
from graphics import *

def main():
    win = GraphWin("Draw a Triangle")
    win.setCoords(0.0, 0.0, 10.0, 10.0)
    message = Text(Point(5, 0.5), "Click on three points")
    message.draw(win)
```

```
# Get and draw three vertices of triangle
p1 = win.getMouse()
p1.draw(win)
p2 = win.getMouse()
p2.draw(win)
p3 = win.getMouse()
p3.draw(win)

# Use Polygon object to draw the triangle
triangle = Polygon(p1,p2,p3)
triangle.setFill("peachpuff")
triangle.setOutline("cyan")
triangle.draw(win)

# Wait for another click to exit
message.setText("Click anywhere to quit.")
win.getMouse()

main()
```

The three-click triangle illustrates a couple of new features of the graphics
module. There is no triangle class; however, there is a general class Polygon
that can be used for any multi-sided, closed shape. The constructor for Polygon
accepts any number of points and creates a polygon by using line segments to
connect the points in the order given and to connect the last point back to the
first. A triangle is just a three-sided polygon. Once we have three Points p1,
p2, and p3, creating the triangle is a snap.

```
triangle = Polygon(p1, p2, p3)
```

You should also study how the Text object is used to provide prompts. A
single Text object is created and drawn near the beginning of the program.

```
message = Text(Point(5, 0.5), "Click on three points")
message.draw(win)
```

To change the prompt, we don't need to create a new Text object, we can just
change the text that is displayed. This is done near the end of the program with
the setText method.

```
message.setText("Click anywhere to quit.")
```

As you can see, the getMouse method of GraphWin provides a simple way of interacting with the user in a graphics-oriented program.

4.7.2   Handling Textual Input

In the triangle example, all of the input was provided through mouse clicks. The graphics module also includes a simple Entry object that can be used to get keyboard input in a GraphWin.

An Entry object draws a box on the screen that can contain text. It understands setText and getText methods just like the Text object does. The difference is that the contents of an Entry can be edited by the user. Here's a version of the temperature conversion program from Chapter 2 with a graphical user interface:

```
# convert_gui.pyw
# Program to convert Celsius to Fahrenheit using a simple
#    graphical interface.

from graphics import *

def main():
    win = GraphWin("Celsius Converter", 400, 300)
    win.setCoords(0.0, 0.0, 3.0, 4.0)

    # Draw the interface
    Text(Point(1,3), "   Celsius Temperature:").draw(win)
    Text(Point(1,1), "Fahrenheit Temperature:").draw(win)
    input = Entry(Point(2,3), 5)
    input.setText("0.0")
    input.draw(win)
    output = Text(Point(2,1),"")
    output.draw(win)
    button = Text(Point(1.5,2.0),"Convert It")
    button.draw(win)
    Rectangle(Point(1,1.5), Point(2,2.5)).draw(win)

    # wait for a mouse click
```

```
win.getMouse()

# convert input
celsius = eval(input.getText())
fahrenheit = 9.0/5.0 * celsius + 32

# display output and change button
output.setText(fahrenheit)
button.setText("Quit")

# wait for click and then quit
win.getMouse()
win.close()

main()
```

When run, this produces a window with an entry box for typing in a Celsius temperature and a "button" for doing the conversion. The button is just for show. The program actually just pauses for a mouse click anywhere in the window. Figure 4.9 shows how the window looks when the program starts.

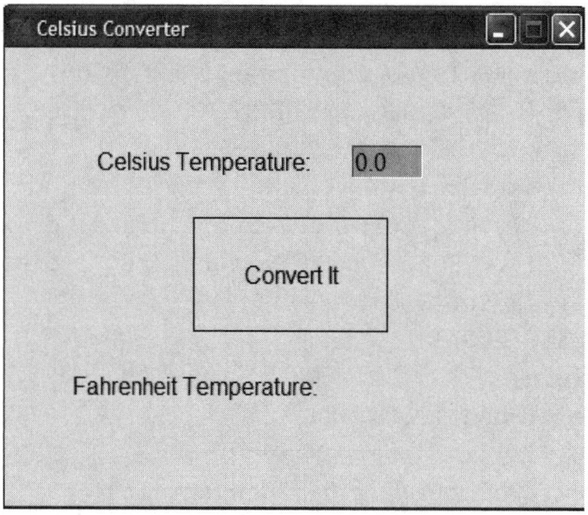

Figure 4.9: Initial screen for graphical temperature converter

Initially, the `input` entry box is set to contain the value 0.0. The user can delete this value and type in another temperature. The program pauses until the user clicks the mouse. Notice that the point where the user clicks is not even saved; the `getMouse` method is just used to pause the program until the user has a chance to enter a value in the input box.

The program then processes the input in four steps. First, the text in the input box is converted into a number (via `eval`). This number is then converted to degrees Fahrenheit. Finally, the resulting number is displayed in the `output` text area. Although `fahrenheit` is an int value, the `setText` method automatically converts it to a string so that it can be displayed in the output text box.

Figure 4.10 shows how the window looks after the user has typed an input and clicked the mouse. Notice that the converted temperature shows up in the output area, and the label on the button has changed to "Quit" to show that clicking again will exit the program. This example could be made much prettier

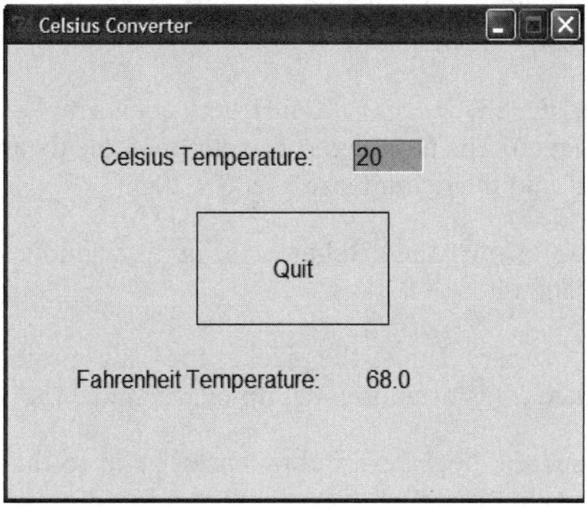

Figure 4.10: Graphical temperature converter after user input

using some of the options in the graphics library for changing the colors, sizes, and line widths of the various widgets. The code for the program is deliberately Spartan to illustrate just the essential elements of GUI design.

Although the basic tools `getMouse` and `Entry` do not provide a full-fledged GUI environment, we will see in later chapters how these simple mechanisms can support surprisingly rich interactions.

4.8   Graphics Module Reference

The examples in this chapter have touched on most of the elements in the
graphics module. This section provides a complete reference to the objects and
functions provided in the graphics library. The set of objects and functions that
are provided by a module is sometimes called an *Applications Programming Interface* or *API*. Experienced programmers study APIs to learn about new libraries.
You should probably read this section over once to see what the graphics library
has to offer. After that, you will probably want to refer back to this section often
when you are writing your own graphical programs.

4.8.1   GraphWin Objects

A GraphWin object represents a window on the screen where graphical images
may be drawn. A program may define any number of GraphWins. A GraphWin
understands the following methods:

GraphWin(title, width, height) Constructs a new graphics window for drawing on the screen. The parameters are optional, the default title is "Graphics Window," and the default size is 200 x 200.

plot(x, y, color) Draws the pixel at (x, y) in the window. Color is optional,
black is the default.

plotPixel(x, y, Color) Draws the pixel at the "raw" position (x, y) ignoring
any coordinate transformations set up by setCoords.

setBackground(color) Sets the window background to the given color. The
initial background is gray. See Section 5.8.5 for information on specifying
colors.

close() Closes the on-screen window.

getMouse() Pauses for the user to click a mouse in the window and returns
where the mouse was clicked as a Point object.

checkMouse() Similar to getMouse, but does not pause for a user click. Returns
the latest point where the mouse was clicked or None if the window as not
been clicked since the previous call to checkMouse or getMouse. This is
particularly useful for controlling simple animation loops.

setCoords(xll, yll, xur, yur) Sets the coordinate system of the window. The lower-left corner is (xll, yll) and the upper-right corner is (xur, yur). All subsequent drawing will be done with respect to the altered coordinate system (except for plotPixel).

4.8.2 Graphics Objects

The module provides the following classes of drawable objects: Point, Line, Circle, Oval, Rectangle, Polygon, and Text. All objects are initially created unfilled with a black outline. All graphics objects support the following generic set of methods:

setFill(color) Sets the interior of the object to the given color.

setOutline(color) Sets the outline of the object to the given color.

setWidth(pixels) Sets the width of the outline of the object to this many pixels. (Does not work for Point.)

draw(aGraphWin) Draws the object into the given GraphWin.

undraw() Undraws the object from a graphics window. This produces an error if the object is not currently drawn.

move(dx,dy) Moves the object dx units in the x direction and dy units in the y direction. If the object is currently drawn, the image is adjusted to the new position.

clone() Returns a duplicate of the object. Clones are always created in an undrawn state. Other than that, they are identical to the cloned object.

Point Methods

Point(x,y) Constructs a point having the given coordinates.

getX() Returns the x coordinate of a point.

getY() Returns the y coordinate of a point.

Line Methods

Line(point1, point2) Constructs a line segment from point1 to point2.

setArrow(string) Sets the arrowhead status of a line. Arrows may be drawn at either the first point, the last point, or both. Possible values of string are 'first', 'last', 'both', and 'none'. The default setting is 'none'.

getCenter() Returns a clone of the midpoint of the line segment.

getP1(), getP2() Returns a clone of the corresponding endpoint of the segment.

Circle Methods

Circle(centerPoint, radius) Constructs a circle with given center point and radius.

getCenter() Returns a clone of the center point of the circle.

getRadius() Returns the radius of the circle.

getP1(), getP2() Returns a clone of the corresponding corner of the circle's bounding box. These are opposite corner points of a square that circumscribes the circle.

Rectangle Methods

Rectangle(point1, point2) Constructs a rectangle having opposite corners at point1 and point2.

getCenter() Returns a clone of the center point of the rectangle.

getP1(), getP2() Returns a clone of corner points originally used to construct the rectangle.

Oval Methods

Oval(point1, point2) Constructs an oval in the bounding box determined by point1 and point2.

getCenter() Returns a clone of the point at the center of the oval.

getP1(), getP2() Returns a clone of the corresponding point used to construct the oval.

Polygon Methods

Polygon(point1, point2, point3, ...) Constructs a polygon having the given points as vertices. Also accepts a single parameter that is a list of the vertices.

getPoints() Returns a list containing clones of the points used to construct the polygon.

Text Methods

Text(anchorPoint, string) Constructs a text object that displays the given string centered at anchorPoint. The text is displayed horizontally.

setText(string) Sets the text of the object to string.

getText() Returns the current string.

getAnchor() Returns a clone of the anchor point.

setFace(family) Changes the font face to the given family. Possible values are 'helvetica', 'courier', 'times roman', and 'arial'.

setSize(point) Changes the font size to the given point size. Sizes from 5 to 36 points are legal.

setStyle(style) Changes font to the given style. Possible values are: 'normal', 'bold', 'italic', and 'bold italic'.

setTextColor(color) Sets the color of the text to color. Note: setFill has the same effect.

4.8.3 Entry Objects

Objects of type Entry are displayed as text entry boxes that can be edited by the user of the program. Entry objects support the generic graphics methods move(), draw(graphwin), undraw(), setFill(color), and clone(). The Entry specific methods are given below.

Entry(centerPoint, width) Constructs an Entry having the given center point and width. The width is specified in number of characters of text that can be displayed.

getAnchor() Returns a clone of the point where the entry box is centered.

getText() Returns the string of text that is currently in the entry box.

setText(string) Sets the text in the entry box to the given string. Changes the font face to the given family. Possible values are: 'helvetica', 'courier', 'times roman', and 'arial'.

setSize(point) Changes the font size to the given point size. Sizes from 5 to 36 points are legal.

setStyle(style) Changes font to the given style. Possible values are: 'normal', 'bold', 'italic', and 'bold italic'.

setTextColor(color) Sets the color of the text to color.

4.8.4 Displaying Images

The graphics module also provides minimal support for displaying and manipulating images in a GraphWin. Most platforms will support at least PPM and GIF images. Display is done with an Image object. Images support the generic methods move(dx,dy), draw(graphwin), undraw(), and clone(). Image-specific methods are given below.

Image(anchorPoint, filename) Constructs an image from contents of the given file, centered at the given anchor point. Can also be called with width and height parameters instead of filename. In this case, a blank (transparent) image is created of the given width and height.

getAnchor() Returns a clone of the point where the image is centered.

getWidth() Returns the width of the image.

getHeight() Returns the height of the image.

getPixel(x, y) Returns a list [red, green, blue] of the RGB values of the pixel at position (x,y). Each value is a number in the range 0–255 indicating the intensity of the corresponding RGB color. These numbers can be turned into a color string using the color_rgb function (see next section).

Note that pixel position is relative to the image itself, not the window where the image may be drawn. The upper-left corner of the image is always pixel (0,0).

setPixel(x, y, color) Sets the pixel at position (x,y) to the given color. Note: this is a slow operation.

save(filename) Saves the image to a file. The type of the resulting file (e.g., GIF or PPM) is determined by the extension on the filename. For example, img.save("myPic.ppm") saves img as a PPM file.

4.8.5 Generating Colors

Colors are indicated by strings. Most normal colors such as 'red', 'purple', 'green', 'cyan', etc. should be available. Many colors come in various shades, such as 'red1', 'red2','red3', 'red4', which are increasingly darker shades of red.

The graphics module also provides a function for mixing your own colors numerically. The function color_rgb(red, green, blue) will return a string representing a color that is a mixture of the intensities of red, green and blue specified. These should be ints in the range 0–255. Thus color_rgb(255, 0, 0) is a bright red, while color_rgb(130, 0, 130) is a medium magenta.

4.8.6 Controlling Display Updates (Advanced)

Usually, the visual display of a GraphWin is updated each time the draw method is called on an object, or an object's visible state is changed in some way. However, under some circumstances, for example when using the graphics library inside some interactive shells, it may be necessary to *force* the window to update in order for changes to be seen. The update() function is provided to do this.

update() Causes any pending graphics operations to be carried out and the results displayed.

For efficiency reasons, it is sometimes desirable to turn off the automatic updating of a window every time one of the objects changes. For example, in an animation, you might want to change the appearance of multiple objects before showing the next "frame" of the animation. The GraphWin constructor includes a special extra parameter called autoflush that controls this automatic updating. By default, autoflush is on when a window is created. To turn it off, the autoflush parameter should be set to False, like this:

```
win = GraphWin("My Animation", 400, 400, autoflush=False)
```

Now changes to the objects in win will only be shown when the graphics system has some idle time or when the changes are forced by a call to update().

4.9 Chapter Summary

This chapter introduced computer graphics and object-based programming. Here is a summary of some of the important concepts:

- An object is a computational entity that combines data and operations. Objects know stuff and can do stuff. An object's data is stored in instance variables, and its operations are called methods.

- Every object is an instance of some class. It is the class that determines what methods an object will have. An instance is created by calling a constructor method.

- An object's attributes are accessed via dot notation. Generally computations with objects are performed by calling on an object's methods. Accessor methods return information about the instance variables of an object. Mutator methods change the value(s) of instance variables.

- The graphics module supplied with this book provides a number of classes that are useful for graphics programming. A GraphWin is an object that represents a window on the screen for displaying graphics. Various graphical objects such as Point, Line, Circle, Rectangle, Oval, Polygon, and Text may be drawn in a GraphWin. Users may interact with a GraphWin by clicking the mouse or typing into an Entry box.

- An important consideration in graphical programming is the choice of an appropriate coordinate system. The graphics library provides a way of automating certain coordinate transformations.

- The situation where two variables refer to the same object is called aliasing. It can sometimes cause unexpected results. Use of the clone method in the graphics library can help prevent these situations.

4.10   Exercises

Review Questions

True/False

1. Using graphics.py allows graphics to be drawn into a Python shell window.

2. Traditionally, the upper-left corner of a graphics window has coordinates (0,0).

3. A single point on a graphics screen is called a pixel.

4. A function that creates a new instance of a class is called an accessor.

5. Instance variables are used to store data inside an object.

6. The statement myShape.move(10,20) moves myShape to the point (10,20).

7. Aliasing occurs when two variables refer to the same object.

8. The copy method is provided to make a copy of a graphics object.

9. A graphics window always has the title "Graphics Window."

10. The method in the graphics library used to get a mouse click is readMouse.

Multiple Choice

1. A method that returns the value of an object's instance variable is called a(n)
   a) mutator   b) function   c) constructor   d) accessor

2. A method that changes the state of an object is called a(n)
   a) stator   b) mutator   c) constructor   d) changor

3. What graphics class would be best for drawing a square?
   a) Square   b) Polygon   c) Line   d) Rectangle

4. What command would set the coordinates of `win` to go from (0,0) in the
   lower-left corner to (10,10) in the upper-right?
   a) `win.setcoords(Point(0,0), Point(10,10))`
   b) `win.setcoords((0,0), (10,10))`
   c) `win.setcoords(0, 0, 10, 10)`
   d) `win.setcoords(Point(10,10), Point(0,0))`

5. What expression would create a line from (2,3) to (4,5)?
   a) `Line(2, 3, 4, 5)`
   b) `Line((2,3), (4,5))`
   c) `Line(2, 4, 3, 5)`
   d) `Line(Point(2,3), Point(4,5))`

6. What command would be used to draw the graphics object `shape` into the
   graphics window `win`?
   a) `win.draw(shape)`   b) `win.show(shape)`
   c) `shape.draw()`   d) `shape.draw(win)`

7. Which of the following computes the horizontal distance between points
   p1 and p2?
   a) `abs(p1-p2)`
   b) `p2.getX() - p1.getX()`
   c) `abs(p1.getY() - p2.getY())`
   d) `abs(p1.getX() - p2.getX())`

8. What kind of object can be used to get text input in a graphics window?
   a) `Text`   b) `Entry`   c) `Input`   d) `Keyboard`

9. A user interface organized around visual elements and user actions is
   called a(n)
   a) GUI   b) application   c) windower   d) API

10. What color is `color_rgb(0,255,255)`?
    a) yellow   b) cyan   c) magenta   d) orange

Discussion

1. Pick an example of an interesting real-world object and describe it as a
   programming object by listing its data (attributes, what it "knows") and
   its methods (behaviors, what it can "do").

2. Describe in your own words the object produced by each of the following operations from the graphics module. Be as precise as you can. Be sure to mention such things as the size, position, and appearance of the various objects. You may include a sketch if that helps.

   (a) `Point(130,130)`

   (b) ```
   c = Circle(Point(30,40),25)
   c.setFill('blue')
   c.setOutline('red')
   ```

   (c) ```
   r = Rectangle(Point(20,20), Point(40,40))
   r.setFill(color_rgb(0,255,150))
   r.setWidth(3)
   ```

   (d) ```
   l = Line(Point(100,100), Point(100,200))
   l.setOutline('red4')
   l.setArrow('first')
   ```

   (e) `Oval(Point(50,50), Point(60,100))`

   (f) ```
   shape = Polygon(Point(5,5), Point(10,10), Point(5,10), Point(10,5))
   shape.setFill('orange')
   ```

   (g) ```
   t = Text(Point(100,100), "Hello World!")
   t.setFace("courier")
   t.setSize(16)
   t.setStyle("italic")
   ```

3. Describe what happens when the following interactive graphics program runs:

```
from graphics import *

def main():
    win = GraphWin()
    shape = Circle(Point(50,50), 20)
    shape.setOutline("red")
    shape.setFill("red")
    shape.draw(win)
    for i in range(10):
        p = win.getMouse()
        c = shape.getCenter()
        dx = p.getX() - c.getX()
```
```

```
              dy = p.getY() - c.getY()
              shape.move(dx,dy)
          win.close()
      main()
```

Programming Exercises

1. Alter the program from the last discussion question in the following ways:

   (a) Make it draw squares instead of circles.

   (b) Have each successive click draw an additional square on the screen (rather than moving the existing one).

   (c) Print a message on the window "Click again to quit" after the loop, and wait for a final click before closing the window.

2. An archery target consists of a central circle of yellow surrounded by concentric rings of red, blue, black and white. Each ring has the same "width," which is the same as the radius of the yellow circle. Write a program that draws such a target. Hint: Objects drawn later will appear on top of objects drawn earlier.

3. Write a program that draws some sort of face.

4. Write a program that draws a winter scene with a Christmas tree and a snowman.

5. Write a program that draws 5 dice on the screen depicting a straight (1, 2, 3, 4, 5 or 2, 3, 4, 5, 6).

6. Modify the graphical future value program so that the input (principal and apr) also are done in a graphical fashion using Entry objects.

7. Circle Intersection. Write a program that computes the intersection of a circle with a horizontal line and displays the information textually and graphically.

   Input: Radius of the circle and the y-intercept of the line.

   Output: Draw a circle centered at $(0, 0)$ with the given radius in a window with coordinates running from -10,-10 to 10,10.
   Draw a horizontal line across the window with the given y-intercept.

Draw the two points of intersection in red.
Print out the x values of the points of intersection.

Formula: $x = \pm\sqrt{r^2 - y^2}$

8. Line Segment Information.

   This program allows the user to draw a line segment and then displays some graphical and textual information about the line segment.

   Input: Two mouse clicks for the end points of the line segment.

   Output: Draw the midpoint of the segment in cyan.
   Draw the line.
   Print the length and the slope of the line.

   Formulas:
   $$dx = x_2 - x_1$$
   $$dy = y_2 - y_1$$
   $$slope = dy/dx$$
   $$length = \sqrt{dx^2 + dy^2}$$

9. Rectangle Information.

   This program displays information about a rectangle drawn by the user.

   Input: Two mouse clicks for the opposite corners of a rectangle.

   Output: Draw the rectangle.
   Print the perimeter and area of the rectangle.

   Formulas:
   $$area = (length)(width)$$
   $$perimeter = 2(length + width)$$

10. Triangle Information.

    Same as previous problem, but with three clicks for the vertices of a triangle.

    Formulas: For perimeter, see length from line problem.
    $area = \sqrt{s(s-a)(s-b)(s-c)}$ where a, b, and c are the lengths of
    the sides and $s = \frac{a+b+c}{2}$

11. Five-click house.

You are to write a program that allows the user to draw a simple house using five mouse-clicks. The first two clicks will be the opposite corners of the rectangular frame of the house. The third click will indicate the center of the top edge of a rectangular door. The door should have a total width that is $\frac{1}{5}$ of the width of the house frame. The sides of the door should extend from the corners of the top down to the bottom of the frame. The fourth click will indicate the *center* of a square window. The window is half as wide as the door. The last click will indicate the peak of the roof. The edges of the roof will extend from the point at the peak to the corners of the top edge of the house frame.

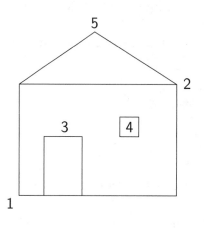

Chapter 5

Sequences: Strings, Lists, and Files

Objectives

- To understand the string data type and how strings are represented in the computer.

- To become familiar with various operations that can be performed on strings through built-in functions and string methods.

- To understand the basic idea of sequences and indexing as they apply to Python strings and lists.

- To be able to apply string formatting to produce attractive, informative program output.

- To understand basic file-processing concepts and techniques for reading and writing text files in Python.

- To understand basic concepts of cryptography.

- To be able to understand and write programs that process textual information.

5.1 The String Data Type

So far, we have been discussing programs designed to manipulate numbers and graphics. But you know that computers are also important for storing and operating on textual information. In fact, one of the most common uses for personal

computers is word processing. This chapter focuses on textual applications to
introduce some important ideas about how text is stored on the computer. You
may not think that word-based applications are all that exciting, but as you'll
soon see, the basic ideas presented here are at work in virtually all areas of
computing, including powering the the World Wide Web.

Text is represented in programs by the *string* data type. You can think of a
string as a sequence of characters. In Chapter 2 you learned that a string literal
is formed by enclosing some characters in quotation marks. Python also allows
strings to be delimited by single quotes (apostrophes). There is no difference;
just be sure to use a matching set.   Strings can also be saved in variables, just
like any other data. Here are some examples illustrating the two forms of string
literals:

```
>>> str1 = "Hello"
>>> str2 = 'spam'
>>> print(str1, str2)
Hello spam
>>> type(str1)
<class 'str'>
>>> type(str2)
<class 'str'>
```

You already know how to print strings. You have also seen how to get string
input from users. Recall that the input function returns whatever the user types
as a string object. That means when you want to get a string, you can use the
input in its "raw" (non evaled) form. Here's a simple interaction to illustrate
the point:

```
>>> firstName = input("Please enter your name: ")
Please enter your name: John
>>> print("Hello", firstName)
Hello John
```

Notice how we saved the user's name with a variable and then used that variable
to print the name back out again.

So far, we have seen how to get strings as input, assign them to variables,
and how to print them out. That's enough to write a parrot program, but not
to do any serious text-based computing. For that, we need some string operations. The rest of this section takes you on a tour of the more important Python
string operations. In the following section, we'll put these ideas to work in some
example programs.

What kinds of things can we do with strings? For starters, remember what a string is: a sequence of characters. One thing we might want to do is access the individual characters that make up the string. In Python, this can be done through the operation of *indexing*. We can think of the positions in a string as being numbered, starting from the left with 0. Figure 5.1 illustrates with the string

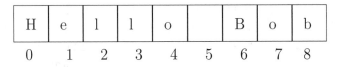

Figure 5.1: Indexing of the string "Hello Bob"

"Hello Bob." Indexing is used in string expressions to access a specific character position in the string. The general form for indexing is `<string>[<expr>]`. The value of the expression determines which character is selected from the string.

Here are some interactive indexing examples:

```
>>> greet = "Hello Bob"
>>> greet[0]
'H'
>>> print(greet[0], greet[2], greet[4])
H l o
>>> x = 8
>>> print(greet[x-2])
B
```

Notice that, in a string of n characters, the last character is at position $n - 1$, because the indexes start at 0. This is probably also a good time to remind you about the difference between string objects and the actual printed output. In the interactions above, the Python shell shows us the value of strings by putting them in single quotes; that's Python's way of communicating to us that we are looking at a string object. When we actually print the string, Python does not put any quotes around the sequence of characters. We just get the text contained in the string.

By the way, Python also allows indexing from the right end of a string using negative indexes.

```
>>> greet[-1]
'b'
```

```
>>> greet[-3]
'B'
```

This is particularly handy for getting at the last character of a string.

Indexing returns a string containing a single character from a larger string. It is also possible to access a contiguous sequence of characters or *substring* from a string. In Python, this is accomplished through an operation called *slicing*. You can think of slicing as a way of indexing a range of positions in the string. Slicing takes the form <string>[<start>:<end>]. Both start and end should be int-valued expressions. A slice produces the substring starting at the position given by start and running up to, *but not including*, position end.

Continuing with our interactive example, here are some slices:

```
>>> greet[0:3]
'Hel'
>>> greet[5:9]
' Bob'
>>> greet[:5]
'Hello'
>>> greet[5:]
' Bob'
>>> greet[:]
'Hello Bob'
```

The last three examples show that if either expression is missing, the start and end of the string are the assumed defaults. The final expression actually hands back the entire string.

Indexing and slicing are useful operations for chopping strings into smaller pieces. The string data type also supports operations for putting strings together. Two handy operators are concatenation (+) and repetition (*). Concatenation builds a string by "gluing" two strings together.   Repetition builds a string by multiple concatenations of a string with itself. Another useful function is len, which tells how many characters are in a string. Finally, since strings are sequences of characters, you can iterate through the characters using a Python for loop.

Here are some examples of various string operations:

```
>>> "spam" + "eggs"
'spameggs'
>>> "Spam" + "And" + "Eggs"
```

Operator	Meaning
+	Concatenation
*	Repetition
<string>[ ]	Indexing
<string>[:]	Slicing
len(<string>)	Length
for <var> in <string>	Iteration through characters

Table 5.1: Python string operations

```
'SpamAndEggs'
>>> 3 * "spam"
'spamspamspam'
>>> "spam" * 5
'spamspamspamspamspam'
>>> (3 * "spam") + ("eggs" * 5)
'spamspamspameggseggseggseggseggs'
>>> len("spam")
4
>>> len("SpamAndEggs")
11
>>> for ch in "Spam!":
        print(ch, end=" ")
S p a m !
```

These basic string operations are summarized in Table 5.1.

5.2   Simple String Processing

Now that you have an idea what various string operations can do, we're ready to write some programs. Our first example is a program to compute the usernames for a computer system.

Many computer systems use a username and password combination to authenticate system users. The system administrator must assign a unique username to each user. Often, usernames are derived from the user's actual name. One scheme for generating usernames is to use the user's first initial followed by up to seven letters of the user's last name. Using this method, the username for

Elmer Thudpucker would be "ethudpuc," and John Smith would just be "jsmith."

We want to write a program that reads a person's name and computes the corresponding username. Our program will follow the basic input, process, output pattern. For brevity, I will skip discussion of the algorithm development and jump right to the code. The outline of the algorithm is included as comments in the final program.

```
# username.py
#    Simple string processing program to generate usernames.

def main():
    print("This program generates computer usernames.\n")

    # get user's first and last names
    first = input("Please enter your first name (all lowercase): ")
    last = input("Please enter your last name (all lowercase): ")

    # concatenate first initial with 7 chars of the last name.
    uname = first[0] + last[:7]

    # output the username
    print("Your username is:", uname)

main()
```

This program first uses input to get strings from the user. Then indexing, slicing, and concatenation are combined to produce the username.

Here's an example run:

```
This program generates computer usernames.

Please enter your first name (all lowercase): elmer
Please enter your last name (all lowercase): thudpucker
Your username is: ethudpuc
```

Do you see where the blank line between the introduction and the prompt for the first name comes from? Putting the newline character (\n) at the end of the string in the first print statement caused the output to skip down an extra line. This is a simple trick for putting some extra white space into the output to make it look a little better.

Here is another problem that we can solve with string operations. Suppose we want to print the abbreviation of the month that corresponds to a given month number. The input to the program is an int that represents a month number (1–12), and the output is the abbreviation for the corresponding month. For example, if the input is 3, then the output should be Mar, for March.

At first, it might seem that this program is beyond your current ability. Experienced programmers recognize that this is a decision problem. That is, we have to decide which of 12 different outputs is appropriate, based on the number given by the user. We will not cover decision structures until later; however, we can write the program now by some clever use of string slicing.

The basic idea is to store all the month names in a big string.

```
months = "JanFebMarAprMayJunJulAugSepOctNovDec"
```

We can look up a particular month by slicing out the appropriate substring. The trick is computing where to slice. Since each month is represented by three letters, if we knew where a given month started in the string, we could easily extract the abbreviation.

```
monthAbbrev = months[pos:pos+3]
```

This would get us the substring of length three that starts in the position indicated by pos.

How do we compute this position? Let's try a few examples and see what we find. Remember that string indexing starts at 0.

month	number	position
Jan	1	0
Feb	2	3
Mar	3	6
Apr	4	9

Of course, the positions all turn out to be multiples of 3. To get the correct multiple, we just subtract 1 from the month number and then multiply by 3. So for 1 we get $(1-1) * 3 = 0 * 3 = 0$ and for 12 we have $(12-1) * 3 = 11 * 3 = 33$.

Now we're ready to code the program. Again, the final result is short and sweet; the comments document the algorithm we've developed.

```
# month.py
#  A program to print the abbreviation of a month, given its number
```

```
def main():
    # months is used as a lookup table
    months = "JanFebMarAprMayJunJulAugSepOctNovDec"

    n = eval(input("Enter a month number (1-12): "))

    # compute starting position of month n in months
    pos = (n-1) * 3

    # Grab the appropriate slice from months
    monthAbbrev = months[pos:pos+3]

    # print the result
    print("The month abbreviation is", monthAbbrev + ".")

main()
```

Notice the last line of this program uses string concatenation to put a period at the end of the month abbreviation.

Here is a sample of program output:

```
Enter a month number (1-12): 4
The month abbreviation is Apr.
```

One weakness of the "string as lookup table" approach used in this example is that it will only work when the substrings all have the same length (in this case, three). Suppose we want to write a program that outputs the complete month name for a given number. How could that be accomplished?

5.3 Lists as Sequences

Strictly speaking the operations in Table 5.1 are not really just string operations. They are operations that apply to sequences. As you know from the discussion in Chapter 2, Python lists are also a kind of sequence. That means we can also index, slice, and concatenate lists, as the following session illustrates:

```
>>> [1,2] + [3,4]
[1, 2, 3, 4]
>>> [1,2]*3
```

```
[1, 2, 1, 2, 1, 2]
>>> grades = ['A','B','C','D','F']
>>> grades[0]
'A'
>>> grades[2:4]
['C', 'D']
>>> len(grades)
5
```

One of the nice things about lists is that they are more general than strings. Strings are always sequences of characters, whereas lists can be sequences of arbitrary objects. You can create a list of numbers or a list of strings. In fact, you can even mix it up and create a list that contains both numbers and strings:

```
myList = [1, "Spam", 4, "U"]
```

In later chapters, we'll put all sorts of things into lists like points, rectangles, dice, buttons, and even students!

Using a list of strings, we can rewrite our month abbreviation program from the previous section and make it even simpler.

```
# month2.py
#  A program to print the month abbreviation, given its number.


def main():

    # months is a list used as a lookup table
    months = ["Jan", "Feb", "Mar", "Apr", "May", "Jun",
              "Jul", "Aug", "Sep", "Oct", "Nov", "Dec"]

    n = eval(input("Enter a month number (1-12): "))

    print("The month abbreviation is", months[n-1] + ".")

main()
```

There are a couple of things you should notice about this program. I have created a list of strings called `months` to use as the lookup table. The code that creates the list is split over two lines. Normally a Python statement is written on a single line, but in this case Python knows that the list isn't finished until the closing bracket "]" is encountered. Breaking the statement across two lines like this makes the code more readable.

Lists, just like strings, are indexed starting with 0, so in this list the value months[0] is the string "Jan". In general, the nth month is at position n-1. Since this computation is straightforward, I didn't even bother to put it in a separate step; the expression months[n-1] is used directly in the print statement.

Not only is this solution to the abbreviation problem a bit simpler, it is also more flexible. For example, it would be trivial to change the program so that it prints out the entire name of the month. All we need is a new definition of the lookup list.

```
months = ["January", "February", "March", "April",
          "May", "June", "July", "August",
          "September", "October", "November", "December"]
```

While strings and lists are both sequences, there is an important difference between the two. Lists are *mutable*. That means that the value of an item in a list can be modified with an assignment statement. Strings, on the other hand, cannot be changed "in place." Here is an example interaction that illustrates the difference:

```
>>> myList = [34, 26, 15, 10]
>>> myList[2]
15
>>> myList[2] = 0
>>> myList
[34, 26, 0, 10]
>>> myString = "Hello World"
>>> myString[2]
'l'
>>> myString[2] = 'z'
Traceback (most recent call last):
  File "<stdin>", line 1, in <module>
TypeError: 'str' object does not support item assignment
```

The first line creates a list of four numbers. Indexing position 2 returns the value 15 (as usual, indexes start at 0). The next command assigns the value 0 to the item in position 2. After the assignment, evaluating the list shows that the new value has replaced the old. Attempting a similar operation on a string produces an error. Strings are not mutable; lists are.

5.4 String Representation and Message Encoding

5.4.1 String Representation

Hopefully, you are starting to get the hang of computing with textual (string) data. However, we haven't yet discussed how computers actually manipulate strings. In Chapter 3, you saw that numbers are stored in binary notation (sequences of zeros and ones); the computer CPU contains circuitry to do arithmetic with these representations. Textual information is represented in exactly the same way. Underneath, when the computer is manipulating text, it is really no different from number crunching.

To understand this, you might think in terms of messages and secret codes. Consider the age-old grade school dilemma. You are sitting in class and want to pass a note to a friend across the room. Unfortunately, the note must pass through the hands, and in front of the curious eyes, of many classmates before it reaches its final destination. And, of course, there is always the risk that the note could fall into enemy hands (the teacher's). So you and your friend need to design a scheme for encoding the contents of your message.

One approach is to simply turn the message into a sequence of numbers. You could choose a number to correspond to each letter of the alphabet and use the numbers in place of letters. Without too much imagination, you might use the numbers 1–26 to represent the letters a–z. Instead of the word "sourpuss," you would write "18, 14, 20, 17, 15, 20, 18, 18." To those who don't know the code, this looks like a meaningless string of numbers. For you and your friend, however, it represents a word.

This is how a computer represents strings. Each character is translated into a number, and the entire string is stored as a sequence of (binary) numbers in computer memory. It doesn't really matter what number is used to represent any given character as long as the computer is consistent about the encoding/decoding process. In the early days of computing, different designers and manufacturers used different encodings. You can imagine what a headache this was for people transferring data between different systems.

Consider a situation that would result if, say, PCs and Macintosh computers each used their own encoding. If you type a term paper on a PC and save it as a text file, the characters in your paper are represented as a certain sequence of numbers. Then, if the file was read into your instructor's Macintosh computer, the numbers would be displayed on the screen as *different* characters from the ones you typed. The result would be gibberish!

To avoid this sort of problem, computer systems today use industry standard encodings. One important standard is called *ASCII* (American Standard Code for Information Interchange). ASCII uses the numbers 0 through 127 to represent the characters typically found on an (American) computer keyboard, as well as certain special values known as *control codes* that are used to coordinate the sending and receiving of information. For example, the capital letters A–Z are represented by the values 65–90, and the lowercase versions have codes 97–122.

One problem with the ASCII encoding, as its name implies, is that it is American-centric. It does not have symbols that are needed in many other languages. Extended ASCII encodings have been developed by the International Standards Organization to remedy this situation. Most modern systems are moving to the support of *Unicode*, a *much* larger standard that includes support for the characters of nearly all written languages. Python strings support the Unicode standard, so you can wrangle characters from just about any language, provided your operating system has appropriate fonts for displaying the characters.

Python provides a couple of built-in functions that allow us to switch back and forth between characters and the numeric values used to represent them in strings. The `ord` function returns the numeric ("ordinal") code of a single-character string, while `chr` goes the other direction. Here are some interactive examples:

```
>>> ord("a")
97
>>> ord("A")
65
>>> chr(97)
'a'
>>> chr(90)
'Z'
```

If you're reading very carefully, you might notice that these results are consistent with the ASCII encoding of characters that I mentioned above. By design, Unicode uses the same codes as ASCII for the 127 characters originally defined there. But Unicode includes many more exotic characters as well. For example, the Greek letter pi is character 960, and the symbol for the Euro is character 8364.

There's one more piece in the puzzle of how to store characters in computer memory. As you know from Chapter 3, the underlying CPU deals with memory in fixed-sized pieces. The smallest addressable piece is typically 8 bits, which is called a *byte* of memory. A single byte can store $2^8 = 256$ different values. That's more than enough to represent every possible ASCII character (in fact, ASCII is only a 7 bit code). But a single byte is nowhere near sufficient for storing all the 100,000+ possible Unicode characters. To get around this problem, the Unicode standard defines various encoding schemes for packing Unicode characters into sequences of bytes. The most common encoding is called UTF-8. UTF-8 is a variable-length encoding that uses a single byte to store characters that are in the ASCII subset, but may need up to four bytes in order to represent some of the more esoteric characters. That means that a string of length 10 characters will end up getting stored in memory as a sequence of between 10 and 40 bytes, depending on the actual characters used in the string. As a rule of thumb for Latin alphabets (the usual, Western, characters), however, it's pretty safe to estimate that a character requires about one byte of storage on average.

5.4.2 Programming an Encoder

Let's return to the note-passing example. Using the Python `ord` and `chr` functions, we can write some simple programs that automate the process of turning messages into sequences of numbers and back again. The algorithm for encoding the message is simple.

```
get the message to encode
for each character in the message:
    print the letter number of the character
```

Getting the message from the user is easy, an `input` will take care of that for us.

```
message = input("Please enter the message to encode: ")
```

Implementing the loop requires a bit more effort. We need to do something for each character of the message. Recall that a `for` loop iterates over a sequence of objects. Since a string is a kind of sequence, we can just use a `for` loop to run through all the characters of the message.

```
for ch in message:
```

Finally, we need to convert each character to a number. The simplest approach is to use the Unicode number (provided by `ord`) for each character in the message.

Here is the final program for encoding the message:

```
# text2numbers.py
#     A program to convert a textual message into a sequence of
#          numbers, utilizing the underlying Unicode encoding.

def main():
    print("This program converts a textual message into a sequence")
    print("of numbers representing the Unicode encoding of the message.\n"

    # Get the message to encode
    message = input("Please enter the message to encode: ")

    print("\nHere are the Unicode codes:")

    # Loop through the message and print out the Unicode values
    for ch in message:
        print(ord(ch), end=" ")

    print() # blank line before prompt

main()
```

We can use the program to encode important messages.

```
This program converts a textual message into a sequence
of numbers representing the Unicode encoding of the message.

Please enter the message to encode: What a Sourpuss!

Here are the Unicode codes:
87 104 97 116 32 97 32 83 111 117 114 112 117 115 115 33
```

One thing to notice about this result is that even the space character has a corresponding Unicode number. It is represented by the value 32.

5.5 String Methods

5.5.1 Programming a Decoder

Now that we have a program to turn a message into a sequence of numbers,
it would be nice if our friend on the other end had a similar program to turn

the numbers back into a readable message. Let's solve that problem next. Our decoder program will prompt the user for a sequence of Unicode numbers and then print out the text message with the corresponding characters. This program presents us with a couple of challenges; we'll address these as we go along.

The overall outline of the decoder program looks very similar to the encoder program. One change in structure is that the decoding version will collect the characters of the message in a string and print out the entire message at the end of the program. To do this, we need to use an accumulator variable, a pattern we saw in the factorial program from Chapter 3. Here is the decoding algorithm:

```
get the sequence of numbers to decode
message = ""
for each number in the input:
    convert the number to the corresponding Unicode character
    add the character to the end of message
print message
```

Before the loop, the accumulator variable `message` is initialized to be an *empty string*; that is, a string that contains no characters (`""`). Each time through the loop a number from the input is converted into an appropriate character and appended to the end of the message constructed so far.

The algorithm seems simple enough, but even the first step presents us with a problem. How exactly do we get the sequence of numbers to decode? We don't even know how many numbers there will be. To solve this problem, we are going to rely on some more string manipulation operations.

First, we will read the entire sequence of numbers as a single string using `input`. Then we will split the big string into a sequence of smaller strings, each of which represents one of the numbers. Finally, we can iterate through the list of smaller strings, convert each into a number, and use that number to produce the corresponding Unicode character. Here is the complete algorithm:

```
get the sequence of numbers as a string, inString
split inString into a sequence of smaller strings
message = ""
for each of the smaller strings:
    change the string of digits into the number it represents
    append the Unicode character for that number to message
print message
```

This looks complicated, but Python provides some functions that do just what we need.

You may have noticed all along that I've been talking about string objects. Remember from last chapter, objects have both data and operations (they "know stuff," and "do stuff.")   By virtue of being objects, strings have some built-in methods in addition to the generic sequence operations that we have used so for. We'll use some of those abilities here to solve our decoder problem.

For our decoder, we will make use of the `split` method. This method splits a string into a list of substrings. By default, it will split the string wherever a space occurs. Here's an example:

```
>>> myString = "Hello, string methods!"
>>> myString.split()
['Hello,', 'string', 'methods!']
```

Naturally, the `split` operation is called using the usual dot notation for invoking one of an object's methods. In the result, you can see how `split` has turned the original string `"Hello, string methods!"` into a list of three substrings: `"Hello,"`, `"string"`, and `"methods!"`.

By the way, `split` can be used to split a string at places other than spaces by supplying the character to split on as a parameter. For example, if we have a string of numbers separated by commas, we could split on the commas.

```
>>> "32,24,25,57".split(",")
['32', '24', '25', '57']
```

Since our decoder program should accept the same format that was produced by the encoder program, namely a sequence of numbers with spaces between, the default version of `split` works nicely.

```
>>> "87 104 97 116 32 97 32 83 111 117 114 112 117 115 115 33".split()
['87', '104', '97', '116', '32', '97', '32', '83', '111', '117',
'114', '112', '117', '115', '115', '33']
```

Notice that the resulting list is not a list of numbers, it is a list of strings. It just so happens these strings contain only digits and *could* be interpreted as numbers.

All that we need now is a way of converting a string containing digits into a Python number. Of course, we already know one way of doing that, we just need to evaluate the string with `eval`. Recall, `eval` takes a string and evaluates it as if it were a Python expression. As a refresher, here are some interactive examples of `eval`:

```
>>> numStr = "500"
>>> eval(numStr)
500
>>> eval("345.67")
345.67
>>> eval("3+4")
7
>>> x = 3.5
>>> y = 4.7
>>> eval("x * y")
16.45
>>> x = eval(input("Enter a number "))
Enter a number 3.14
>>> print(x)
3.14
```

Using split and eval we can write our decoder program.

```
# numbers2text.py
#      A program to convert a sequence of Unicode numbers into
#          a string of text.

def main():
    print("This program converts a sequence of Unicode numbers into")
    print("the string of text that it represents.\n")

    # Get the message to encode
    inString = input("Please enter the Unicode-encoded message: ")

    # Loop through each substring and build Unicode message
    message = ""
    for numStr in inString.split():
        codeNum = eval(numStr)                # convert digits to a number
        message = message + chr(codeNum) # concatentate character to message

    print("\nThe decoded message is:", message)

main()
```

Study this program a bit and you should be able to understand exactly how it accomplishes its task. The heart of the program is the loop.

```
for numStr in inString.split():
    codeNum = eval(numStr)
    message = message + chr(codeNum)
```

The `split` function produces a list of (sub)strings, and `numStr` takes on each successive string in the list. I called the loop variable `numStr` to emphasize that its value is a string of digits that represents some number. Each time through the loop, the next substring is converted to a number by `eval`ing it. This number is converted to the corresponding Unicode character via `chr` and appended to the end of the accumulator, `message`. When the loop is finished, every number in `inString` has been processed and `message` contains the decoded text.

Here is an example of the program in action:

```
>>> import numbers2text
This program converts a sequence of Unicode numbers into
the string of text that it represents.

Please enter the Unicode-encoded message:
83 116 114 105 110 103 115 32 97 114 101 32 70 117 110 33

The decoded message is: Strings are Fun!
```

5.5.2 More String Methods

Now we have a couple of programs that can encode and decode messages as sequences of Unicode values. These programs turned out to be quite simple due to the power both of Python's string data type and its built-in sequence operations and string methods.

Python is a very good language for writing programs that manipulate textual data. Table 5.2 lists some other useful string methods. A good way to learn about these operations is to try them out interactively.

```
>>> s = "hello, I came here for an argument"
>>> s.capitalize()
'Hello, i came here for an argument'
>>> s.title()
'Hello, I Came Here For An Argument'
>>> s.lower()
```

```
'hello, i came here for an argument'
>>> s.upper()
'HELLO, I CAME HERE FOR AN ARGUMENT'
>>> s.replace("I", "you")
'hello, you came here for an argument'
>>> s.center(30)
'hello, I came here for an argument'
>>> s.center(50)
'         hello, I came here for an argument         '
>>> s.count('e')
5
>>> s.find(',')
5
>>> " ".join(["Number", "one,", "the", "Larch"])
'Number one, the Larch'
>>> "spam".join(["Number", "one,", "the", "Larch"])
'Numberspamone,spamthespamLarch'
```

I should mention that many of these functions, like `split`, accept additional parameters to customize their operation. Python also has a number of other standard libraries for text-processing that are not covered here. You can consult the online documentation or a Python reference to find out more.

5.6 Lists Have Methods, Too

In the last section we took a look at some of the methods for manipulating string objects. Like strings, lists are also objects and come with their own set of "extra" operations. Since this chapter is primarily concerned with text-processing, we'll save the detailed discussion of various list methods for a for a later chapter. However, I do want to introduce one important list method here, just to whet your appetite.

The append method can be used to add an item at the end of a list. This is often used to build a list one item at a time. Here's a fragment of code that creates a list of the squares of the first 100 natural numbers:

```
squares = []
for x in range(1,101):
    squares.append(x*x)
```

Function	Meaning
s.capitalize()	Copy of s with only the first character capitalized.
s.center(width)	Copy of s centered in a field of given width.
s.count(sub)	Count the number of occurrences of sub in s.
s.find(sub)	Find the first position where sub occurs in s.
s.join(list)	Concatenate list into a string, using s as separator.
s.ljust(width)	Like center, but s is left-justified.
s.lower()	Copy of s in all lowercase characters.
s.lstrip()	Copy of s with leading white space removed.
s.replace(oldsub,newsub)	Replace all occurrences of oldsub in s with newsub.
s.rfind(sub)	Like find, but returns the rightmost position.
s.rjust(width)	Like center, but s is right-justified.
s.rstrip()	Copy of s with trailing white space removed.
s.split()	Split s into a list of substrings (see text).
s.title()	Copy of s with first character of each word capitalized.
s.upper()	Copy of s with all characters converted to uppercase.

Table 5.2: Some string methods

In this example we start with an empty list ([]) and each number from 1 to 100 is squared and appended to the list. When the loop is done, squares will be the list: [1, 4, 9, ..., 10000]. This is really just the accumulator pattern at work again, this time with our accumulated value being a list.

With the append method in hand, we can go back and address a weakness in our little decoder program. As we left it, our program used a string variable as an accumulator for the decoded output message. Because strings are immutable, this is somewhat inefficient. The statement

```
message = message + chr(codeNum)
```

essentially creates a complete copy of the message so far and tacks one more character on the end. As the we build up the message, we keep recopying a longer and longer string, just to add a single new character at the end.

One way to avoid recopying the message over and over again is to use a list. The message can be accumulated as a list of characters where each new character is appended to the end of the existing list. Remember, lists are mutable, adding at the end of the list changes the list "in place," without having to copy the existing contents over to a new object. Once we have accumulated all the characters in a list, we can use the `join` operation to concatenate the characters into a string in one fell swoop.

Here's a version of the decoder that uses this more efficient approach.

```
# numbers2text2.py
#       A program to convert a sequence of Unicode numbers into
#             a string of text. Efficient version using a list accumulator.

def main():
    print("This program converts a sequence of Unicode numbers into")
    print("the string of text that it represents.\n")

    # Get the message to encode
    inString = input("Please enter the Unicode-encoded message: ")

    # Loop through each substring and build Unicode message
    chars = []
    for numStr in inString.split():
        codeNum = eval(numStr)              # convert digits to a number
        chars.append(chr(codeNum))          # accumulate new character

    message = "".join(chars)
    print("\nThe decoded message is:", message)

main()
```

In this code, we collect the characters by appending them to a list called `chars`. The final message is obtained by `join`ing these characters together using an empty string as the separator. So the original characters are concatenated together without any extra spaces between. This is the standard way of accumulating a string in Python.

5.7 From Encoding to Encryption

We have looked at how computers represent strings as a sort of encoding problem. Each character in a string is represented by a number that is stored in the computer as a binary representation. You should realize that there is nothing really secret about this code at all. In fact, we are simply using an industry-standard mapping of characters into numbers. Anyone with a little knowledge of computer science would be able to crack our code with very little effort.

The process of encoding information for the purpose of keeping it secret or transmitting it privately is called *encryption*. The study of encryption methods is an increasingly important sub-field of mathematics and computer science known as *cryptography*. For example, if you shop over the Internet, it is important that your personal information such as your name and credit card number be transmitted using encodings that keep it safe from potential eavesdroppers on the network.

Our simple encoding/decoding programs use a very weak form of encryption known as a *substitution cipher*. Each character of the original message, called the *plaintext*, is replaced by a corresponding symbol (in our case a number) from a *cipher alphabet*. The resulting code is called the *ciphertext*.

Even if our cipher were not based on the well-known Unicode encoding, it would still be easy to discover the original message. Since each letter is always encoded by the same symbol, a code-breaker could use statistical information about the frequency of various letters and some simple trial and error testing to discover the original message. Such simple encryption methods may be sufficient for grade-school note passing, but they are certainly not up to the task of securing communication over global networks.

Modern approaches to encryption start by translating a message into numbers, much like our encoding program. Then sophisticated mathematical algorithms are employed to transform these numbers into other numbers. Usually, the transformation is based on combining the message with some other special value called the *key*. In order to decrypt the message, the party on the receiving end needs to have an appropriate key so that the encoding can be reversed to recover the original message.

Encryption approaches come in two flavors: *private key* and *public key*. In a private key (also called *shared key*) system the same key is used for encrypting and decrypting messages. All parties that wish to communicate need to know the key, but it must be kept secret from the outside world. This is the usual system that people think of when considering secret codes.

In public key systems, there are separate but related keys for encrypting and decrypting. Knowing the encryption key does not allow you to decrypt messages or discover the decryption key. In a public key system, the encryption key can be made publicly available, while the decryption key is kept private. Anyone can safely send a message using the public key for encryption. Only the party holding the decryption key will be able to decipher it. For example, a secure web site can send your web browser its public key, and the browser can use it to encode your credit card information before sending it on the Internet. Then only the company that is requesting the information will be able to decrypt and read it using the proper private key.

5.8 Input/Output as String Manipulation

Even programs that we may not view as primarily doing text manipulation often need to make use of string operations. For example, consider a program that does financial analysis. Some of the information (e.g., dates) must be entered as strings. After doing some number crunching, the results of the analysis will typically be a nicely formatted report including textual information that is used to label and explain numbers, charts, tables, and figures. String operations are needed to handle these basic input and output tasks.

5.8.1 Example Application: Date Conversion

As a concrete example, let's extend our month abbreviation program to do date conversions. The user will input a date such as "05/24/2003," and the program will display the date as "May 24, 2003." Here is the algorithm for our program:

```
Input the date in mm/dd/yyyy format (dateStr)
Split dateStr into month, day and year strings
Convert the month string into a month number
Use the month number to look up the month name
Create a new date string in form Month Day, Year
Output the new date string
```

We can implement the first two lines of our algorithm directly in code using string operations we have already discussed.

```
dateStr = input("Enter a date (mm/dd/yyyy): ")
monthStr, dayStr, yearStr = dateStr.split("/")
```

Here I have gotten the date as a string and split it at the slashes. I then "unpacked" the list of three strings into the variables monthStr, dayStr, and yearStr using simultaneous assignment.

The next step is to convert monthStr into an appropriate number. In the Unicode decoding program, we used the eval function to convert from a string

data type into a numeric data type. Recall that `eval` evaluates a string as a
Python expression. It is very general and can be used to turn strings into nearly
any other Python data type. It's the Swiss army knife of string conversion.

You can also convert strings into numbers using the Python numeric type
conversion functions (`int()`, `float()`), which were covered in Chapter 3. Here
are some quick examples.

```
>>> int("3")
3
>>> float("3")
3.0
>>> float("3.5")
3.5
>>> int("3.5")
Traceback (most recent call last):
  File "<stdin>", line 1, in <module>
ValueError: invalid literal for int() with base 10: '3.5'
```

As the last example shows, the string passed to these conversion functions must
be a numeric literal of the appropriate form, otherwise you will get an error.

There is one subtle "gotcha" to consider when choosing between `eval()` and
`int()` to convert strings into numbers. Python does not allow an int literal to
have any leading zeroes.[1] As a result, attempting to `eval` a string that contains
a leading 0 will produce an error. On the other hand, the `int` function handles
this case without a problem.

```
>>> int("008")
8
>>> int("05")
5
>>> int("009")
9
>>> eval("05")
Traceback (most recent call last):
  File "<stdin>", line 1, in <module>
  File "<string>", line 1
    05
     ^
SyntaxError: invalid token
```

---

[1] In older versions of Python, literals with a leading 0 were taken to be octal (base 8) values.

In general then, if you're converting something that supposed to be an int, it's safest to use int rather than eval.

Returning to the date conversion algorithm, we can turn monthStr into a number using int and then use this value to look up the correct month name. Here is the code:

```
months = ["January", "February", "March", "April",
          "May", "June", "July", "August",
          "September", "October", "November", "December"]
monthStr = months[int(monthStr)-1]
```

Remember the indexing expression int(monthStr)-1 is used because list indexes start at 0.

The last step in our program is to piece together the date in the new format.

```
print("The converted date is:", monthStr, dayStr+",", yearStr)
```

Notice how I have used concatenation for the comma immediately after the day.

Here's the complete program:

```
# dateconvert.py
#   Converts a date in form "mm/dd/yyyy" to "month day, year"

def main():
    # get the date
    dateStr = input("Enter a date (mm/dd/yyyy): ")

    # split into components
    monthStr, dayStr, yearStr = dateStr.split("/")

    # convert monthStr to the month name
    months = ["January", "February", "March", "April",
              "May", "June", "July", "August",
              "September", "October", "November", "December"]
    monthStr = months[int(monthStr)-1]

    # output result in month day, year format
    print("The converted date is:", monthStr, dayStr+",", yearStr)

main()
```

When run, the output looks like this:

```
Enter a date (mm/dd/yyyy): 05/24/2003
The converted date is: May 24, 2003
```

This example didn't show it, but often it is also necessary to turn a number into a string. In Python, most data types can be converted into strings using the str function. Here are a couple of simple examples:

```
>>> str(500)
'500'
>>> value = 3.14
>>> str(value)
'3.14'
>>> print("The value is", str(value) + ".")
The value is 3.14.
```

Notice particularly the last example. By turning value into a string, we can use string concatenation to put a period at the end of a sentence. If we didn't first turn value into a string, Python would interpret the + as a numerical operation and produce an error, because "." is not a number.

We now have a complete set of operations for converting values among various Python data types. Table 5.3 summarizes these four Python type conversion functions:

Function	Meaning
float(<expr>)	Convert expr to a floating point value.
int(<expr>)	Convert expr to an integer value.
str(<expr>)	Return a string representation of expr.
eval(<string>)	Evaluate string as an expression.

Table 5.3: Type conversion functions

One common reason for converting a number into a string is so that string operations can be used to control the way the value is printed. For example, a program performing date calculations would have to manipulate the month, day, and year as numbers. For nicely formatted output, these numbers would be converted back to strings.

Just for fun, here is a program that inputs the day, month, and year as numbers and then prints out the date in two different formats:

```
# dateconvert2.py
#     Converts day month and year numbers into two date formats

def main():
    # get the day month and year
    day, month, year = eval(input("Enter day, month, and year numbers: "))

    date1 = str(month)+"/"+str(day)+"/"+str(year)

    months = ["January", "February", "March", "April",
              "May", "June", "July", "August",
              "September", "October", "November", "December"]
    monthStr = months[month-1]
    date2 = monthStr+" " + str(day) + ", " + str(year)

    print("The date is", date1, "or", date2+".")

main()
```

Notice how string concatenation is used to produce the required output. Here is how the result looks:

```
Please enter day, month, and year numbers: 24, 5, 2003
The date is 5/24/2003 or May 24, 2003.
```

5.8.2 String Formatting

As you have seen, basic string operations can be used to build nicely formatted output. This technique is useful for simple formatting, but building up a complex output through slicing and concatenation of smaller strings can be tedious. Python provides a powerful string formatting operation that makes the job much easier.

Let's start with a simple example. Here is a run of the change-counting program from last chapter:

```
Change Counter

Please enter the count of each coin type.
How many quarters do you have? 6
How many dimes do you have? 0
```

```
How many nickels do you have? 0
How many pennies do you have? 0
The total value of your change is 1.5
```

Notice that the final value is given as a fraction with only one decimal place. This looks funny, since we expect the output to be something like $1.50.

We can fix this problem by changing the very last line of the program as follows:

```
print("The total value of your change is ${0:0.2f}".format(total))
```

Now the program prints this message:

```
The total value of your change is $1.50
```

Let's try to make some sense of this. The `format` method is a built-in for Python strings. The idea is that the string serves as a sort of template, and values supplied as parameters are plugged into this template to form a new string. So string formatting takes the form:

```
<template-string>.format(<values>)
```

Curly braces (`{}`) inside the `template-string` mark "slots" into which the provided `values` are inserted. The information inside the curly braces tells which value goes in the slot and how the value should be formatted. The Python formatting operator is very flexible, we'll cover just some basics here; you can consult a Python reference if you'd like all of the details. In this book, the slot descriptions will always have the form:

```
{<index>:<format-specifier>}
```

The `index` tells which of the parameters is inserted into the slot.[2] As usual in Python, indexing starts with 0. In the example above, there is a single slot and the index 0 is used to say that the first (and only) parameter is inserted into that slot.

The part of the description after the colon specifies how the value should look when it is inserted into the slot. Again returning to the example, the format specifier is `0.2f`. The format of this specifier is `<width>.<precision><type>`. The width specifies how many "spaces" the value should take up. If the value

---

[2]As of Python 3.1, the index portion of the slot description is optional. When the indexes are omitted, the parameters are just filled into the slots in a left-to-right fashion.

takes up less than the specified width, it is padded (by default space characters). If the value requires more space than allotted, it will take as much space as is required to show the value. So putting a 0 here essentially says "use as much space as you need." The precision is 2, which tells Python to round the value to two decimal places. Finally, the type character f says the value should be displayed as a fixed point number. That means that the specified number of decimal places will always be shown, even if they are zero.

A complete description of format specifiers is pretty hairy, but you can get a good handle on what's possible just by looking at a few examples. The simplest template strings just specify where to plug in the parameters.

```
>>> "Hello {0} {1}, you may have won ${2}".format("Mr.", "Smith", 10000)
'Hello Mr. Smith, you may have won $10000'
```

Often, you'll want to control the width and/or precision of a numeric value.

```
>>> "This int, {0:5}, was placed in a field of width 5".format(7)
'This int,     7, was placed in a field of width 5'

>>> "This int, {0:10}, was placed in a field of width 10".format(7)
'This int,          7, was placed in a field of width 10'

>>> "This float, {0:10.5}, has width 10 and precision 5".format(3.1415926)
'This float,    3.1416, has width 10 and precision 5'

>>> "This float, {0:10.5f}, is fixed at 5 decimal places".format(3.1415926)
'This float,    3.14159, is fixed at 5 decimal places'

>>> "This float, {0:0.5}, has width 0 and precision 5".format(3.1415926)
'This float, 3.1416, has width 0 and precision 5'

>>> "Compare {0} and {0:0.20}".format(3.14)
'Compare 3.14 and 3.1400000000000001243'
```

Notice that for normal (not fixed-point) floating point numbers, the precision specifies the number of significant digits to print. For fixed-point (indicated by the f at the end of the specifier) the precision gives the number of decimal places. In the last example, the same number is printed out in two different formats. It illustrates that if you print enough digits of a floating-point number, you will almost always find a "surprise." The computer can't represent 3.14 exactly as a floating-point number. The closest value it can represent is ever so slightly larger than 3.14. If not given an explicit precision, Python will print the number out to a few decimal places. The slight extra amount shows up if you print lots of digits. Generally, Python only displays a closely rounded version of a float. Using explicit formatting allows you to see the full result down to the last bit.

You may notice that, by default, numeric values are right-justified. This is helpful for lining up numbers in columns. Strings, on the other hand, are left-justified in their fields. You can change the default behaviors by including an explicit justification character at the beginning of the format specifier. The necessary characters are $<$, $>$, and $\char`\^$ for left, right, and center justification, respectively.

```
>>> "left justification: {0:<5}".format("Hi!")
'left justification: Hi!  '

>>> "right justification: {0:>5}".format("Hi!")
'right justification:   Hi!'

>>> "centered: {0:^5}".format("Hi!")
'centered:  Hi! '
```

5.8.3   Better Change Counter

Let's close our formatting discussion with one more example program. Given what you have learned about floating point numbers, you might be a little uneasy about using them to represent money.

Suppose you are writing a computer system for a bank. Your customers would not be too happy to learn that a check went through for an amount "very close to $107.56." They want to know that the bank is keeping precise track of their money. Even though the amount of error in a given value is very small, the small errors can be compounded when doing lots of calculations, and the resulting error could add up to some real cash. That's not a satisfactory way of doing business.

A better approach would be to make sure that our program used exact values to represent money. We can do that by keeping track of the money in cents and using an int to store it. We can then convert this into dollars and cents in the output step. Assuming we are dealing with positive amounts, if total represents the value in cents, then we can get the number of dollars by integer division total // 100 and the cents from total % 100. Both of these are integer calculations and, hence, will give us exact results. Here is the updated program:

```python
# change2.py
#    A program to calculate the value of some change in dollars
#    This version represents the total cash in cents.

def main():
    print("Change Counter\n")

    print("Please enter the count of each coin type.")
    quarters = eval(input("Quarters: "))
    dimes = eval(input("Dimes: "))
    nickels = eval(input("Nickels: "))
    pennies = eval(input("Pennies: "))

    total = quarters * 25 + dimes * 10 + nickels * 5 + pennies

    print("The total value of your change is ${0}.{1:0>2}"
          .format(total//100, total%100))

main()
```

I have split the final `print` statement across two lines. Normally a statement ends at the end of the line. Sometimes it is nicer to break a long statement into smaller pieces. Because this line is broken in the middle of the `print` function, Python knows that the statement is not finished until the final closing parenthesis is reached. In this case, it is OK, and preferable, to break the statement across two lines rather than having one really long line.

The string formatting in the print statement contains two slots, one for dollars as an int and one for cents. The cents slot illustrates one additional twist on format specifiers. The value of cents is printed with the specifier 0>2. The zero in front of the justification character tells Python to pad the field (if necessary) with zeroes instead of spaces. This ensures that a value like 10 dollars and 5 cents prints as $10.05 rather than $10.   5.

By the way, string formatting would also be useful in the `dateconvert2.py` program. You might want to try redoing that program using string formatting in place of `str()` and concatenation.

5.9 File Processing

I began the chapter with a reference to word processing as an application of the string data type. One critical feature of any word processing program is the ability to store and retrieve documents as files on disk. In this section, we'll take a look at file input and output, which, as it turns out, is really just another form of string processing.

5.9.1 Multi-line Strings

Conceptually, a file is a sequence of data that is stored in secondary memory (usually on a disk drive). Files can contain any data type, but the easiest files to work with are those that contain text. Files of text have the advantage that they can be read and understood by humans, and they are easily created and edited using general-purpose text editors and word processors. In Python, text files can be very flexible, since it is easy to convert back and forth between strings and other types.

You can think of a text file as a (possibly long) string that happens to be stored on disk. Of course, a typical file generally contains more than a single line of text. A special character or sequence of characters is used to mark the end of each line. There are numerous conventions for end-of-line markers. Python takes care of these different conventions for us and just uses the regular newline character (designated with \n) to indicate line breaks.

Let's take a look at a concrete example. Suppose you type the following lines into a text editor exactly as shown here:

```
Hello
World

Goodbye 32
```

When stored to a file, you get this sequence of characters.

```
Hello\nWorld\n\nGoodbye 32\n
```

Notice that the blank line becomes a bare newline in the resulting file/string.

By the way, this is really no different than when we embed newline characters into output strings, to produce multiple lines of output with a single `print` statement. Here is the example from above printed interactively:

```
>>> print("Hello\nWorld\n\nGoodbye 32\n")
Hello
World

Goodbye 32

>>>
```

Remember if you simply evaluate a string containing newline characters in the shell, you will just get the embedded newline representation back again.

```
>>>"Hello\nWorld\n\nGoodbye 32\n"
'Hello\nWorld\n\nGoodbye 32\n'
```

It's only when a string is printed that the special characters affect how the string is displayed.

5.9.2 File Processing

The exact details of file-processing differ substantially among programming languages, but virtually all languages share certain underlying file-manipulation concepts. First, we need some way to associate a file on disk with an object in a program. This process is called *opening* a file. Once a file has been opened, it's contents can be accessed through the associated file object.

Second, we need a set of operations that can manipulate the file object. At the very least, this includes operations that allow us to read the information from a file and write new information to a file. Typically, the reading and writing operations for text files are similar to the operations for text-based, interactive input and output.

Finally, when we are finished with a file, it is *closed*. Closing a file makes sure that any bookkeeping that was necessary to maintain the correspondence between the file on disk and the file object is finished up. For example, if you write information to a file object, the changes might not show up on the disk version until the file has been closed.

This idea of opening and closing files is closely related to how you might work with files in an application program like a word processor. However, the concepts are not exactly the same. When you open a file in a program like Microsoft Word, the file is actually read from the disk and stored into RAM. In programming terminology, the file is opened for reading and the contents of the file are then read into memory via file-reading operations. At this point, the file is closed (again in the programming sense). As you "edit the file," you are really making changes to data in memory, not the file itself. The changes will not show up in the file on the disk until you tell the application to "save" it.

Saving a file also involves a multi-step process. First, the original file on the disk is reopened, this time in a mode that allows it to store information—the file on disk is opened for writing. Doing so actually *erases* the old contents of the file. File writing operations are then used to copy the current contents of the in-memory version into the new file on the disk. From your perspective, it appears that you have edited an existing file. From the program's perspective, you have actually opened a file, read its contents into memory, closed the file, created a new file (having the same name), written the (modified) contents of memory into the new file, and closed the new file.

Working with text files is easy in Python. The first step is to create a file object corresponding to a file on disk. This is done using the `open` function. Usually, a file object is immediately assigned to a variable like this.

```
<variable> = open(<name>, <mode>)
```

Here `name` is a string that provides the name of the file on the disk. The `mode` parameter is either the string `"r"` or `"w"` depending on whether we intend to *read* from the file or *write* to the file.

For example, to open a file called "numbers.dat" for reading, we could use a statement like the following:

```
infile = open("numbers.dat", "r")
```

Now we can use the file object `infile` to read the contents of `numbers.dat` from the disk.

Python provides three related operations for reading information from a file:

`<file>.read()` Returns the entire remaining contents of the file as a single (potentially large, multi-line) string.

`<file>.readline()` Returns the next line of the file. That is all text up to *and including* the next newline character.

`<file>.readlines()` Returns a list of the remaining lines in the file. Each list item is a single line including the newline character at the end.

Here's an example program that prints the contents of a file to the screen using the `read` operation:

```
# printfile.py
#      Prints a file to the screen.

def main():
    fname = input("Enter filename: ")
    infile = open(fname,"r")
    data = infile.read()
    print(data)

main()
```

The program first prompts the user for a file name and then opens the file for reading through the variable infile. You could use any name for the variable; I used infile to emphasize that the file was being used for input. The entire contents of the file is then read as one large string and stored in the variable data. Printing data causes the contents to be displayed.

The readline operation can be used to read the next line from a file. Successive calls to readline get successive lines from the file. This is analogous to input, which reads characters interactively until the user hits the <Enter> key; each call to input gets another line from the user. One thing to keep in mind, however, is that the string returned by readline will always end with a newline character, whereas input discards the newline character.

As a quick example, this fragment of code prints out the first five lines of a file:

```
infile = open(someFile, "r")
for i in range(5):
    line = infile.readline()
    print(line[:-1])
```

Notice the use of slicing to strip off the newline character at the end of the line. Since print automatically jumps to the next line (i.e., it outputs a newline), printing with the explicit newline at the end would put an extra blank line of output between the lines of the file. Alternatively, you could print the whole line, but simply tell print not to add its own newline character.

```
print(line, end="")
```

One way to loop through the entire contents of a file is to read in all of the file using readlines and then loop through the resulting list.

```
infile = open(someFile, "r")
for line in infile.readlines():
    # process the line here
infile.close()
```

Of course, a potential drawback of this approach is the fact that the file may be
very large, and reading it into a list all at once may take up too much RAM.

Fortunately, there is a simple alternative. Python treats the file itself as a
sequence of lines. So looping through the lines of a file can be done directly like
this:

```
infile = open(someFile, "r")
for line in infile:
    # process the line here
infile.close()
```

This is a particularly handy way to process the lines of a file one at a time.

Opening a file for writing prepares that file to receive data. If no file with
the given name exists, a new file will be created. A word of warning: if a file
with the given name *does* exist, Python will delete it and create a new, empty
file. When writing to a file, make sure you do not clobber any files you will need
later! Here is an example of opening a file for output:

```
outfile = open("mydata.out", "w")
```

The easiest way to write information into a text file is to use the already-
familiar print function. To print to a file, we just need to add an extra keyword
parameter that specifies the file:

```
print(..., file=<outputFile>)
```

This behaves exactly like a normal print except that the result is sent to outputFile
instead of being displayed on the screen.

5.9.3 Example Program: Batch Usernames

To see how all these pieces fit together, let's redo the username generation program. Our previous version created usernames interactively by having the user
type in his or her name. If we were setting up accounts for a large number of
users, the process would probably not be done interactively, but in *batch* mode.
In batch processing, program input and output is done through files.

Our new program is designed to process a file of names. Each line of the input file will contain the first and last names of a new user separated by one or more spaces. The program produces an output file containing a line for each generated username.

```python
# userfile.py
#     Program to create a file of usernames in batch mode.

def main():
    print("This program creates a file of usernames from a")
    print("file of names.")

    # get the file names
    infileName = input("What file are the names in? ")
    outfileName = input("What file should the usernames go in? ")

    # open the files
    infile = open(infileName, "r")
    outfile = open(outfileName, "w")

    # process each line of the input file
    for line in infile:
        # get the first and last names from line
        first, last = line.split()
        # create the username
        uname = (first[0]+last[:7]).lower()
        # write it to the output file
        print(uname, file=outfile)

    # close both files
    infile.close()
    outfile.close()

    print("Usernames have been written to", outfileName)

main()
```

There are a couple of things worth noticing in this program. I have two files open at the same time, one for input (infile) and one for output (outfile).

It's not unusual for a program to operate on several files simultaneously. Also, when creating the username, I used the `lower` string method. Notice that the method is applied to the string that results from the concatenation. This ensures that the username is all lowercase, even if the input names are mixed case.

5.10 Chapter Summary

This chapter has covered important elements of the Python types: strings, lists, and files. Here is a summary of the highlights:

- Strings are sequences of characters. String literals can be delimited with either single or double quotes.

- Strings and lists can be manipulated with the built-in sequence operations for concatenation (+), repetition (*), indexing ([]), slicing ([:]), and length (`len()`). A `for` loop can be used to iterate through the characters of a string, items in a list, or lines of a file.

- One way of converting numeric information into string information is to use a string or a list as a lookup table.

- Lists are more general than strings.

  - Strings are always sequences of characters, whereas lists can contain values of any type.

  - Lists are mutable, which means that items in a list can be modified by assigning new values.

- Strings are represented in the computer as numeric codes. ASCII and Unicode are compatible standards that are used for specifying the correspondence between characters and the underlying codes. Python provides the `ord` and `chr` functions for translating between Unicode codes and characters.

- Python string and list objects include many useful built-in methods for string and list processing.

- The process of encoding data to keep it private is called encryption. There are two different kinds of encryption systems: private key and public key.

- Program input and output often involve string processing. Python provides numerous operators for converting back and forth between numbers and strings. The string formatting method (format) is particularly useful for producing nicely formatted output.

- Text files are multi-line strings stored in secondary memory. A file may be opened for reading or writing. When opened for writing, the existing contents of the file are erased. Python provides three file-reading methods: read(), readline(), and readlines(). It is also possible to iterate through the lines of a file with a for loop. Data is written to a file using the print function. When processing is finished, a file should be closed.

5.11 Exercises

Review Questions

True/False

1. A Python string literal is always enclosed in double quotes.

2. The last character of a string s is at position len(s)-1.

3. A string always contains a single line of text.

4. In Python "4" + "5" is "45".

5. Python lists are mutable, but strings are not.

6. ASCII is a standard for representing characters using numeric codes.

7. The split method breaks a string into a list of substrings, and join does the opposite.

8. A substitution cipher is a good way to keep sensitive information secure.

9. The add method can be used to add an item to the end of a list.

10. The process of associating a file with an object in a program is called "reading" the file.

Multiple Choice

1. Accessing a single character out of a string is called:
   a) slicing   b) concatenation   c) assignment   d) indexing

2. Which of the following is the same as s[0:-1]?
   a) s[-1]   b) s[:]   c) s[:len(s)-1]   d) s[0:len(s)]

3. What function gives the Unicode value of a character?
   a) ord   b) ascii   c) chr   d) eval

4. Which of the following can *not* be used to convert a string of digits into a number?
   a) int   b) float   c) str   d) eval

5. A successor to ASCII that includes characters from (nearly) all written languages is
   a) TELLI   b) ASCII++   c) Unicode   d) ISO

6. Which string method converts all the characters of a string to upper case?
   a) capitalize   b) capwords   c) uppercase   d) upper

7. The string "slots" that are filled in by the format method are marked by:
   a) %   b) $ c) []   d) {}

8. Which of the following is *not* a file-reading method in Python?
   a) read   b) readline   c) readall   d) readlines

9. The term for a program that does its I/O with files is
   a) file-oriented   b) multi-line   c) batch   d) lame

10. Before reading or writing to a file, a file object must be created via
    a) open   b) create   c) File   d) Folder

Discussion

1. Given the initial statements:

```
s1 = "spam"
s2 = "ni!"
```

Show the result of evaluating each of the following string expressions.

    (a) `"The Knights who say, " + s2`

    (b) `3 * s1 + 2 * s2`

    (c) `s1[1]`

    (d) `s1[1:3]`

    (e) `s1[2] + s2[:2]`

    (f) `s1 + s2[-1]`

    (g) `s1.upper()`

    (h) `s2.upper().ljust(4) * 3`

2. Given the same initial statements as in the previous problem, show a Python expression that could construct each of the following results by performing string operations on s1 and s2.

    (a) `"NI"`

    (b) `"ni!spamni!"`

    (c) `"Spam Ni!  Spam Ni!  Spam Ni!"`

    (d) `"spam"`

    (e) `["sp","m"]`

    (f) `"spm"`

3. Show the output that would be generated by each of the following program fragments:

    (a)
```
for ch in "aardvark":
    print(ch)
```

    (b)
```
for w in "Now is the winter of our discontent...".split():
    print(w)
```

    (c)
```
for w in "Mississippi".split("i"):
    print(w, end=" ")
```

    (d)
```
msg = ""
for s in "secret".split("e"):
    msg = msg + s
print(msg)
```

    (e)
```
msg = ""
for ch in "secret":
    msg = msg + chr(ord(ch)+1)
print(msg)
```

4. Show the string that would result from each of the following string formatting operations. If the operation is not legal, explain why.

   (a) `"Looks like {1} and {0} for breakfast".format("eggs", "spam")`

   (b) `"There is {0} {1} {2} {3}".format(1,"spam", 4, "you")`

   (c) `"Hello {0}".format("Susan", "Computewell")`

   (d) `"{0:0.2f} {0:0.2f}".format(2.3, 2.3468)`

   (e) `"{7.5f} {7.5f}".format(2.3, 2.3468)`

   (f) `"Time left {0:02}:{1:05.2f}".format(1, 37.374)`

   (g) `"{1:3}".format("14")`

5. Explain why public key encryption is more useful for securing communications on the Internet than private (shared) key encryption.

Programming Exercises

1. As discussed in the chapter, string formatting could be used to simplify the `dateconvert2.py` program. Go back and redo this program making use of the string-formatting method.

2. A certain CS professor gives 5-point quizzes that are graded on the scale 5-A, 4-B, 3-C, 2-D, 1-F, 0-F. Write a program that accepts a quiz score as an input and prints out the corresponding grade.

3. A certain CS professor gives 100-point exams that are graded on the scale 90–100:A, 80–89:B, 70–79:C, 60–69:D, <60:F. Write a program that accepts an exam score as input and prints out the corresponding grade.

4. An acronym is a word formed by taking the first letters of the words in a phrase and making a word from them. For example, RAM is an acronym for "random access memory." Write a program that allows the user to type in a phrase and then outputs the acronym for that phrase. Note: the acronym should be all uppercase, even if the words in the phrase are not capitalized.

5. Numerologists claim to be able to determine a person's character traits based on the "numeric value" of a name. The value of a name is determined by summing up the values of the letters of the name where "a" is 1, "b" is 2, "c" is 3 etc., up to "z" being 26. For example, the name "Zelle"

would have the value $26 + 5 + 12 + 12 + 5 = 60$ (which happens to be a very auspicious number, by the way). Write a program that calculates the numeric value of a single name provided as input.

6. Expand your solution to the previous problem to allow the calculation of a complete name such as "John Marvin Zelle" or "John Jacob Jingleheimer Smith." The total value is just the sum of the numeric values of all the names.

7. A Caesar cipher is a simple substitution cipher based on the idea of shifting each letter of the plaintext message a fixed number (called the key) of positions in the alphabet. For example, if the key value is 2, the word "Sourpuss" would be encoded as "Uqwtrwuu." The original message can be recovered by "reencoding" it using the negative of the key.

   Write a program that can encode and decode Caesar ciphers. The input to the program will be a string of plaintext and the value of the key. The output will be an encoded message where each character in the original message is replaced by shifting it *key* characters in the Unicode character set. For example, if ch is a character in the string and key is the amount to shift, then the character that replaces ch can be calculated as: chr(ord(ch) + key).

8. One problem with the previous exercise is that it does not deal with the case when we "drop off the end" of the alphabet. A true Caesar cipher does the shifting in a circular fashion where the next character after "z" is "a." Modify your solution to the previous problem to make it circular. You may assume that the input consists only of letters and spaces. Hint: make a string containing all the characters of your alphabet and use positions in this string as your code. You do not have to shift "z" into "a" just make sure that you use a circular shift over the entire sequence of characters in your alphabet string.

9. Write a program that counts the number of words in a sentence entered by the user.

10. Write a program that calculates the average word length in a sentence entered by the user.

11. Write an improved version of the Chaos program from Chapter 1 that allows a user to input two initial values and the number of iterations and

then prints a nicely formatted table showing how the values change over time. For example, if the starting values were .25 and .26 with 10 iterations, the table might look like this:

```
index     0.25           0.26
---------------------------------
   1     0.731250       0.750360
   2     0.766441       0.730547
   3     0.698135       0.767707
   4     0.821896       0.695499
   5     0.570894       0.825942
   6     0.955399       0.560671
   7     0.166187       0.960644
   8     0.540418       0.147447
   9     0.968629       0.490255
  10     0.118509       0.974630
```

12. Write an improved version of the future value program from Chapter 2. Your program will prompt the user for the amount of the investment, the annualized interest rate, and the number of years of the investment. The program will then output a nicely formatted table that tracks the value of the investment year by year. Your output might look something like this:

```
Year     Value
-----------------
   0     $2000.00
   1     $2200.00
   2     $2420.00
   3     $2662.00
   4     $2928.20
   5     $3221.02
   6     $3542.12
   7     $3897.43
```

13. Redo any of the previous programming problems to make them batch-oriented (using text files for input and output).

14. Word count. A common utility on Unix/Linux systems is a small program called "wc." This program analyzes a file to determine the number of

lines, words, and characters contained therein. Write your own version of wc. The program should accept a file name as input and then print three numbers showing the count of lines, words, and characters in the file.

15. Write a program to plot a horizontal bar chart of student exam scores. Your program should get input from a file. The first line of the file contains the count of the number of students in the file, and each subsequent line contains a student's last name followed by a score in the range 0 to 100. Your program should draw a horizontal rectangle for each student where the length of the bar represents the student's score. The bars should all line up on their left-hand edges. Hint: use the number of students to determine the size of the window and its coordinates. Bonus: label the bars at the left end with the student name.

Computewell

Dibblebit

Jones

Smith

16. Write a program to draw a quiz score histogram. Your program should read data from a file. Each line of the file contains a number in the range 0–10. Your program must count the number of occurrences of each score and then draw a vertical bar chart with a bar for each possible score (0–10) with a height corresponding to the count of that score. For example, if 15 students got an 8, then the height of the bar for 8 should be 15. Hint: use a list that stores the count for each possible score.

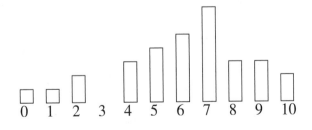

Chapter 6

Defining Functions

Objectives

- To understand why programmers divide programs up into sets of cooperating functions.

- To be able to define new functions in Python.

- To understand the details of function calls and parameter passing in Python.

- To write programs that use functions to reduce code duplication and increase program modularity.

6.1 The Function of Functions

The programs that we have written so far comprise a single function, usually called main. We have also been using pre-written functions and methods including built-in Python functions (e.g., abs, eval), functions and methods from the Python standard libraries (e.g., math.sqrt), and methods from the graphics module (e.g., myPoint.getX()). Functions are an important tool for building sophisticated programs. This chapter covers the whys and hows of designing your own functions to make your programs easier to write and understand.

In Chapter 4, we looked at a graphic solution to the future value problem. Recall, this program makes use of the graphics library to draw a bar chart showing the growth of an investment. Here is the program as we left it:

```
# futval_graph2.py

from graphics import *
```

167

```
def main():
    # Introduction
    print("This program plots the growth of a 10-year investment.")

    # Get principal and interest rate
    principal = eval(input("Enter the initial principal: "))
    apr = eval(input("Enter the annualized interest rate: "))

    # Create a graphics window with labels on left edge
    win = GraphWin("Investment Growth Chart", 320, 240)
    win.setBackground("white")
    win.setCoords(-1.75,-200, 11.5, 10400)
    Text(Point(-1, 0), ' 0.0K').draw(win)
    Text(Point(-1, 2500), ' 2.5K').draw(win)
    Text(Point(-1, 5000), ' 5.0K').draw(win)
    Text(Point(-1, 7500), ' 7.5k').draw(win)
    Text(Point(-1, 10000), '10.0K').draw(win)

    # Draw bar for initial principal
    bar = Rectangle(Point(0, 0), Point(1, principal))
    bar.setFill("green")
    bar.setWidth(2)
    bar.draw(win)

    # Draw a bar for each subsequent year
    for year in range(1, 11):
        principal = principal * (1 + apr)
        bar = Rectangle(Point(year, 0), Point(year+1, principal))
        bar.setFill("green")
        bar.setWidth(2)
        bar.draw(win)

    input("Press <Enter> to quit.")
    win.close()

main()
```

This is certainly a workable program, but there is a nagging issue of program style that really should be addressed. Notice that this program draws bars in two different places. The initial bar is drawn just before the loop, and the subsequent bars are drawn inside the loop.

Having similar code like this in two places has some drawbacks. Obviously, one issue is having to write the code twice. A more subtle problem is that the code has to be maintained in two different places. Should we decide to change the color or other facets of the bars, we would have to make sure these changes occur in both places. Failing to keep related parts of the code in sync is a common problem in program maintenance.

Functions can be used to reduce code duplication and to make programs more understandable and easier to maintain. Before fixing up the future value program, let's take look at what functions have to offer.

6.2 Functions, Informally

You can think of a function as a *subprogram*—a small program inside a program. The basic idea of a function is that we write a sequence of statements and give that sequence a name. The instructions can then be executed at any point in the program by referring to the function name.

The part of the program that creates a function is called a *function definition*. When a function is subsequently used in a program, we say that the definition is *called* or *invoked*. A single function definition may be called at many different points of a program.

Let's take a concrete example. Suppose you want to write a program that prints out the lyrics to the "Happy Birthday" song. The standard lyrics look like this.

```
Happy birthday to you!
Happy birthday to you!
Happy birthday, dear <insert-name>.
Happy birthday to you!
```

We're going to play with this example in the interactive Python environment. You might want to fire up Python and try some of this out yourself.

A simple approach to this problem is to use four print statements. Here's an interactive session that creates a program for singing "Happy Birthday" to Fred.

```
>>> def main():
        print("Happy birthday to you!")
```

```
print("Happy birthday to you!")
print("Happy birthday, dear Fred.")
print("Happy birthday to you!")
```

We can then run this program to get our lyrics.

```
>>> main()
Happy birthday to you!
Happy birthday to you!
Happy birthday, dear Fred.
Happy birthday to you!
```

Obviously, there is some duplicated code in this program. For such a simple program, that's not a big deal, but even here it's a bit annoying to keep retyping the same line. Let's introduce a function that prints the lyrics of the first, second, and fourth lines.

```
>>> def happy():
        print("Happy birthday to you!")
```

We have defined a new function called happy. Here is an example of what it does:

```
>>> happy()
Happy birthday to you!
```

Invoking the happy command causes Python to print a line of the song.

Now we can redo the verse for Fred using happy. Let's call our new version singFred.

```
>>> def singFred():
        happy()
        happy()
        print("Happy birthday, dear Fred.")
        happy()
```

This version required much less typing, thanks to the happy command. Let's try printing the lyrics for Fred just to make sure it works.

```
>>> singFred()
Happy birthday to you!
Happy birthday to you!
Happy birthday, dear Fred.
Happy birthday to you!
```

So far, so good. Now suppose that it's also Lucy's birthday, and we want to sing a verse for Fred followed by a verse for Lucy. We've already got the verse for Fred; we can prepare one for Lucy as well.

```
>>> def singLucy():
        happy()
        happy()
        print("Happy birthday, dear Lucy.")
        happy()
```

Now we can write a main program that sings to both Fred and Lucy.

```
>>> def main():
        singFred()
        print()
        singLucy()
```

The bare print between the two function calls puts a space between the verses in our output. And here's the final product in action:

```
>>> main()
Happy birthday to you!
Happy birthday to you!
Happy birthday, dear Fred.
Happy birthday to you!

Happy birthday to you!
Happy birthday to you!
Happy birthday, dear Lucy.
Happy birthday to you!
```

Well now, that certainly seems to work, and we've removed some of the duplication by defining the happy function. However, something still doesn't feel quite right. We have two functions, singFred and singLucy, that are almost identical. Following this approach, adding a verse for Elmer would have us create a singElmer function that looks just like those for Fred and Lucy. Can't we do something about the proliferation of verses?

Notice that the only difference between singFred and singLucy is the name at the end of the third print statement. The verses are exactly the same except for this one changing part. We can collapse these two functions together by using a *parameter*. Let's write a generic function called sing.

```
>>> def sing(person):
        happy()
        happy()
        print("Happy Birthday, dear", person + ".")
        happy()
```

This function makes use of a parameter named person. A parameter is a variable that is initialized when the function is called. We can use the sing function to print a verse for either Fred or Lucy. We just need to supply the name as a parameter when we invoke the function.

```
>>> sing("Fred")
Happy birthday to you!
Happy birthday to you!
Happy Birthday, dear Fred.
Happy birthday to you!

>>> sing("Lucy")
Happy birthday to you!
Happy birthday to you!
Happy Birthday, dear Lucy.
Happy birthday to you!
```

Let's finish with a program that sings to all three of our birthday people.

```
>>> def main():
        sing("Fred")
        print()
        sing("Lucy")
        print()
        sing("Elmer")
```

It doesn't get much easier than that.

Here is the complete program as a module file.

```
# happy.py

def happy():
    print("Happy Birthday to you!")

def sing(person):
    happy()
    happy()
    print("Happy birthday, dear", person + ".")
    happy()

def main():
    sing("Fred")
    print()
    sing("Lucy")
    print()
    sing("Elmer")

main()
```

6.3 Future Value with a Function

Now that you've seen how defining functions can help solve the code duplication problem, let's return to the future value graph. Remember, the problem is that bars of the graph are drawn at two different places in the program.

The code just before the loop looks like this:

```
# Draw bar for initial principal
bar = Rectangle(Point(0, 0), Point(1, principal))
bar.setFill("green")
bar.setWidth(2)
bar.draw(win)
```

And the code inside the loop is as follows.

```
bar = Rectangle(Point(year, 0), Point(year+1, principal))
bar.setFill("green")
bar.setWidth(2)
bar.draw(win)
```

Let's try to combine these two into a single function that draws a bar on the screen.

In order to draw the bar, we need some information. Specifically, we need to know what year the bar will be for, how tall the bar will be, and what window the bar will be drawn in. These three values will be supplied as parameters for the function. Here's the function definition:

```
def drawBar(window, year, height):
    # Draw a bar in window for given year with given height
    bar = Rectangle(Point(year, 0), Point(year+1, height))
    bar.setFill("green")
    bar.setWidth(2)
    bar.draw(window)
```

To use this function, we just need to supply values for the three parameters. For example, if win is a GraphWin, we can draw a bar for year 0 and a principal of $2,000 by invoking drawBar like this:

```
drawBar(win, 0, 2000)
```

Incorporating the drawBar function, here is the latest version of our future value program:

```
# futval_graph3.py
from graphics import *

def drawBar(window, year, height):
    # Draw a bar in window starting at year with given height
    bar = Rectangle(Point(year, 0), Point(year+1, height))
    bar.setFill("green")
    bar.setWidth(2)
    bar.draw(window)

def main():
    # Introduction
    print("This program plots the growth of a 10-year investment.")

    # Get principal and interest rate
    principal = eval(input("Enter the initial principal: "))
    apr = eval(input("Enter the annualized interest rate: "))
```

```
# Create a graphics window with labels on left edge
win = GraphWin("Investment Growth Chart", 320, 240)
win.setBackground("white")
win.setCoords(-1.75,-200, 11.5, 10400)
Text(Point(-1, 0),   ' 0.0K').draw(win)
Text(Point(-1, 2500),  ' 2.5K').draw(win)
Text(Point(-1, 5000),  ' 5.0K').draw(win)
Text(Point(-1, 7500),  ' 7.5k').draw(win)
Text(Point(-1, 10000), '10.0K').draw(win)

drawBar(win, 0, principal)
for year in range(1, 11):
    principal = principal * (1 + apr)
    drawBar(win, year, principal)

input("Press <Enter> to quit.")
win.close()
main()
```

You can see how drawBar has eliminated the duplicated code. Should we wish to change the appearance of the bars in the graph, we only need to change the code in one spot, the definition of drawBar. Don't worry yet if you don't understand every detail of this example. You still have some things to learn about functions.

6.4 Functions and Parameters: The Exciting Details

You may be wondering about the choice of parameters for the drawBar function. Obviously, the year for which a bar is being drawn and the height of the bar are the changeable parts in the drawing of a bar. But why is window also a parameter to this function? After all, we will be drawing all of the bars in the same window; it doesn't seem to change.

The reason for making window a parameter has to do with the *scope* of variables in function definitions. Scope refers to the places in a program where a given variable may be referenced. Remember each function is its own little subprogram. The variables used inside one function are *local* to that function, even if they happen to have the same name as variables that appear inside another function.

The only way for a function to see a variable from another function is for that variable to be passed as a parameter.[1] Since the GraphWin (assigned to the variable win) is created inside main, it is not directly accessible in drawBar. However, the window parameter in drawBar gets assigned the value of win from main when drawBar is called. To see how this happens, we need to take a more detailed look at the function invocation process.

A function definition looks like this:

```
def <name>(<formal-parameters>):
    <body>
```

The name of the function must be an identifier, and formal-parameters is a (possibly empty) list of variable names (also identifiers). The formal parameters, like all variables used in the function, are only accessible in the body of the function. Variables with identical names elsewhere in the program are distinct from the formal parameters and variables inside the function body.

A function is called by using its name followed by a list of *actual parameters* or *arguments*.

```
<name>(<actual-parameters>)
```

When Python comes to a function call, it initiates a four-step process:

1. The calling program suspends execution at the point of the call.

2. The formal parameters of the function get assigned the values supplied by the actual parameters in the call.

3. The body of the function is executed.

4. Control returns to the point just after where the function was called.

Returning to the Happy Birthday example, let's trace through the singing of two verses. Here is part of the body from main:

```
sing("Fred")
print()
sing("Lucy")
...
```

---

[1]Technically, it is possible to reference a variable from a function that is nested inside another function, but function nesting is beyond the scope of this discussion.

When Python gets to sing("Fred"), execution of main is temporarily suspended. At this point, Python looks up the definition of sing and sees that it has a single formal parameter, person. The formal parameter is assigned the value of the actual, so it is as if we had executed this statement:

person = "Fred"

A snapshot of this situation is shown in Figure 6.1. Notice the variable person inside sing has just been initialized.

```
def main():           person = "Fred"   def sing(person):
    sing("Fred")                          happy()
    print()                               happy()
    sing("Lucy")                          print ("Happy birthday, dear", person + ".")
                                          happy()


                      person: "Fred"
```

Figure 6.1: Illustration of control transferring to sing

At this point, Python begins executing the body of sing. The first statement is another function call, this one to happy. Python suspends execution of sing and transfers control to the called function. The body of happy consists of a single print. This statement is executed, and then control returns to where it left off in sing. Figure 6.2 shows a snapshot of the execution so far.

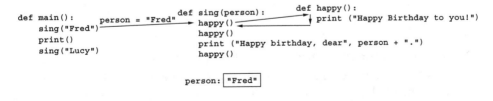

```
                                 def sing(person):    def happy():
def main():     person = "Fred"    happy()            print ("Happy Birthday to you!")
    sing("Fred")                   happy()
    print()                        print ("Happy birthday, dear", person + ".")
    sing("Lucy")                   happy()


                     person: "Fred"
```

Figure 6.2: Snapshot of completed call to happy

Execution continues in this manner with Python making two more side trips
back to happy to complete the execution of sing. When Python gets to the end
of sing, control then returns to main and continues immediately after the function call. Figure 6.3 shows where we are at that point. Notice that the person
variable in sing has disappeared. The memory occupied by local function variables is reclaimed when the function finishes. Local variables do not retain any
values from one function execution to the next.

Figure 6.3: Snapshot of completed call to sing

The next statement to execute is the bare print statement in main. This
produces a blank line in the output. Then Python encounters another call to
sing. As before, control transfers to the function definition. This time the formal
parameter is "Lucy". Figure 6.4 shows the situation as sing begins to execute
for the second time.

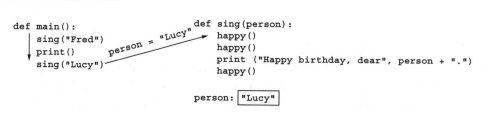

Figure 6.4: Snapshot of second call to sing

Now we'll fast forward to the end. The function body of sing is executed
for Lucy (with three side trips through happy) and control returns to main just
after the point of the function call. Now we have reached the bottom of our
code fragment, as illustrated by Figure 6.5. These three statements in main have
caused sing to execute twice and happy to execute six times. Overall, nine total
lines of output were generated.

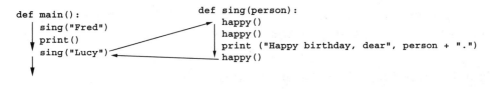

Figure 6.5: Completion of second call to `sing`

Hopefully you're getting the hang of how function calls actually work. One point that this example did not address is the use of multiple parameters. Usually when a function definition has several parameters, the actual parameters are matched up with the formal parameters by *position*. The first actual parameter is assigned to the first formal parameter, the second actual is assigned to the second formal, etc. It's possible to modify this behavior using keyword parameters, which are matched up by name (e.g., `end=""` in a call to `print`). However, we will rely on positional matching for all of our example functions.

As an example, look again at the use of the `drawBar` function from the future value program. Here is the call to draw the initial bar:

```
drawBar(win, 0, principal)
```

When Python transfers control to `drawBar`, these parameters are matched up to the formal parameters in the function heading.

```
def drawBar(window, year, height):
```

The net effect is as if the function body had been prefaced with three assignment statements.

```
window = win
year = 0
height = principal
```

You must always be careful when calling a function that you get the actual parameters in the correct order to match the function definition.

6.5   Getting Results from a Function

You have seen that parameter passing provides a mechanism for initializing the variables in a function. In a way, parameters act as inputs to a function. We can call a function many times and get different results by changing the input parameters. Oftentimes we also want to get information back out of a function.

6.5.1   Functions That Return Values

One way to get information from a function is by having it return a value to the caller. You have already seen numerous examples of this type of function. For example, consider this call to the sqrt function from the math library:

```
discRt = math.sqrt(b*b - 4*a*c)
```

Here the value of b*b - 4*a*c is the actual parameter of math.sqrt. This function call occurs on the right side of an assignment statement; that means it is an expression. The math.sqrt function must somehow produce a value that is then assigned to the variable discRt.   Technically, we say that sqrt *returns* the square root of its argument.

It's very easy to write functions that return values. Here's an example value-returning function that does the opposite of sqrt; it returns the square of its argument:

```
def square(x):
    return x * x
```

The body of this function consists of a single return statement. When Python encounters return, it exits the function and returns control to the point where the function was called. In addition, the value(s) provided in the return statement are sent back to the caller as an expression result.

We can use our square function any place that an expression would be legal. Here are some interactive examples:

```
>>> square(3)
9
>>> print(square(4))
16
>>> x = 5
>>> y = square(x)
>>> print(y)
25
>>> print(square(x) + square(3))
34
```

Let's use the square function to write another function that finds the distance between two points. Given two points (x_1, y_1) and (x_2, y_2), the distance between them is calculated from the Pythagorean Theorem as $\sqrt{(x_2 - x_1)^2 + (y_2 - y_1)^2}$. Here is a Python function to compute the distance between two Point objects:

```
def distance(p1, p2):
    dist = math.sqrt(square(p2.getX() - p1.getX())
                         + square(p2.getY() - p1.getY())
    return dist
```

Using the distance function, we can augment the interactive triangle program from Chapter 4 to calculate the perimeter of the triangle. Here's the complete program:

```
# Program: triangle2.py
import math
from graphics import *

def square(x):
    return x * x

def distance(p1, p2):
    dist = math.sqrt(square(p2.getX() - p1.getX())
                         + square(p2.getY() - p1.getY()))
    return dist

def main():
    win = GraphWin("Draw a Triangle")
    win.setCoords(0.0, 0.0, 10.0, 10.0)
    message = Text(Point(5, 0.5), "Click on three points")
    message.draw(win)

    # Get and draw three vertices of triangle
    p1 = win.getMouse()
    p1.draw(win)
    p2 = win.getMouse()
    p2.draw(win)
    p3 = win.getMouse()
    p3.draw(win)
```

```
    # Use Polygon object to draw the triangle
    triangle = Polygon(p1,p2,p3)
    triangle.setFill("peachpuff")
    triangle.setOutline("cyan")
    triangle.draw(win)

    # Calculate the perimeter of the triangle
    perim = distance(p1,p2) + distance(p2,p3) + distance(p3,p1)
    message.setText("The perimeter is: {0:0.2f}".format(perim))

    # Wait for another click to exit
    win.getMouse()
    win.close()

main()
```

You can see how `distance` is called three times in one line to compute the perimeter of the triangle. Using a function here saves quite a bit of tedious coding.

Sometimes a function needs to return more than one value. This can be done by simply listing more than one expression in the `return` statement. As a silly example, here is a function that computes both the sum and the difference of two numbers.

```
def sumDiff(x,y):
    sum = x + y
    diff = x - y
    return sum, diff
```

As you can see, this `return` hands back two values. When calling this function, we would place it in a simultaneous assignment.

```
num1, num2 = eval(input("Please enter two numbers (num1, num2) "))
s, d   = sumDiff(num1, num2)
print("The sum is", s, "and the difference is", d)
```

As with parameters, when multiple values are returned from a function, they are assigned to variables by position. In this example, s will get the first value listed in the `return` (sum), and d will get the second value (diff).

That's just about all there is to know about value-returning functions in Python. There is one "gotcha" to warn you about. Technically, all functions in Python return a value, regardless of whether the function actually contains a `return` statement. Functions without a `return` always hand back a special object, denoted `None`. This object is often used as a sort of default value for variables that don't currently hold anything useful. A common mistake that new (and not-so-new) programmers make is writing what should be a value-returning function but forgetting to include a `return` statement at the end.

Suppose we forget to include the `return` statement at the end of the `distance` function.

```
def distance(p1, p2):
    dist = math.sqrt(square(p2.getX() - p1.getX())
                     + square(p2.getY() - p1.getY()))
```

Running the revised triangle program with this version of `distance` generates this Python error message:

```
Traceback (most recent call last):
  File "triangle2.py", line 42, in <module>
    main()
  File "triangle2.py", line 35, in main
    perim = distance(p1,p2) + distance(p2,p3) + distance(p3,p1)
TypeError: unsupported operand type(s) for +: 'NoneType' and 'NoneType'
```

The problem here is that this version of `distance` does not return a number; it always hands back the value `None`. Addition is not defined for `None` (which has the special type `NoneType`), and so Python complains. If your value-returning functions are producing strange error messages involving `None`, check to make sure you remembered to include the `return`.

6.5.2 Functions that Modify Parameters

Return values are the main way to send information from a function back to the part of the program that called the function. In some cases, functions can also communicate back to the calling program by making changes to the function parameters. Understanding when and how this is possible requires the mastery of some subtle details about how assignment works in Python and the effect this has on the relationship between the actual and formal parameters used in a function call.

Let's start with a simple example. Suppose you are writing a program that manages bank accounts or investments. One of the common tasks that must be performed is to accumulate interest on an account (as we did in the future value program). We might consider writing a function that automatically adds the interest to the account balance. Here is a first attempt at such a function:

```
# addinterest1.py
def addInterest(balance, rate):
    newBalance = balance * (1+rate)
    balance = newBalance
```

The intent of this function is to set the balance of the account to a value that has been updated by the amount of interest.

Let's try out our function by writing a very small test program.

```
def test():
    amount = 1000
    rate = 0.05
    addInterest(amount, rate)
    print(amount)
```

What do you think this program will print? Our intent is that 5% should be added to amount, giving a result of 1050. Here's what actually happens:

```
>>>addinterest.test()
1000
```

As you can see, amount is unchanged! What has gone wrong?

Actually, nothing has gone wrong. If you consider carefully what we have discussed so far regarding functions and parameters, you will see that this is exactly the result that we should expect. Let's trace the execution of this example to see what happens. The first two lines of the test function create two local variables called amount and rate which are given the initial values of 1000 and 0.05, respectively.

Next, control transfers to the addInterest function. The formal parameters balance and rate are assigned the values from the actual parameters amount and rate. Remember, even though the name rate appears in both functions, these are two separate variables. The situation as addInterest begins to execute is shown in Figure 6.6. Notice that the assignment of parameters causes the variables balance and rate in addInterest to refer to the *values* of the actual parameters.

Executing the first line of addInterest creates a new variable newBalance. Now comes the key step. The next statement in addInterest assigns balance

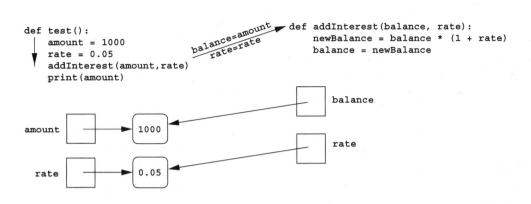

Figure 6.6: Transfer of control to `addInterest`

to have the same value as newBalance. The result is shown in Figure 6.7. Notice that balance now refers to the same value as newBalance, but this *had no effect on* amount in the test function.

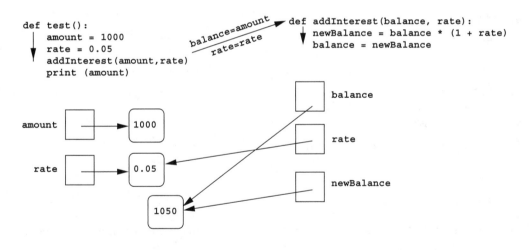

Figure 6.7: Assignment of `balance`

At this point, execution of addInterest has completed and control returns to test. The local variables (including parameters) in addInterest go away, but amount and rate in the test function still refer to the initial values of 1000 and 0.05, respectively. Of course, the program prints the value of amount as 1000.

To summarize the situation, the formal parameters of a function only receive the *values* of the actual parameters. The function does not have any access to the variable that holds the actual parameter; therefore, assigning a new value to a formal parameter has no effect on the variable that contains the actual parameter. In programming language parlance, Python is said to pass all parameters *by value*.

Some programming languages (e.g., C++ and Ada), do allow variables themselves to be sent as parameters to a function. Such a mechanism is called passing parameters *by reference*. When a variable is passed by reference, assigning a new value to the formal parameter actually changes the value of the parameter variable in the calling program.

Since Python does not allow passing parameters by reference, an obvious alternative is to change our `addInterest` function so that it returns the `newBalance`. This value can then be used to update the `amount` in the `test` function. Here's a working version:

```
# addinterest2.py

def addInterest(balance, rate):
    newBalance = balance * (1+rate)
    return newBalance

def test():
    amount = 1000
    rate = 0.05
    amount = addInterest(amount, rate)
    print(amount)


test()
```

You should easily be able to trace through the execution of this program to see how we get this output.

```
>>>addinterest2.test()
1050
```

Now suppose instead of looking at a single account, we are writing a program that deals with many bank accounts. We could store the account balances in a Python list. It would be nice to have an `addInterest` function that adds the accrued interest to all of the balances in the list. If `balances` is a list of account balances, we can update the first amount in the list (the one at index 0) with a line of code like this:

```
balances[0] = balances[0] * (1 + rate)
```

Remember, this works because lists are mutable. This line of code essentially says, "multiply the value in the 0th position of the list by $(1 + rate)$ and store the result back into the 0th position of the list." Of course, a very similar line of code would work to update the balance of the next location in the list; we just replace the 0s with 1s.

```
balances[1] = balances[1] * (1 + rate)
```

A more general way of updating all the balances in a list is to use a loop that goes through positions $0, 1, \ldots, length - 1$. Here is a program that implements this idea.

```python
# addinterest3.py

def addInterest(balances, rate):
    for i in range(len(balances)):
        balances[i] = balances[i] * (1+rate)

def test():
    amounts = [1000, 2200, 800, 360]
    rate = 0.05
    addInterest(amounts, rate)
    print(amounts)

test()
```

Take a moment to study this program. The `test` function starts by setting `amounts` to be a list of four values. Then the `addInterest` function is called sending `amounts` as the first parameter. After the function call, the value of `amounts` is printed out. What do you expect to see? Let's run this little program and see what happens.

```
>>> addinterest3.test()
[1050.0, 2310.0, 840.0, 378.0]
```

Isn't that interesting? In this example, the function seems to change the value of the `amounts` variable. But I just told you that Python passes parameters by value, so the variable itself (amounts) *can't* be changed by the function. So what's going on here?

The first two lines of test create the variables amounts and rates, and then control transfers to the addInterest function. The situation at this point is depicted in Figure 6.8. Notice that the value of the variable amounts is now a

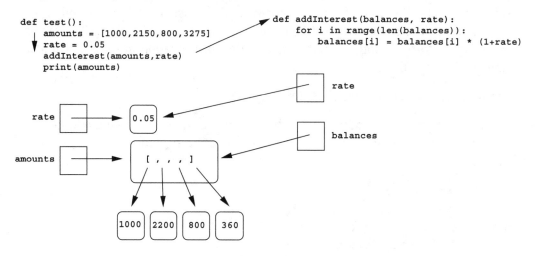

Figure 6.8: Transfer of list parameter to addInterest

list object that itself contains four int values. It is this list object that gets passed to addInterest and is therefore also the value of balances.

Next addInterest executes. The loop goes through each index in the range $0, 1, \ldots, length - 1$ and updates that item in balances. The result is shown in Figure 6.9. You'll notice in the diagram that I left the old values (1000, 2200, 800, 360) just hanging around. I did this to emphasize that the numbers in the value boxes have not changed. Instead what has happened is that new values were created, and the assignments into the list caused it to refer to the new values. The old values will actually get cleaned up when Python does garbage collection.

It should be clear now why the list version of the addInterest program produces the answer that it does. When addInterest terminates, the list stored in amounts now contains the new balances, and that is what gets printed. Notice that the variable amounts was never changed. It still refers to the same list that it did before the call to addInterest. What has happened is that the state of that list has changed, and this change is visible back in the calling program.

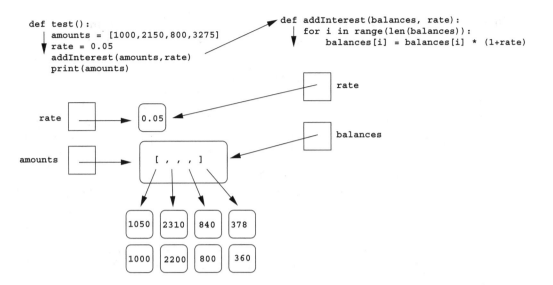

Figure 6.9: List modified in addInterest

Now you really know everything there is to know about how Python passes parameters to functions. Parameters are always passed by value. However, if the value of the variable is a mutable object (like a list or graphics object), then changes to the state of the object *will* be visible to the calling program. This latter situation is another example of the aliasing issue discussed in Chapter 4.

6.6 Functions and Program Structure

So far, we have been discussing functions as a mechanism for reducing code duplication, thus shortening and simplifying our programs. Surprisingly, functions are often used even when doing so actually makes a program longer. A second reason for using functions is to make programs more *modular*.

As the algorithms that you design get more complex, it gets more and more difficult to make sense of programs. Humans are pretty good at keeping track of eight to ten things at a time. When presented with an algorithm that is hundreds of lines long, even the best programmers will throw up their hands in bewilderment.

One way to deal with this complexity is to break an algorithm into smaller subprograms, each of which makes sense on its own. I'll have a lot more to say about this later when we discuss program design in Chapter 9. For now, we'll just take a look at an example. Let's return to the future value problem one more time. Here is the `main` program as we left it:

```python
def main():
    # Introduction
    print("This program plots the growth of a 10-year investment.")

    # Get principal and interest rate
    principal = eval(input("Enter the initial principal: "))
    apr = eval(input("Enter the annualized interest rate: "))

    # Create a graphics window with labels on left edge
    win = GraphWin("Investment Growth Chart", 320, 240)
    win.setBackground("white")
    win.setCoords(-1.75,-200, 11.5, 10400)
    Text(Point(-1, 0), ' 0.0K').draw(win)
    Text(Point(-1, 2500), ' 2.5K').draw(win)
    Text(Point(-1, 5000), ' 5.0K').draw(win)
    Text(Point(-1, 7500), ' 7.5k').draw(win)
    Text(Point(-1, 10000), '10.0K').draw(win)

    # Draw bar for initial principal
    drawBar(win, 0, principal)

    # Draw a bar for each subsequent year
    for year in range(1, 11):
        principal = principal * (1 + apr)
        drawBar(win, year, principal)

    input("Press <Enter> to quit.")
    win.close()

main()
```

Although we have already shortened this algorithm through the use of the drawBar function, it is still long enough to make reading through it awkward. The comments help to explain things, but—not to put too fine a point on it— this function is just too long. One way to make the program more readable is to move some of the details into a separate function. For example, there are eight lines in the middle that simply create the window where the chart will be drawn. We could put these steps into a value-returning function.

```
def createLabeledWindow():
    # Returns a GraphWin with title and labels drawn
    window = GraphWin("Investment Growth Chart", 320, 240)
    window.setBackground("white")
    window.setCoords(-1.75,-200, 11.5, 10400)
    Text(Point(-1, 0), ' 0.0K').draw(window)
    Text(Point(-1, 2500), ' 2.5K').draw(window)
    Text(Point(-1, 5000), ' 5.0K').draw(window)
    Text(Point(-1, 7500), ' 7.5k').draw(window)
    Text(Point(-1, 10000), '10.0K').draw(window)
    return window
```

As its name implies, this function takes care of all the nitty-gritty details of drawing the initial window. It is a self-contained entity that performs this one well-defined task.

Using our new function, the main algorithm seems much simpler.

```
def main():
    print("This program plots the growth of a 10-year investment.")

    principal = input("Enter the initial principal: ")
    apr = input("Enter the annualized interest rate: ")

    win = createLabeledWindow()
    drawBar(win, 0, principal)
    for year in range(1, 11):
        principal = principal * (1 + apr)
        drawBar(win, year, principal)

    input("Press <Enter> to quit.")
    win.close()
```

Notice that I have removed the comments; the intent of the algorithm is now clear. With suitably named functions, the code has become nearly self-documenting.

Here is the final version of our future value program:

```python
# futval_graph4.py

from graphics import *

def createLabeledWindow():
    window = GraphWin("Investment Growth Chart", 320, 240)
    window.setBackground("white")
    window.setCoords(-1.75,-200, 11.5, 10400)
    Text(Point(-1, 0), ' 0.0K').draw(window)
    Text(Point(-1, 2500), ' 2.5K').draw(window)
    Text(Point(-1, 5000), ' 5.0K').draw(window)
    Text(Point(-1, 7500), ' 7.5k').draw(window)
    Text(Point(-1, 10000), '10.0K').draw(window)
    return window

def drawBar(window, year, height):
    bar = Rectangle(Point(year, 0), Point(year+1, height))
    bar.setFill("green")
    bar.setWidth(2)
    bar.draw(window)

def main():
    print("This program plots the growth of a 10 year investment.")

    principal = eval(input("Enter the initial principal: "))
    apr = eval(input("Enter the annualized interest rate: "))

    win = createLabeledWindow()
    drawBar(win, 0, principal)
    for year in range(1, 11):
        principal = principal * (1 + apr)
        drawBar(win, year, principal)

    input("Press <Enter> to quit.")
    win.close()

main()
```

Although this version is longer than the previous version, experienced programmers would find it much easier to understand. As you get used to reading and writing functions, you too will learn to appreciate the elegance of more modular code.

6.7   Chapter Summary

- A function is a kind of subprogram. Programmers use functions to reduce code duplication and to help structure or modularize programs. Once a function is defined, it may be called multiple times from many different places in a program. Parameters allow functions to have changeable parts. The parameters appearing in the function definition are called formal parameters, and the expressions appearing in a function call are known as actual parameters.

- A call to a function initiates a four-step process:

  1. The calling program is suspended.

  2. The values of actual parameters are assigned to the formal parameters.

  3. The body of the function is executed.

  4. Control returns immediately following the function call in the calling program.

- The scope of a variable is the area of the program where it may be referenced. Formal parameters and other variables inside function definitions are local to the function. Local variables are distinct from variables of the same name that may be used elsewhere in the program.

- Functions can communicate information back to the caller through return values. Python functions may return multiple values. Value-returning functions should generally be called from inside an expression. Functions that don't explicitly return a value return the special object None.

- Python passes parameters by value. If the value being passed is a mutable object, then changes made to the object may be visible to the caller.

6.8   Exercises

Review Questions

True/False

1. Programmers rarely define their own functions.

2. A function may only be called at one place in a program.

3. Information can be passed into a function through parameters.

4. Every Python function returns some value.

5. In Python, some parameters are passed by reference.

6. In Python, a function can return only one value.

7. Python functions can never modify a parameter.

8. One reason to use functions is to reduce code duplication.

9. Variables defined in a function are local to that function.

10. It's a bad idea to define new functions if it makes a program longer.

Multiple Choice

1. The part of a program that uses a function is called the
   a) user   b) caller   c) callee   d) statement

2. A Python function definition begins with
   a) `def`   b) `define`   c) `function`   d) `defun`

3. A function can send output back to the program with a(n)
   a) `return`   b) `print`   c) assignment   d) SASE

4. Formal and actual parameters are matched up by
   a) name   b) position   c) id   d) interests

5. Which of the following is *not* a step in the function-calling process?
   a) The calling program suspends.
   b) The formal parameters are assigned the value of the actual parameters.
   c) The body of the function executes.
   d) Control returns to the point just before the function was called.

6. In Python, actual parameters are passed to functions
   a) by value   b) by reference   c) at random   d) by networking

7. Which of the following is *not* a reason to use functions?
   a) to reduce code duplication
   b) to make a program more modular
   c) to make a program more self-documenting
   d) to demonstrate intellectual superiority

8. If a function returns a value, it should generally be called from
   a) an expression   b) a different program
   c) `main`   d) a cell phone

9. A function with no `return` statement returns
   a) nothing   b) its parameters   c) its variables   d) `None`

10. A function can modify the value of an actual parameter only if it's
    a) mutable   b) a list   c) passed by reference   d) a variable

Discussion

1. In your own words, describe the two motivations for defining functions in your programs.

2. We have been thinking about computer programs as sequences of instructions where the computer methodically executes one instruction and then moves on to the next one. Do programs that contain functions fit this model? Explain your answer.

3. Parameters are an important concept in defining functions.

   (a) What is the purpose of parameters?

   (b) What is the difference between a formal parameter and an actual parameter?

   (c) In what ways are parameters similar to and different from ordinary variables?

4. Functions can be thought of as miniature (sub)programs inside other programs. Like any other program, we can think of functions as having input and output to communicate with the main program.

(a) How does a program provide "input" to one of its functions?

(b) How does a function provide "output" to the program?

5. Consider this very simple function:

```
def cube(x):
    answer = x * x * x
    return answer
```

(a) What does this function do?

(b) Show how a program could use this function to print the value of y^3, assuming y is a variable.

(c) Here is a fragment of a program that uses this function:

```
answer = 4
result = cube(3)
print(answer, result)
```

The output from this fragment is 4 27. Explain why the output is not 27 27, even though cube seems to change the value of answer to 27.

Programming Exercises

1. Write a program to print the lyrics of the song "Old MacDonald." Your program should print the lyrics for five different animals, similar to the example verse below.

> Old MacDonald had a farm, Ee-igh, Ee-igh, Oh!
> And on that farm he had a cow, Ee-igh, Ee-igh, Oh!
> With a moo, moo here and a moo, moo there.
> Here a moo, there a moo, everywhere a moo, moo.
> Old MacDonald had a farm, Ee-igh, Ee-igh, Oh!

2. Write a program to print the lyrics for ten verses of "The Ants Go Marching." A couple of sample verses are given below. You may choose your own activity for the little one in each verse, but be sure to choose something that makes the rhyme work (or almost work).

> The ants go marching one by one, hurrah! hurrah!
> The ants go marching one by one, hurrah! hurrah!

The ants go marching one by one,
The little one stops to suck his thumb,
And they all go marching down...
In the ground...
To get out....
Of the rain.
Boom! Boom! Boom!

The ants go marching two by two, hurrah! hurrah!
The ants go marching two by two, hurrah! hurrah!
The ants go marching two by two,
The little one stops to tie his shoe,
And they all go marching down...
In the ground...
To get out...
Of the rain.
Boom! Boom! Boom!

3. Write definitions for these functions:

   sphereArea(radius) Returns the surface area of a sphere having the given radius.

   sphereVolume(radius) Returns the volume of a sphere having the given radius.

   Use your functions to solve Programming Exercise 1 from Chapter 3.

4. Write definitions for the following two functions:

   sumN(n) returns the sum of the first n natural numbers.

   sumNCubes(n) returns the sum of the cubes of the first n natural numbers.

   Then use these functions in a program that prompts a user for n and prints out the sum of the first n natural numbers and the sum of the cubes of the first n natural numbers.

5. Redo Programming Exercise 2 from Chapter 3. Use two functions—one to compute the area of a pizza, and one to compute cost per square inch.

6. Write a function that computes the area of a triangle given the length of its three sides as parameters (see Programming Exercise 9 from Chapter 3).

Use your function to augment `triangle2.py` so that it also displays the area of the triangle.

7. Write a function to compute the nth Fibonacci number. Use your function to solve Programming Exercise 16 from Chapter 3.

8. Solve Programming Exercise 17 from Chapter 3 using a function `nextGuess(guess, x)` that returns the next guess.

9. Do Programming Exercise 3 from Chapter 5 using a function `grade(score)` that returns the letter grade for a score.

10. Do Programming Exercise 5 from Chapter 5 using a function `acronym(phrase)` that returns an acronym for a phrase supplied as a string.

11. Write and test a function to meet this specification.

    `squareEach(nums)` `nums` is a list of numbers. Modifies the list by squaring each entry.

12. Write and test a function to meet this specification.

    `sumList(nums)` `nums` is a list of numbers. Returns the sum of the numbers in the list.

13. Write and test a function to meet this specification.

    `toNumbers(strList)` `strList` is a list of strings, each of which represents a number. Modifies each entry in the list by converting it to a number.

14. Use the functions from the previous three problems to implement a program that computes the sum of the squares of numbers read from a file. Your program should prompt for a file name and print out the sum of the squares of the values in the file. Hint: use `readlines()`

15. Write and test a function to meet this specification.

    `drawFace(center, size, win)` `center` is a `Point`, `size` is an `int`, and `win` is a `GraphWin`. Draws a simple face of the given size in `win`.

    Your function can draw a simple smiley (or grim) face. Demonstrate the function by writing a program that draws several faces of varying size in a single window.

16. Use your `drawFace` function from the previous exercise to write a photo anonymizer. This program allows a user to load an image file (such as a PPM or GIF) and to draw cartoon faces over the top of existing faces in the photo. The user first inputs the name of the file containing the image. The image is displayed and the user is asked how many faces are to be blocked. The program then enters a loop for the user to click on two points for each face: the center and somewhere on the edge of the face (to determine the size of the face). The program should then draw a face in that location using the `drawFace` function.

    Hints: Section 4.8.4 describes the image-manipulation methods in the graphics library. If you display the image centered in a `GraphWin` that is the same width and height as the image, the window coordinates will match the pixel positions in the image. Drawing graphics on top of the original image will not actually change the image, but you can use a screen capture application to grab and save your modified image, should you wish to preserve it.

17. Write a function to meet this specification.

    `moveTo(shape, newCenter)` shape is a graphics object that supports the `getCenter` method and `newCenter` is a `Point`. Moves shape so that `newCenter` is its center.

    Use your function to write a program that draws a circle and then allows the user to click the window 10 times. Each time the user clicks, the circle is moved where the user clicked.

Chapter 7

Decision Structures

Objectives

- To understand the simple decision programming pattern and its implementation using a Python `if` statement.

- To understand the two-way decision programming pattern and its implementation using a Python `if-else` statement.

- To understand the multi-way decision programming pattern and its implementation using a Python `if-elif-else` statement.

- To understand the idea of exception handling and be able to write simple exception handling code that catches standard Python run-time errors.

- To understand the concept of Boolean expressions and the `bool` data type.

- To be able to read, write, and implement algorithms that employ decision structures, including those that employ sequences of decisions and nested decision structures.

7.1 Simple Decisions

So far, we have mostly viewed computer programs as sequences of instructions that are followed one after the other. Sequencing is a fundamental concept of programming, but alone it is not sufficient to solve every problem. Often it is necessary to alter the sequential flow of a program to suit the needs of a particular situation. This is done with special statements known as *control structures*. In this chapter, we'll take a look at *decision structures*, which are statements that allow a program to execute different sequences of instructions for different cases, effectively allowing the program to "choose" an appropriate course of action.

7.1.1 Example: Temperature Warnings

Let's start by getting the computer to make a simple decision. For an easy example, we'll return to the Celsius to Fahrenheit temperature conversion program from Chapter 2. Remember, this was written by Susan Computewell to help her figure out how to dress each morning in Europe. Here is the program as we left it:

```
# convert.py
#      A program to convert Celsius temps to Fahrenheit
# by: Susan Computewell

def main():
    celsius = eval(input("What is the Celsius temperature? "))
    fahrenheit = 9/5 * celsius + 32
    print("The temperature is", fahrenheit, "degrees fahrenheit.")

main()
```

This is a fine program as far as it goes, but we want to enhance it. Susan Computewell is not a morning person, and even though she has a program to convert the temperatures, sometimes she does not pay very close attention to the results. Our enhancement to the program will ensure that when the temperatures are extreme, the program prints out a suitable warning so that Susan takes notice.

The first step is to fully specify the enhancement. An extreme temperature is either quite hot or quite cold. Let's say that any temperature over 90 degrees Fahrenheit deserves a heat warning, and a temperature under 30 degrees warrants a cold warning. With this specification in mind, we can design an enhanced algorithm.

```
Input the temperature in degrees Celsius (call it celsius)
Calculate fahrenheit as 9/5 celsius + 32
Output fahrenheit
```

```
if fahrenheit > 90
    print a heat warning
if fahrenheit < 30
    print a cold warning
```

This new design has two simple *decisions* at the end. The indentation indicates that a step should be performed only if the condition listed in the previous line is met. The idea here is that the decision introduces an alternative flow of control through the program. The exact set of steps taken by the algorithm will depend on the value of `fahrenheit`.

Figure 7.1 is a flowchart showing the possible paths that can be taken through the algorithm. The diamond boxes show conditional decisions. If the condition is false, control passes to the next statement in the sequence (the one below). If the condition holds, however, control transfers to the instructions in the box to the right. Once these instructions are done, control then passes to the next statement.

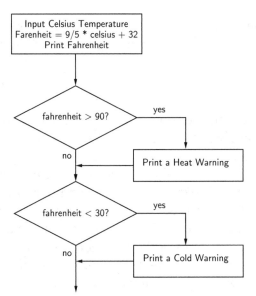

Figure 7.1: Flowchart of temperature conversion program with warnings

Here is how the new design translates into Python code:

```
# convert2.py
#       A program to convert Celsius temps to Fahrenheit.
#       This version issues heat and cold warnings.

def main():
    celsius = eval(input("What is the Celsius temperature? "))
    fahrenheit = 9/5 * celsius + 32
    print("The temperature is", fahrenheit, "degrees Fahrenheit.")

    # Print warnings for extreme temps
    if fahrenheit > 90:
        print("It's really hot out there. Be careful!")
    if fahrenheit < 30:
        print("Brrrrr. Be sure to dress warmly!")

main()
```

You can see that the Python `if` statement is used to implement the decision.
The form of the `if` is very similar to the pseudocode in the algorithm.

```
if <condition>:
    <body>
```

The `body` is just a sequence of one or more statements indented under the `if`
heading. In `convert2.py` there are two `if` statements, both of which have a
single statement in the body.

The semantics of the `if` should be clear from the example above. First, the
condition in the heading is evaluated. If the condition is true, the sequence of
statements in the body is executed, and then control passes to the next statement
in the program. If the condition is false, the statements in the body are skipped.
Figure 7.2 shows the semantics of the `if` as a flowchart. Notice that the body
of the `if` either executes or not depending on the condition. In either case,
control then passes to the next statement after the `if`. This is a *one-way* or
simple decision.

7.1.2   Forming Simple Conditions

One point that has not yet been discussed is exactly what a condition looks like.
For the time being, our programs will use simple conditions that compare the
values of two expressions.

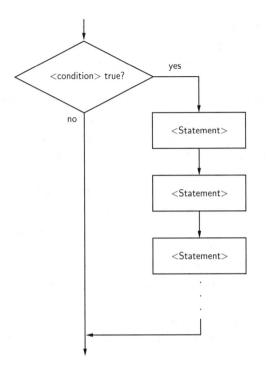

Figure 7.2: Control flow of simple if-statement

```
<expr> <relop> <expr>
```

`<relop>` is short for *relational operator*. That's just a fancy name for the mathematical concepts like "less than" or "equal to." There are six relational operators in Python, shown in the following table.

Python	Mathematics	Meaning
$<$	$<$	Less than
$<=$	$\leq$	Less than or equal to
$==$	$=$	Equal to
$>=$	$\geq$	Greater than or equal to
$>$	$>$	Greater than
$!=$	$\neq$	Not equal to

Notice especially the use of $==$ for equality. Since Python uses the $=$ sign to indicate an assignment statement, a different symbol is required for the concept of equality. A common mistake in Python programs is using $=$ in conditions, where a $==$ is required.

Conditions may compare either numbers or strings. When comparing strings, the ordering is *lexicographic*. Basically, this means that strings are put in alphabetic order according to the underlying Unicode values. So all uppercase Latin letters come before lowercase equivalents (e.g., "Bbbb" comes before "aaaa," since "B" precedes "a").

I should mention that conditions are actually a type of expression, called a *Boolean* expression, after George Boole, a 19th century English mathematician. When a Boolean expression is evaluated, it produces a value of either *true* (the condition holds) or *false* (it does not hold). Some languages such as C++ and older versions of Python just use the ints 1 and 0 to represent these values. Other languages like Java and modern Python have a dedicated data type for Boolean expressions.

In Python, Boolean expressions are of type `bool` and the Boolean values true and false are represented by the literals `True` and `False`. Here are a few interactive examples:

```
>>> 3 < 4
True
>>> 3 * 4 < 3 + 4
False
>>> "hello" == "hello"
True
>>> "hello" < "hello"
False
>>> "Hello" < "hello"
True
```

7.1.3   Example: Conditional Program Execution

Back in Chapter 1, I mentioned that there are several different ways of running Python programs. Some Python module files are designed to be run directly. These are usually referred to as "programs" or "scripts." Other Python modules are designed primarily to be imported and used by other programs; these are often called "libraries." Sometimes we want to create a sort of hybrid module that can be used both as a stand-alone program and as a library that can be imported by other programs.

So far, most of our programs have had a line at the bottom to invoke the `main` function.

```
main()
```

As you know, this is what actually starts a program running. These programs are suitable for running directly. In a windowing environment, you might run a file by (double-)clicking its icon. Or you might type a command like `python <myfile>.py`.

Since Python evaluates the lines of a module during the import process, our current programs also run when they are imported into either an interactive Python session or into another Python program. Generally, it is nicer not to have modules run as they are imported. When testing a program interactively, the usual approach is to first import the module and then call its `main` (or some other function) each time we want to run it.

In a program designed to be *either* imported (without running) *or* run directly, the call to `main` at the bottom must be made conditional. A simple decision should do the trick.

```
if <condition>:
    main()
```

We just need to figure out a suitable condition.

Whenever a module is imported, Python sets a special variable in the module called `__name__` to be the name of the imported module. Here is an example interaction showing what happens with the `math` library:

```
>>> import math
>>> math.__name__
'math'
```

You can see that, when imported, the `__name__` variable inside the `math` module is assigned the string `'math'`.

However, when Python code is being run directly (not imported), Python sets the value of `__name__` to be `'__main__'`. To see this in action, you just need to start a Python shell and look at the value.

```
>>> __name__
'__main__'
```

So, if a module is imported, the code in that module will see a variable called __name__ whose value is the name of the module. When a file is run directly, the code will see that __name__ has the value '__main__'. A module can determine how it is being used by inspecting this variable.

Putting the pieces together, we can change the final lines of our programs to look like this:

```
if __name__ == '__main__':
    main()
```

This guarantees that main will automatically run when the program is invoked directly, but it will not run if the module is imported. You will see a line of code similar to this at the bottom of virtually every Python program.

7.2 Two-Way Decisions

Now that we have a way to selectively execute certain statements in a program using decisions, it's time to go back and spruce up the quadratic equation solver from Chapter 3. Here is the program as we left it:

```
# quadratic.py
#    A program that computes the real roots of a quadratic equation.
#    Note: this program crashes if the equation has no real roots.

import math

def main():
    print("This program finds the real solutions to a quadratic\n")

    a, b, c = eval(input("Please enter the coefficients (a, b, c): "))

    discRoot = math.sqrt(b * b - 4 * a * c)
    root1 = (-b + discRoot) / (2 * a)
    root2 = (-b - discRoot) / (2 * a)

    print("\nThe solutions are:", root1, root2 )

main()
```

As noted in the comments, this program crashes when it is given coefficients of a quadratic equation that has no real roots. The problem with this code is that when $b^2 - 4ac$ is less than 0, the program attempts to take the square root of a negative number. Since negative numbers do not have real roots, the math library reports an error. Here's an example:

```
>>> quadratic.main()
This program finds the real solutions to a quadratic

Please enter the coefficients (a, b, c): 1,2,3
Traceback (most recent call last):
  File "quadratic.py", line 18, in <module>
    main()
  File "quadratic.py", line 12, in main
    discRoot = math.sqrt(b * b - 4 * a * c)
ValueError: math domain error
>>>
```

We can use a decision to check for this situation and make sure that the program can't crash. Here's a first attempt:

```
# quadratic2.py
import math

def main():
    print("This program finds the real solutions to a quadratic\n")

    a, b, c = eval(input("Please enter the coefficients (a, b, c): "))

    discrim = b * b - 4 * a * c
    if discrim >= 0:
        discRoot = math.sqrt(discrim)
        root1 = (-b + discRoot) / (2 * a)
        root2 = (-b - discRoot) / (2 * a)
        print("\nThe solutions are:", root1, root2 )

main()
```

This version first computes the value of the discriminant ($b^2 - 4ac$) and then checks to make sure it is not negative. Only then does the program proceed to take the square root and calculate the solutions. This program will never attempt to call `math.sqrt` when `discrim` is negative.

Unfortunately, this updated version is not really a complete solution. Study the program for a moment. What happens when the equation has no real roots? According to the semantics for a simple `if`, when `b*b - 4*a*c` is less than zero, the program will simply skip the calculations and go to the next statement. Since there is no next statement, the program just quits. Here's what happens in an interactive session:

```
>>> quadratic2.main()
This program finds the real solutions to a quadratic

Please enter the coefficients (a, b, c): 1,2,3
>>>
```

This is almost worse than the previous version, because it does not give users any indication of what went wrong; it just leaves them hanging. A better program would print a message telling users that their particular equation has no real solutions. We could accomplish this by adding another simple decision at the end of the program.

```
if discrim < 0:
    print("The equation has no real roots!")
```

This will certainly solve our problem, but this solution just doesn't feel right. We have programmed a sequence of two decisions, but the two outcomes are mutually exclusive. If `discrim >= 0` is true then `discrim < 0` must be false and vice versa. We have two conditions in the program, but there is really only one decision to make. Based on the value of `discrim` the program should *either* print that there are no real roots *or* it should calculate and display the roots. This is an example of a two-way decision. Figure 7.3 illustrates the situation.

In Python, a two-way decision can be implemented by attaching an `else` clause onto an `if` clause. The result is called an `if-else` statement.

```
if <condition>:
    <statements>
else:
    <statements>
```

When the Python interpreter encounters this structure, it will first evaluate the condition. If the condition is true, the statements under the `if` are executed.

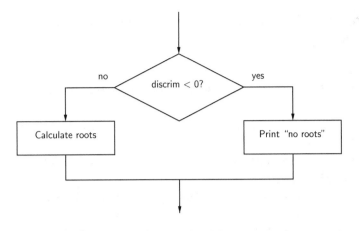

Figure 7.3: Quadratic solver as a two-way decision

If the condition is false, the statements under the else are executed. In either case, control then passes to the statement following the if-else.

Using a two-way decision in the quadratic solver yields a more elegant solution.

```
# quadratic3.py
import math

def main():
    print("This program finds the real solutions to a quadratic\n")
    a, b, c = eval(input("Please enter the coefficients (a, b, c): "))

    discrim = b * b - 4 * a * c
    if discrim < 0:
        print("\nThe equation has no real roots!")
    else:
        discRoot = math.sqrt(b * b - 4 * a * c)
        root1 = (-b + discRoot) / (2 * a)
        root2 = (-b - discRoot) / (2 * a)
        print("\nThe solutions are:", root1, root2)
main()
```

This program fills the bill nicely. Here is a sample session that runs the new program twice:

```
>>> quadratic3.main()
This program finds the real solutions to a quadratic

Please enter the coefficients (a, b, c): 1,2,3

The equation has no real roots!
>>> quadratic3.main()
This program finds the real solutions to a quadratic

Please enter the coefficients (a, b, c): 2,4,1

The solutions are: -0.292893218813 -1.70710678119
```

7.3 Multi-Way Decisions

The newest version of the quadratic solver is certainly a big improvement, but it still has some quirks. Here is another example run:

```
>>> quadratic3.main()
This program finds the real solutions to a quadratic

Please enter the coefficients (a, b, c): 1, 2, 1

The solutions are: -1.0 -1.0
```

This is technically correct; the given coefficients produce an equation that has a double root at -1. However, the output might be confusing to some users. It looks like the program has mistakenly printed the same number twice. Perhaps the program should be a bit more informative to avoid confusion.

The double-root situation occurs when discrim is exactly 0. In this case, discRoot is also 0, and both roots have the value $\frac{-b}{2a}$. If we want to catch this special case, our program actually needs a three-way decision. Here's a quick sketch of the design:

```
...
Check the value of discrim
```

```
when < 0: handle the case of no roots
when = 0: handle the case of a double root
when > 0: handle the case of two distinct roots.
```

One way to code this algorithm is to use two `if-else` statements. The body of an `if` or `else` clause can contain any legal Python statements, including other `if` or `if-else` statements. Putting one compound statement inside another is called *nesting*. Here's a fragment of code that uses nesting to achieve a three-way decision: :

```
if discrim < 0:
    print("Equation has no real roots")
else:
    if discrim == 0:
        root = -b / (2 * a)
        print("There is a double root at", root)
    else:
        # Do stuff for two roots
```

If you trace through this code carefully, you will see that there are exactly three possible paths. The sequencing is determined by the value of `discrim`. A flowchart of this solution is shown in Figure 7.4. You can see that the top-level structure is just an `if-else`. (Treat the dashed box as one big statement.) The dashed box contains the second `if-else` nested comfortably inside the `else` part of the top-level decision.

Once again, we have a working solution, but the implementation doesn't feel quite right. We have finessed a three-way decision by using two two-way decisions. The resulting code does not reflect the true three-fold decision of the original problem. Imagine if we needed to make a five-way decision using this technique. The `if-else` structures would nest four levels deep, and the Python code would march off the right-hand edge of the page.

There is another way to write multi-way decisions in Python that preserves the semantics of the nested structures but gives it a more appealing look. The idea is to combine an `else` followed immediately by an `if` into a single clause called an `elif` (pronounced "ell-if").

```
if <condition1>:
    <case1 statements>
elif <condition2>:
    <case2 statements>
```

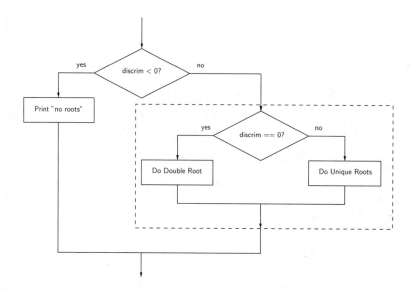

Figure 7.4: Three-way decision for quadratic solver using nested `if-else`

```
elif <condition3>:
    <case3 statements>
...
else:
    <default statements>
```

This form is used to set off any number of mutually exclusive code blocks. Python will evaluate each condition in turn looking for the first one that is true. If a true condition is found, the statements indented under that condition are executed, and control passes to the next statement after the entire `if-elif-else`. If none of the conditions are true, the statements under the `else` are performed. The `else` clause is optional; if omitted, it is possible that no indented statement block will be executed.

Using an `if-elif-else` to show the three-way decision in our quadratic solver yields a nicely finished program.

```
# quadratic4.py
import math

def main():
```

```
print("This program finds the real solutions to a quadratic\n")

a, b, c = eval(input("Please enter the coefficients (a, b, c): "))

discrim = b * b - 4 * a * c
if discrim < 0:
    print("\nThe equation has no real roots!")
elif discrim == 0:
    root = -b / (2 * a)
    print("\nThere is a double root at", root)
else:
    discRoot = math.sqrt(b * b - 4 * a * c)
    root1 = (-b + discRoot) / (2 * a)
    root2 = (-b - discRoot) / (2 * a)
    print("\nThe solutions are:", root1, root2 )
main()
```

7.4 Exception Handling

Our quadratic program uses decision structures to avoid taking the square root of a negative number and generating an error at run-time. This is a common pattern in many programs: using decisions to protect against rare but possible errors.

In the case of the quadratic solver, we checked the data *before* the call to the sqrt function. Sometimes functions themselves check for possible errors and return a special value to indicate that the operation was unsuccessful. For example, a different square root operation might return a negative number (say, -1) to indicate an error. Since the square root function should always return the non-negative root, this value could be used to signal that an error has occurred. The program would check the result of the operation with a decision.

```
discRt = otherSqrt(b*b - 4*a*c)
if discRt < 0:
    print "No real roots."
else:
    . . .
```

Sometimes programs become so peppered with decisions to check for special cases that the main algorithm for handling the run-of-the-mill cases seems

completely lost. Programming language designers have come up with mechanisms for *exception handling* that help to solve this design problem. The idea of
an exception-handling mechanism is that the programmer can write code that
catches and deals with errors that arise when the program is running. Rather
than explicitly checking that each step in the algorithm was successful, a program
with exception handling can in essence say, "Do these steps, and if any problem
crops up, handle it this way."

We're not going to discuss all the details of the Python exception-handling
mechanism here, but I do want to give you a concrete example so you can see
how exception handling works and understand programs that use it. In Python,
exception handling is done with a special control structure that is similar to a
decision. Let's start with a specific example and then take a look at the general
approach.

Here is a version of the quadratic program that uses Python's exception
mechanism to catch potential errors in the math.sqrt function:

```python
# quadratic5.py
import math

def main():
    print ("This program finds the real solutions to a quadratic\n")

    try:
        a, b, c = eval(input("Please enter the coefficients (a, b, c): "))
        discRoot = math.sqrt(b * b - 4 * a * c)
        root1 = (-b + discRoot) / (2 * a)
        root2 = (-b - discRoot) / (2 * a)
        print("\nThe solutions are:", root1, root2)
    except ValueError:
        print("\nNo real roots")

main()
```

Notice that this is basically the very first version of the quadratic program
with the addition of a try . . . except around the heart of the program. A try
statement has the general form:

```python
try:
    <body>
except <ErrorType>:
    <handler>
```

When Python encounters a `try` statement, it attempts to execute the statements inside the body. If these statements execute without error, control then passes to the next statement after the `try...except`. If an error occurs somewhere in the body, Python looks for an `except` clause with a matching error type. If a suitable `except` is found, the handler code is executed.

The original program *without the exception handling* produced the following error:

```
Traceback (most recent call last):
  File "quadratic.py", line 18, in <module>
    main()
  File "quadratic.py", line 12, in main
    discRoot = math.sqrt(b * b - 4 * a * c)
ValueError: math domain error
```

The last line of this error message indicates the type of error that was generated, namely a `ValueError`. The updated version of the program provides an `except` clause to catch the `ValueError`.

Here is the error-handling version in action:

```
This program finds the real solutions to a quadratic

Please enter the coefficients (a, b, c): 1,2,3

No real roots
```

Instead of crashing, the exception handler catches the error and prints a message indicating that the equation does not have real roots.

The nice thing about the `try...except` statement is that it can be used to catch any kind of error, even ones that might be difficult to test for, and hopefully, provide a graceful exit. For example, in the quadratic solver, there are lots of other things that could go wrong besides having a bad set of coefficients. If the user fails to type the correct number of inputs, the program generates a different kind of `ValueError`. If the user accidentally types an identifier instead of a number, the program generates a `NameError`. If the input is not a valid Python expression, it generates a `SyntaxError`. If the user types in a valid Python expression that produces non-numeric results, the program generates a `TypeError`. A single `try` statement can have multiple `except` clauses to catch various possible classes of errors.

Here's one last version of the program designed to robustly handle any possible errors in the input:

```python
# quadratic6.py
import math

def main():
    print("This program finds the real solutions to a quadratic\n")

    try:
        a, b, c = eval(input("Please enter the coefficients (a, b, c): "))
        discRoot = math.sqrt(b * b - 4 * a * c)
        root1 = (-b + discRoot) / (2 * a)
        root2 = (-b - discRoot) / (2 * a)
        print("\nThe solutions are:", root1, root2 )
    except ValueError as excObj:
        if str(excObj) == "math domain error":
            print("No Real Roots")
        else:
            print("You didn't give me the right number of coefficients.")
    except NameError:
        print("\nYou didn't enter three numbers.")
    except TypeError:
        print("\nYour inputs were not all numbers.")
    except SyntaxError:
        print("\nYour input was not in the correct form. Missing comma?")
    except:
        print("\nSomething went wrong, sorry!")

main()
```

The multiple excepts are similar to elifs. If an error occurs, Python will try each except in turn looking for one that matches the type of error. The bare except at the bottom acts like an else and will be used if none of the others match. If there is no default at the bottom and none of the except types match the error, then the program crashes and Python reports the error.

Notice how I handled the two different kinds of ValueErrors. Exceptions are actually a kind of object. If you follow the error type with an as <variable> in an except clause, Python will assign that variable the actual exception object. In this case, I turned the exception into a string and looked at the message to see what caused the ValueError. Notice that this text is exactly what Python prints out if the error is not caught (e.g., "ValueError: math domain error"). If the exception doesn't match any of the expected types, this program just prints a general apology. As a challenge, you might see if you can find an erroneous input that produces the apology.

You can see how the try...except statement allows us to write bullet-proof programs. You can use this same technique by observing the error messages that Python prints and designing except clauses to catch and handle them. Whether you need to go to this much trouble depends on the type of program you are writing. In your beginning programs, you might not worry too much about bad input; however, professional-quality software should do whatever is feasible to shield users from unexpected results.

7.5 Study in Design: Max of Three

Now that we have decisions that can alter the control flow of a program, our algorithms are liberated from the monotony of step-by-step, strictly sequential processing. This is both a blessing and a curse. The positive side is that we can now develop more sophisticated algorithms, as we did for our quadratic solver. The negative side is that designing these more sophisticated algorithms is much harder. In this section, we'll step through the design of a more difficult decision problem to illustrate some of the challenge and excitement of the design process.

Suppose we need an algorithm to find the largest of three numbers. This algorithm could be part of a larger problem such as determining grades or computing taxes, but we are not interested in the final details, just the crux of the problem. That is, how can a computer determine which of three user inputs is the largest? Here is a program outline. We need to fill in the missing part.

```
def main():
    x1, x2, x3 = eval(input("Please enter three values: "))

    # missing code sets max to the value of the largest

    print("The largest value is", max)
```

Before reading the following analysis, you might want to try your hand at solving this problem.

7.5.1   Strategy 1: Compare Each to All

Obviously, this program presents us with a decision problem. We need a sequence of statements that sets the value of max to the largest of the three inputs x1, x2, and x3. At first glance, this looks like a three-way decision; we need to execute *one* of the following assignments:

```
max = x1
max = x2
max = x3
```

It would seem we just need to preface each one with the appropriate condition(s), so that it is executed only in the proper situation.

Let's consider the first possibility, that x1 is the largest. To determine that x1 is actually the largest, we just need to check that it is at least as large as the other two. Here is a first attempt:

```
if x1 >= x2 >= x3:
    max = x1
```

Your first concern here should be whether this statement is syntactically correct. The condition x1 >= x2 >= x3 does not match the template for conditions shown above. Most computer languages would not accept this as a valid expression. It turns out that Python does allow this *compound condition*, and it behaves exactly like the mathematical relations $x1 \geq x2 \geq x3$. That is, the condition is true when x1 is at least as large as x2 and x2 is at least as large as x3. So, fortunately, Python has no problem with this condition.

Whenever you write a decision, you should ask yourself two crucial questions. First, when the condition is true, are you absolutely certain that executing the body of the decision is the right action to take? In this case, the condition clearly states that x1 is at least as large as x2 and x3, so assigning its value to max should be correct. Always pay particular attention to borderline values. Notice that our condition includes equal as well as greater. We should convince ourselves that this is correct. Suppose that x1, x2, and x3 are all the same; this condition will return true. That's OK because it doesn't matter which we choose, the first is at least as big as the others, and hence, the max.

The second question to ask is the converse of the first. Are we certain that this condition is true in all cases where x1 is the max? Unfortunately, our condition does not meet this test. Suppose the values are 5, 2, and 4. Clearly, x1 is the largest, but our condition returns false since the relationship $5 \geq 2 \geq 4$ does not hold. We need to fix this.

We want to ensure that x1 is the largest, but we don't care about the relative ordering of x2 and x3. What we really need is two separate tests to determine that x1 >= x2 *and* that x2 >= x3. Python allows us to test multiple conditions like this by combining them with the keyword and. We'll discuss the exact semantics of and in Chapter 8. Intuitively, the following condition seems to be what we are looking for:

```
if x1 >= x2 and x1 >= x3:    # x1 is greater than each of the others
    max = x1
```

To complete the program, we just need to implement analogous tests for the other possibilities.

```
if x1 >= x2 and x1 >= x3:
    max = x1
elif x2 >= x1 and x2 >= x3:
    max = x2
else:
    max = x3
```

Summing up this approach, our algorithm is basically checking each possible value against all the others to determine if it is the largest.

With just three values the result is quite simple, but how would this solution look if we were trying to find the max of five values? Then we would need three Boolean expressions, each consisting of four conditions anded together. The complex expressions result from the fact that each decision is designed to stand on its own; information from one test is ignored in the subsequent tests. To see what I mean, look back at our simple max of three code. Suppose the first decision discovers that x1 is greater than x2, but not greater than x3. At this point, we know that x3 must be the max. Unfortunately, our code ignores this; Python will go ahead and evaluate the next expression, discover it to be false, and finally execute the else.

7.5.2 Strategy 2: Decision Tree

One way to avoid the redundant tests of the previous algorithm is to use a *decision tree* approach. Suppose we start with a simple test x1 >= x2. This knocks either x1 or x2 out of contention to be the max. If the condition is true, we just need to see which is larger, x1 or x3. Should the initial condition be false, the result boils down to a choice between x2 and x3. As you can see, the first decision "branches" into two possibilities, each of which is another decision, hence the name *decision tree*. Figure 7.5 shows the situation in a flowchart. This flowchart translates easily into nested `if-else` statements.

```
if x1 >= x2:
    if x1 >= x3:
        max = x1
    else:
        max = x3
else:
    if x2 >= x3:
        max = x2
    else:
        max = x3
```

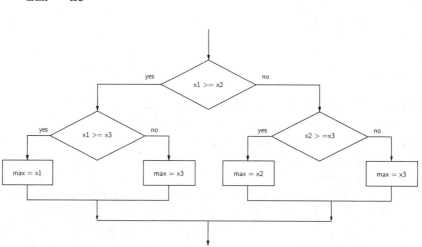

Figure 7.5: Flowchart of the decision tree approach to max of three

The strength of this approach is its efficiency. No matter what the ordering of the three values, this algorithm will make exactly two comparisons and assign the correct value to `max`. However, the structure of this approach is more complicated than the first, and it suffers a similar complexity explosion should we try this design with more than three values. As a challenge, you might see if you can design a decision tree to find the max of four values. (You will need `if-elses` nested three levels deep leading to eight assignment statements.)

7.5.3 | Strategy 3: Sequential Processing

So far, we have designed two very different algorithms, but neither one seems particularly elegant. Perhaps there is yet a third way. When designing an algorithm, a good starting place is to ask yourself how you would solve the problem if you were asked to do the job. For finding the max of three numbers, you probably don't have a very good intuition about the steps you go through. You'd just look at the numbers and *know* which is the largest. But what if you were handed a book containing hundreds of numbers in no particular order? How would you find the largest in this collection?

When confronted with the larger problem, most people develop a simple strategy. Scan through the numbers until you find a big one, and put your finger on it. Continue scanning; if you find a number bigger than the one your finger is on, move your finger to the new one. When you get to the end of the list, your finger will remain on the largest value. In a nutshell, this strategy has us look through the list sequentially, keeping track of the largest number seen so far.

A computer doesn't have fingers, but we can use a variable to keep track of the max so far. In fact, the easiest approach is just to use max to do this job. That way, when we get to the end, max automatically contains the value of the largest. A flowchart depicting this strategy for the max of three problem is shown in Figure 7.6. Here is the translation into Python code:

```
max = x1
if x2 > max:
    max = x2
if x3 > max:
    max = x3
```

Clearly, the sequential approach is the best of our three algorithms. The code itself is quite simple, containing only two simple decisions, and the sequencing is easier to understand than the nesting used in the previous algorithm. Furthermore, the idea scales well to larger problems; adding a fourth item adds only one more statement.

```
max = x1
if x2 > max:
    max = x2
if x3 > max:
    max = x3
if x4 > max:
```

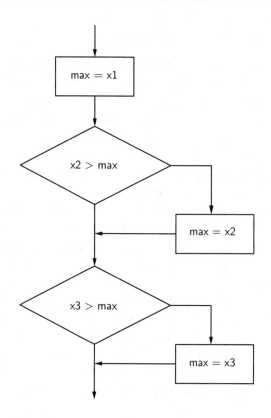

Figure 7.6: Flowchart of a sequential approach to the max of three problem

```
    max = x4
```

It should not be surprising that the last solution scales to larger problems; we invented the algorithm by explicitly considering how to solve a more complex problem. In fact, you can see that the code is very repetitive. We can easily write a program that allows the user to find the largest of n numbers by folding our algorithm into a loop. Rather than having separate variables for x1, x2, x3, etc., we can just get the values one at a time and keep reusing a single variable x. Each time, we compare the newest x against the current value of max to see if it is larger.

```
# program: maxn.py
#   Finds the maximum of a series of numbers
```

```
def main():
    n = eval(input("How many numbers are there? "))

    # Set max to be the first value
    max = eval(input("Enter a number >> "))

    # Now compare the n-1 successive values
    for i in range(n-1):
        x = eval(input("Enter a number >> "))
        if x > max:
            max = x

    print("The largest value is", max)

main()
```

This code uses a decision nested inside of a loop to get the job done. On each iteration of the loop, max contains the largest value seen so far.

7.5.4 Strategy 4: Use Python

Before leaving this problem, I really should mention that none of the algorithm development we have so painstakingly pursued was necessary. Python actually has a built-in function called max that returns the largest of its parameters. Here is the simplest version of our program:

```
def main():
    x1, x2, x3 = eval(input("Please enter three values: "))
    print("The largest value is", max(x1, x2, x3))
```

Of course, this version didn't require any algorithm development at all, which rather defeats the point of the exercise! Sometimes Python is just too simple for our own good.

7.5.5 Some Lessons

The max of three problem is not particularly earth shattering, but the attempt to solve this problem has illustrated some important ideas in algorithm and program design.

- There is more than one way to do it. For any non-trivial computing problem, there are many ways to approach the problem. While this may seem obvious, many beginning programmers do not really take this point to heart. What does this mean for you? Don't rush to code up the first idea that pops into your head. Think about your design, ask yourself if there is a better way to approach the problem. Once you have written the code, ask yourself again if there might be a better way. Your first task is to find a correct algorithm. After that, strive for clarity, simplicity, efficiency, scalability, and elegance. Good algorithms and programs are like poems of logic. They are a pleasure to read and maintain.

- Be the computer. Especially for beginning programmers, one of the best ways to formulate an algorithm is to simply ask yourself how you would solve the problem. There are other techniques for designing good algorithms (see Chapter 13); however, the straightforward approach is often simple, clear, and efficient enough.

- Generality is good. We arrived at the best solution to the max of three problem by considering the more general max of n numbers problem. It is not unusual that consideration of a more general problem can lead to a better solution for some special case. Don't be afraid to step back and think about the overarching problem. Similarly, when designing programs, you should always have an eye toward making your program more generally useful. If the max of n program is just as easy to write as max of three, you may as well write the more general program because it is more likely to be useful in other situations. That way you get the maximum utility from your programming effort.

- Don't reinvent the wheel. Our fourth solution was to use Python's max function. You may think that was cheating, but this example illustrates an important point. A lot of very smart programmers have designed countless good algorithms and programs. If the problem you are trying to solve seems to be one that lots of others must have encountered, you might begin by finding out if the problem has already been solved for you. As you are learning to program, designing from scratch is great experience. Truly expert programmers, however, know when to borrow.

7.6 Chapter Summary

This chapter has laid out the basic control structures for making decisions. Here are the key points.

- Decision structures are control structures that allow a program to execute different sequences of instructions for different cases.

- Decisions are implemented in Python with `if` statements. Simple decisions are implemented with a plain `if`. Two-way decisions generally use an `if-else`. Multi-way decisions are implemented with `if-elif-else`.

- Decisions are based on the evaluation of conditions, which are simple Boolean expressions. A Boolean expression is either true or false. Python has a dedicated `bool` data type with literals `True` and `False`. Conditions are formed using the relational operators: <, <=, !=, ==, >, and >=.

- Some programming languages provide exception handling mechanisms which help to make programs more "bulletproof." Python provides a `try-except` statement for exception handling.

- Algorithms that incorporate decisions can become quite complicated as decision structures are nested. Usually a number of solutions are possible, and careful thought should be given to produce a correct, efficient, and understandable program.

7.7 Exercises

Review Questions

True/False

1. A simple decision can be implemented with an `if` statement.

2. In Python conditions, $\neq$ is written as /=.

3. Strings are compared by lexicographic ordering.

4. A two-way decision is implemented using an `if-elif` statement.

5. The `math.sqrt` function cannot compute the square root of a negative number.

6. A single `try` statement can catch multiple kinds of errors.

7. Multi-way decisions must be handled by nesting multiple `if-else` statements.

8. There is usually only one correct solution to a problem involving decision structures.

9. The condition x `<=` y `<=` z is allowed in Python.

10. Input validation means prompting a user when input is required.

Multiple Choice

1. A statement that controls the execution of other statements is called a
   a) boss structure   b) super structure
   c) control structure   d) branch

2. The best structure for implementing a multi-way decision in Python is
   a) `if`   b) `if-else`   c) `if-elif-else`   d) `try`

3. An expression that evaluates to either true or false is called
   a) operational   b) Boolean   c) simple   d) compound

4. When a program is being run directly (not imported), the value of `__name__` is
   a) `script`   b) `main`   c) `__main__`   d) `True`

5. The literals for type `bool` are
   a) T, F   b) `True, False`   c) `true, false`   d) 1, 0

6. Placing a decision inside of another decision is an example of
   a) cloning   b) spooning   c) nesting   d) procrastination

7. In Python, the body of a decision is indicated by
   a) indentation   b) parentheses   c) curly braces   d) a colon

8. A structure in which one decision leads to another set of decisions, which leads to another set of decisions, etc., is called a decision
   a) network   b) web   c) tree   d) trap

9. Taking the square root of a negative value with `math.sqrt` produces a(n)
   a) ValueError   b) imaginary number
   c) program crash   d) stomachache

10. A multiple choice question is most similar to
    a) simple decision   b) two-way decision
    c) multi-way decisions   d) an exception handler

Discussion

1. Explain the following patterns in your own words:

   (a) simple decision

   (b) two-way decision

   (c) multi-way decision

2. The following is a (silly) decision structure:

```
a, b, c = eval(input('Enter three numbers: '))
if a > b:
    if b > c:
        print("Spam Please!")
    else:
        print("It's a late parrot!")
elif b > c:
    print("Cheese Shoppe")
    if a >= c:
        print("Cheddar")
    elif a < b:
        print("Gouda")
    elif c == b:
        print("Swiss")
else:
    print("Trees")
    if a == b:
        print("Chestnut")
    else:
        print("Larch")
print("Done")
```

   Show the output that would result from each of the following possible inputs:

   (a) 3, 4, 5

   (b) 3, 3, 3

   (c) 5, 4, 3

   (d) 3, 5, 2

   (e) 5, 4, 7

   (f) 3, 3, 2

3. How is exception handling using `try/except` similar to and different from handling exceptional cases using ordinary decision structures (variations on `if`)?

Programming Exercises

1. Many companies pay time-and-a-half for any hours worked above 40 in a given week. Write a program to input the number of hours worked and the hourly rate and calculate the total wages for the week.

2. A certain CS professor gives five-point quizzes that are graded on the scale 5-A, 4-B, 3-C, 2-D, 1-F, 0-F. Write a program that accepts a quiz score as an input and uses a decision structure to calculate the corresponding grade.

3. A certain CS professor gives 100-point exams that are graded on the scale 90–100:A, 80–89:B, 70–79:C, 60–69:D, <60:F. Write a program that accepts an exam score as input and uses a decision structure to calculate the corresponding grade.

4. A certain college classifies students according to credits earned. A student with less than 7 credits is a Freshman. At least 7 credits are required to be a Sophomore, 16 to be a Junior and 26 to be classified as a Senior. Write a program that calculates class standing from the number of credits earned.

5. The body mass index (BMI) is calculated as a person's weight (in pounds) times 720, divided by the square of the person's height (in inches). A BMI in the range 19–25, inclusive, is considered healthy. Write a program that calculates a person's BMI and prints a message telling whether they are above, within, or below the healthy range.

6. The speeding ticket fine policy in Podunksville is $50 plus $5 for each mph over the limit plus a penalty of $200 for any speed over 90 mph. Write a program that accepts a speed limit and a clocked speed and either prints

a message indicating the speed was legal or prints the amount of the fine, if the speed is illegal.

7. A babysitter charges $2.50 an hour until 9:00 PM when the rate drops to $1.75 an hour (the children are in bed). Write a program that accepts a starting time and ending time in hours and minutes and calculates the total babysitting bill. You may assume that the starting and ending times are in a single 24-hour period. Partial hours should be appropriately prorated.

8. A person is eligible to be a US senator if they are at least 30 years old and have been a US citizen for at least 9 years. To be a US representative these numbers are 25 and 7, respectively. Write a program that accepts a person's age and years of citizenship as input and outputs their eligibility for the Senate and House.

9. A formula for computing Easter in the years 1982–2048, inclusive, is as follows: let $a = year\%19$, $b = year\%4$, $c = year\%7$, $d = (19a + 24)\%30$, $e = (2b + 4c + 6d + 5)\%7$. The date of Easter is March $22 + d + e$ (which could be in April). Write a program that inputs a year, verifies that it is in the proper range, and then prints out the date of Easter that year.

10. The formula for Easter in the previous problem works for every year in the range 1900–2099 except for 1954, 1981, 2049, and 2076. For these 4 years it produces a date that is one week too late. Modify the above program to work for the entire range 1900–2099.

11. A year is a leap year if it is divisible by 4, unless it is a century year that is not divisible by 400. (1800 and 1900 are *not* leap years while 1600 and 2000 *are*.) Write a program that calculates whether a year is a leap year.

12. Write a program that accepts a date in the form month/day/year and outputs whether or not the date is valid. For example 5/24/1962 is valid, but 9/31/2000 is not. (September has only 30 days.)

13. The days of the year are often numbered from 1 through 365 (or 366). This number can be computed in three steps using int arithmetic:

    (a) dayNum $= 31(\text{month} - 1) + \text{day}$

    (b) if the month is after February subtract $(4(\text{month}) + 23)//10$

    (c) if it's a leap year and after February 29, add 1

Write a program that accepts a date as month/day/year, verifies that it is a valid date (see previous problem), and then calculates the corresponding day number.

14. Do Programming Exercise 7 from Chapter 4, but add a decision to handle the case where the line does not intersect the circle.

15. Do Programming Exercise 8 from Chapter 4, but add a decision to prevent the program from dividing by zero if the line is vertical.

16. Archery Scorer. Write a program that draws an archery target (see Programming Exercise 2 from Chapter 4) and allows the user to click five times to represent arrows shot at the target. Using five-band scoring, a bulls-eye (yellow) is worth 9 points and each successive ring is worth 2 fewer points down to 1 for white. The program should output a score for each click and keep track of a running sum for the entire series.

17. Write a program to animate a circle bouncing around a window. The basic idea is to start the circle somewhere in the interior of the window. Use variables dx and dy (both initialized to 1) to control the movement of the circle. Use a large counted loop (say 10000 iterations), and each time through the loop move the circle using dx and dy. When the x-value of the center of the circle gets too high (it hits the edge), change dx to -1. When it gets too low, change dx back to 1. Use a similar approach for dy.

Note: Your animation will probably run too fast. You can slow it down by using the sleep function from the time library module.

```
from time import sleep
...
sleep(0.005) # pauses the program for 5 thousandths of a second.
```

18. Take a favorite programming problem from a previous chapter and add decisions and/or exception handling as required to make it truly robust (will not crash on any inputs). Trade your program with a friend and have a contest to see who can "break" the other's program.

Chapter 8

Loop Structures and Booleans

Objectives

- To understand the concepts of definite and indefinite loops as they are realized in the Python `for` and `while` statements.

- To understand the programming patterns interactive loop and sentinel loop and their implementations using a Python `while` statement.

- To understand the programming pattern end-of-file loop and ways of implementing such loops in Python.

- To be able to design and implement solutions to problems involving loop patterns including nested loop structures.

- To understand the basic ideas of Boolean algebra and be able to analyze and write Boolean expressions involving Boolean operators.

8.1 For Loops: A Quick Review

In Chapter 7, we looked in detail at the Python `if` statement and its use in implementing programming patterns such as one-way, two-way, and multi-way decisions. In this chapter, we'll wrap up our tour of control structures with a detailed look at loops and Boolean expressions.

You already know that the Python `for` statement provides a kind of loop. It allows us to iterate through a sequence of values.

233

```
for <var> in <sequence>:
    <body>
```

The loop index variable var takes on each successive value in the sequence, and the statements in the body of the loop are executed once for each value.

Suppose we want to write a program that can compute the average of a series of numbers entered by the user. To make the program general, it should work for any size set of numbers. You know that an average is calculated by summing up the numbers and dividing by the count of how many numbers there are. We don't need to keep track of all the numbers that have been entered; we just need a running sum so that we can calculate the average at the end.

This problem description should start some bells ringing in your head. It suggests the use of some design patterns you have seen before. We are dealing with a series of numbers—that will be handled by some form of loop. If there are n numbers, the loop should execute n times; we can use the counted loop pattern. We also need a running sum; that calls for a loop accumulator. Putting the two ideas together, we can generate a design for this problem.

```
Input the count of the numbers, n
Initialize sum to 0
Loop n times
    Input a number, x
    Add x to sum
Output average as sum / n
```

Hopefully, you see both the counted loop and accumulator patterns integrated into this design. We can translate this design almost directly into a Python implementation.

```python
# average1.py

def main():
    n = eval(input("How many numbers do you have? "))
    sum = 0.0
    for i in range(n):
        x = eval(input("Enter a number >> "))
        sum = sum + x
    print("\nThe average of the numbers is", sum / n)

main()
```

The running sum starts at 0, and each number is added in turn. After the loop, the sum is divided by n to compute the average.

Here is the program in action:

```
How many numbers do you have? 5
Enter a number >> 32
Enter a number >> 45
Enter a number >> 34
Enter a number >> 76
Enter a number >> 45

The average of the numbers is 46.4
```

Well, that wasn't too bad. Knowing a couple of common patterns, counted loop and accumulator, got us to a working program with minimal difficulty in design and implementation. Hopefully, you can see the worth of committing these sorts of programming clichés to memory.

8.2 Indefinite Loops

Our averaging program is certainly functional, but it doesn't have the best user interface. It begins by asking the user how many numbers there are. For a handful of numbers this is OK, but what if I have a whole page of numbers to average? It might be a significant burden to go through and count them up.

It would be much nicer if the computer could take care of counting the numbers for us. Unfortunately, as you no doubt recall, the for loop (in its usual form) is a definite loop, and that means the number of iterations is determined when the loop starts. We can't use a definite loop unless we know the number of iterations ahead of time, and we can't know how many iterations this loop needs until all of the numbers have been entered. We seem to be stuck.

The solution to this dilemma lies in another kind of loop, the *indefinite* or *conditional* loop. An indefinite loop keeps iterating until certain conditions are met. There is no guarantee ahead of time regarding how many times the loop will go around.

In Python, an indefinite loop is implemented using a while statement. Syntactically, the while is very simple.

```
while <condition>:
    <body>
```

Here condition is a Boolean expression, just like in if statements. The body is, as usual, a sequence of one or more statements.

The semantics of while is straightforward. The body of the loop executes repeatedly as long as the condition remains true. When the condition is false, the loop terminates. Figure 8.1 shows a flowchart for the while. Notice that the condition is always tested at the top of the loop, before the loop body is executed. This kind of structure is called a *pre-test* loop. If the loop condition is initially false, the loop body will not execute at all.

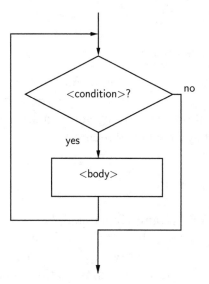

Figure 8.1: Flowchart of a while loop

Here is an example of a simple while loop that counts from 0 to 10:

```
i = 0
while i <= 10:
    print(i)
    i = i + 1
```

This code will have the same output as if we had written a for loop like this:

```
for i in range(11):
    print(i)
```

Notice that the `while` version requires us to take care of initializing `i` before the loop and incrementing `i` at the bottom of the loop body. In the `for` loop, the loop variable is handled automatically.

The simplicity of the `while` statement makes it both powerful and dangerous. Because it is less rigid, it is more versatile; it can do more than just iterate through sequences. But it is also a common source of errors.

Suppose we forget to increment `i` at the bottom of the loop body in the counting example.

```
i = 0
while i <= 10:
    print(i)
```

What will the output from this program be? When Python gets to the loop, `i` will be 0, which is less than 10, so the loop body executes, printing a 0. Now control returns to the condition; `i` is still 0, so the loop body executes again, printing a 0. Now control returns to the condition; `i` is still 0, so the loop body executes again, printing a 0....

You get the picture. This is an example of an *infinite loop*. Usually, infinite loops are a bad thing. Clearly this version of the program does nothing useful. That reminds me, did you hear about the computer scientist who died of exhaustion while washing his hair? The instructions on the bottle said: "Lather. Rinse. Repeat."

As a beginning programmer, it would be surprising if you did not accidentally write a few programs with infinite loops—it's a rite of passage for programmers. Even more experienced programmers have been known to do this from time to time. Usually, you can break out of a loop by pressing <Ctrl>-c (holding down the <Ctrl> key and pressing "c"). If your loop is really tight, this might not work, and you'll have to resort to more drastic means (such as <Ctrl>-<Alt>-<Delete> on a PC). If all else fails, there is always the trusty *reset* button on your computer. The best idea is to avoid writing infinite loops in the first place.

8.3   Common Loop Patterns

8.3.1   Interactive Loops

One good use of the indefinite loop is to write *interactive loops*. The idea behind an interactive loop is that it allows the user to repeat certain portions of a program on demand. Let's take a look at this loop pattern in the context of our number averaging problem.

Recall that the previous version of the program forced the user to count up how many numbers there were to be averaged. We want to modify the program so that it keeps track of how many numbers there are. We can do this with another accumulator—call it count—that starts at zero and increases by 1 each time through the loop.

To allow the user to stop at any time, each iteration of the loop will ask whether there is more data to process. The general pattern for an interactive loop looks like this:

```
set moredata to "yes"
while moredata is "yes"
    get the next data item
    process the item
    ask user if there is moredata
```

Combining the interactive loop pattern with accumulators for the sum and count yields this algorithm for the averaging program:

```
initialize sum to 0.0
initialize count to 0
set moredata to "yes"
while moredata is "yes"
    input a number, x
    add x to sum
    add 1 to count
    ask user if there is moredata
output sum / count
```

Notice how the two accumulators are interleaved into the basic structure of the interactive loop.

Here is the corresponding Python program:

```
# average2.py

def main():
    sum = 0.0
    count = 0
    moredata = "yes"
```

```
    while moredata[0] == "y":
        x = eval(input("Enter a number >> "))
        sum = sum + x
        count = count + 1
        moredata = input("Do you have more numbers (yes or no)? ")
    print("\nThe average of the numbers is", sum / count)

main()
```

Notice this program uses string indexing (`moredata[0]`) to look just at the first letter of the user's input. This allows for varied responses such as "yes," "y," "yeah," etc. All that matters is that the first letter is a "y."

Here is sample output from this program:

```
Enter a number >> 32
Do you have more numbers (yes or no)? yes
Enter a number >> 45
Do you have more numbers (yes or no)? y
Enter a number >> 34
Do you have more numbers (yes or no)? y
Enter a number >> 76
Do you have more numbers (yes or no)? y
Enter a number >> 45
Do you have more numbers (yes or no)? nope

The average of the numbers is 46.5
```

In this version, the user doesn't have to count the data values, but the interface is still not good. The user will almost certainly be annoyed by the constant prodding for more data. The interactive loop has many good applications; this is not one of them.

8.3.2 Sentinel Loops

A better solution to the number averaging problem is to employ a pattern commonly known as a *sentinel loop*. A sentinel loop continues to process data until reaching a special value that signals the end. The special value is called the *sentinel*. Any value may be chosen for the sentinel. The only restriction is that it be distinguishable from actual data values. The sentinel is not processed as part of the data.

Here is a general pattern for designing sentinel loops:

```
get the first data item
while item is not the sentinel
    process the item
    get the next data item
```

Notice how this pattern avoids processing the sentinel item. The first item is retrieved before the loop starts. This is sometimes called the *priming read*, as it gets the process started. If the first item is the sentinel, the loop immediately terminates and no data is processed. Otherwise, the item is processed and the next one is read. The loop test at the top ensures this next item is not the sentinel before processing it. When the sentinel is reached, the loop terminates.

We can apply the sentinel pattern to our number averaging problem. The first step is to pick a sentinel. Suppose we are using the program to average exam scores. In that case, we can safely assume that no score will be below 0. The user can enter a negative number to signal the end of the data. Combining the sentinel loop with the two accumulators from the interactive loop version yields this program:

```python
# average3.py

def main():
    sum = 0.0
    count = 0
    x = eval(input("Enter a number (negative to quit) >> "))
    while x >= 0:
        sum = sum + x
        count = count + 1
        x = eval(input("Enter a number (negative to quit) >> "))
    print("\nThe average of the numbers is", sum / count)

main()
```

I have changed the prompt so that the user knows how to signal the end of the data. Notice that the prompt is identical at the priming read and the bottom of the loop body.

Now we have a useful form of the program. Here it is in action:

```
Enter a number (negative to quit) >> 32
```

```
Enter a number (negative to quit) >> 45
Enter a number (negative to quit) >> 34
Enter a number (negative to quit) >> 76
Enter a number (negative to quit) >> 45
Enter a number (negative to quit) >> -1
```

```
The average of the numbers is 46.4
```

This version provides the ease of use of the interactive loop without the hassle of having to type "yes" all the time. The sentinel loop is a very handy pattern for solving all sorts of data processing problems. It's another cliché that you should commit to memory.

This sentinel loop solution is quite good, but there is still a limitation. The program can't be used to average a set of numbers containing negative as well as positive values. Let's see if we can't generalize the program a bit. What we need is a sentinel value that is distinct from any possible valid number, positive or negative. Of course, this is impossible as long as we restrict ourselves to working with numbers. No matter what number or range of numbers we pick as a sentinel, it is always possible that some data set may contain such a number.

In order to have a truly unique sentinel, we need to broaden the possible inputs. Suppose that we get the input from the user as a string. We can have a distinctive, non-numeric string that indicates the end of the input; all others would be converted into numbers and treated as data. One simple solution is to have the sentinel value be an *empty string*. Remember, an empty string is represented in Python as "" (quotes with no space between). If the user types a blank line in response to a input (just hits <Enter>), Python returns an empty string. We can use this as a simple way to terminate input. The design looks like this:

```
Initialize sum to 0.0
Initialize count to 0
Input data item as a string, xStr
while xStr is not empty
    Convert xStr to a number, x
    Add x to sum
    Add 1 to count
    Input next data item as a string, xStr
Output sum / count
```

Comparing this to the previous algorithm, you can see that converting the string to a number has been added to the processing section of the sentinel loop.

Translating it into Python yields this program:

```
# average4.py

def main():
    sum = 0.0
    count = 0
    xStr = input("Enter a number (<Enter> to quit) >> ")
    while xStr != "":
        x = eval(xStr)
        sum = sum + x
        count = count + 1
        xStr = input("Enter a number (<Enter> to quit) >> ")
    print("\nThe average of the numbers is", sum / count)

main()
```

This code does not turn the input into a number (via eval) until after it has checked to make sure the input was not the sentinel (""").

Here is an example run, showing that it is now possible to average arbitrary sets of numbers:

```
Enter a number (<Enter> to quit) >> 34
Enter a number (<Enter> to quit) >> 23
Enter a number (<Enter> to quit) >> 0
Enter a number (<Enter> to quit) >> -25
Enter a number (<Enter> to quit) >> -34.4
Enter a number (<Enter> to quit) >> 22.7
Enter a number (<Enter> to quit) >>

The average of the numbers is 3.38333333333
```

We finally have an excellent solution to our original problem. You should study this solution so that you can incorporate these techniques into your own programs.

8.3.3   File Loops

One disadvantage of all the averaging programs presented so far is that they are interactive. Imagine you are trying to average 87 numbers and you happen to make a typo near the end. With our interactive program, you will need to start all over again.

A better approach to the problem might be to type all of the numbers into a file. The data in the file can be perused and edited before sending it to a program that generates a report. This file-oriented approach is typically used for data-processing applications.

Back in Chapter 5, we looked at reading data from files by using the file object as a sequence in a for loop. We can apply this technique directly to the number averaging problem. Assuming that the numbers are typed into a file one per line, we can compute the average with this program:

```python
# average5.py

def main():
    fileName = input("What file are the numbers in? ")
    infile = open(fileName,'r')
    sum = 0.0
    count = 0
    for line in infile:
        sum = sum + eval(line)
        count = count + 1
    print("\nThe average of the numbers is", sum / count)

main()
```

In this code, the loop variable line iterates through the file as a sequence of lines; each line is converted to a number and added to the running sum.

Many programming languages do not have a special mechanism for looping through files like this. In these languages, the lines of a file can be read one at a time using a form of sentinel loop. We can illustrate this method in Python by using readline(). Remember, the readline() method gets the next line from a file as a string. At the end of the file, readline() returns an empty string, which we can use as a sentinel value. Here is a general pattern for an *end-of-file loop* using readline()in Python.

```python
line = infile.readline()
while line != "":
    # process line
    line = infile.readline()
```

At first glance, you may be concerned that this loop stops prematurely if it encounters an empty line in the file. This is not the case. Remember, a blank line in a text file contains a single newline character ("\n"), and the `readline` method includes the newline character in its return value. Since "\n" != "", the loop will continue.

Here is the code that results from applying the end-of-file sentinel loop to our number averaging problem:

```
# average6.py

def main():
    fileName = input("What file are the numbers in? ")
    infile = open(fileName,'r')
    sum = 0.0
    count = 0
    line = infile.readline()
    while line != "":
        sum = sum + eval(line)
        count = count + 1
        line = infile.readline()
    print("\nThe average of the numbers is", sum / count)

main()
```

Obviously, this version is not quite as concise as the version using the `for` loop. In Python, you might as well use the latter, but it is still good to know about end-of-file loops in case you're stuck programming in a less elegant language.

8.3.4   Nested Loops

In the last chapter, you saw how control structures such as decisions and loops could be nested inside one another to produce sophisticated algorithms. One particularly useful but somewhat tricky technique is the nesting of loops.

Let's take a look at an example program. How about one last version of our number averaging problem? I promise this is the last time I'll use this example.[1] Suppose we modify the specification of our file averaging problem slightly. This time, instead of typing the numbers into the file one-per-line, we'll allow any

---

[1]until Chapter 11.

number of values on a line. When multiple values appear on a line, they will be separated by commas.

At the top level, the basic algorithm will be some sort of file-processing loop that computes a running sum and count. For practice, let's use an end-of-file loop. Here is the code comprising the top-level loop:

```
sum = 0.0
count = 0
line = infile.readline()
while line != "":
    # update sum and count for values in line
    line = infile.readline()
print("\nThe average of the numbers is", sum / count)
```

Now we need to figure out how to update the sum and count in the body of the loop. Since each individual line of the file contains one or more numbers separated by commas, we can split the line into substrings, each of which represents a number. Then we need to loop through these substrings, convert each to a number, and add it to sum. We also need to add 1 to count for each number. Here is a code fragment that processes a line:

```
for xStr in line.split(","):
    sum = sum + eval(xStr)
    count = count +1
```

Notice that the iteration of the for loop in this fragment is controlled by the value of line, which just happens to be the loop-control variable for the file-processing loop we outlined above. Knitting these two loops together, here is our program:

```
# average7.py

def main():
    fileName = input("What file are the numbers in? ")
    infile = open(fileName,'r')
    sum = 0.0
    count = 0
    line = infile.readline()
    while line != "":
        # update sum and count for values in line
```

```
        for xStr in line.split(","):
            sum = sum + eval(xStr)
            count = count + 1
        line = infile.readline()
    print("\nThe average of the numbers is", sum / count)

main()
```

As you can see, the loop that processes the numbers in a line is indented inside the file processing loop. The outer `while` loop iterates once for each line of the file. On each iteration of the outer loop, the inner `for` loop iterates as many times as there are numbers on that line. When the inner loop finishes, the next line of the file is read, and the outer loop goes through its next iteration.

The individual fragments of this problem are not complex when taken separately, but the final result is fairly intricate. The best way to design nested loops is to follow the process we did here. First design the outer loop without worrying about what goes inside. Then design what goes inside, ignoring the outer loop(s). Finally, put the pieces together, taking care to preserve the nesting. If the individual loops are correct, the nested result will work just fine; trust it. With a little practice, you'll be implementing double-, even triple-nested loops with ease.

8.4   Computing with Booleans

We now have two control structures, `if` and `while`, that use conditions, which are Boolean expressions. Conceptually, a Boolean expression evaluates to one of two values: false or true. In Python, these values are represented by the literals `False` and `True`. So far, we have used simple Boolean expressions that compare two values (e.g., `while x >= 0`).

8.4.1   Boolean Operators

Sometimes the simple conditions that we have been using do not seem expressive enough. For example, suppose you need to determine whether two point objects are in the same position—that is, they have equal x coordinates and equal y coordinates. One way of handling this would be a nested decision.

```
if p1.getX() == p2.getX():
    if p1.getY() == p2.getY():
```

```
        # points are the same
    else:
        # points are different
else:
    # points are different
```

You can see how awkward this is.

Instead of working around this problem with a decision structure, another approach would be to construct a more complex expression using *Boolean operations*. Like most programming languages, Python provides three Boolean operators: and, or, and not. Let's take a look at these three operators and then see how they can be used to simplify our problem.

The Boolean operators and and or are used to combine two Boolean expressions and produce a Boolean result.

```
<expr> and <expr>
<expr> or <expr>
```

The and of two expressions is true exactly when both of the expressions are true. We can represent this definition in a *truth table*.

P	Q	P and Q
T	T	T
T	F	F
F	T	F
F	F	F

In this table, P and Q represent smaller Boolean expressions. Since each expression has two possible values, there are four possible combinations of values, each shown as one row in the table. The last column gives the value of P and Q for each possible combination. By definition, the and is true only in the case where both P and Q are true.

The or of two expressions is true when either expression is true. Here is the truth table defining or:

P	Q	P or Q
T	T	T
T	F	T
F	T	T
F	F	F

The only time the or is false is when both expressions are false. Notice especially that or is true when both expressions are true. This is the mathematical definition of or, but the word "or" is sometimes used in an exclusive sense in everyday English. If your mom said that you could have cake or cookies for dessert, she would probably scold you for taking both.

The not operator computes the opposite of a Boolean expression. It is a *unary* operator, meaning that it operates on a single expression. The truth table is very simple.

P	not P
T	F
F	T

Using Boolean operators, it is possible to build arbitrarily complex Boolean expressions. As with arithmetic operators, the exact meaning of a complex expression depends on the precedence rules for the operators. Consider this expression:

```
a or not b and c
```

How should this be evaluated?

Python follows a standard convention that the order of precedence from high to low is not, followed by and, followed by or. So the expression would be equivalent to this parenthesized version:

```
(a or ((not b) and c))
```

Unlike arithmetic, however, most people don't tend to know or remember the precedence rules for Booleans. I suggest that you always parenthesize your complex expressions to prevent confusion.

Now that we have some Boolean operators, we are ready to return to our example problem. To test for the co-location of two points, we could use an and operation.

```
if p1.getX() == p2.getX() and p2.getY() == p1.getY():
    # points are the same
else:
    # points are different
```

Here the entire expression will only be true when both of the simple conditions are true. This ensures that both the *x* and *y* coordinates match for the points to be the same. Obviously, this is much simpler and clearer than the nested `if`s from the previous version.

Let's look at a slightly more complex example. In the next chapter, we will develop a simulation for the game of racquetball. Part of the simulation will need to determine when a game has ended. Suppose that `scoreA` and `scoreB` represent the scores of two racquetball players. The game is over as soon as either of the players has reached 15 points. Here is a Boolean expression that is true when the game is over:

```
scoreA == 15 or scoreB == 15
```

When either score reaches 15, one of the two simple conditions becomes true, and, by definition of or, the entire Boolean expression is true. As long as both conditions remain false (neither player has reached 15) the entire expression is false.

Our simulation will need a loop that continues as long as the game is *not* over. We can construct an appropriate loop condition by taking the negation of the game-over condition.

```
while not (scoreA == 15 or scoreB == 15):
    # continue playing
```

We can also construct more complex Boolean expressions that reflect different possible stopping conditions. Some racquetball players play shutouts (sometimes called a skunk). For these players, a game also ends when one of the players reaches 7 and the other has not yet scored a point. For brevity, I'll use a for `scoreA` and b for `scoreB`. Here is an expression for game-over when shutouts are included:

```
a == 15 or b == 15 or (a == 7 and b == 0) or (b == 7 and a == 0)
```

Do you see how I have added two more situations to the original condition? The new parts reflect the two possible ways a shutout can occur, and each requires checking both scores. The result is a fairly complex expression.

While we're at it, let's try one more example. Suppose we were writing a simulation for volleyball, rather than racquetball. Traditional volleyball does not have shutouts, but it requires a team to win by at least two points. If the score is 15 to 14, or even 21 to 20, the game continues.

Let's write a condition that computes when a volleyball game is over. Here's one approach:

```
(a >= 15 and a - b >= 2) or (b >= 15 and b - a >= 2)
```

Do you see how this expression works? It basically says the game is over when team A has won (scored at least 15 and leading by at least 2) or when team B has won.

Here is another way to do it:

```
(a >= 15 or b >= 15) and abs(a - b) >= 2
```

This version is a bit more succinct. It states that the game is over when one of the teams has reached a winning total and the difference in the scores is at least 2. Remember that abs returns the absolute value of an expression.

8.4.2   Boolean Algebra

All decisions in computer programs boil down to appropriate Boolean expressions. The ability to formulate, manipulate, and reason with these expressions is an important skill for programmers and computer scientists. Boolean expressions obey certain algebraic laws similar to those that apply to numeric operations. These laws are called *Boolean logic* or *Boolean algebra*.

Let's look at a few examples. The following table shows some rules of algebra with their correlates in Boolean algebra:

Algebra	Boolean algebra
$a * 0 = 0$	a and false $==$ false
$a * 1 = a$	a and true $==$ a
$a + 0 = a$	a or false $==$ a

From these examples, you can see that and has similarities to multiplication, and or has similarities to addition; while 0 and 1 correspond to false and true.

Here are some other interesting properties of Boolean operations. Anything ored with true is just true.

```
a or true == true
```

Both and and or distribute over each other.

```
a or (b and c) == (a or b) and (a or c)
a and (b or c) == (a and b) or (a and c)
```

A double negative cancels out.

```
not(not a) == a
```

The next two identities are known as DeMorgan's laws.

```
not(a or b) == (not a) and (not b)
not(a and b) == (not a) or (not b)
```

Notice how the operator changes between and and or when the not is pushed into an expression.

One application of Boolean algebra is the analysis and simplification of Boolean expressions inside programs. For example, let's go back to the racquetball game one more time. Above, we developed a loop condition for continuing the game that looked like this:

```
while not (scoreA == 15 or scoreB == 15):
    # continue playing
```

You can read this condition as something like: *While it is not the case that player A has 15 or player B has 15, continue playing.* We're pretty sure that's correct, but negating complex conditions like this can be somewhat awkward, to say the least. Using a little Boolean algebra, we can transform this result.

Applying DeMorgan's law, we know that the expression is equivalent to this:

```
(not scoreA == 15)  and  (not scoreB == 15)
```

Remember, we have to change the or to and when "distributing" the not. This condition is no better than the first, but we can go one step farther by pushing the nots into the conditions themselves.

```
while scoreA != 15 and scoreB != 15:
    # continue playing
```

Now we have a version that is much easier to understand. This reads simply as *while player A has not reached 15 and player B has not reached 15, continue playing.*

This particular example illustrates a generally useful approach to loop conditions. Sometimes it's easier to figure out when a loop should stop, rather than when the loop should continue. In that case, simply write the loop *termination* condition and then put a not in front of it. An application or two of DeMorgan's laws can then get you to a simpler but equivalent version suitable for use in a while statement.

8.5   Other Common Structures

Taken together, the decision structure (if) along with a pre-test loop (while) provide a complete set of control structures. This means that every algorithm can be expressed using just these. Once you've mastered the while and the if, you can write every conceivable algorithm, in principle. However, for certain kinds of problems, alternative structures can sometimes be convenient. This section outlines some of those alternatives.

8.5.1   Post-Test Loop

Suppose you are writing an input algorithm that is supposed to get a non-negative number from the user. If the user types an incorrect input, the program asks for another value. It continues to reprompt until the user enters a valid value. This process is called *input validation*. Well-engineered programs validate inputs whenever possible.

Here is a simple algorithm:

```
repeat
    get a number from the user
until number is >= 0
```

The idea here is that the loop keeps getting inputs until the value is acceptable. The flowchart depicting this design in shown in Figure 8.2. Notice how this algorithm contains a loop where the condition test comes after the loop body. This is a *post-test loop*. A post-test loop must always execute the body of the loop at least once.

Unlike some other languages, Python does not have a statement that directly implements a post-test loop. However, this algorithm can be implemented with a while by "seeding" the loop condition for the first iteration.

```
number = -1  # Start with an illegal value to get into the loop.
while number < 0:
    number = eval(input("Enter a positive number: "))
```

This forces the loop body to execute at least once and is equivalent to the post-test algorithm. You might notice that this is similar to the structure given earlier for the interactive loop pattern. Interactive loops are naturally suited to a post-test implementation.

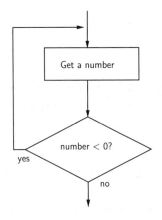

Figure 8.2: Flowchart of a post-test loop

Some programmers prefer to simulate a post-test loop more directly by using a Python break statement. Executing break causes Python to immediately
exit the enclosing loop. Often a break statement is used to leave what looks
syntactically like an infinite loop.

Here is the same algorithm implemented with a break:

```
while True:
    number = eval(input("Enter a positive number: "))
    if number >= 0: break # Exit loop if number is valid.
```

The first line may look a bit strange to you. Remember that a while loop continues as long as the expression in the loop heading evaluates to true. Since True
is always true, this appears to be an infinite loop.   However, when the value
of x is non-negative, the break statement executes, which terminates the loop.
Notice that I placed the break on the same line as the if. This is legal when
the body of the if contains only one statement. It's common to see a one-line
if–break combination used as a loop exit.

Even this small example can be improved. It would be nice if the program
issued a warning explaining why the input was invalid. In the while version
of the post-test loop, this is a bit awkward. We need to add an if so that the
warning is not displayed for valid inputs.

```
number = -1  # Start with an illegal value to get into the loop.
while number < 0:
```

```
number = eval(input("Enter a positive number: "))
if number < 0:
    print("The number you entered was not positive")
```

Do you see how the validity check gets repeated in two places?

Adding a warning to the version using break only requires adding an else to the existing if.

```
while True:
    number = eval(input("Enter a positive number: "))
    if number >= 0:
        break # Exit loop if number is valid.
    else:
        print("The number you entered was not positive")
```

8.5.2   Loop and a Half

Some programmers would solve the warning problem from the previous section using a slightly different style.

```
while True:
    number = eval(input("Enter a positive number: "))
    if number >= 0: break   # Loop exit
    print("The number you entered was not positive")
```

Here the loop exit is actually in the middle of the loop body. This is called a *loop and a half*. Some purists frown on exits in the midst of a loop like this, but the pattern can be quite handy.

The loop and a half is an elegant way to avoid the priming read in a sentinel loop. Here is the general pattern of a sentinel loop implemented as a loop and a half:

```
while True:
    Get next data item
    if the item is the sentinel: break
    process the item
```

Figure 8.3 shows a flowchart of this approach to sentinel loops. You can see that this implementation is faithful to the first rule of sentinel loops: *avoid processing the sentinel value.*

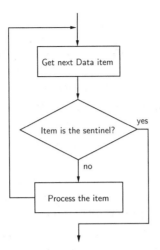

Figure 8.3: Loop-and-a-half implementation of sentinel loop pattern

The choice of whether to use break statements or not is largely a matter of taste. Either style is acceptable. One temptation that should generally be avoided is peppering the body of a loop with multiple break statements. The logic of a loop is easily lost when there are multiple exits. However, there are times when even this rule should be broken to provide the most elegant solution to a problem.

8.5.3 Boolean Expressions as Decisions

So far, we have talked about Boolean expressions only within the context of other control structures. Sometimes Boolean expressions themselves can act as control structures. In fact, Boolean expressions are so flexible in Python that they can sometimes lead to subtle programming errors.

Consider writing an interactive loop that keeps going as long as the user response starts with a "y." To allow the user to type either an upper- or lowercase response, you could use a loop like this:

```
while response[0] == "y" or response[0] == "Y":
```

You must be careful not to abbreviate this condition as you might think of it in English: "While the first letter is 'y' or 'Y'". The following form *does not work*.

```
while response[0] == "y" or "Y":
```

In fact, this is an infinite loop. Understanding why this condition is always true requires digging into some idiosyncrasies of Python Boolean expressions.

You already know that Python has a bool type. Actually, this is a fairly recent addition to the language (version 2.3). Before that, Python just used the ints 1 and 0 to represent true and false. In fact, the bool type is just a "special" int where the values of 0 and 1 print as `False` and `True`. You can test this out by evaluating the Expression `True + True`.

We have been using the bool literals `True` and `False` to represent the Boolean values true and false, respectively. The Python condition operators (i.e., `==`) always evaluate to a value of type bool. However, Python is actually very flexible about what data type can appear as a Boolean expression. Any built-in type can be interpreted as a Boolean. For numbers (ints and floats) a zero value is considered as false, anything other than zero is taken as true. You can see how a value will be interpreted when used as a Boolean expression by explicitly converting the value to type bool. Here are a few examples:

```
>>> bool(0)
False
>>> bool(1)
True
>>> bool(32)
True
>>> bool("hello")
True
>>> bool("")
False
>>> bool([1,2,3])
True
>>> bool([])
False
```

As you can see, for sequence types, an empty sequence is interpreted as false whereas any non-empty sequence is taken to indicate true.

The flexibility of Python Booleans extends to the Boolean operators. Although the main use of these operators is forming Boolean expressions, they have operational definitions that make them useful for other purposes as well. This table summarizes the behavior of these operators:

operator	operational definition
x and y	If x is false, return x. Otherwise, return y.
x or y	If x is true, return x. Otherwise, return y.
not x	If x is false, return `True`. Otherwise, return `False`.

The definition of `not` is straightforward. It might take a bit of thinking to convince yourself that these descriptions of `and` and `or` faithfully reflect the truth tables you saw at the beginning of the chapter.

Consider the expression x and y. In order for this to be true, both expressions x and y must be true. As soon as one of them is discovered to be false, the party is over. Python looks at the expressions left to right. If x is false, Python should return a false result. Whatever the false value of x was, that is what is returned. If x turns out to be true, then the truth or falsity of the whole expression turns on the result of y. Simply returning y guarantees that if y is true, the whole result is true, and if y is false, the whole result is false. Similar reasoning can be used to show that the description of `or` is faithful to the logical definition of `or` given in the truth table.

These operational definitions show that Python's Boolean operators are *short-circuit* operators. That means that a true or false value is returned as soon as the result is known. In an `and` where the first expression is false and in an `or` where the first expression is true, Python will not even evaluate the second expression.

Now let's take a look at our infinite loop problem:

```
response[0] == "y" or "Y"
```

Treated as a Boolean expression, this will always evaluate to true. The first thing to notice is that the Boolean operator is combining two expressions; the first is a simple condition, and the second is a string. Here is an equivalent parenthesized version:

```
(response[0] == "y") or ("Y"):
```

By the operational description of `or`, this expression returns either `True` (returned by `==` when `response[0]` is "y") or `"Y"` (when `response[0]` is not a "y"). Either of these results is interpreted by Python as true.

A more logic-oriented way to think about this is to simply look at the second expression. It is a nonempty string, so Python will always interpret it as true. Since at least one of the two expressions is always true, the `or` of the expressions must always be true as well.

So, the strange behavior of this example is due to some quirks in the definitions of the Boolean operators. This is one of the few places where the design of

Python has a potential pitfall for the beginning programmer. You may wonder about the wisdom of this design, yet the flexibility of Python allows for certain succinct programming idioms that many programmers find useful. Let's look at an example.

Frequently, programs prompt users for information but offer a default value for the response. The default value, sometimes listed in square brackets, is used if the user simply hits the <Enter> key. Here is an example code fragment:

```
ans = input("What flavor do you want [vanilla]: ")
if ans != "":
    flavor = ans
else:
    flavor = "vanilla"
```

Exploiting the fact that the string in ans can be treated as a Boolean, the condition in this code can be simplified as follows:

```
ans = input("What flavor do you want [vanilla]: ")
if ans:
    flavor = ans
else:
    flavor = "vanilla"
```

Here a Boolean condition is being used to decide how to set a string variable. If the user just hits <Enter>, ans will be an empty string, which Python interprets as false. In this case, the empty string will be replaced by "vanilla" in the else clause.

The same idea can be more succinctly coded by treating the strings themselves as Booleans and using an or.

```
ans = input("What flavor do you want [vanilla]: ")
flavor = ans or "vanilla"
```

The operational definition of or guarantees that this is equivalent to the if-else version. Remember, any nonempty answer is interpreted as "true."

In fact, this task can easily be accomplished in a single line of code.

```
flavor = input("What flavor do you want [vanilla]: ") or "vanilla"
```

I don't know whether it's really worthwhile to save a few lines of code using Boolean operators this way. If you like this style, by all means, feel free to use it. Just make sure that your code doesn't get so tricky that others (or you) have trouble understanding it.

8.6 Chapter Summary

This chapter has filled in details of Python loops and Boolean expressions. Here are the highlights:

- A Python `for` loop is a definite loop that iterates through a sequence.

- A Python `while` statement is an example of an indefinite loop. It continues to iterate as long as the loop condition remains true. When using an indefinite loop, programmers must guard against the possibility of accidentally writing an infinite loop.

- One important use for an indefinite loop is for implementing the programming pattern interactive loop. An interactive loop allows portions of a program to be repeated according to the wishes of the user.

- A sentinel loop is a loop that handles input until a special value (the sentinel) is encountered. Sentinel loops are a common programming pattern. In writing a sentinel loop, a programmer must be careful that the sentinel is not processed.

- Loops are useful for reading files. Python treats a file as a sequence of lines, so it is particularly easy to process a file line-by-line using a `for` loop. In other languages, a file loop is generally implemented using a sentinel loop pattern.

- Loops, like other control structures, can be nested. When designing nested loop algorithms, it is best to consider the loops one at a time.

- Complex Boolean expressions can be built from simple conditions using the Boolean operators `and`, `or`, and `not`. Boolean operators obey the rules of Boolean algebra. DeMorgan's laws describe how to negate Boolean expressions involving and and or.

- Nonstandard loop structures such as a loop-and-a-half can be built using a `while` loop having a loop condition of `True` and using a `break` statement to provide a loop exit.

- Python Boolean operators and and or employ short-circuit evaluation. They also have operational definitions that allow them to be used in certain decision contexts. Even though Python has a built-in `bool` data type, other data types (e.g., int) may also be used where Boolean expressions are expected.

8.7 Exercises

Review Questions

True/False

1. A Python `while` implements a definite loop.

2. The counted loop pattern uses a definite loop.

3. A sentinel loop asks the user whether to continue on each iteration.

4. A sentinel loop should not actually process the sentinel value.

5. The easiest way to iterate through the lines of a file in Python is to use a `while` loop.

6. A `while` is a post-test loop.

7. The Boolean operator `or` returns `True` when both of its operands are true.

8. `a and (b or c) == (a and b) or (a and c)`

9. `not(a or b) == (not a) or not(b)`

10. `True or False`

Multiple Choice

1. A loop pattern that asks the user whether to continue on each iteration is called a(n)
   a) interactive loop   b) end-of-file loop
   c) sentinel loop   d) infinite loop

2. A loop pattern that continues until a special value is input is called a(n)
   a) interactive loop   b) end-of-file loop
   c) sentinel loop   d) infinite loop

3. A loop structure that tests the loop condition after executing the loop body is called a
   a) pre-test loop   b) loop-and-a-half
   c) sentinel loop   d) post-test loop

4. A priming read is part of the pattern for a(n)
   a) interactive loop   b) end-of-file loop
   c) sentinel loop   d) infinite loop

5. What statement can be executed in the body of a loop to cause it to terminate?
   a) if   b) input   c) break   d) exit

6. Which of the following is not a valid rule of Boolean algebra?
   a) (True or x) == True
   b) (False and x) == False
   c) not(a and b) == not(a) and not(b)
   d) (True or False) == True

7. A loop that never terminates is called
   a) busy   b) indefinite   c) tight   d) infinite

8. Which line would *not* be found in a truth table for and?
   a) T T T   b) T F T   c) F T F   d) F F F

9. Which line would *not* be found in a truth table for or?
   a) T T T   b) T F T   c) F T F   d) F F F

10. The term for an operator that may not evaluate one of its subexpressions is
    a) short-circuit   b) faulty   c) exclusive   d) indefinite

Discussion

1. Compare and contrast the following pairs of terms:

   (a) Definite loop vs. Indefinite loop

   (b) For loop vs. While loop

   (c) Interactive loop vs. Sentinel loop

   (d) Sentinel loop vs. End-of-file loop

2. Give a truth table that shows the (Boolean) value of each of the following Boolean expressions, for every possible combination of "input" values. Hint: including columns for intermediate expressions is helpful.

(a) not $(P$ and $Q)$

(b) (not $P)$ and Q

(c) (not $P)$ or (not $Q)$

(d) $(P$ and $Q)$ or R

(e) $(P$ or $R)$ and $(Q$ or $R)$

3. Write a while loop fragment that calculates the following values:

(a) Sum of the first n *counting* numbers: $1 + 2 + 3 + \ldots + n$

(b) Sum of the first n odd numbers: $1 + 3 + 5 + \ldots + 2n - 1$

(c) Sum of a series of numbers entered by the user until the value 999 is entered. Note: 999 should not be part of the sum.

(d) The number of times a whole number n can be divided by 2 (using integer division) before reaching 1 (i.e., $log_2 n$).

Programming Exercises

1. The Fibonacci sequence starts $1, 1, 2, 3, 5, 8, \ldots$. Each number in the sequence (after the first two) is the sum of the previous two. Write a program that computes and outputs the nth Fibonacci number, where n is a value entered by the user.

2. The National Weather Service computes the windchill index using the following formula:

$$35.74 + 0.6215T - 35.75(V^{0.16}) + 0.4275T(V^{0.16})$$

Where T is the temperature in degrees Fahrenheit, and V is the wind speed in miles per hour.

Write a program that prints a nicely formatted table of windchill values. Rows should represent wind speed for 0 to 50 in 5 mph increments, and the columns represent temperatures from -20 to +60 in 10-degree increments. Note: the formula only applies for wind speeds in excess of 3 miles per hour.

3. Write a program that uses a while loop to determine how long it takes for an investment to double at a given interest rate. The input will be an annualized interest rate, and the output is the number of years it takes an investment to double. Note: the amount of the initial investment does not matter; you can use $1.

4. The Syracuse (also called Collatz or Hailstone) sequence is generated by starting with a natural number and repeatedly applying the following function until reaching 1:

$$syr(x) = \begin{cases} x/2 & \text{if x is even} \\ 3x + 1 & \text{if x is odd} \end{cases}$$

For example, the Syracuse sequence starting with 5 is: $5, 16, 8, 4, 2, 1$. It is an open question in mathematics whether this sequence will always go to 1 for every possible starting value.

Write a program that gets a starting value from the user and then prints the Syracuse sequence for that starting value.

5. A positive whole number $n > 2$ is prime if no number between 2 and $\sqrt{n}$ (inclusive) evenly divides n. Write a program that accepts a value of n as input and determines if the value is prime. If n is not prime, your program should quit as soon as it finds a value that evenly divides n.

6. Modify the previous program to find every prime number less than or equal to n.

7. The Goldbach conjecture asserts that every even number is the sum of two prime numbers. Write a program that gets a number from the user, checks to make sure that it is even, and then finds two prime numbers that add up to the number.

8. The greatest common divisor (GCD) of two values can be computed using Euclid's algorithm. Starting with the values m and n, we repeatedly apply the formula: n, m = m, n%m until m is 0. At that point, n is the GCD of the original m and n. Write a program that finds the GCD of two numbers using this algorithm.

9. Write a program that computes the fuel efficiency of a multi-leg journey. The program will first prompt for the starting odometer reading and then get information about a series of legs. For each leg, the user enters the current odometer reading and the amount of gas used (separated by a space). The user signals the end of the trip with a blank line. The program should print out the miles per gallon achieved on each leg and the total MPG for the trip.

10. Modify the previous program to get its input from a file.

11. Heating and cooling degree-days are measures used by utility companies to estimate energy requirements. If the average temperature for a day is below 60, then the number of degrees below 60 is added to the heating degree-days. If the temperature is above 80, the amount over 80 is added to the cooling degree-days. Write a program that accepts a sequence of average daily temps and computes the running total of cooling and heating degree-days. The program should print these two totals after all the data has been processed.

12. Modify the previous program to get its input from a file.

13. Write a program that graphically plots a regression line, that is, the line with the best fit through a collection of points. First ask the user to specify the data points by clicking on them in a graphics window. To find the end of input, place a small rectangle labeled "Done" in the lower left corner of the window; the program will stop gathering points when the user clicks inside that rectangle.

    The regression line is the line with the following equation:

    $$y = \bar{y} + m(x - \bar{x})$$

    where

    $$m = \frac{\sum x_i y_i - n\bar{x}\bar{y}}{\sum x_i^2 - n\bar{x}^2}$$

    $\bar{x}$ is the mean of the x-values, $\bar{y}$ is the mean of the y-values, and n is the number of points.

    As the user clicks on points, the program should draw them in the graphics window and keep track of the count of input values and the running sum of x, y, x^2, and xy values. When the user clicks inside the "Done" rectangle, the program then computes value of y (using the equations above) corresponding to the x values at the left and right edges of the window to compute the endpoints of the regression line spanning the window. After the line is drawn, the program will pause for another mouse click before closing the window and quitting.

14. Write a program that converts a color image to grayscale. The user supplies the name of a file containing a GIF or PPM image, and the program loads the image and displays the file. At the click of the mouse, the program converts the image to grayscale. The user is then prompted for a filename to store the grayscale image in.

You will probably want to go back and review the Image object from the graphics libarary (Section 4.8.4). The basic idea for converting the image is to go through it pixel by pixel and convert each one from color to an appropriate shade of gray. A gray pixel created by setting its red, green, and blue components to have the same brightness. So, color_rgb(0,0,0) is black, color_rgb(255,255,255) is white, and color_rgb(127,127,127) is a gray "halfway" between. You should use a weighted average of the original RGB values to determine the brightness of the gray. Here is the pseudocode for the grayscale algorithm:

```
for each row in the image:
    for each column in the image:
        r, g, b = get pixel information for current row and column
        brightness = int(round(0.299r + 0.587g + 0.114b))
        set pixel to color_rgb(brightness, brightness, brightness)
    update the image # to see progress row by row
```

Note: the pixel operations in the Image class are rather slow, so you will want to use relatively small images (*not* 12 megapixels) to test your program.

15. Write a program to convert an image to its color negative. The general form of the program will be similar to that of the previous problem. The negative of a pixel is formed by subtracting each color value from 255. So the new pixel color is color_rgb(255-r, 255-g, 255-b).

Chapter 9   Simulation and Design

Objectives

- To understand the potential applications of simulation as a way to solve real-world problems.

- To understand pseudo random numbers and their application in Monte Carlo simulations.

- To understand and be able to apply top-down and spiral design techniques in writing complex programs.

- To understand unit-testing and be able to apply this technique in the implementation and debugging of complex programs.

9.1 Simulating Racquetball

You may not realize it, but you have reached a significant milestone in the journey to becoming a computer scientist. You now have all the tools to write programs that solve interesting problems. By interesting, I mean problems that would be difficult or impossible to solve without the ability to write and implement computer algorithms. You are probably not yet ready to write the next great killer application, but you can do some nontrivial computing.

One particularly powerful technique for solving real-world problems is *simulation*. Computers can model real-world processes to provide otherwise unobtainable information. Computer simulation is used every day to perform myriad

267

tasks such as predicting the weather, designing aircraft, creating special effects for movies, and entertaining video game players, to name just a few. Most of these applications require extremely complex programs, but even relatively modest simulations can sometimes shed light on knotty problems.

In this chapter we are going to develop a simple simulation of the game of racquetball. Along the way, you will learn some important design and implementation strategies that will help you in tackling your own problems.

9.1.1   A Simulation Problem

Susan Computewell's friend, Denny Dibblebit, plays racquetball. Over years of playing, he has noticed a strange quirk in the game. He often competes with players who are just a little bit better than he is. In the process, he always seems to get thumped, losing the vast majority of matches. This has led him to question what is going on. On the surface, one would think that players who are *slightly* better should win *slightly* more often, but against Denny, they seem to win the lion's share.

One obvious possibility is that Denny Dibblebit's problem is in his head. Maybe his mental game isn't up to par with his physical skills. Or perhaps the other players are really *much* better than he is, and he just refuses to see it.

One day, Denny was discussing racquetball with Susan, when she suggested another possibility. Maybe it is the nature of the game itself that small differences in ability lead to lopsided matches on the court. Denny was intrigued by the idea; he didn't want to waste money on an expensive sports psychologist if it wasn't going to help. But how could he figure out if the problem was mental or just part of the game?

Susan suggested she could write a computer program to simulate certain aspects of racquetball. Using the simulation, they could let the computer model thousands of games between players of differing skill levels. Since there would not be any mental aspects involved, the simulation would show whether Denny is losing more than his share of matches.

Let's write our own racquetball simulation and see what Susan and Denny discovered.

9.1.2   Analysis and Specification

Racquetball is a sport played between two players using racquets to strike a ball in a four-walled court. It has aspects similar to many other ball and racquet games such as tennis, volleyball, badminton, squash, table tennis, etc. We don't need to understand all the rules of racquetball to write the program, just the basic outline of the game.

To start the game, one of the players puts the ball into play—this is called *serving*. The players then alternate hitting the ball to keep it in play; this is a *rally*. The rally ends when one of the players fails to hit a legal shot. The player who misses the shot loses the rally. If the loser is the player who served, then service passes to the other player. If the server wins the rally, a point is awarded. Players can only score points during their own service. The first player to reach 15 points wins the game.

In our simulation, the ability-level of the players will be represented by the probability that the player wins the rally when he or she serves. Thus, players with a 0.6 probability win a point on 60% of their serves. The program will prompt the user to enter the service probability for both players and then simulate multiple games of racquetball using those probabilities. The program will then print a summary of the results.

Here is a detailed specification:

Input The program first prompts for and gets the service probabilities of the two players (called "Player A" and "Player B"). Then the program prompts for and gets the number of games to be simulated.

Output The program will provide a series of initial prompts such as the following:

```
What is the prob. player A wins a serve?
What is the prob. player B wins a serve?
How many games to simulate?
```

The program will print out a nicely formatted report showing the number of games simulated and the number of wins and winning percentage for each player. Here is an example:

```
Games Simulated: 500
Wins for A: 268 (53.6%)
Wins for B: 232 (46.4%)
```

Notes: All inputs are assumed to be legal numeric values, no error or validity checking is required.

In each simulated game, player A serves first.

9.2 Pseudo Random Numbers

Our simulation program will have to deal with uncertain events. When we say that a player wins 50% of the serves, that does not mean that every other serve is a winner. It's more like a coin toss. Overall, we expect that half the time the coin will come up heads and half the time it will come up tails, but there is nothing to prevent a run of five tails in a row. Similarly, our racquetball player should win or lose rallies randomly. The service probability provides a likelihood that a given serve will be won, but there is no set pattern.

Many simulations share this property of requiring events to occur with a certain likelihood. A driving simulation must model the unpredictability of other drivers; a bank simulation has to deal with the random arrival of customers. These sorts of simulations are sometimes called *Monte Carlo* algorithms because the results depend on "chance" probabilities.[1] Of course, you know that there is nothing random about computers; they are instruction-following machines. How can computer programs model seemingly random happenings?

Simulating randomness is a well-studied problem in computer science. Remember the chaos program from Chapter 1? The numbers produced by that program seemed to jump around randomly between zero and one. This apparent randomness came from repeatedly applying a function to generate a sequence of numbers. A similar approach can be used to generate random (actually *pseudo random*) numbers.

A pseudo random number generator works by starting with some *seed* value. This value is fed to a function to produce a "random" number. The next time a random number is needed, the current value is fed back into the function to produce a new number. With a carefully chosen function, the resulting sequence of values looks essentially random. Of course, if you start the process over again with the same seed value, you end up with exactly the same sequence of numbers. It's all determined by the generating function and the value of the seed.

Python provides a library module that contains a number of useful functions for generating pseudo random numbers. The functions in this module derive an initial seed value from the date and time when the module is loaded, so you get a different seed value each time the program is run. This means that you will also get a unique sequence of pseudo random values. The two functions of greatest interest to us are `randrange` and `random`.

---

[1]So probabilistic simulations written in Python *could* be called Monte Python programs (nudge, nudge; wink,wink).

The randrange function is used to select a pseudo random int from a given range. It can be used with one, two, or three parameters to specify a range exactly as with the range function. For example, randrange(1,6) returns some number from the range [1,2,3,4,5], and randrange(5,105,5) returns a multiple of 5 between 5 and 100, inclusive. (Remember, ranges go up to, but do not include, the stopping value.)

Each call to randrange generates a new pseudo random int. Here is an interactive session that shows randrange in action:

```
>>> from random import randrange
>>> randrange(1,6)
3
>>> randrange(1,6)
3
>>> randrange(1,6)
5
>>> randrange(1,6)
5
>>> randrange(1,6)
5
>>> randrange(1,6)
1
>>> randrange(1,6)
5
>>> randrange(1,6)
4
>>> randrange(1,6)
2
```

Notice it took nine calls to randrange to eventually generate every number in the range 1–5. The value 5 came up almost half of the time. This shows the probabilistic nature of random numbers. Over the long haul, this function produces a uniform distribution, which means that all values will appear an (approximately) equal number of times.

The random function can be used to generate pseudo random floating point values. It takes no parameters and returns values uniformly distributed between 0 and 1 (including 0, but excluding 1). Here are some interactive examples:

```
>>> from random import random
>>> random()
```

```
0.545146406725
>>> random()
0.221621655814
>>> random()
0.928877335157
>>> random()
0.258660828538
>>> random()
0.859346793436
```

The name of the module (random) is the same as the name of the function, which gives rise to the funny-looking import line.

Our racquetball simulation can make use of the random function to determine whether or not a player wins a serve. Let's look at a specific example. Suppose a player's service probability is 0.70. This means that they should win 70% of their serves. You can imagine a decision in the program something like this:

```
if <player wins serve>:
    score = score + 1
```

We need to insert a probabilistic condition that will succeed 70% of the time.

Suppose we generate a random value between 0 and 1. Exactly 70% of the interval 0...1 is to the left of 0.7. So 70% of the time the random number will be < 0.7, and it will be ≥ 0.7 the other 30% of the time. (The = goes on the upper end, because the random generator can produce a 0, but never a 1.) In general, if prob represents the probability that the player wins a serve, the condition random() < prob will succeed with just the right probability. Here is how the decision will look:

```
if random() < prob:
    score = score + 1
```

9.3 Top-Down Design

Now you have the complete specification for our simulation and the necessary knowledge of random numbers to get the job done. Go ahead and take a few minutes to write up the program; I'll wait.

OK, seriously, this is a more complicated program than you've probably attempted so far. You may not even know where to begin. If you're going to make it through with minimal frustration, you'll need a systematic approach.

One proven technique for tackling complex problems is called *top-down design*. The basic idea is to start with the general problem and try to express a solution in terms of smaller problems. Then each of the smaller problems is attacked in turn using the same technique. Eventually the problems get so small that they are trivial to solve. Then you just put all the pieces back together and, voilà, you've got a program.

9.3.1 Top-Level Design

Top-down design is easier to illustrate than it is to define. Let's give it a try on our racquetball simulation and see where it takes us. As always, a good start is to study the program specification. In very broad brush strokes, this program follows the basic input, process, output pattern. We need to get the simulation inputs from the user, simulate a bunch of games, and print out a report. Here is a basic algorithm:

```
Print an Introduction
Get the inputs: probA, probB, n
Simulate n games of racquetball using probA and probB
Print a report on the wins for playerA and playerB
```

Now that we've got an algorithm, we're ready to write a program. I know what you're thinking: this design is too high-level; you don't have any idea yet how it's all going to work. That's OK. Whatever we don't know how to do, we'll just ignore for now. Imagine that all of the components you need to implement the algorithm have already been written for you. Your job is to finish this top-level algorithm using those components.

First we have to print an introduction. I think I know how to do this. It just requires a few print statements, but I don't really want to bother with it right now. It seems an unimportant part of the algorithm. I'll procrastinate and pretend that someone else will do it for me. Here's the beginning of the program:

```
def main():
    printIntro()
```

Do you see how this works? I'm just assuming there is a printIntro function that takes care of printing the instructions. That step was easy! Let's move on.

Next, I need to get some inputs from the user. I also know how to do that—I just need a few input statements. Again, that doesn't seem very interesting, and I feel like putting off the details. Let's assume that a component already exists to solve that problem. We'll call the function getInputs. The point of this function is to get values for variables probA, probB, and n. The function must return these values for the main program to use. Here is our program so far:

```
def main():
    printIntro()
    probA, probB, n = getInputs()
```

We're making progress, let's move on to the next line.

Here we've hit the crux of the problem. We need to simulate n games of racquetball using the values of probA and probB. This time, I really don't have a very good idea how that will even be accomplished. Let's procrastinate again and push the details off into a function. (Maybe we can get someone else to write that part for us later.) But what should we put into main? Let's call our function simNGames. We need to figure out what the call of this function looks like.

Suppose you were asking a friend to actually carry out a simulation of n games. What information would you have to give him? Your friend would need to know how many games he was supposed to simulate and what the values of probA and probB should be for those simulations. These three values will, in a sense, be inputs to the function.

What information do you need to get back from your friend? Well, in order to finish out the program (print a report) you need to know how many games were won by player A and how many games were won by Player B. These must be outputs from the simNGames function. Remember in the discussion of functions in Chapter 6, I said that parameters were used as function inputs, and return values serve as function outputs. Given this analysis, we now know how the next step of the algorithm can be coded.

```
def main():
    printIntro()
    probA, probB, n = getInputs()
    winsA, winsB = simNGames(n, probA, probB)
```

Are you getting the hang of this? The last step is to print a report. If you told your friend to type up the report, you would have to tell him how many wins there were for each player; these values are inputs to the function. Here's the complete program:

```
def main():
    printIntro()
    probA, probB, n = getInputs()
    winsA, winsB = simNGames(n, probA, probB)
    printSummary(winsA, winsB)
```

That wasn't very hard. The main function is only five lines long, and the program looks like a more precise formulation of the rough algorithm.

9.3.2 Separation of Concerns

Of course, the main function alone won't do very much; we've put off all of the interesting details. In fact, you may think that we have not yet accomplished anything at all, but that is far from true.

We have broken the original problem into four independent tasks: printIntro, getInputs, simNGames and printSummary. Further, we have specified the name, parameters, and expected return values of the functions that perform these tasks. This information is called the *interface* or *signature* of a function.

Having signatures allows us to tackle pieces independently. For the purposes of main, we don't care *how* simNGames does its job. The only concern is that, when given the number of games to simulate and the two probabilities, it must hand back the correct number of wins for each player. The main function only cares *what* each (sub-)function does.

Our work so far can be represented as a *structure chart* (also called a *module hierarchy chart*). Figure 9.1 illustrates this. Each component in the design is a rectangle. A line connecting two rectangles indicates that the one above uses the one below. The arrows and annotations show the interfaces between the components in terms of information flow.

At each level of a design, the interface tells us which details of the lower level are important. Anything else can be ignored (for the moment). The general process of determining the important characteristics of something and ignoring other details is called *abstraction*. Abstraction is *the* fundamental tool of design. You might view the entire process of top-down design as a systematic method for discovering useful abstractions.

9.3.3 Second-Level Design

Now all we need to do is repeat the design process for each of the remaining components. Let's take them in order. The printIntro function should print

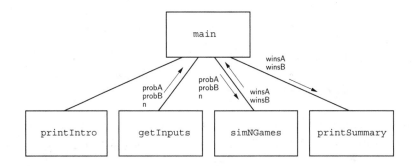

Figure 9.1: First-level structure chart for racquetball simulation

an introduction to the program. Let's compose a suitable sequence of `print` statements.

```
def printIntro():
    print("This program simulates a game of racquetball between two")
    print('players called "A" and "B".  The abilities of each player is')
    print("indicated by a probability (a number between 0 and 1) that")
    print("the player wins the point when serving. Player A always")
    print("has the first serve.")
```

Notice the second line. I wanted to put double quotes around "A" and "B" so that the entire string is enclosed in apostrophes. This function comprises only primitive Python instructions. Since we didn't introduce any new functions, there is no change to our structure chart.

Now let's tackle `getInputs`. We need to prompt for and get three values, which are returned to the main program. Again, this is simple to code.

```
def getInputs():
    # Returns the three simulation parameters probA, probB and n
    a = eval(input("What is the prob. player A wins a serve? "))
    b = eval(input("What is the prob. player B wins a serve? "))
    n = eval(input("How many games to simulate? "))
    return a, b, n
```

Notice that I have taken some shortcuts with the variable names. Remember, variables inside a function are local to that function. This function is so short, it's very easy to see what the three values represent. The main concern here is to make sure the values are returned in the correct order to match with the interface we established between `getInputs` and `main`.

9.3.4 Designing simNGames

Now that we are getting some experience with the top-down design technique, we are ready to try our hand at the real problem, `simNGames`. This one requires a bit more thought. The basic idea is to simulate n games and keep track of how many wins there are for each player. Well, "simulate n games" sounds like a counted loop, and tracking wins sounds like the job for a couple of accumulators. Using our familiar patterns, we can piece together an algorithm.

```
Initialize winsA and winsB to 0
loop n times
    simulate a game
    if playerA wins
        Add one to winsA
    else
        Add one to winsB
```

It's a pretty rough design, but then so was our top-level algorithm. We'll fill in the details by turning it into Python code.

Remember, we already have the signature for our function.

```
def simNGames(n, probA, probB):
    # Simulates n games and returns winsA and winsB
```

We'll add to this by initializing the two accumulator variables and adding the counted loop heading.

```
def simNGames(n, probA, probB):
    # Simulates n games and returns winsA and winsB
    winsA = 0
    winsB = 0
    for i in range(n):
```

The next step in the algorithm calls for simulating a game of racquetball. I'm not quite sure how to do that, so as usual, I'll put off the details. Let's just assume there's a function called `simOneGame` to take care of this.

We need to figure out what the interface for this function will be. The inputs for the function seem straightforward. In order to accurately simulate a game, we need to know what the probabilities are for each player. But what should the output be? In the next step of the algorithm, we will need to know who won the game. How do you know who won? Generally, you look at the final score.

Let's have `simOneGame` return the final scores for the two players. We can update our structure chart to reflect these decisions. The result is shown in Figure 9.2. Translating this structure into code yields this nearly completed function:

```
def simNGames(n, probA, probB):
    # Simulates n games and returns winsA and winsB
    winsA = 0
    winsB = 0
    for i in range(n):
        scoreA, scoreB = simOneGame(probA, probB)
```

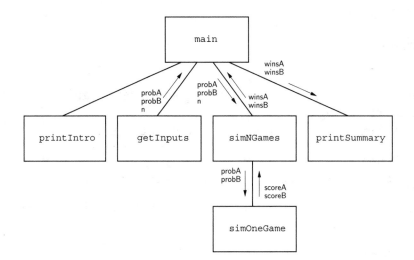

Figure 9.2: Level 2 structure chart for racquetball simulation

Finally, we need to check the scores to see who won and update the appropriate accumulator. Here is the result:

```
def simNGames(n, probA, probB):
    winsA = winsB = 0
    for i in range(n):
```

```
        scoreA, scoreB = simOneGame(probA, probB)
        if scoreA > scoreB:
            winsA = winsA + 1
        else:
            winsB = winsB + 1
    return winsA, winsB
```

9.3.5 Third-Level Design

Everything seems to be coming together nicely. Let's keep working on the guts of the simulation. The next obvious point of attack is simOneGame. Here's where we actually have to code up the logic of the racquetball rules. Players keep doing rallies until the game is over. That suggests some kind of indefinite loop structure; we don't know how many rallies it will take before one of the players gets to 15. The loop just keeps going until the game is over.

Along the way, we need to keep track of the score(s), and we also need to know who is currently serving. The scores will probably just be a couple of int-valued accumulators, but how do we keep track of who's serving? It's either player A or player B. One approach is to use a string variable that stores either "A" or "B". It's also an accumulator of sorts, but to update its value we just switch it from one value to the other.

That's enough analysis to put together a rough algorithm. Let's try this:

```
Initialize scores to 0
Set serving to "A"
Loop while game is not over:
    Simulate one serve of whichever player is serving
    update the status of the game
Return scores
```

It's a start, at least. Clearly there's still some work to be done on this one.

We can quickly fill in the first couple of steps of the algorithm to get the following:

```
def simOneGame(probA, probB):
    scoreA = 0
    scoreB = 0
    serving = "A"
    while <condition>:
```

The question at this point is exactly what the condition will be. We need to keep looping as long as the game is not over. We should be able to tell if the game is over by looking at the scores. We discussed a number of possibilities for this condition in the previous chapter, some of which were fairly complex. Let's hide the details in another function, gameOver, that looks at the scores and returns True if the game is over, and False if it is not. That gets us on to the rest of the loop for now.

Figure 9.3 shows the structure chart with our new function. The code for simOneGame now looks like this:

```
def simOneGame(probA, probB):
    scoreA = 0
    scoreB = 0
    serving = "A"
    while not gameOver(scoreA, scoreB):
```

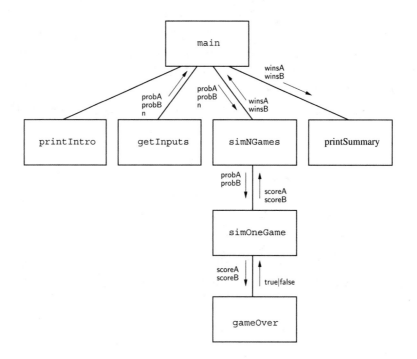

Figure 9.3: Level 3 structure chart for racquetball simulation

Inside the loop, we need to do a single serve. Remember, we are going to compare a random number to a probability in order to determine if the server wins the point (random() < prob). The correct probability to use is determined by the value of serving. We will need a decision based on this value. If A is serving, then we need to use A's probability, and, based on the result of the serve, update either A's score or change the service to B. Here is the code:

```
if serving == "A":
    if random() < probA:  # A wins the serve
        scoreA = scoreA + 1
    else:                 # A loses the serve
        serving = "B"
```

Of course, if A is not serving, we need to do the same thing, only for B. We just need to attach a mirror image else clause.

```
if serving == "A":
    if random() < probA:     # A wins the serve
        scoreA = scoreA + 1
    else:                    # A loses serve
        serving = "B"
else:
    if random() < probB:     # B wins the serve
        scoreB = scoreB + 1
    else:                    # B loses the serve
        serving = "A"
```

That pretty much completes the function. It got a bit complicated, but seems to reflect the rules of the simulation as they were laid out. Putting the function together, here is the result:

```
def simOneGame(probA, probB):
    scoreA = 0
    scoreB = 0
    serving = "A"
    while not gameOver(scoreA, scoreB):
        if serving == "A":
            if random() < probA:
                scoreA = scoreA + 1
            else:
```

```
                serving = "B"
        else:
            if random() < probB:
                scoreB = scoreB + 1
            else:
                serving = "A"
    return scoreA, scoreB
```

9.3.6 Finishing Up

Whew! We have just one more troublesome function left, gameOver. Here is what we know about it so far:

```
def gameOver(a,b):
    # a and b represent scores for a racquetball game
    # Returns True if the game is over, False otherwise.
```

According to the rules for our simulation, a game is over when either player reaches a total of 15. We can check this with a simple Boolean condition.

```
def gameOver(a,b):
    # a and b represent scores for a racquetball game
    # Returns True if the game is over, False otherwise.
    return a==15 or b==15
```

Notice how this function directly computes and returns the Boolean result all in one step.

We've done it! Except for printSummary, the program is complete. Let's fill in the missing details and call it a wrap. Here is the complete program from start to finish:

```
# rball.py
from random import random

def main():
    printIntro()
    probA, probB, n = getInputs()
    winsA, winsB = simNGames(n, probA, probB)
    printSummary(winsA, winsB)

def printIntro():
```

```
    print("This program simulates a game of racquetball between two")
    print('players called "A" and "B".  The abilities of each player is')
    print("indicated by a probability (a number between 0 and 1) that")
    print("the player wins the point when serving. Player A always")
    print("has the first serve.")

def getInputs():
    # Returns the three simulation parameters
    a = eval(input("What is the prob. player A wins a serve? "))
    b = eval(input("What is the prob. player B wins a serve? "))
    n = eval(input("How many games to simulate? "))
    return a, b, n

def simNGames(n, probA, probB):
    # Simulates n games of racquetball between players whose
    #    abilities are represented by the probability of winning a serve.
    # Returns number of wins for A and B
    winsA = winsB = 0
    for i in range(n):
        scoreA, scoreB = simOneGame(probA, probB)
        if scoreA > scoreB:
            winsA = winsA + 1
        else:
            winsB = winsB + 1
    return winsA, winsB

def simOneGame(probA, probB):
    # Simulates a single game or racquetball between players whose
    #    abilities are represented by the probability of winning a serve.
    # Returns final scores for A and B
    serving = "A"
    scoreA = 0
    scoreB = 0
    while not gameOver(scoreA, scoreB):
        if serving == "A":
            if random() < probA:
                scoreA = scoreA + 1
            else:
```

```
                    serving = "B"
          else:
              if random() < probB:
                  scoreB = scoreB + 1
              else:
                  serving = "A"
      return scoreA, scoreB

def gameOver(a, b):
    # a and b represent scores for a racquetball game
    # Returns True if the game is over, False otherwise.
    return a==15 or b==15

def printSummary(winsA, winsB):
    # Prints a summary of wins for each player.
    n = winsA + winsB
    print("\nGames simulated:", n)
    print("Wins for A: {0} ({1:0.1%})".format(winsA, winsA/n))
    print("Wins for B: {0} ({1:0.1%})".format(winsB, winsB/n))

if __name__ == '__main__': main()
```

You might take notice of the string formatting in printSummary. The type specifier % is useful for printing percentages. Python automatically multiplies the number by 100 and adds a trailing percent sign.

9.3.7   Summary of the Design Process

You have just seen an example of top-down design in action. Now you can really see why it's called top-down design. We started at the highest level of our structure chart and worked our way down. At each level, we began with a general algorithm and then gradually refined it into precise code. This approach is sometimes called *step-wise refinement*. The whole process can be summarized in four steps:

1. Express the algorithm as a series of smaller problems.

2. Develop an interface for each of the small problems.

3. Detail the algorithm by expressing it in terms of its interfaces with the smaller problems.

4. Repeat the process for each smaller problem.

Top-down design is an invaluable tool for developing complex algorithms. The process may seem easy, since I've walked you through it step by step. When you first try it out for yourself, though, things probably won't go quite so smoothly. Stay with it—the more you do it, the easier it will get. Initially, you may think writing all of those functions is a lot of trouble. The truth is, developing any sophisticated system is virtually impossible without a modular approach. Keep at it, and soon expressing your own programs in terms of cooperating functions will become second nature.

9.4 Bottom-Up Implementation

Now that we've got a program in hand, your inclination might be to run off, type the whole thing in, and give it a try. If you do that, the result will probably be disappointment and frustration. Even though we have been very careful in our design, there is no guarantee that we haven't introduced some silly errors. Even if the code is flawless, you'll probably make some mistakes when you enter it. Just as designing a program one piece at a time is easier than trying to tackle the whole problem at once, implementation is best approached in small doses.

9.4.1 Unit Testing

A good way to approach the implementation of a modest size program is to start at the lowest levels of the structure chart and work your way up, testing each component as you complete it. Looking back at the structure chart for our simulation, we could start with the gameOver function. Once this function is typed into a module file, we can immediately import the file and test it. Here is a sample session testing out just this function:

```
>>> import rball
>>> rball1.gameOver(0,0)
False
>>> rball1.gameOver(5,10)
False
>>> rball1.gameOver(15,3)
True
>>> rball1.gameOver(3,15)
True
```

I have selected test data that tries all the important cases for the function. The first time it is called, the score will be 0 to 0. The function correctly responds with `False`; the game is not over. As the game progresses, the function will be called with intermediate scores. The second example shows that the function again responded that the game is still in progress. The last two examples show that the function correctly identifies that the game is over when either player reaches 15.

Having confidence that `gameOver` is functioning correctly, now we can go back and implement the `simOneGame` function. This function has some probabilistic behavior, so I'm not sure exactly what the output will be. The best we can do in testing it is to see that it behaves reasonably. Here is a sample session:

```
>>> import rball
>>> rball1.simOneGame(.5,.5)
(13, 15)
>>> rball1.simOneGame(.5,.5)
(15, 11)
>>> rball1.simOneGame(.3,.3)
(15, 11)
>>> rball1.simOneGame(.3,.3)
(11, 15)
>>> rball1.simOneGame(.4,.9)
(4, 15)
>>> rball1.simOneGame(.4,.9)
(1, 15)
>>> rball1.simOneGame(.9,.4)
(15, 3)
>>> rball1.simOneGame(.9,.4)
(15, 0)
>>> rball1.simOneGame(.4,.6)
(9, 15)
>>> rball1.simOneGame(.4,.6)
(6, 15)
```

Notice that when the probabilities are equal, the scores are close. When the probabilities are farther apart, the game is a rout. That squares with how we think this function should behave.

We can continue this piecewise implementation, testing out each component as we add it into the code. Software engineers call this process *unit testing*.

Testing each function independently makes it easier to spot errors. By the time you get around to testing the entire program, chances are that everything will work smoothly.

Separating concerns through a modular design makes it possible to design sophisticated programs. Separating concerns through unit testing makes it possible to implement and debug sophisticated programs. Try these techniques for yourself, and you'll see that you are getting your programs working with less overall effort and far less frustration.

9.4.2 Simulation Results

Finally, we can take a look at Denny Dibblebit's question. Is it the nature of racquetball that small differences in ability lead to large differences in the outcome? Suppose Denny wins about 60% of his serves and his opponent is 5% better. How often should Denny win the game? Here's an example run where Denny's opponent always serves first.

```
This program simulates a game of racquetball between two
players called "A" and "B".  The abilities of each player is
indicated by a probability (a number between 0 and 1) that
the player wins the point when serving. Player A always
has the first serve.

What is the prob. player A wins a serve? .65
What is the prob. player B wins a serve? .6
How many games to simulate? 5000

Games simulated: 5000
Wins for A: 3360 (67.2%)
Wins for B: 1640 (32.8%)
```

Even though there is only a small difference in ability, Denny should win only about one in three games. His chances of winning a three- or five-game match are pretty slim. Apparently, Denny is winning his share. He should skip the shrink and work harder on his game.

Speaking of matches, expanding this program to compute the probability of winning multi-game matches would be a great exercise. Why don't you give it a try?

9.5 Other Design Techniques

Top-down design is a very powerful technique for program design, but it is not the only way to go about creating a program. Sometimes you may get stuck at a step and not know how to go about refining it. Or the original specification might be so complicated that refining it level-by-level is just too daunting.

9.5.1 Prototyping and Spiral Development

Another approach to design is to start with a simple version of a program or program component and then try to gradually add features until it meets the full specification. The initial stripped-down version is called a *prototype*. Prototyping often leads to a sort of *spiral* development process. Rather than taking the entire problem and proceeding through specification, design, implementation, and testing, we first design, implement, and test a prototype. Then new features are designed, implemented, and tested. We make many mini-cycles through the development process as the prototype is incrementally expanded into the final program.

As an example, consider how we might have approached the racquetball simulation. The very essence of the problem is simulating a game of racquetball. We might have started with just the simOneGame function. Simplifying even further, our prototype could assume that each player has a 50-50 chance of winning any given point and just play a series of 30 rallies. That leaves the crux of the problem, which is handling the awarding of points and change of service. Here is an example prototype:

```
from random import random

def simOneGame():
    scoreA = 0
    scoreB = 0
    serving = "A"
    for i in range(30):
        if serving == "A":
            if random() < .5:
                scoreA = scoreA + 1
            else:
                serving = "B"
        else:
```

```
        if random() < .5:
            scoreB = scoreB + 1
        else:
            serving = "A"
    print(scoreA, scoreB)

if __name__ == '__main__': simOneGame()
```

You can see that I have added a print statement at the bottom of the loop. Printing out the scores as we go along allows us to see that the prototype is playing a game. Here is some example output:

```
1 0
1 0
2 0
...
7 7
7 8
```

It's not pretty, but it shows that we have gotten the scoring and change of service working.

We could then work on augmenting the program in phases. Here's a project plan:

Phase 1 Initial prototype. Play 30 rallies where the server always has a 50% chance of winning. Print out the scores after each serve.

Phase 2 Add two parameters to represent different probabilities for the two players.

Phase 3 Play the game until one of the players reaches 15 points. At this point, we have a working simulation of a single game.

Phase 4 Expand to play multiple games. The output is the count of games won by each player.

Phase 5 Build the complete program. Add interactive inputs and a nicely formatted report of the results.

Spiral development is particularly useful when dealing with new or unfamiliar features or technologies. It's helpful to "get your hands dirty" with a quick prototype just to see what you can do. As a novice programmer, everything may seem new to you, so prototyping might prove useful. If full-blown top-down design does not seem to be working for you, try some spiral development.

9.5.2   The Art of Design

It is important to note that spiral development is not an alternative to top-down design. Rather, they are complementary approaches. When designing the prototype, you will still use top-down techniques. In Chapter 12, you will see yet another approach called object-oriented design.

There is no "one true way" of design. The truth is that good design is as much a creative process as a science. Designs can be meticulously analyzed after the fact, but there are no hard-and-fast rules for producing a design. The best software designers seem to employ a variety of techniques. You can learn about techniques by reading books like this one, but books can't teach how and when to apply them. That you have to learn for yourself through experience. In design, as in almost anything, the key to success is *practice*.

9.6   Chapter Summary

- Computer simulation is a powerful technique for answering questions about real-world processes. Simulation techniques that rely on probabilistic or chance events are known as Monte Carlo simulations. Computers use pseudo random numbers to perform Monte Carlo simulations.

- Top-down design is a technique for designing complex programs. The basic steps are:

  1. Express an algorithm in terms of smaller problems.
  2. Develop an interface for each of the smaller problems.
  3. Express the algorithm in terms of its interfaces with the smaller problems.
  4. Repeat the process for each of the smaller problems.

- Top-down design was illustrated by the development of a program to simulate the game of racquetball.

- Unit-testing is the process of trying out each component of a larger program independently. Unit-testing and bottom-up implementation are useful in coding complex programs.

- Spiral development is the process of first creating a simple version (prototype) of a complex program and gradually adding more features. Prototyping and spiral development are often useful in conjunction with top-down design.

- Design is a combination of art and science. Practice is the best way to become a better designer.

9.7 | Exercises

Review Questions

True/False

1. Computers can generate truly random numbers.

2. The Python `random` function returns a pseudo random int.

3. Top-down design is also called stepwise refinement.

4. In top-down design, the main algorithm is written in terms of functions that don't yet exist.

5. The `main` function is at the top of a functional structure chart.

6. A top-down design is best implemented from the top down.

7. Unit-testing is the process of trying out a component of a larger program in isolation.

8. A developer should use either top-down or spiral design, but not both.

9. Reading design books alone will make you a great designer.

10. A simplified version of a program is called a simulation.

Multiple Choice

1. Which expression is true approximately 66% of the time?
   a) `random() >= 66`   c) `random() < 66`
   b) `random() < 0.66`   d) `random() >= 0.66`

2. Which of the following is *not* a step in pure top-down design?
   a) Repeat the process on smaller problems.
   b) Detail the algorithm in terms of its interfaces with smaller problems.
   c) Construct a simplified prototype of the system.
   d) Express the algorithm in terms of smaller problems.

3. A graphical view of the dependencies among components of a design is called a(n)
   a) flowchart   b) prototype   c) interface   d) structure chart

4. The arrows in a module hierarchy chart depict
   a) information flow   b) control flow   c) sticky-note attachment
   d) one-way streets

5. In top-down design, the subcomponents of the design are
   a) objects   b) loops   c) functions   d) programs

6. A simulation that uses probabilistic events is called
   a) Monte Carlo   b) pseudo random   c) Monty Python   d) chaotic

7. The initial version of a system used in spiral development is called a
   a) starter kit   b) prototype   c) mock-up   d) beta-version

8. In the racquetball simulation, what data type is returned by the gameOver function?
   a) bool   b) int   c) string   d) float

9. How is a percent sign indicated in a string formatting template?
   a) %   b) \%   c) %%   d) \%%

10. The easiest place in a system structure to start unit-testing is
    a) the top   b) the bottom   c) the middle   d) the main function

Discussion

1. Draw the top levels of a structure chart for a program having the following main function:

```
def main():
    printIntro()
    length, width = getDimensions()
    amtNeeded = computeAmount(length,width)
```

```
printReport(length, width, amtNeeded)
```

2. Write an expression using either `random` or `randrange` to calculate the following:

   - A random int in the range 0–10
   - A random float in the range -0.5–0.5
   - A random number representing the roll of a six-sided die
   - A random number representing the *sum* resulting from rolling two six-sided dice
   - A random float in the range -10.0–10.0

3. In your own words, describe what factors might lead a designer to choose spiral development over a top-down approach.

Programming Exercises

1. Revise the racquetball simulation so that it computes the results for best of n game matches. First service alternates, so player A serves first in the odd games of the match, and player B serves first in the even games.

2. Revise the racquetball simulation to take shutouts into account. Your updated version should report for both players the number of wins, percentage of wins, number of shutouts, and percentage of wins that are shutouts.

3. Design and implement a simulation of the game of volleyball. Normal volleyball is played like racquetball, in that a team can only score points when it is serving. Games are played to 15, but must be won by at least two points.

4. Most sanctioned volleyball is now played using rally scoring. In this system, the team that wins a rally is awarded a point, even if they were not the serving team. Games are played to a score of 25. Design and implement a simulation of volleyball using rally scoring.

5. Design and implement a system that compares regular volleyball games to those using rally scoring. Your program should be able to investigate whether rally scoring magnifies, reduces, or has no effect on the relative advantage enjoyed by the better team.

6. Design and implement a simulation of some other racquet sport (e.g., tennis or table tennis).

7. Craps is a dice game played at many casinos. A player rolls a pair of normal six-sided dice. If the initial roll is 2, 3, or 12, the player loses. If the roll is 7 or 11, the player wins. Any other initial roll causes the player to "roll for point." That is, the player keeps rolling the dice until either rolling a 7 or re-rolling the value of the initial roll. If the player re-rolls the initial value before rolling a 7, it's a win. Rolling a 7 first is a loss.

    Write a program to simulate multiple games of craps and estimate the probability that the player wins. For example, if the player wins 249 out of 500 games, then the estimated probability of winning is $249/500 = 0.498$

8. Blackjack (twenty-one) is a casino game played with cards. The goal of the game is to draw cards that total as close to 21 points as possible without going over. All face cards count as 10 points, aces count as 1 or 11, and all other cards count their numeric value.

    The game is played against a dealer. The player tries to get closer to 21 (without going over) than the dealer. If the dealer busts (goes over 21), the player automatically wins (provided the player had not already busted). The dealer must always take cards according to a fixed set of rules. The dealer takes cards until he or she achieves a total of at least 17. If the dealer's hand contains an ace, it will be counted as 11 when that results in a total between 17 and 21 inclusive; otherwise, the ace is counted as 1.

    Write a program that simulates multiple games of blackjack and estimates the probability that the dealer will bust. Hints: treat the deck of cards as infinite (casinos use a "shoe" containing many decks). You do not need to keep track of the cards in the hand, just the total so far (treating an ace as 1) and a bool variable hasAce that tells whether or not the hand contains an ace. A hand containing an ace should have 10 points added to the total exactly when doing so would produce a stopping total (something between 17 and 21 inclusive).

9. A blackjack dealer always starts with one card showing. It would be useful for a player to know the dealer's bust probability (see previous problem) for each possible starting value. Write a simulation program that runs multiple hands of blackjack for each possible starting value (ace–10) and estimates the probability that the dealer busts for each starting value.

10. Monte Carlo techniques can be used to estimate the value of pi. Suppose you have a round dart board that just fits inside of a square cabinet. If you throw darts randomly, the proportion that hit the dart board vs. those that hit the cabinet (in the corners not covered by the board) will be determined by the relative area of the dart board and the cabinet. If n is the total number of darts randomly thrown (that land within the confines of the cabinet), and h is the number that hit the board, it is easy to show that

$$\pi \approx 4(\frac{h}{n})$$

Write a program that accepts the "number of darts" as an input and then performs a simulation to estimate π. Hint: you can use 2*random() - 1 to generate the x and y coordinates of a random point inside a 2x2 square centered at $(0, 0)$. The point lies inside the inscribed circle if $x^2 + y^2 \leq 1$.

11. Write a program that performs a simulation to estimate the probability of rolling five-of-a-kind in a single roll of five six-sided dice.

12. A *random walk* is a particular kind of probabilistic simulation that models certain statistical systems such as the Brownian motion of molecules. You can think of a one-dimensional random walk in terms of coin flipping. Suppose you are standing on a very long straight sidewalk that extends both in front of and behind you. You flip a coin. If it comes up heads, you take a step forward; tails means to take a step backward.

    Suppose you take a random walk of n steps. On average, how many steps away from the starting point will you end up? Write a program to help you investigate this question.

13. Suppose you are doing a random walk (see previous problem) on the blocks of a city street. At each "step" you choose to walk one block (at random) either forward, backward, left or right. In n steps, how far do you expect to be from your starting point? Write a program to help answer this question.

14. Write a graphical program to trace a random walk (see previous two problems) in two dimensions. In this simulation you should allow the step to be taken in *any* direction. You can generate a random direction as an angle off of the x axis.

```
angle = random() * 2 * math.pi
```

The new x and y positions are then given by these formulas:

```
x = x + cos(angle)
y = y + sin(angle)
```

The program should take the number of steps as an input. Start your walker at the center of a 100x100 grid and draw a line that traces the walk as it progresses.

15. (Advanced) Here is a puzzle problem that can be solved with either some fancy analytic geometry (calculus) or a (relatively) simple simulation.

Suppose you are located at the exact center of a cube. If you could look all around you in every direction, each wall of the cube would occupy $\frac{1}{6}$ of your field of vision. Suppose you move toward one of the walls so that you are now half-way between it and the center of the cube. What fraction of your field of vision is now taken up by the closest wall? Hint: use a Monte Carlo simulation that repeatedly "looks" in a random direction and counts how many times it sees the wall.

Chapter 10

Defining Classes

Objectives

- To appreciate how defining new classes can provide structure for a complex program.

- To be able to read and write Python class definitions.

- To understand the concept of encapsulation and how it contributes to building modular and maintainable programs.

- To be able to write programs involving simple class definitions.

- To be able to write interactive graphics programs involving novel (programmer designed) widgets.

10.1 Quick Review of Objects

In the last three chapters, we have developed techniques for structuring the *computations* of a program. In the next few chapters, we will take a look at techniques for structuring the *data* that our programs use. You already know that objects are one important tool for managing complex data. So far, our programs have made use of objects created from pre-defined classes such as `Circle`. In this chapter, you will learn how to write your own classes so that you can create novel objects.

Remember back in Chapter 4 I defined an *object* as an active data type that knows stuff and can do stuff. More precisely, an object consists of

1. A collection of related information.

2. A set of operations to manipulate that information.

The information is stored inside the object in *instance variables*. The operations, called *methods*, are functions that "live" inside the object. Collectively, the instance variables and methods are called the *attributes* of an object.

To take a now-familiar example, a `Circle` object will have instance variables such as `center`, which remembers the center point of the circle, and `radius`, which stores the length of the circle's radius. The methods of the circle will need this data to perform actions. The `draw` method examines the `center` and `radius` to decide which pixels in a window should be colored. The `move` method will change the value of `center` to reflect the new position of the circle.

Recall that every object is said to be an *instance* of some *class*. The class of the object determines what attributes the object will have. Basically a class is a description of what its instances will know and do. New objects are created from a class by invoking a *constructor*. You can think of the class itself as a sort of factory for stamping out new instances.

Consider making a new circle object:

```
myCircle = Circle(Point(0,0), 20)
```

`Circle`, the name of the class, is used to invoke the constructor. This statement creates a new `Circle` instance and stores a reference to it in the variable `myCircle`. The parameters to the constructor are used to initialize some of the instance variables (namely `center` and `radius`) inside `myCircle`. Once the instance has been created, it is manipulated by calling on its methods:

```
myCircle.draw(win)
myCircle.move(dx, dy)
. . .
```

10.2   Example Program: Cannonball

Before launching into a detailed discussion of how to write your own classes, let's take a short detour to see how useful new classes can be.

10.2.1   Program Specification

Suppose we want to write a program that simulates the flight of a cannonball (or any other projectile such as a bullet, baseball, or shot put). We are particularly interested in finding out how far the cannonball will travel when fired at various launch angles and initial velocities. The input to the program will be the launch angle (in degrees), the initial velocity (in meters per second), and the initial height (in meters) of the cannonball. The output will be the distance that the projectile travels before striking the ground (in meters).

If we ignore the effects of wind resistance and assume that the cannonball stays close to earth's surface (i.e., we're not trying to put it into orbit), this is a relatively simple classical physics problem. The acceleration of gravity near the earth's surface is about 9.8 meters per second, per second. That means if an object is thrown upward at a speed of 20 meters per second, after one second has passed, its upward speed will have slowed to $20 - 9.8 = 10.2$ meters per second. After another second, the speed will be only 0.4 meters per second, and shortly thereafter it will start coming back down.

For those who know a little bit of calculus, it's not hard to derive a formula that gives the position of our cannonball at any given moment in its flight. Rather than take the calculus approach, however, our program will use simulation to track the cannonball moment by moment. Using just a bit of simple trigonometry to get started, along with the obvious relationship that the distance an object travels in a given amount of time is equal to its rate times the amount of time ($d = rt$), we can solve this problem algorithmically.

10.2.2 Designing the Program

Let's start by designing an algorithm for this problem. Given the problem statement, it's clear that we need to consider the flight of the cannonball in two dimensions: height, so we know when it hits the ground; and distance, to keep track of how far it goes. We can think of the position of the cannonball as a point (x, y) in a 2D graph where the value of y gives the height above the ground and the value of x gives the distance from the starting point.

Our simulation will have to update the position of the cannonball to account for its flight. Suppose the ball starts at position $(0, 0)$, and we want to check its position, say, every tenth of a second. In that interval, it will have moved some distance upward (positive y) and some distance forward (positive x). The exact distance in each dimension is determined by its velocity in that direction.

Separating out the x and y components of the velocity makes the problem easier. Since we are ignoring wind resistance, the x velocity remains constant for the entire flight. However, the y velocity changes over time due to the influence of gravity. In fact, the y velocity will start out being positive and then become negative as the cannonball starts back down.

Given this analysis, it's pretty clear what our simulation will have to do. Here is a rough outline:

```
Input the simulation parameters: angle, velocity, height, interval.
Calculate the initial position of the cannonball: xpos, ypos
Calculate the initial velocities of the cannonball: xvel, yvel
While the cannonball is still flying:
    update the values of xpos, ypos, and yvel for interval seconds
        further into the flight
Output the distance traveled as xpos
```

Let's turn this into a program using stepwise refinement.

The first line of the algorithm is straightforward. We just need an appropriate sequence of input statements. Here's a start:

```
def main():
    angle = eval(input("Enter the launch angle (in degrees): "))
    vel = eval(input("Enter the initial velocity (in meters/sec): "))
    h0 = eval(input("Enter the initial height (in meters): "))
    time = eval(input(
            "Enter the time interval between position calculations: "))
```

Calculating the initial position for the cannonball is also easy. It will start at distance 0 and height h0. We just need a couple of assignment statements.

```
    xpos = 0.0
    ypos = h0
```

Next we need to calculate the x and y components of the initial velocity. We'll need a little high-school trigonometry. (See, they told you you'd use that some day.) If we consider the initial velocity as consisting of some amount of change in y and some amount of change in x, then these three components (velocity, x-velocity and y-velocity) form a right triangle. Figure 10.1 illustrates the situation. If we know the magnitude of the velocity and the launch angle (labeled *theta*, because the Greek letter θ is often used as the measure of angles), we can easily calculate the magnitude of $xvel$ by the equation $xvel = velocity \cos theta$. A similar formula (using $\sin theta$) provides $yvel$.

Even if you don't completely understand the trigonometry, the important thing is that we can translate these formulas into Python code. There's still one subtle issue to consider. Our input angle is in degrees, and the Python math library uses radian measures. We'll have to convert our angle before applying

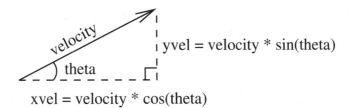

Figure 10.1: Finding the x and y components of velocity

the formulas. There are 2π radians in a circle (360 degrees); so $theta = \frac{\pi*angle}{180}$. This is such a common conversion that the math library provides a convenient function called `radians` that does this computation. These three formulas give us the code for computing the initial velocities:

```
theta = math.radians(angle)
xvel = velocity * math.cos(theta)
yvel = velocity * math.sin(theta)
```

That brings us to the main loop in our program. We want to keep updating the position and velocity of the cannonball until it reaches the ground. We can do this by examining the value of ypos.

```
while ypos >= 0.0:
```

I used $>=$ as the relationship so that we can start with the cannonball on the ground ($= 0$) and still get the loop going. The loop will quit as soon as the value of ypos dips just below 0, indicating the cannonball has embedded itself slightly in the ground.

Now we arrive at the crux of the simulation. Each time we go through the loop, we want to update the state of the cannonball to move it `time` seconds farther in its flight. Let's start by considering movement in the horizontal direction. Since our specification says that we can ignore wind resistance, the horizontal speed of the cannonball will remain constant and is given by the value of `xvel`.

As a concrete example, suppose the ball is traveling at 30 meters per second and is currently 50 meters from the firing point. In another second, it will go 30 more meters and be 80 meters from the firing point. If the interval is only 0.1 second (rather than a full second), then the cannonball will only fly another $0.1(30) = 3$ meters and be at a distance of 53 meters. You can see that the distance traveled is always given by `time * xvel`. To update the horizontal position, we need just one statement:

```
xpos = xpos + time * xvel
```

The situation for the vertical component is slightly more complicated, since gravity causes the y-velocity to change over time. Each second, `yvel` must decrease by 9.8 meters per second, the acceleration of gravity. In 0.1 seconds the velocity will decrease by $0.1(9.8) = 0.98$ meters per second. The new velocity at the *end* of the interval is calculated as

```
yvel1 = yvel - time * 9.8
```

To calculate how far the cannonball travels during this interval, we need to know its *average* vertical velocity. Since the acceleration due to gravity is constant, the average velocity will just be the average of the starting and ending velocities: `(yvel+yvel1)/2.0`. Multiplying this average velocity by the amount of time in the interval gives us the change in height.

Here is the completed loop:

```
while ypos >= 0.0:
    xpos = xpos + time * xvel
    yvel1 = yvel - time * 9.8
    ypos = ypos + time * (yvel + yvel1)/2.0
    yvel = yvel1
```

Notice how the velocity at the end of the time interval is first stored in the temporary variable `yvel1`. This is done to preserve the initial `yvel` so that the average velocity can be computed from the two values. Finally, the value of `yvel` is assigned its new value at the end of the loop. This represents the correct vertical velocity of the cannonball at the end of the interval.

The last step of our program simply outputs the distance traveled. Adding this step gives us the complete program.

```
# cball1.py
from math import sin, cos, radians

def main():
    angle = eval(input("Enter the launch angle (in degrees): "))
    vel = eval(input("Enter the initial velocity (in meters/sec): "))
    h0 = eval(input("Enter the initial height (in meters): "))
```

```
time = eval(input(
        "Enter the time interval between position calculations: "))

# convert angle to radians
theta = radians(angle)

# set the initial position and velocities in x and y directions
xpos = 0
ypos = h0
xvel = vel * cos(theta)
yvel = vel * sin(theta)

# loop until the ball hits the ground
while ypos >= 0.0:
    # calculate position and velocity in time seconds
    xpos = xpos + time * xvel
    yvel1 = yvel - time * 9.8
    ypos = ypos + time * (yvel + yvel1)/2.0
    yvel = yvel1

print("\nDistance traveled: {0:0.1f} meters.".format(xpos))
```

10.2.3 Modularizing the Program

You may have noticed during the design discussion that I employed stepwise
refinement (top-down design) to develop the program, but I did not divide the
program into separate functions. We are going to modularize the program in
two different ways. First, we'll use functions (á la top-down design).

While the final program is not too long, it is fairly complex for its length.
One cause of the complexity is that it uses ten variables, and that is a lot for the
reader to keep track of. Let's try dividing the program into functional pieces to
see if that helps. Here's a version of the main algorithm using helper functions:

```
def main():
    angle, vel, h0, time = getInputs()
    xpos, ypos = 0, h0
    xvel, yvel = getXYComponents(vel, angle)
    while ypos >= 0:
        xpos, ypos, yvel = updateCannonBall(time, xpos, ypos, xvel, yvel)
    print("\nDistance traveled: {0:0.1f} meters.".format(xpos))
```

It should be obvious what each of these functions does based on their names
and the original program code. You might take a couple of minutes to code the
three helper functions.

This second version of the main algorithm is certainly more concise. The
number of variables has been reduced to eight, since theta and yvel1 have been
eliminated from the main algorithm. Do you see where they went? The value
of theta is only needed locally inside of getXYComponents. Similarly, yvel1 is
now local to updateCannonBall. Being able to hide some of the intermediate
variables is a major benefit of the separation of concerns provided by top-down
design.

Even this version seems overly complicated. Look especially at the loop.
Keeping track of the state of the cannonball requires four pieces of information,
three of which must change from moment to moment. All four variables along
with the value of time are needed to compute the new values of the three that
change. That results in an ugly function call having five parameters and three
return values. An explosion of parameters is often an indication that there might
be a better way to organize a program. Let's try another approach.

The original problem specification itself suggests a better way to look at the
variables in our program. There is a single real-world cannonball object, but
describing it in the current program requires four pieces of information: xpos,
ypos, xvel, and yvel. Suppose we had a Projectile class that "understood"
the physics of objects like cannonballs. Using such a class, we could express the
main algorithm in terms of creating and updating a suitable object using a single
variable. With this *object-based* approach, we might write main like this:

```
def main():
    angle, vel, h0, time = getInputs()
    cball = Projectile(angle, vel, h0)
    while cball.getY() >= 0:
        cball.update(time)
    print("\nDistance traveled: {0:0.1f} meters.".format(cball.getX()))
```

Obviously, this is a much simpler and more direct expression of the algorithm.
The initial values of angle, vel, and h0 are used as parameters to create a
Projectile called cball. Each time through the loop, cball is asked to update
its state to account for time. We can get the position of cball at any moment
by using its getX and getY methods. To make this work, we just need to define
a suitable Projectile class that implements the methods update, getX, and
getY.

10.3 Defining New Classes

Before designing a Projectile class, let's take an even simpler example to examine the basic ideas.

10.3.1 Example: Multi-sided Dice

You know that a normal die (the singular of dice) is a cube, and each face shows a number from one to six. Some games employ nonstandard dice that may have fewer (e.g., four) or more (e.g., thirteen) sides. Let's design a general class MSDie to model multi-sided dice. We could use such an object in any number of simulation or game programs.

Each MSDie object will know two things:

1. How many sides it has.

2. Its current value.

When a new MSDie is created, we specify how many sides it will have, n. We can then operate on the die through three provided methods: roll, to set the die to a random value between 1 and n, inclusive; setValue, to set the die to a specific value (i.e., cheat); and getValue, to see what the current value is.

Here is an interactive example showing what our class will do:

```
>>> die1 = MSDie(6)
>>> die1.getValue()
1
>>> die1.roll()
>>> die1.getValue()
4
>>> die2 = MSDie(13)
>>> die2.getValue()
1
>>> die2.roll()
>>> die2.getValue()
12
>>> die2.setValue(8)
>>> die2.getValue()
8
```

Do you see how this might be useful? I can define any number of dice having
arbitrary numbers of sides. Each die can be rolled independently and will always
produce a random value in the proper range determined by the number of sides.

Using our object-oriented terminology, we create a die by invoking the `MSDie`
constructor and providing the number of sides as a parameter. Our die object
will keep track of this number internally using an instance variable. Another
instance variable will be used to store the current value of the die. Initially, the
value of the die will be set to be 1, since that is a legal value for any die. The
value can be changed by the `roll` and `setRoll` methods and returned from the
`getValue` method.

Writing a definition for the `MSDie` class is really quite simple. A class is a collection of methods, and methods are just functions. Here is the class definition
for `MSDie`:

```
# msdie.py
#    Class definition for an n-sided die.

from random import randrange

class MSDie:

    def __init__(self, sides):
        self.sides = sides
        self.value = 1

    def roll(self):
        self.value = randrange(1,self.sides+1)

    def getValue(self):
        return self.value

    def setValue(self, value):
        self.value = value
```

As you can see, a class definition has a simple form:

```
class <class-name>:
    <method-definitions>
```

Each method definition looks like a normal function definition. Placing the function inside a class makes it a method of that class, rather than a stand-alone function.

Let's take a look at the three methods defined in this class. You'll notice that each method has a first parameter named `self`. The first parameter of a method is special—it always contains a reference to the object on which the method is acting. As usual, you can use any name you want for this parameter, but the traditional name is `self`, so that is what I will always use.

An example might be helpful in making sense of `self`. Suppose we have a `main` function that executes `die1.setValue(8)`. A method invocation is a function call. Just as in normal function calls, Python executes a four-step sequence:

1. The calling program (`main`) suspends at the point of the method application. Python locates the appropriate method definition inside the class of the object to which the method is being applied. In this case, control is transferring to the `setValue` method in the `MSDie` class, since `die1` is an instance of `MSDie`.

2. The formal parameters of the method get assigned the values supplied by the actual parameters of the call. In the case of a method call, the first formal parameter corresponds to the object. In our example, it is as if the following assignments are done before executing the method body:

```
self = die1
value = 8
```

3. The body of the method is executed.

4. Control returns to the point just after where the method was called, in this case, the statement immediately following `die1.setValue(8)`.

Figure 10.2 illustrates the method-calling sequence for this example. Notice how the method is called with one parameter (the value), but the method definition has two parameters, due to `self`. Generally speaking, we would say `setValue` requires one parameter. The `self` parameter in the definition is a bookkeeping detail. Some languages do this implicitly; Python requires us to add the extra parameter. To avoid confusion, I will always refer to the first formal parameter of a method as the *self* parameter and any others as *normal* parameters. So, I would say `setValue` uses one normal parameter.

OK, so `self` is a parameter that represents an object. But what exactly can we do with it? The main thing to remember is that objects contain their own

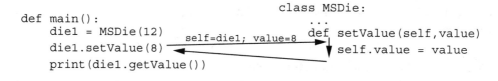

Figure 10.2: Flow of control in call: `die1.setValue(8)`

data. Conceptually, instance variables provide a way to remember data inside an object. Just as with regular variables, instance variables are accessed by name. We can use our familiar dot notation: <object>.<instance-var>. Look at the definition of setValue; self.value refers to the instance variable value that is associated with the object. Each instance of a class has its own instance variables, so each MSDie object has its very own value.

Certain methods in a class have special meaning to Python. These methods have names that begin and end with two underscores. The special method __init__ is the object constructor. Python calls this method to initialize a new MSDie. The role of __init__ is to provide initial values for the instance variables of an object.

From outside the class, the constructor is referred to by the class name.

```
die1 = MSDie(6)
```

This statement causes Python to create a new MSDie and execute __init__ on that object. The net result is that die1.sides is 6 and die1.value is 1.

The power of instance variables is that we can use them to remember the state of a particular object, and this information then gets passed around the program as part of the object. The values of instance variables can be referred to again in other methods or even in successive calls to the same method. This is different from regular local function variables, whose values disappear once the function terminates.

Here is a simple illustration:

```
>>> die1 = Die(13)
>>> print(die1.getValue())
1
>>> die1.setValue(8)
>>> print(die1.getValue())
8
```

The call to the constructor sets the instance variable die1.value to 1. The next line prints out this value. The value set by the constructor persists as part of the object, even though the constructor is over and done with. Similarly, executing die1.setValue(8) changes the object by setting its value to 8. When the object is asked for its value the next time, it responds with 8.

That's just about all there is to know about defining new classes in Python. Now it's time to put this new knowledge to use.

10.3.2 Example: The Projectile Class

Returning to the cannonball example, we want a class that can represent projectiles. This class will need a constructor to initialize instance variables, an update method to change the state of the projectile, and getX and getY methods so that we can find the current position.

Let's start with the constructor. In the main program, we will create a cannonball from the initial angle, velocity and height.

```
cball = Projectile(angle, vel, h0)
```

The Projectile class must have an __init__ method that uses these values to initialize the instance variables of cball. But what should the instance variables be? Of course, they will be the four pieces of information that characterize the flight of the cannonball: xpos, ypos, xvel, and yvel. We will calculate these values using the same formulas that were in the original program.

Here is how our class looks with the constructor:

```
class Projectile:

    def __init__(self, angle, velocity, height):
        self.xpos = 0.0
        self.ypos = height
        theta = math.radians(angle)
        self.xvel = velocity * math.cos(theta)
        self.yvel = velocity * math.sin(theta)
```

Notice how we have created four instance variables inside the object using the self dot notation. The value of theta is not needed after __init__ terminates, so it is just a normal (local) function variable.

The methods for accessing the position of our projectiles are straightforward; the current position is given by the instance variables xpos and ypos. We just need a couple of methods that return these values.

```
def getX(self):
    return self.xpos

def getY(self):
    return self.ypos
```

Finally, we come to the update method. This method takes a single normal parameter that represents an interval of time. We need to update the state of the projectile to account for the passage of that much time. Here's the code:

```
def update(self, time):
    self.xpos = self.xpos + time * self.xvel
    yvel1 = self.yvel - time * 9.8
    self.ypos = self.ypos + time * (self.yvel + yvel1)/2.0
    self.yvel = yvel1
```

Basically, this is the same code that we used in the original program updated to use and modify instance variables. Notice the use of yvel1 as a temporary (ordinary) variable. This new value is saved by storing it into the object in the last line of the method.

That completes our projectile class. We now have a complete object-based solution to the cannonball problem.

```
# cball3.py
from math import sin, cos, radians

class Projectile:

    def __init__(self, angle, velocity, height):
        self.xpos = 0.0
        self.ypos = height
        theta = radians(angle)
        self.xvel = velocity * cos(theta)
        self.yvel = velocity * sin(theta)

    def update(self, time):
        self.xpos = self.xpos + time * self.xvel
        yvel1 = self.yvel - 9.8 * time
        self.ypos = self.ypos + time * (self.yvel + yvel1) / 2.0
        self.yvel = yvel1
```

```
    def getY(self):
        return self.ypos

    def getX(self):
        return self.xpos

def getInputs():
    a = eval(input("Enter the launch angle (in degrees): "))
    v = eval(input("Enter the initial velocity (in meters/sec): "))
    h = eval(input("Enter the initial height (in meters): "))
    t = eval(input(
            "Enter the time interval between position calculations: "))
    return a,v,h,t

def main():
    angle, vel, h0, time = getInputs()
    cball = Projectile(angle, vel, h0)
    while cball.getY() >= 0:
        cball.update(time)
    print("\nDistance traveled: {0:0.1f} meters.".format(cball.getX()))
```

10.4   Data Processing with Class

The projectile example shows how useful a class can be for modeling a real-world object that has complex behavior. Another common use for objects is simply to group together a set of information that describes a person or thing. For example, a company needs to keep track of information about all of its employees. Their personnel system might make use of an Employee object that contains data such as the employee's name, social security number, address, salary, department, etc. A grouping of information of this sort is often called a *record*.

Let's try our hand at some simple data processing involving university students. In a typical university, courses are measured in terms of credit hours, and grade point averages are calculated on a 4 point scale where an "A" is 4 points, a "B" is 3 points, etc. Grade point averages are generally computed using quality points. If a class is worth 3 credit hours and the student gets an "A," then he or she earns 3(4) = 12 quality points. To calculate a student's grade point average (GPA), we divide the total quality points by the number of credit hours completed.

Suppose we have a data file that contains student grade information. Each line of the file consists of a student's name, credit-hours, and quality points. These three values are separated by a tab character. For example, the contents of the file might look something like this:

```
Adams, Henry      127      228
Computewell, Susan         100      400
DibbleBit, Denny           18       41.5
Jones, Jim        48.5     155
Smith, Frank      37       125.33
```

Our job is to write a program that reads through this file to find the student with the best GPA and print out his/her name, credits-hours, and GPA. We can begin by creating a Student class. An object of type Student will be a record of information for a single student. In this case, we have three pieces of information: name, credit-hours, and quality points. We can save this information as instance variables that are initialized in the constructor.

```
class Student:
    def __init__(self, name, hours, qpoints):
        self.name = name
        self.hours = float(hours)
        self.qpoints = float(qpoints)
```

Notice that I have used parameter names that match the instance variable names. This looks a bit strange at first, but it is a very common style for this sort of class. I have also floated the values of hours and qpoints. This makes the constructor a bit more versatile by allowing it to accept parameters that may be floats, ints, or even strings.

Now that we have a constructor, it's easy to create student records. For example, we can make a record for Henry Adams like this.

```
aStudent = Student("Adams, Henry", 127, 228)
```

Using objects allows us to collect all of the information about an individual in a single variable.

Next we must decide what methods a student object should have. Obviously, we would like to be able to access the student's information, so we should define a set of accessor methods.

```
def getName(self):
    return self.name

def getHours(self):
    return self.hours

def getQPoints(self):
    return self.qpoints
```

These methods allow us to get information back out of a student record. For example, to print a student's name we could write:

```
print(aStudent.getName())
```

One method that we have not yet included in our class is a way of computing GPA. We *could* compute it separately using the getHours and getQPoints methods, but GPA is so handy that it probably warrants its own method.

```
def gpa(self):
    return self.qpoints/self.hours
```

With this class in hand, we are ready to attack the problem of finding the best student. Our algorithm will be similar to the one used for finding the max of n numbers. We'll look through the file of students one by one, keeping track of the best student seen so far. Here's the algorithm for our program:

```
Get the file name from the user
Open the file for reading
Set best to be the first student
For each student s in the file
    if s.gpa() > best.gpa()
        set best to s
print out information about best
```

The completed program looks like this:

```
# gpa.py
#    Program to find student with highest GPA

class Student:
```

```
    def __init__(self, name, hours, qpoints):
        self.name = name
        self.hours = float(hours)
        self.qpoints = float(qpoints)

    def getName(self):
        return self.name

    def getHours(self):
        return self.hours

    def getQPoints(self):
        return self.qpoints

    def gpa(self):
        return self.qpoints/self.hours

def makeStudent(infoStr):
    # infoStr is a tab-separated line: name hours qpoints
    # returns a corresponding Student object
    name, hours, qpoints = infoStr.split("\t")
    return Student(name, hours, qpoints)

def main():
    # open the input file for reading
    filename = input("Enter the name of the grade file: ")
    infile = open(filename, 'r')

    # set best to the record for the first student in the file
    best = makeStudent(infile.readline())

    # process subsequent lines of the file
    for line in infile:
        # turn the line into a student record
        s = makeStudent(line)
        # if this student is best so far, remember it.
        if s.gpa() > best.gpa():
            best = s
```

```
    infile.close()

    # print information about the best student
    print("The best student is:", best.getName())
    print("hours:", best.getHours())
    print("GPA:", best.gpa())

if __name__ == '__main__':
    main()
```

You will notice that I added a helper function called makeStudent. This function takes a single line of the file, splits it into its three tab-separated fields, and returns a corresponding Student object. Right before the loop, this function is used to create a record for the first student in the file:

```
    best = makeStudent(infile.readline())
```

It is called again inside the loop to process each subsequent line of the file.

```
    s = makeStudent(line)
```

Here's how it looks running the program on the sample data:

```
Enter name the grade file: students.dat
The best student is: Computewell, Susan
hours: 100.0
GPA: 4.0
```

One unresolved issue with this program is that it only reports back a single student. If multiple students are tied for the best GPA, only the first one found is reported. I leave it as an interesting design issue for you to modify the program so that it reports all students having the highest GPA.

10.5 Objects and Encapsulation

10.5.1 Encapsulating Useful Abstractions

Hopefully, you are seeing how defining new classes like Projectile and Student can be a good way to modularize a program. Once we identify some useful

objects, we can write an algorithm using those objects and push the implementation details into a suitable class definition. This gives us the same kind of
separation of concerns that we had using functions in top-down design. The
main program only has to worry about what objects can do, not about how they
are implemented.

Computer scientists call this separation of concerns *encapsulation*. The implementation details of an object are encapsulated in the class definition, which
insulates the rest of the program from having to deal with them. This is another
application of abstraction (ignoring irrelevant details), which is the essence of
good design.

For completeness, I should mention that encapsulation is only a programming convention in Python. It is not enforced by the language, per se. In our
`Projectile` class we included two short methods, `getX` and `getY`, that simply returned the values of instance variables `xpos` and `ypos`, respectively. Our
`Student` class has similar accessor methods for its instance variables. Strictly
speaking, these methods are not absolutely necessary. In Python, you can access
the instance variables of any object with the regular dot notation. For example,
we could test the constructor for the `Projectile` class interactively by creating
an object and then directly inspecting the values of the instance variables.

```
>>> c = Projectile(60, 50, 20)
>>> c.xpos
0.0
>>> c.ypos
20
>>> c.xvel
25.0
>>> c.yvel
43.301270
```

Accessing the instance variables of an object is very handy for testing purposes, but it is generally considered poor practice to do this in programs. One
of the main reasons for using objects is to hide the internal complexities of
those objects from the programs that use them. References to instance variables
should generally remain inside the class definition with the rest of the implementation details. From outside the class, all interaction with an object should
generally be done using the interface provided by its methods. However, this
is not a hard-and-fast rule, and Python program designers often specify that
certain instance variables are accessible as part of the interface.

One immediate advantage of encapsulation is that it allows us to modify and improve classes independently, without worrying about "breaking" other parts of the program. As long as the interface provided by a class stays the same, the rest of the program can't even tell that a class has changed. As you begin to design classes of your own, you should strive to provide each with a complete set of methods to make it useful.

10.5.2 Putting Classes in Modules

Often a well-defined class or set of classes provides useful abstractions that can be leveraged in many different programs. For example, we might want to turn our projectile class into its own module file so that it can be used in other programs. In doing so, it would be a good idea to add documentation that describes how the class can be used so that programmers who want to use the module don't have to study the code to figure out (or remember) what the class and its methods do.

10.5.3 Module Documentation

You are already familiar with one way of documenting programs, namely comments. It's always a good idea to provide comments explaining the contents of a module and its uses. In fact, comments of this sort are so important that Python incorporates a special kind of commenting convention called a *docstring*. You can insert a plain string literal as the first line of a module, class, or function to document that component. The advantage of docstrings is that, while ordinary comments are simply ignored by Python, docstrings are actually carried along during execution in a special attribute called __doc__. These strings can be examined dynamically.

Most of the Python library modules have extensive docstrings that you can use to get help on using the module or its contents. For example, if you can't remember how to use the random function, you can print its docstring directly like this:

```
>>> import random
>>> print(random.random.__doc__)
random() -> x in the interval [0, 1).
```

Docstrings are also used by the Python online help system and by a utility called PyDoc that automatically builds documentation for Python modules. You could get the same information using interactive help like this:

```
>>> import random
>>> help(random.random)
Help on built-in function random:

random(...)
    random() -> x in the interval [0, 1).
```

If you want to see a whole bunch of information about the entire random
module, try typing `help(random)`.

Here is a version of our `Projectile` class as a module file with docstrings
included:

```
# projectile.py

"""projectile.py
Provides a simple class for modeling the
flight of projectiles."""

from math import sin, cos, radians

class Projectile:

    """Simulates the flight of simple projectiles near the earth's
    surface, ignoring wind resistance. Tracking is done in two
    dimensions, height (y) and distance (x)."""

    def __init__(self, angle, velocity, height):
        """Create a projectile with given launch angle, initial
        velocity and height."""
        self.xpos = 0.0
        self.ypos = height
        theta = radians(angle)
        self.xvel = velocity * cos(theta)
        self.yvel = velocity * sin(theta)

    def update(self, time):
        """Update the state of this projectile to move it time seconds
        farther into its flight"""
        self.xpos = self.xpos + time * self.xvel
```

```
        yvel1 = self.yvel - 9.8 * time
        self.ypos = self.ypos + time * (self.yvel + yvel1) / 2.0
        self.yvel = yvel1

    def getY(self):
        "Returns the y position (height) of this projectile."
        return self.ypos

    def getX(self):
        "Returns the x position (distance) of this projectile."
        return self.xpos
```

You might notice that many of the docstrings in this code are enclosed in triple quotes ("""). This is a third way that Python allows string literals to be delimited. Triple quoting allows us to directly type multi-line strings. Here is an example of how the docstrings appear when they are printed:

```
>>> print(projectile.Projectile.__doc__)
Simulates the flight of simple projectiles near the earth's
    surface, ignoring wind resistance. Tracking is done in two
    dimensions, height (y) and distance (x).
```

You might try `help(projectile)` to see how the complete documentation looks for this module.

10.5.4 Working with Multiple Modules

Our main program can now simply import from the `projectile` module in order to solve the original problem.

```
# cball4.py
from projectile import Projectile

def getInputs():
    a = eval(input("Enter the launch angle (in degrees): "))
    v = eval(input("Enter the initial velocity (in meters/sec): "))
    h = eval(input("Enter the initial height (in meters): "))
    t = eval(input("Enter the time interval between position calculations: "))
    return a,v,h,t
```

```
def main():
    angle, vel, h0, time = getInputs()
    cball = Projectile(angle, vel, h0)
    while cball.getY() >= 0:
        cball.update(time)
    print("\nDistance traveled: {0:0.1f} meters.".format(cball.getX()))
```

In this version, details of projectile motion are now hidden in the `projectile` module file.

If you are testing multi-module Python projects interactively (a good thing to do), you need to be aware of a subtlety in the Python module importing mechanism. When Python first imports a given module, it creates a module object that contains all of the things defined in the module (technically, this is called a *namespace*). If a module imports successfully (it has no syntax errors), subsequent imports do not reload the module, they just create additional references to the existing module object. Even if a module has been changed (its source file edited) re-importing it into an ongoing interactive session will not get you an updated version.

It *is* possible to interactively replace a module object using the function `reload(<module>)` in the `imp` module of the standard library (consult the Python documentation for details). But often this won't give you the results you want. That's because `reloading` a module doesn't change the values of any identifiers in the current session that already refer to objects from the old version of the module. In fact, it's pretty easy to create a situation where objects from both the old and new version of a module are active at the same time, which is confusing to say the least.

The simplest way to avoid this confusion is to make sure you start a new interactive session for testing each time any of the modules involved in your tests is modified. That way you are guaranteed to get a fresh (updated) import of all the modules that you are using.

10.6 Widgets

One very common use of objects is in the design of graphical user interfaces (GUIs). Back in Chapter 4, we talked about GUIs being composed of visual interface objects called *widgets*. The `Entry` object defined in our `graphics` library is one example of a widget. Now that we know how to define new classes, we can create our own custom widgets.

10.6.1 Example Program: Dice Roller

Let's try our hand at building a couple of useful widgets. As an example application, consider a program that rolls a pair of standard (six-sided) dice. The program will display the dice graphically and provide two buttons, one for rolling the dice and one for quitting the program. Figure 10.3 shows a snapshot of the user interface.

Figure 10.3: Snapshot of dice roller in action

You can see that this program has two kinds of widgets: buttons and dice. We can start by developing suitable classes. The two buttons will be instances of a Button class, and the class that provides a graphical view of the value of a die will be DieView.

10.6.2 Building Buttons

Buttons, of course, are standard elements of virtually every GUI these days. Modern buttons are very sophisticated, usually having a 3-dimensional look and feel. Our simple graphics package does not have the machinery to produce buttons that appear to depress as they are clicked. The best we can do is find out

where the mouse was clicked after the click has already completed. Nevertheless, we can make a useful, if less pretty, button class.

Our buttons will be rectangular regions in a graphics window where user
clicks can influence the behavior of the running application. We will need to
create buttons and determine when they have been clicked. In addition, it is
also nice to be able to activate and deactivate individual buttons. That way, our
applications can signal which options are available to the user at any given moment. Typically, an inactive button is grayed-out to show that it is not available.

Summarizing this description, our buttons will support the following methods:

constructor Create a button in a window. We will have to specify the window
in which the button will be displayed, the location/size of the button, and
the label that will be on the button.

activate Set the state of the button to active.

deactivate Set the state of the button to inactive.

clicked Indicate if the button was clicked. If the button is active, this method
will determine if the point clicked is inside the button region. The point
will have to be sent as a parameter to the method.

getLabel Returns the label string of the button. This is provided so that we can
identify a particular button.

In order to support these operations, our buttons will need a number of instance variables. For example, the button itself will be drawn as a rectangle with
some text centered in it. Invoking the `activate` and `deactivate` methods will
change the appearance of the button. Saving the `Rectangle` and `Text` objects as
instance variables will allow us to change the width of the outline and the color
of the label. We might start by implementing the various methods to see what
other instance variables might be needed. Once we have identified the relevant
variables, we can write a constructor that initializes these values.

Let's start with the `activate` method. We can signal that the button is active
by making the outline thicker and making the label text black. Here is the code
(remember the `self` parameter refers to the button object):

```
def activate(self):
    "Sets this button to 'active'."
    self.label.setFill('black')
```

```
        self.rect.setWidth(2)
        self.active = True
```

As I mentioned above, in order for this code to work, our constructor will have to initialize self.label as an appropriate Text object and self.rect as a Rectangle object. In addition, the self.active instance variable stores a Boolean value to remember whether or not the button is currently active.

Our deactivate method will do the inverse of activate. It looks like this:

```
def deactivate(self):
    "Sets this button to 'inactive'."
    self.label.setFill('darkgrey')
    self.rect.setWidth(1)
    self.active = False
```

Of course, the main point of a button is being able to determine if it has been clicked. Let's try to write the clicked method. As you know, the graphics package provides a getMouse method that returns the point where the mouse was clicked. If an application needs to get a button click, it will first have to call getMouse and then see which active button (if any) the point is inside of. We could imagine the button processing code looking something like the following:

```
pt = win.getMouse()
if button1.clicked(pt):
    # Do button1 stuff
elif button2.clicked(pt):
    # Do button2 stuff
elif button3.clicked(pt)
    # Do button3 stuff
...
```

The main job of the clicked method is to determine whether a given point is inside the rectangular button. The point is inside the rectangle if its x and y coordinates lie between the extreme x and y values of the rectangle. This would be easiest to figure out if we just assume that the button object has instance variables that record the min and max values of x and y.

Assuming the existence of instance variables xmin, xmax, ymin, and ymax, we can implement the clicked method with a single Boolean expression.

```
def clicked(self, p):
    "Returns true if button is active and p is inside"
```

```
return (self.active and
        self.xmin <= p.getX() <= self.xmax and
        self.ymin <= p.getY() <= self.ymax)
```

Here we have a single large Boolean expression composed by anding together three simpler expressions; all three must be true for the function to return a true value.

The first of the three subexpressions simply retrieves the value of the instance variable self.active. This ensures that only active buttons will report that they have been clicked. If self.active is false, then clicked will return false. The second two subexpressions are compound conditions to check that the x and y values of the point fall between the edges of the button rectangle. (Remember, x <= y <= z means the same as the mathematical expression $x \le y \le z$ (section 7.5.1)).

Now that we have the basic operations of the button ironed out, we just need a constructor to get all the instance variables properly initialized. It's not hard, but it is a bit tedious. Here is the complete class with a suitable constructor:

```
# button.py
from graphics import *

class Button:

    """A button is a labeled rectangle in a window.
    It is activated or deactivated with the activate()
    and deactivate() methods. The clicked(p) method
    returns true if the button is active and p is inside it."""

    def __init__(self, win, center, width, height, label):
        """ Creates a rectangular button, eg:
        qb = Button(myWin, centerPoint, width, height, 'Quit') """

        w,h = width/2.0, height/2.0
        x,y = center.getX(), center.getY()
        self.xmax, self.xmin = x+w, x-w
        self.ymax, self.ymin = y+h, y-h
        p1 = Point(self.xmin, self.ymin)
        p2 = Point(self.xmax, self.ymax)
        self.rect = Rectangle(p1,p2)
```

```
        self.rect.setFill('lightgray')
        self.rect.draw(win)
        self.label = Text(center, label)
        self.label.draw(win)
        self.deactivate()

    def clicked(self, p):
        "Returns true if button active and p is inside"
        return (self.active and
                    self.xmin <= p.getX() <= self.xmax and
                    self.ymin <= p.getY() <= self.ymax)

    def getLabel(self):
        "Returns the label string of this button."
        return self.label.getText()

    def activate(self):
        "Sets this button to 'active'."
        self.label.setFill('black')
        self.rect.setWidth(2)
        self.active = True

    def deactivate(self):
        "Sets this button to 'inactive'."
        self.label.setFill('darkgrey')
        self.rect.setWidth(1)
        self.active = False
```

You should study the constructor in this class to make sure you understand all of the instance variables and how they are initialized. A button is positioned by providing a center point, width, and height. Other instance variables are calculated from these parameters.

10.6.3 Building Dice

Now we'll turn our attention to the DieView class. The purpose of this class is to display the value of a die in a graphical fashion. The face of the die will be a square (via Rectangle) and the pips will be circles.

Our DieView will have the following interface:

constructor Create a die in a window. We will have to specify the window, the center point of the die, and the size of the die as parameters.

setValue Change the view to show a given value. The value to display will be passed as a parameter.

Obviously, the heart of `DieView` is turning various pips "on" and "off" to indicate the current value of the die. One simple approach is to pre-place circles in all the possible locations where a pip might be and then turn them on or off by changing their colors.

Using the standard position of pips on a die, we will need seven circles: three down the left edge, three down the right edge, and one in the center. The constructor will create the background square and the seven circles. The `setValue` method will set the colors of the circles based on the value of the die.

Without further ado, here is the code for our `DieView` class. The comments will help you to follow how it works:

```
# dieview.py
from graphics import *
class DieView:
    """ DieView is a widget that displays a graphical representation
    of a standard six-sided die."""

    def __init__(self, win, center, size):
        """"""Create a view of a die, e.g.:
           d1 = DieView(myWin, Point(40,50), 20)
        creates a die centered at (40,50) having sides
        of length 20."""

        # first define some standard values
        self.win = win              # save this for drawing pips later
        self.background = "white" # color of die face
        self.foreground = "black" # color of the pips
        self.psize = 0.1 * size    # radius of each pip
        hsize = size / 2.0         # half the size of the die
        offset = 0.6 * hsize       # distance from center to outer pips

        # create a square for the face
        cx, cy = center.getX(), center.getY()
        p1 = Point(cx-hsize, cy-hsize)
```

```
        p2 = Point(cx+hsize, cy+hsize)
        rect = Rectangle(p1,p2)
        rect.draw(win)
        rect.setFill(self.background)

        # Create 7 circles for standard pip locations
        self.pip1 = self.__makePip(cx-offset, cy-offset)
        self.pip2 = self.__makePip(cx-offset, cy)
        self.pip3 = self.__makePip(cx-offset, cy+offset)
        self.pip4 = self.__makePip(cx, cy)
        self.pip5 = self.__makePip(cx+offset, cy-offset)
        self.pip6 = self.__makePip(cx+offset, cy)
        self.pip7 = self.__makePip(cx+offset, cy+offset)

        # Draw an initial value
        self.setValue(1)

    def __makePip(self, x, y):
        "Internal helper method to draw a pip at (x,y)"
        pip = Circle(Point(x,y), self.psize)
        pip.setFill(self.background)
        pip.setOutline(self.background)
        pip.draw(self.win)
        return pip

    def setValue(self, value):
        "Set this die to display value."
        # turn all pips off
        self.pip1.setFill(self.background)
        self.pip2.setFill(self.background)
        self.pip3.setFill(self.background)
        self.pip4.setFill(self.background)
        self.pip5.setFill(self.background)
        self.pip6.setFill(self.background)
        self.pip7.setFill(self.background)

        # turn correct pips on
        if value == 1:
```

```
            self.pip4.setFill(self.foreground)
        elif value == 2:
            self.pip1.setFill(self.foreground)
            self.pip7.setFill(self.foreground)
        elif value == 3:
            self.pip1.setFill(self.foreground)
            self.pip7.setFill(self.foreground)
            self.pip4.setFill(self.foreground)
        elif value == 4:
            self.pip1.setFill(self.foreground)
            self.pip3.setFill(self.foreground)
            self.pip5.setFill(self.foreground)
            self.pip7.setFill(self.foreground)
        elif value == 5:
            self.pip1.setFill(self.foreground)
            self.pip3.setFill(self.foreground)
            self.pip4.setFill(self.foreground)
            self.pip5.setFill(self.foreground)
            self.pip7.setFill(self.foreground)
        else:
            self.pip1.setFill(self.foreground)
            self.pip2.setFill(self.foreground)
            self.pip3.setFill(self.foreground)
            self.pip5.setFill(self.foreground)
            self.pip6.setFill(self.foreground)
            self.pip7.setFill(self.foreground)
```

There are a couple of things worth noticing in this code. First, in the constructor, I have defined a set of values that determine various aspects of the
die such as its color and the size of the pips. Calculating these values in the
constructor and then using them in other places allows us to easily tweak the
appearance of the die without having to search through the code to find all the
places where those values are used. I actually figured out the specific calculations (such as the pip size being one-tenth of the die size) through a process of
trial and error.

Another important thing to notice is that I have added an extra method
__makePip that was not part of the original specification. This method is just a
helper function that executes the four lines of code necessary to draw each of
the seven pips. Since this is a function that is only useful within the DieView

class, it is appropriate to make it a class method. Inside the constructor, it is invoked by lines such as `self.__makePip(cx, cy)`. Method names beginning with a single or double underscore are used in Python to indicate that a method is "private" to the class and not intended for use by outside programs.

10.6.4 The Main Program

Now we are ready to write our main program. The `Button` and `Dieview` classes are imported from their respective modules. Here is the program that uses our new widgets:

```
# roller.py
# Graphics program to roll a pair of dice. Uses custom widgets
# Button and DieView.

from random import randrange
from graphics import GraphWin, Point

from button import Button
from dieview import DieView

def main():

    # create the application window
    win = GraphWin("Dice Roller")
    win.setCoords(0, 0, 10, 10)
    win.setBackground("green2")

    # Draw the interface widgets
    die1 = DieView(win, Point(3,7), 2)
    die2 = DieView(win, Point(7,7), 2)
    rollButton = Button(win, Point(5,4.5), 6, 1, "Roll Dice")
    rollButton.activate()
    quitButton = Button(win, Point(5,1), 2, 1, "Quit")

    # Event loop
    pt = win.getMouse()
    while not quitButton.clicked(pt):
        if rollButton.clicked(pt):
```

```
            value1 = randrange(1,7)
            die1.setValue(value1)
            value2 = randrange(1,7)
            die2.setValue(value2)
            quitButton.activate()
        pt = win.getMouse()

    # close up shop
    win.close()

main()
```

Notice that near the top of the program I have built the visual interface by creating the two DieViews and two Buttons. To demonstrate the activation feature of buttons, the Roll Dice button is initially active, but the Quit button is left deactivated. The Quit button is activated inside the event loop below when the Roll Dice button is clicked. This approach forces the user to roll the dice at least once before quitting.

The heart of the program is the event loop. It is just a sentinel loop that gets mouse clicks and processes them until the user successfully clicks the Quit button. The if inside the loop ensures that the rolling of the dice only happens when the Roll Dice button is clicked. Clicking a point that is not inside either button causes the loop to iterate, but nothing is actually done.

10.7 Chapter Summary

This chapter has shown you how to work with class definitions. Here is a summary of some key points:

- An object comprises a collection of related data and a set of operations to manipulate that data. Data is stored in instance variables and manipulated via methods.

- Every object is an instance of some class. It is the class definition that determines what the attributes of the object will be. Programmers can create new kinds of objects by writing suitable class definitions.

- A Python class definition is a collection of function definitions. These functions implement the methods of the class. Every method definition has a special first parameter called self. The actual parameter of self is the object to which the method is being applied. The self parameter is used to access the attributes of the object via dot notation.

- The special method __init__ is the constructor for a class. Its job is to initialize the instance variables of an object.

- Defining new objects (via class) can simplify the structure of a program by allowing a single variable to store a constellation of related data. Objects are useful for modeling real world entities. These entities may have complex behavior that is captured in method algorithms (e.g., a projectile), or they may be little more than a collection of relevant information about some individual (e.g., a student record).

- Correctly designed classes provide encapsulation. The internal details of an object are hidden inside the class definition so that other portions of the program do not need to know how an object is implemented. This separation of concerns is a programming convention in Python; the instance variables of an object should only be accessed or modified through the interface methods of the class.

- Most GUI systems are built using an object-oriented approach. We can build novel GUI widgets by defining suitable classes.

10.8 Exercises

Review Questions

True/False

1. New objects are created by invoking a constructor.

2. Functions that live in objects are called instance variables.

3. The first parameter of a Python method definition is called this.

4. An object may have only one instance variable.

5. In data processing, a collection of information about a person or thing is called a file.

6. In a Python class, the constructor is called __init__.

7. A Docstring is the same thing as a comment.

8. Instance variables go away once a method terminates.

9. Method names should always begin with one or two underscores.

10. It is considered bad style to directly access an instance variable outside of a class definition.

Multiple Choice

1. What Python reserved word starts a class definition?
   a) def   b) class   c) object   d) __init__

2. A method definition with four formal parameters is generally called with how many actual parameters?
   a) three   b) four   c) five   d) it depends

3. A method definition is similar to a(n)
   a) loop   b) module   c) import statement   d) function definition

4. Within a method definition, the instance variable x could be accessed via which expression?
   a) x   b) self.x   c) self[x]   d) self.getX()

5. A Python convention for defining methods that are "private" to a class is to begin the method name with
   a) "private"   b) a pound sign (#)
   c) an underscore (_)   d) a hyphen (-)

6. The term applied to hiding details inside class definitions is
   a) obscuring   b) subclassing
   c) documentation   d) encapsulation

7. A Python string literal can span multiple lines if enclosed with
   a) "   b) '   c) """   d) \

8. In a Button widget, what is the data type of the instance variable active?
   a) bool   b) int   c) float   d) str

9. Which of the following methods is *not* part of the Button class in this chapter?
   a) activate   b) deactivate   c) setLabel   d) clicked

10. Which of the following methods is part of the `DieView` class in this chapter?
    a) `activate`   b) `setColor`   c) `setValue`   d) `clicked`

Discussion

1. Explain the similarities and differences between instance variables and "regular" function variables.

2. Explain the following in terms of actual code that might be found in a class definition:

    (a) method

    (b) instance variable

    (c) constructor

    (d) accessor

    (e) mutator

3. Show the output that would result from the following nonsense program:

```
class Bozo:

    def __init__(self, value):
        print("Creating a Bozo from:", value)
        self.value = 2 * value

    def clown(self, x):
        print("Clowning:", x)
        print(x * self.value)
        return x + self.value

def main():
    print("Clowning around now.")
    c1 = Bozo(3)
    c2 = Bozo(4)
    print c1.clown(3)
    print c2.clown(c1.clown(2))

main()
```

Programming Exercises

1. Modify the cannonball simulation from the chapter so that it also calculates the maximum height achieved by the cannonball.

2. Use the Button class discussed in this chapter to build a GUI for one (or more) of your projects from previous chapters.

3. Write a program to play "Three Button Monte." Your program should draw three buttons labeled "Door 1", "Door 2," and "Door 3" in a window and randomly select one of the buttons (without telling the user which one is selected). The program then prompts the user to click on one of the buttons. A click on the special button is a win, and a click on one of the other two is a loss. You should tell the user whether they won or lost, and in the case of a loss, which was the correct button. Your program should be entirely graphical; that is, all prompts and messages should be displayed in the graphics window.

4. Extend the program from the previous problem by allowing the player to play multiple rounds and displaying the number of wins and losses. Add a "Quit" button for ending the game.

5. Modify the Student class from the chapter by adding a mutator method that records a grade for the student. Here is the specification of the new method:

   addGrade(self, gradePoint, credits) gradePoint is a float that represents a grade (e.g., A = 4.0, A– = 3.7 B+ = 3.3, etc.), and credits is a float indicating the number of credit hours for the class. Modifies the student object by adding this grade information.

   Use the updated class to implement a simple program for calculating GPA. Your program should create a new student object that has 0 credits and 0 quality points (the name is irrelevant). Your program should then prompt the user to enter course information (gradepoint and credits) and then print out the final GPA achieved.

6. Extend the previous exercise by implementing an addLetterGrade method. This is similar to addGrade except that it accepts a letter grade as a string (instead of a gradepoint). Use the updated class to improve the GPA calculator by allowing the entry of letter grades.

7. Write a modified Button class that creates circular buttons. Call your class CButton and implement the exact same methods that are in the existing Button class. Your constructor should take the center of the button and its radius as normal parameters. Place your class in a module called cbutton.py. Test your class by modifying roller.py to use your buttons.

8. Modify the DieView class from the chapter by adding a method that allows the color of the pips to be specified.

   setColor(self, color) Changes the color of the pips to color.

   Hints: You can change the color by changing the value of the instance variable foreground, but you also need to redraw the die after doing this. Modify setValue so that it remembers the value of the die in an instance variable. Then setColor can call setValue and pass the stored value to redraw the die. You can test your new class with the roller.py program. Have the dice change to a random color after each roll (you can generate a random color with the color_rgb function).

9. Write a class to represent the geometric solid sphere. Your class should implement the following methods:

   __init__(self, radius) Creates a sphere having the given radius.

   getRadius(self) Returns the radius of this sphere.

   surfaceArea(self) Returns the surface area of the sphere.

   volume(self) Returns the volume of the sphere.

   Use your new class to solve Programming Exercise 1 from Chapter 3.

10. Same as the previous problem, but for a cube. The constructor should accept the length of a side as a parameter.

11. Implement a class to represent a playing card. Your class should have the following methods:

    __init__(self, rank, suit) rank is an int in the range 1–13 indicating the ranks Ace–King, and suit is a single character "d," "c," "h," or "s" indicating the suit (diamonds, clubs, hearts, or spades). Create the corresponding card.

    getRank(self) Returns the rank of the card.

getSuit(self) Returns the suit of the card.

BJValue(self) Returns the Blackjack value of a card. Ace counts as 1, face cards count as 10.

__str__(self) Returns a string that names the card. For example, "Ace of Spades".

Note: A method named __str__ is special in Python. If asked to convert an object into a string, Python uses this method, if it's present. For example,

```
c = Card(1,"s")
print c
```

will print "Ace of Spades."

Test your card class with a program that prints out n randomly generated cards and the associated Blackjack value where n is a number supplied by the user.

12. Extend your card class from the previous problem with a draw(self, win, center) method that displays the card in a graphics window. Use your extended class to create and display a hand of five random cards. Hint: the easiest way to do this is to search the Internet for a free set of card images and use the Image object in the graphics library to display them.

13. Here is a simple class that draws a (grim) face in a graphics window:

```
# face.py
from graphics import *

class Face:

    def __init__(self, window, center, size):
        eyeSize = 0.15 * size
        eyeOff = size / 3.0
        mouthSize = 0.8 * size
        mouthOff = size / 2.0
        self.head = Circle(center, size)
        self.head.draw(window)
        self.leftEye = Circle(center, eyeSize)
```

```
self.leftEye.move(-eyeOff, -eyeOff)
self.rightEye = Circle(center, eyeSize)
self.rightEye.move(eyeOff, -eyeOff)
self.leftEye.draw(window)
self.rightEye.draw(window)
p1 = center.clone()
p1.move(-mouthSize/2, mouthOff)
p2 = center.clone()
p2.move(mouthSize/2, mouthOff)
self.mouth = Line(p1,p2)
self.mouth.draw(window)
```

Add methods to this class that cause the face to change expression. For example you might add methods such as smile, wink, frown, flinch, etc. Your class should implement at least three such methods.

Use your class to write a program that draws a face and provides the user with buttons to change the facial expression.

14. Modify the face class from the previous problem to include a move method similar to other graphics objects. Using the move method, create a program that makes a face bounce around in a window (see Programming Exercise 17 from Chapter 7). Bonus: have the face change expression each time it "hits" the edge of the window.

15. Create a Tracker class that displays a circle in a graphics window to show the current location of an object. Here is a quick specification of the class:

```
class Tracker:

    def __init__(self, window, objToTrack):

        # window is a graphWin and objToTrack is an object whose
        #    position is to be shown in the window. objToTrack is
        #    an object that has getX() and getY() methods that
        #    report its current position.

        # Creates a Tracker object and draws a circle in window
        #    at the current position of objToTrack.
```

```
def update():
    # Moves the circle in the window to the current position
    #    of the object being tracked.
```

Use your new `Tracker` class in conjunction with the `Projectile` class to write a program that graphically depicts the flight of a cannonball.

16. Advanced: Add a `Target` class to the cannonball program from the previous problem. A target should be a rectangle placed at a random x position at the bottom of the window. Allow users to keep firing until they hit the target.

17. Redo the regression problem from Chapter 8 (Programming Exercise 13) using a `Regression` class. Your new class will keep track of the various quantities that are needed to compute a line of regression (the running sums of x, y, x^2, and xy). The regression class should have the following methods:

   __init__ Creates a new regression object to which points can be added.

   addPoint Adds a point to the regression object.

   predict Accepts a value of x as a parameter, and returns the value of the corresponding y on the line of best fit.

   Note: Your class might also use some internal helper methods to do such things as compute the slope of the regression line.

Chapter 11　　　　　Data Collections

Objectives

- To understand the use of lists (arrays) to represent a collection of related data.

- To be familiar with the functions and methods available for manipulating Python lists.

- To be able to write programs that use lists to manage a collection of information.

- To be able to write programs that use lists and classes to structure complex data.

- To understand the use of Python dictionaries for storing non-sequential collections.

11.1　Example Problem: Simple Statistics

As you saw in the last chapter, classes are one mechanism for structuring the data in our programs. Classes alone, however, are not enough to satisfy all of our data-handling needs.

If you think about the kinds of data that most real-world programs manipulate, you will quickly realize that many programs deal with large collections of similar information. A few examples of the collections that you might find in a modern program include:

- Words in a document.

- Students in a course.

- Data from an experiment.

- Customers of a business.

- Graphics objects drawn on the screen.

- Cards in a deck.

In this chapter, you will learn techniques for writing programs that manipulate collections like these.

Let's start with a simple example: a collection of numbers. Back in Chapter 8, we wrote a simple but useful program to compute the mean (average) of a set of numbers entered by the user. Just to refresh your memory (as if you could forget it), here is the program again:

```
# average4.py
def main():
    sum = 0.0
    count = 0
    xStr = input("Enter a number (<Enter> to quit) >> ")
    while xStr != "":
        x = eval(xStr)
        sum = sum + x
        count = count + 1
        xStr = input("Enter a number (<Enter> to quit) >> ")
    print("\nThe average of the numbers is", sum / count)

main()
```

This program allows the user to enter a sequence of numbers, but the program itself does not keep track of what numbers were entered. Instead, it just keeps a summary of the numbers in the form of a running sum. That's all that's needed to compute the mean.

Suppose we want to extend this program so that it computes not only the mean, but two other standard statistical measures—*median* and *standard devia-tion* —of the data. You are probably familiar with the concept of a median. This is the value that splits the data set into equal-sized parts. For the data 2, 4, 6, 9, 13, the median value is 6, since there are two values greater than 6 and two that are smaller. One way to calculate the median is to store all the numbers and put them in order so that we can identify the middle value.

The standard deviation is a measure of how spread out the data is relative to the mean. If the data is tightly clustered around the mean, then the standard deviation is small. When the data is more spread out, the standard deviation is larger. The standard deviation provides a yardstick for determining how exceptional a value is. For example, some teachers define an "A" as any score that is at least two standard deviations above the mean.

The standard deviation, s, is defined as

$$s = \sqrt{\frac{\sum (\bar{x} - x_i)^2}{n - 1}}$$

In this formula $\bar{x}$ is the mean, x_i represents the ith data value and n is the number of data values. The formula looks complicated, but it is not hard to compute. The expression $(\bar{x} - x_i)^2$ is the square of the "deviation" of an individual item from the mean. The numerator of the fraction is the sum of the deviations (squared) across all the data values.

Let's take a simple example. If we again use the values 2, 4, 6, 9, and 13, the mean of this data ($\bar{x}$) is 6.8. So the numerator of the fraction is computed as

$$(6.8 - 2)^2 + (6.8 - 4)^2 + (6.8 - 6)^2 + (6.8 - 9)^2 + (6.8 - 13)^2 = 74.8$$

Finishing out the calculation gives us

$$s = \sqrt{\frac{74.8}{5 - 1}} = \sqrt{18.7} = 4.32$$

The standard deviation is about 4.3. You can see how the first step of this calculation uses both the mean (which can't be computed until all of the numbers have been entered) and each individual value as well. Computing the standard deviation this way requires some method to remember all of the individual values that were entered.

11.2 Applying Lists

In order to complete our enhanced statistics program, we need a way to store and manipulate an entire collection of numbers. We can't just use a bunch of independent variables, because we don't know how many numbers there will be.

What we need is some way of combining an entire collection of values into one object. Actually, we've already done something like this, but we haven't discussed all of the details. Take a look at these interactive examples:

```
>>> list(range(10))
[0, 1, 2, 3, 4, 5, 6, 7, 8, 9]
>>> "This is an ex-parrot!".split()
['This', 'is', 'an', 'ex-parrot!']
```

Both of these familiar functions return a collection of values denoted by the enclosing square brackets. These are lists, of course.

11.2.1 Lists and Arrays

As you know, Python lists are ordered sequences of items. In fact, the ideas and notations that we use for manipulating lists are borrowed from the mathematical notion of sequence. Mathematicians sometimes give an entire sequence of items a single name. For instance, a sequence of n numbers might just be called S:

$$S = s_0, s_1, s_2, s_3, ..., s_{n-1}$$

When they want to refer to specific values in the sequence, these values are denoted by *subscripts*. In this example, the first item in the sequence is denoted with the subscript 0, s_0.

By using numbers as subscripts, mathematicians are able to succinctly summarize computations over items in the sequence using subscript variables. For example, the sum of the sequence is written using standard summation notation as

$$\sum_{i=0}^{n-1} s_i$$

A similar idea can be applied to computer programs. With a list, we can use a single variable to represent an entire sequence, and the individual items in the sequence can be accessed through subscripting. Well, almost; we don't have a way of typing subscripts, but we use indexing instead.

Suppose that our sequence is stored in a variable called s. We could write a loop to calculate the sum of the items in the sequence like this:

```
sum = 0
for i in range(n):
    sum = sum + s[i]
```

Virtually all computer languages provide some sort of sequence structure similar to Python's list; in other languages, it is called an *array*. To summarize, a list or array is a sequence of items where the entire sequence is referred to by a single name (in this case, s) and individual items can be selected by indexing (e.g., s[i]).

Arrays in other programming languages are generally fixed size. When you create an array, you have to specify how many items it will hold. If you don't know how many items you will have, then you have to allocate a large array, just in case, and keep track of how many "slots" you actually fill. Arrays are also usually *homogeneous*. That means they are restricted to holding objects of a single data type. You can have an array of ints or an array of strings but cannot mix strings and ints in a single array.

In contrast, Python lists are dynamic. They can grow and shrink on demand. They are also *heterogeneous*. You can mix arbitrary data types in a single list. In a nutshell, Python lists are mutable sequences of arbitrary objects.

11.2.2 List Operations

Because lists are sequences, you know that all of the Python built-in sequence operations also apply to lists. To jog your memory, here's a summary of those operations:

Operator	Meaning
<seq> + <seq>	Concatenation
<seq> * <int-expr>	Repetition
<seq>[ ]	Indexing
len(<seq>)	Length
<seq>[:]	Slicing
for <var> in <seq>:	Iteration
<expr> in <seq>	Membership check (Returns a Boolean)

Except for the last (membership check), these are the same operations that we used before on strings. The membership operation can be used to see if a certain value appears anywhere in a sequence. Here are a couple of quick examples checking for membership in lists and string:

```
>>> lst = [1,2,3,4]
>>> 3 in lst
True
```

```
>>> 5 in lst
False
>>> ans = 'Y'
>>> ans in 'Yy'
True
```

By the way, since we can iterate through lists, the summing example from above can be written more simply and clearly this way:

```
sum = 0
for x in s:
    sum = sum + x
```

Recall that one important difference between lists and strings is that lists are mutable. You can use assignment to change the value of items in a list.

```
>>> lst = [1, 2, 3, 4]
>>> lst[3]
4
>>> lst[3] = "Hello"
>>> lst
[1, 2, 3, 'Hello']
>>> lst[2] = 7
>>> lst
[1, 2, 7, 'Hello']
>>> lst[1:3] = ["Slice", "Assignment"]
>>> lst
[1, 'Slice', 'Assignment', 'Hello']
```

As the last example shows, it's even possible to change an entire subsequence in a list by assigning a list into a slice. Python lists are very flexible. Don't attempt this in other languages!

As you know, lists can be created by listing items inside square brackets.

```
odds = [1, 3, 5, 7, 9]
food = ["spam", "eggs", "back bacon"]
silly = [1, "spam", 4, "U"]
empty = []
```

In the last example, empty is a list containing no items at all—an empty list.

A list of identical items can be created using the repetition operator. This example creates a list containing 50 zeroes:

```
zeroes = [0] * 50
```

As we discussed in Chapter 5, lists are often built up one piece at a time using the append method. Here is a fragment of code that fills a list with positive numbers typed by the user:

```
nums = []
x = input('Enter a number: ')
while x >= 0:
    nums.append(x)
    x = input("Enter a number: ")
```

In essence, nums is being used as an accumulator. The accumulator starts out empty, and each time through the loop a new value is tacked on.

The append method is just one example of a number of useful list-specific methods. This table briefly summarizes some things you can do to a list:

Method	Meaning
\<list\>.append(x)	Add element x to end of list.
\<list\>.sort()	Sort (order) the list.
\<list\>.reverse()	Reverse the list.
\<list\>.index(x)	Returns index of first occurrence of x.
\<list\>.insert(i,x)	Insert x into list at index i.
\<list\>.count(x)	Returns the number of occurrences of x in list.
\<list\>.remove(x)	Deletes the first occurrence of x in list.
\<list\>.pop(i)	Deletes the ith element of the list and returns its value.

We have seen how lists can grow by appending new items. Lists can also shrink when items are deleted. Individual items or entire slices can be removed from a list using the del operator.

```
>>> myList
[34, 26, 0, 10]
>>> del myList[1]
>>> myList
[34, 0, 10]
>>> del myList[1:3]
>>> myList
[34]
```

Notice that del is not a list method, but a built-in operation that can be used on list items.

As you can see, Python lists provide a very flexible mechanism for handling arbitrarily large sequences of data. Using lists is easy if you keep these basic principles in mind:

- A list is a sequence of items stored as a single object.

- Items in a list can be accessed by indexing, and sublists can be accessed by slicing.

- Lists are mutable; individual items or entire slices can be replaced through assignment statements.

- Lists support a number of convenient and frequently used methods.

- Lists will grow and shrink as needed.

11.2.3 Statistics with Lists

Now that you know more about lists, we are ready to solve our little statistics problem. Recall that we are trying to develop a program that can compute the mean, median, and standard deviation of a sequence of numbers entered by the user. One obvious way to approach this problem is to store the numbers in a list. We can write a series of functions—mean, stdDev, and median—that take a list of numbers and calculate the corresponding statistics.

Let's start by using lists to rewrite our original program that only computes the mean. First, we need a function that gets the numbers from the user. Let's call it getNumbers. This function will implement the basic sentinel loop from our original program to input a sequence of numbers. We will use an initially empty list as an accumulator to collect the numbers. The list will then be returned from the function.

Here's the code for getNumbers:

```
def getNumbers():
    nums = []       # start with an empty list

    # sentinel loop to get numbers
    xStr = input("Enter a number (<Enter> to quit) >> ")
    while xStr != "":
        x = eval(xStr)
```

```
        nums.append(x)    # add this value to the list
        xStr = input("Enter a number (<Enter> to quit) >> ")
    return nums
```

Using this function, we can get a list of numbers from the user with a single line of code.

```
data = getNumbers()
```

Next, let's implement a function that computes the mean of the numbers in a list. This function takes a list of numbers as a parameter and returns the mean. We will use a loop to go through the list and compute the sum.

```
def mean(nums):
    sum = 0.0
    for num in nums:
        sum = sum + num
    return sum / len(nums)
```

Notice how the average is computed and returned in the last line of this function. The `len` operation returns the length of a list; we don't need a separate loop accumulator to determine how many numbers there are.

With these two functions, our original program to average a series of numbers can now be done in two simple lines:

```
def main():
    data = getNumbers()
    print('The mean is', mean(data))
```

Next, let's tackle the standard deviation function, `stdDev`. In order use the standard deviation formula discussed above, we first need to compute the mean. We have a design choice here. The value of the mean can either be calculated inside `stdDev` or passed to the function as a parameter. Which way should we do it?

On the one hand, calculating the mean inside `stdDev` seems cleaner, as it makes the interface to the function simpler. To get the standard deviation of a set of numbers, we just call `stdDev` and pass it the list of numbers. This is exactly analogous to how `mean` (and `median` below) works. On the other hand, programs that need to compute the standard deviation will almost certainly need to compute the mean as well. Computing it again in `stdDev` results in the calculations being done twice. If our data set is large, this seems inefficient.

Since our program is going to output both the mean and the standard deviation, let's have the main program compute the mean and pass it as a parameter to stdDev. Other options are explored in the exercises at the end of the chapter.

Here is the code to compute the standard deviation using the mean (xbar) as a parameter:

```
def stdDev(nums, xbar):
    sumDevSq = 0.0
    for num in nums:
        dev = xbar - num
        sumDevSq = sumDevSq + dev * dev
    return sqrt(sumDevSq/(len(nums)-1))
```

Notice how the summation from the standard deviation formula is computed using a loop with an accumulator. The variable sumDevSq stores the running sum of the squares of the deviations. Once this sum has been computed, the last line of the function calculates the rest of the formula.

Finally, we come to the median function. This one is a little bit trickier, as we do not have a formula to calculate the median. We need an algorithm that picks out the middle value. The first step is to arrange the numbers in increasing order. Whatever value ends up in the middle of the pack is, by definition, the median. There is just one small complication. If we have an even number of values, there is no exact middle number. In that case, the median is determined by averaging the two middle values. So the median of 3, 5, 6, and 9 is $(5 + 6)/2 = 5.5$.

In pseudocode our median algorithm looks like this:

```
sort the numbers into ascending order
if the size of  data is odd:
    median = the middle value
else:
    median = the average of the two middle values
return median
```

This algorithm translates almost directly into Python code. We can take advantage of the sort method to put the list in order. To test whether the size is even, we need to see if it is divisible by two. This is a perfect application of the remainder operation. The size is even if size % 2 == 0, that is, dividing by 2 leaves a remainder of 0.

With these insights, we are ready to write the code.

```
def median(nums):
    nums.sort()
    size = len(nums)
    midPos = size // 2
    if size % 2 == 0:
        median = (nums[midPos] + nums[midPos-1]) / 2
    else:
        median = nums[midPos]
    return median
```

You should study this code carefully to be sure you understand how it selects the correct median from the sorted list.

The middle position of the list is calculated using integer division as `size // 2`. If `size` is 3, then `midPos` is 1 (2 goes into 3 just one time). This is the correct middle position, since the three values in the list will have the indexes 0, 1, 2. Now suppose `size` is 4. In this case, `midPos` will be 2, and the four values will be in locations 0, 1, 2, 3. The correct median is found by averaging the values at `midPos` (2) and `midPos-1` (1).

Now that we have all the basic functions, finishing out the program is a cinch.

```
def main():
    print("This program computes mean, median, and standard deviation.")

    data = getNumbers()
    xbar = mean(data)
    std = stdDev(data, xbar)
    med = median(data)

    print("\nThe mean is", xbar)
    print("The standard deviation is", std)
    print("The median is", med)
```

Many computational tasks from assigning grades to monitoring flight systems on the space shuttle require some sort of statistical analysis. By using the `if __name__ == '__main__'` technique, we can make our code useful as a standalone program and as a general statistical library module.

Here's the complete program:

```
# stats.py
```

```python
from math import sqrt

def getNumbers():
    nums = []        # start with an empty list

    # sentinel loop to get numbers
    xStr = input("Enter a number (<Enter> to quit) >> ")
    while xStr != "":
        x = eval(xStr)
        nums.append(x)   # add this value to the list
        xStr = input("Enter a number (<Enter> to quit) >> ")
    return nums

def mean(nums):
    sum = 0.0
    for num in nums:
        sum = sum + num
    return sum / len(nums)

def stdDev(nums, xbar):
    sumDevSq = 0.0
    for num in nums:
        dev = num - xbar
        sumDevSq = sumDevSq + dev * dev
    return sqrt(sumDevSq/(len(nums)-1))

def median(nums):
    nums.sort()
    size = len(nums)
    midPos = size // 2
    if size % 2 == 0:
        median = (nums[midPos] + nums[midPos-1]) / 2.0
    else:
        median = nums[midPos]
    return median

def main():
    print("This program computes mean, median, and standard deviation.")
```

```
data = getNumbers()
xbar = mean(data)
std = stdDev(data, xbar)
med = median(data)

print("\nThe mean is", xbar)
print("The standard deviation is", std)
print("The median is", med)

if __name__ == '__main__': main()
```

11.3 Lists of Records

All of the list examples we've looked at so far have involved lists of simple types like numbers and strings. However, a list can be used to store collections of any type. One particularly useful application is storing a collection of records. We can illustrate this idea by building on the student GPA data processing program from last chapter.

Recall that our previous grade processing program read through a file of student grade information to find and print information about the student with the highest GPA. One of the most common operations performed on this kind of data is sorting. We might want the list in different orders for different purposes. An academic advisor might like to have a file with grade information sorted alphabetically by the name of the student. To determine which students have enough credit hours for graduation, it would be useful to have the file in order according to credit-hours. And a GPA sort would be useful for deciding which students are in the top 10% of the class.

Let's write a program that sorts a file of students according to their GPA. The program will make use of a list of Student objects. We just need to borrow the Student class from our previous program and add a bit of list processing. The basic algorithm for our program is very simple.

```
Get the name of the input file from the user
Read student information into a list
Sort the list by GPA
Get the name of the output file from the user
Write the student information from the list into a file
```

Let's begin with the file processing. We want to read through the data file and create a list of students. Here's a function that takes a filename as a parameter and returns a list of Student objects from the file:

```
def readStudents(filename):
    infile = open(filename, 'r')
    students = []
    for line in infile:
        students.append(makeStudent(line))
    infile.close()
    return students
```

This function first opens the file for reading and then reads line by line, appending a student object to the students list for each line of the file. Notice that I am borrowing the makeStudent function from the gpa program; it creates a student object from a line of the file. We will have to be sure to import this function (along with the Student class) at the top of our program.

While we're thinking about files, let's also write a function that can write the list of students back out to a file. Remember, each line of the file should contain three pieces of information (name, credit hours, and quality points) separated by tabs. The code to do this is straightforward.

```
def writeStudents(students, filename):
    # students is a list of Student objects
    outfile = open(filename, 'w')
    for s in students:
        print("{0}\t{1}\t{2}".
                    format(s.getName(), s.getHours(), s.getQPoints()),
              file=outfile)
    outfile.close()
```

Notice that I used the string formatting method to generate the appropriate line of output; the \t represents a tab character.

Using the functions readStudents and writeStudents, we can easily convert our data file into a list of students and then write it back out to a file. All we have to do now is figure how to sort the records by GPA.

In the statistics program, we used the sort method to sort a list of numbers. What happens if we try to sort a list that contains something other than numbers? In this case, we want to sort a list of student objects. Let's try that out and see what happens.

```
>>> lst = gpasort.readStudents("students.dat")
>>> lst
[<gpa.Student object at 0xb7b1554c>, <gpa.Student object at 0xb7b156cc>,
 <gpa.Student object at 0xb7b1558c>, <gpa.Student object at 0xb7b155cc>,
 <gpa.Student object at 0xb7b156ec>]
>>> lst.sort()
Traceback (most recent call last):
  File "<stdin>", line 1, in <module>
TypeError: unorderable types: Student() < Student()
```

As you can see, Python gives us an error message because it does not know
how our Student objects should be ordered. If you think about it, that makes
sense. We have not defined any implicit ordering for students, and we might
want to arrange them in different order for different purposes. In this example,
we want them ranked by GPA; in another context, we may want them in alphabetical order. In data processing, the field on which records are sorted is called
a key. To put the students in alphabetical order, we would use their name as the
key. For our GPA problem, obviously, we want the GPA to be used as the key for
sorting the students.

The built-in sort method gives us a way to specify the key that is used when
sorting a list. By supplying an optional keyword parameter, key, we can pass
along a function that computes a key value for each item in the list.

```
<list>.sort(key=<key_function>)
```

The key_function must be a function that takes an item from the list as a parameter and returns the key value for that item. In our case, the list item will
be an instance of Student, and we want to use GPA as the key. Here's a suitable
key function:

```
def use_gpa(aStudent):
    return aStudent.gpa()
```

As you can see this function simply uses the gpa method defined in the Student
class to provide the key value. Having defined this little helper function, we can
use it to sort a list of Students with call to sort.

```
data.sort(key=use_gpa)
```

An important point to notice here is that I did not put parentheses on the function name (use_gpa()). I do not want to *call* the function. Rather, I am sending

use_gpa to the sort method, and it will call this function anytime it needs to compare two items to see what their relative ordering should be in the sorted list.

It's often useful to write this sort of helper function to provide keys for sorting a list; however, in this particular case, writing an additional function is not really necessary. We have already written a function that computes the GPA for a student, it's the gpa method in the Student class. If you go back and look at the definition of that method, you'll see that it takes a single parameter (self) and returns the computed GPA. Since methods are just functions, we can use this as our key and save us the trouble of writing the helper. In order to use a method as a stand-alone function, we just need to use our standard dot notation.

```
data.sort(key=Student.gpa)
```

This snippet says to use the function/method called gpa defined in the Student class.

I think we now have all the components in place for our program. Here's the completed code:

```
# gpasort.py
#    A program to sort student information into GPA order.

from gpa import Student, makeStudent

def readStudents(filename):
    infile = open(filename, 'r')
    students = []
    for line in infile:
        students.append(makeStudent(line))
    infile.close()
    return students


def writeStudents(students, filename):
    outfile = open(filename, 'w')
    for s in students:
        print("{0}\t{1}\t{2}".
              format(s.getName(), s.getHours(), s.getQPoints()),
            file=outfile)
    outfile.close()
```

```
def main():
    print("This program sorts student grade information by GPA")
    filename = input("Enter the name of the data file: ")
    data = readStudents(filename)
    data.sort(key=Student.gpa)
    filename = input("Enter a name for the output file: ")
    writeStudents(data, filename)
    print("The data has been written to", filename)

if __name__ == '__main__':
    main()
```

11.4 Designing with Lists and Classes

Lists and classes taken together give us powerful tools for structuring the data in our programs. Let's put these tools to work in some more sophisticated examples.

Remember the DieView class from last chapter? In order to display the six possible values of a die, each DieView object keeps track of seven circles representing the position of pips on the face of a die. In the previous version, we saved these circles using instance variables, pip1, pip2, pip3, etc.

Let's consider how the code looks using a collection of circle objects stored as a list. The basic idea is to replace our seven instance variables with a single list called pips. Our first problem is to create a suitable list. This will be done in the constructor for the DieView class.

In our previous version, the pips were created with this sequence of statements inside __init__:

```
self.pip1 = self.__makePip(cx-offset, cy-offset)
self.pip2 = self.__makePip(cx-offset, cy)
self.pip3 = self.__makePip(cx-offset, cy+offset)
self.pip4 = self.__makePip(cx, cy)
self.pip5 = self.__makePip(cx+offset, cy-offset)
self.pip6 = self.__makePip(cx+offset, cy)
self.pip7 = self.__makePip(cx+offset, cy+offset)
```

Recall that __makePip is a local method of the DieView class that creates a circle
centered at the position given by its parameters.

We want to replace these lines with code to create a list of pips. One approach would be to start with an empty list of pips and build up the final list one
pip at a time.

```
pips = []
pips.append(self.__makePip(cx-offset, cy-offset))
pips.append(self.__makePip(cx-offset, cy))
pips.append(self.__makePip(cx-offset, cy+offset))
pips.append(self.__makePip(cx, cy))
pips.append(self.__makePip(cx+offset, cy-offset))
pips.append(self.__makePip(cx+offset, cy))
pips.append(self.__makePip(cx+offset, cy+offset))
self.pips = pips
```

An even more straightforward approach is to create the list directly, enclosing
the calls to __makePip inside list construction brackets, like this:

```
self.pips = [ self.__makePip(cx-offset, cy-offset)),
              self.__makePip(cx-offset, cy)),
              self.__makePip(cx-offset, cy+offset)),
              self.__makePip(cx, cy)),
              self.__makePip(cx+offset, cy-offset)),
              self.__makePip(cx+offset, cy)),
              self.__makePip(cx+offset, cy+offset))
            ]
```

Notice how I have formatted this statement. Rather than making one giant line,
I put one list element on each line. Again, Python is smart enough to know that
the end of the statement has not been reached until it finds the matching square
bracket. Listing complex objects one per line like this makes it much easier to
see what is happening. Just make sure to include the commas at the end of
intermediate lines to separate the items of the list.

The advantage of a pip list is that it is much easier to perform actions on the
entire set. For example, we can blank out the die by setting all of the pips to
have the same color as the background.

```
for pip in self.pips:
    pip.setFill(self.background)
```

See how these two lines of code loop through the entire collection of pips to change their color? This required seven lines of code in the previous version using separate instance variables.

Similarly, we can turn a set of pips back on by indexing the appropriate spot in the pips list. In the original program, pips 1, 4, and 7 were turned on for the value 3.

```
self.pip1.setFill(self.foreground)
self.pip4.setFill(self.foreground)
self.pip7.setFill(self.foreground)
```

In the new version, this corresponds to pips in positions 0, 3, and 6, since the pips list is indexed starting at 0. A parallel approach could accomplish this task with these three lines of code:

```
self.pips[0].setFill(self.foreground)
self.pips[3].setFill(self.foreground)
self.pips[6].setFill(self.foreground)
```

Doing it this way makes explicit the correspondence between the individual instance variables used in the first version and the list elements used in the second version. By subscripting the list, we can get at the individual pip objects, just as if they were separate variables. However, this code does not really take advantage of the new representation.

Here is an easier way to turn on the same three pips:

```
for i in [0,3,6]:
    self.pips[i].setFill(self.foreground)
```

Using an index variable in a loop, we can turn all three pips on using the same line of code.

The second approach considerably shortens the code needed in the setValue method of the DieView class. Here is the updated algorithm:

```
Loop through pips and turn all off
Determine the list of pip indexes to turn on
Loop through the list of indexes and turn on those pips.
```

We could implement this algorithm using a multi-way selection followed by a loop.

```
for pip in self.pips:
    self.pip.setFill(self.background)
if value == 1:
    on = [3]
elif value == 2:
    on = [0,6]
elif value == 3:
    on = [0,3,6]
elif value == 4:
    on = [0,2,4,6]
elif value == 5:
    on = [0,2,3,4,6]
else:
    on = [0,1,2,4,5,6]
for i in on:
    self.pips[i].setFill(self.foreground)
```

The version without lists required 36 lines of code to accomplish the same task. But we can do even better than this.

Notice that this code still uses the if-elif structure to determine which pips should be turned on. The correct list of indexes is determined by value; we can make this decision *table-driven* instead. The idea is to use a list where each item in the list is itself a list of pip indexes. For example, the item in position 3 should be the list [0,3,6], since these are the pips that must be turned on to show a value of 3.

Here is how a table-driven approach can be coded:

```
onTable = [ [], [3], [2,4], [2,3,4],
            [0,2,4,6], [0,2,3,4,6], [0,1,2,4,5,6] ]

for pip in self.pips:
    self.pip.setFill(self.background)
on = onTable[value]
for i in on:
    self.pips[i].setFill(self.foreground)
```

I have called the table of pip indexes onTable. Notice that I padded the table by placing an empty list in the first position. If value is 0, the DieView will be blank. Now we have reduced our 36 lines of code to seven. In addition, this version is much easier to modify; if you want to change which pips are displayed for various values, you simply modify the entries in onTable.

There is one last issue to address. The onTable will remain unchanged throughout the life of any particular DieView. Rather than (re)creating this table each time a new value is displayed, it would be better to create the table in the constructor and save it in an instance variable.[1] Putting the definition of onTable into __init__ yields this nicely completed class:

```
# dieview2.py
from graphics import *
class DieView:
    """ DieView is a widget that displays a graphical
    representation of a standard six-sided die."""

    def __init__(self, win, center, size):
        """Create a view of a die, e.g.:
           d1 = GDie(myWin, Point(40,50), 20)
        creates a die centered at (40,50) having sides
        of length 20."""

        # first define some standard values
        self.win = win
        self.background = "white" # color of die face
        self.foreground = "black" # color of the pips
        self.psize = 0.1 * size   # radius of each pip
        hsize = size / 2.0        # half of size
        offset = 0.6 * hsize      # distance from center
                                  #     to outer pips

        # create a square for the face
        cx, cy = center.getX(), center.getY()
        p1 = Point(cx-hsize, cy-hsize)
        p2 = Point(cx+hsize, cy+hsize)
        rect = Rectangle(p1,p2)
        rect.draw(win)
        rect.setFill(self.background)
```

----

[1]An even better approach would be to use a class variable, but class variables are beyond the scope of the current discussion.

```
    # Create 7 circles for standard pip locations
    self.pips = [ self.__makePip(cx-offset, cy-offset),
                  self.__makePip(cx-offset, cy),
                  self.__makePip(cx-offset, cy+offset),
                  self.__makePip(cx, cy),
                  self.__makePip(cx+offset, cy-offset),
                  self.__makePip(cx+offset, cy),
                  self.__makePip(cx+offset, cy+offset) ]

    # Create a table for which pips are on for each value
    self.onTable = [ [], [3], [2,4], [2,3,4],
        [0,2,4,6], [0,2,3,4,6], [0,1,2,4,5,6] ]

    self.setValue(1)

def __makePip(self, x, y):
    """Internal helper method to draw a pip at (x,y)"""
    pip = Circle(Point(x,y), self.psize)
    pip.setFill(self.background)
    pip.setOutline(self.background)
    pip.draw(self.win)
    return pip

def setValue(self, value):
    """ Set this die to display value."""
    # Turn all the pips off
    for pip in self.pips:
        pip.setFill(self.background)

    # Turn the appropriate pips back on
    for i in self.onTable[value]:
        self.pips[i].setFill(self.foreground)
```

This example also showcases the advantages of encapsulation that I talked about in Chapter 10. We have significantly improved the implementation of the DieView class, but we have not changed the set of methods that it supports. We can substitute this improved version into any program that uses a DieView without having to modify any of the other code. The encapsulation of objects allows us to build complex software systems as a set of "pluggable modules."

11.5 Case Study: Python Calculator

The reworked DieView class shows how lists can be used effectively as instance variables of objects. Interestingly, our pips list and onTable list contain circles and lists, respectively, which are themselves objects. By nesting and combining collections and objects we can devise elegant ways of storing data in our programs.

We can even go one step further and view a program itself as a collection of data structures (collections and objects) and a set of algorithms that operate on those data structures. Now, if a program contains data and operations, one natural way to organize the program is to treat the entire application itself as an object.

11.5.1 A Calculator as an Object

As an example, we'll develop a program that implements a simple Python calculator. Our calculator will have buttons for the ten digits (0–9), a decimal point (.), four operations (+, -, *, /), and a few special keys: "C" to clear the display, "<-" to backspace over characters in the display, and "=" to do the calculation.

We'll take a very simple approach to performing calculations. As buttons are clicked, the corresponding characters will show up in the display, allowing the user to create a formula. When the "=" key is pressed, the formula will be evaluated and the resulting value shown in the display. Figure 11.1 shows a snapshot of the calculator in action.

Basically, we can divide the functioning of the calculator into two parts: creating the interface and interacting with the user. The user interface in this case consists of a display widget and a bunch of buttons. We can keep track of these GUI widgets with instance variables. The user interaction can be managed by a set of methods that manipulate the widgets.

To implement this division of labor, we will create a Calculator class that represents the calculator in our program. The constructor for the class will create the initial interface. We will make the calculator respond to user interaction by invoking a special run method.

11.5.2 Constructing the Interface

Let's take a detailed look at the constructor for the Calculator class. First, we'll need to create a graphics window to draw the interface.

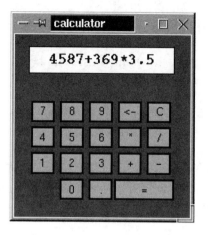

Figure 11.1: Python calculator in action

```
def __init__(self):
    # create the window for the calculator
    win = GraphWin("Calculator")
    win.setCoords(0,0,6,7)
    win.setBackground("slategray")
    self.win = win
```

The coordinates for the window were chosen to simplify the layout of the buttons. In the last line, the window object is tucked into an instance variable so that other methods can refer to it.

The next step is to create the buttons. We will reuse the button class from last chapter. Since there are a lot of similar buttons, we will use a list to store them. Here is the code that creates the button list:

```
# create list of buttons
# start with all the standard sized buttons
# bSpecs gives center coords and label of buttons
bSpecs = [(2,1,'0'), (3,1,'.'),
          (1,2,'1'), (2,2,'2'), (3,2,'3'), (4,2,'+'), (5,2,'-'),
          (1,3,'4'), (2,3,'5'), (3,3,'6'), (4,3,'*'), (5,3,'/'),
          (1,4,'7'), (2,4,'8'), (3,4,'9'), (4,4,'<-'),(5,4,'C')]
self.buttons = []
for (cx,cy,label) in bSpecs:
```

```
        self.buttons.append(Button(self.win,Point(cx,cy),
                                   .75,.75,label))
    # create the larger '=' button
    self.buttons.append(Button(self.win, Point(4.5,1),
                                   1.75, .75, "="))
    # activate all buttons
    for b in self.buttons:
        b.activate()
```

Study this code carefully. A button is normally specified by providing a center point, width, height, and label. Typing out calls to the Button constructor with all this information for each button would be tedious. Rather than creating the buttons directly, this code first creates a list of button specifications, bSpecs. This list of specifications is then used to create the buttons.

Each specification is a *tuple* consisting of the x and y coordinates of the center of the button and its label. A tuple looks like a list except that it is enclosed in round parentheses () instead of square brackets []. A tuple is just another kind of sequence in Python. Tuples are like lists except that tuples are immutable— the items can't be changed. If the contents of a sequence won't be changed after it is created, using a tuple is more efficient than using a list.

The next step is to iterate through the specification list and create a corresponding button for each entry. Take a look at the loop heading:

```
    for (cx,cy,label) in bSpecs:
```

According to the definition of a for loop, the tuple (cx,cy,label) will be assigned each successive item in the list bSpecs.

Put another way, conceptually, each iteration of the loop starts with an assignment.

```
(cx,cy,label) = <next item from bSpecs>
```

Of course, each item in bSpecs is also a tuple. When a tuple of variables is used on the left side of an assignment, the corresponding components of the tuple on the right side are *unpacked* into the variables on the left side. In fact, this is how Python actually implements all simultaneous assignments.

The first time through the loop, it is as if we had done this simultaneous assignment:

```
cx, cy, label = 2, 1, "0"
```

Each time through the loop, another tuple from bSpecs is unpacked into the variables in the loop heading. The values are then used to create a Button that is appended to the list of buttons.

After all of the standard-sized buttons have been created, the larger = button is created and tacked onto the list.

```
self.buttons.append(Button(self.win, Point(4.5,1), 1.75, .75, "="))
```

I could have written a line like this for each of the previous buttons, but I think you can see the appeal of the specification-list/loop approach for creating the 17 similar buttons.

In contrast to the buttons, creating the calculator display is quite simple. The display will just be a rectangle with some text centered on it. We need to save the text object as an instance variable so that its contents can be accessed and changed during processing of button clicks. Here is the code that creates the display:

```
bg = Rectangle(Point(.5,5.5), Point(5.5,6.5))
bg.setFill('white')
bg.draw(self.win)
text = Text(Point(3,6), "")
text.draw(self.win)
text.setFace("courier")
text.setStyle("bold")
text.setSize(16)
self.display = text
```

11.5.3 Processing Buttons

Now that we have an interface drawn, we need a method that actually gets the calculator running. Our calculator will use a classic event loop that waits for a button to be clicked and then processes that button. Let's encapsulate this in a method called run.

```
def run(self):
    while True:
        key = self.getKeyPress()
        self.processKey(key)
```

Notice that this is an infinite loop. To quit the program, the user will have to "kill" the calculator window. All that's left is to implement the `getKeyPress` and `processKey` methods.

Getting key presses is easy; we continue getting mouse clicks until one of those mouse clicks is on a button. To determine whether a button has been clicked, we loop through the list of buttons and check each one. The result is a nested loop.

```
def getKeyPress(self):
    # Waits for a button to be clicked
    # Returns the label of the button that was clicked.
    while True:
        # loop for each mouse click
        p = self.win.getMouse()
        for b in self.buttons:
            # loop for each button
            if b.clicked(p):
                return b.getLabel() # method exit
```

You can see how having the buttons in a list is a big win here. We can use a `for` loop to look at each button in turn. If the clicked point p turns out to be in one of the buttons, the label of that button is returned, providing an exit from the otherwise infinite `while` loop.

The last step is to update the display of the calculator according to which button was clicked. This is accomplished in `processKey`. Basically, this is a multi-way decision that checks the key label and takes the appropriate action.

A digit or operator is simply appended to the display. If `key` contains the label of the button, and `text` contains the current contents of the display, the appropriate line of code looks like this:

```
self.display.setText(text+key)
```

The clear key blanks the display.

```
self.display.setText("")
```

The backspace strips off one character.

```
self.display.setText(text[:-1])
```

Finally, the equal key causes the expression in the display to be evaluated and the result displayed.

```
    try:
        result = eval(text)
    except:
        result = 'ERROR'
    self.display.setText(str(result))
```

The try-except here is necessary to catch run-time errors caused by entries that
are not legal Python expressions. If an error occurs, the calculator will display
ERROR rather than causing the program to crash.

Here is the complete program:

```
# calc.pyw -- A four function calculator using Python arithmetic.
#      Illustrates use of objects and lists to build a simple GUI.

from graphics import *
from button import Button

class Calculator:
    # This class implements a simple calculator GUI

    def __init__(self):
        # create the window for the calculator
        win = GraphWin("calculator")
        win.setCoords(0,0,6,7)
        win.setBackground("slategray")
        self.win = win
        # Now create the widgets
        self.__createButtons()
        self.__createDisplay()

    def __createButtons(self):
        # create list of buttons
        # start with all the standard sized buttons
        # bSpecs gives center coords and label of buttons
        bSpecs = [(2,1,'0'), (3,1,'.'),
                  (1,2,'1'), (2,2,'2'), (3,2,'3'), (4,2,'+'), (5,2,'-'),
                  (1,3,'4'), (2,3,'5'), (3,3,'6'), (4,3,'*'), (5,3,'/'),
                  (1,4,'7'), (2,4,'8'), (3,4,'9'), (4,4,'<-'),(5,4,'C')]
        self.buttons = []
```

```
    for (cx,cy,label) in bSpecs:
        self.buttons.append(Button(self.win,Point(cx,cy),.75,.75,label))
    # create the larger = button
    self.buttons.append(Button(self.win, Point(4.5,1), 1.75, .75, "="))
    # activate all buttons
    for b in self.buttons:
        b.activate()

def __createDisplay(self):
    bg = Rectangle(Point(.5,5.5), Point(5.5,6.5))
    bg.setFill('white')
    bg.draw(self.win)
    text = Text(Point(3,6), "")
    text.draw(self.win)
    text.setFace("courier")
    text.setStyle("bold")
    text.setSize(16)
    self.display = text

def getButton(self):
    # Waits for a button to be clicked and returns the label of
    #    the button that was clicked.
    while True:
        p = self.win.getMouse()
        for b in self.buttons:
            if b.clicked(p):
                return b.getLabel() # method exit

def processButton(self, key):
    # Updates the display of the calculator for press of this key
    text = self.display.getText()
    if key == 'C':
        self.display.setText("")
    elif key == '<-':
        # Backspace, slice off the last character.
        self.display.setText(text[:-1])
    elif key == '=':
        # Evaluate the expresssion and display the result.
```

```
# the try...except mechanism "catches" errors in the
# formula being evaluated.
try:
    result = eval(text)
except:
    result = 'ERROR'
self.display.setText(str(result))
else:
    # Normal key press, append it to the end of the display
    self.display.setText(text+key)

def run(self):
    # Infinite 'event loop' to process button clicks.
    while True:
        key = self.getButton()
        self.processButton(key)

# This runs the program.
if __name__ == '__main__':
    # First create a calculator object
    theCalc = Calculator()
    # Now call the calculator's run method.
    theCalc.run()
```

Notice especially the very end of the program. To run the application, we create an instance of the Calculator class and then call its run method.

11.6   Non-sequential Collections

Python provides another built-in data type for collections, called a *dictionary*. While dictionaries are incredibly useful, they are not as common in other languages as lists (arrays). The example programs in the rest of the book will not use dictionaries, so you can skip the rest of this section if you've learned all you want to about collections for the moment.

11.6.1   Dictionary Basics

Lists allow us to store and retrieve items from sequential collections. When we want to access an item in the collection, we look it up by index—its position in the collection. Many applications require a more flexible way to look up information. For example, we might want to retrieve information about students or employees based on their social security numbers. In programming terminology, this is a *key-value pair*. We access the value (student information) associated with a particular key (social security number). If you think a bit, you can come up with lots of other examples of useful key-value pairs: names and phone numbers, usernames and passwords, zip codes and shipping costs, state names and capitals, sales items and quantity in stock, etc.

A collection that allows us to look up information associated with arbitrary keys is called a *mapping*. Python dictionaries are mappings. Some other programming languages provide similar structures called *hashes* or *associative arrays*. A dictionary can be created in Python by listing key-value pairs inside of curly braces. Here is a simple dictionary that stores some fictional usernames and passwords:

```
>>> passwd = {"guido":"superprogrammer", "turing":"genius",
            "bill":"monopoly"}
```

Notice that keys and values are joined with a ":", and commas are used to separate the pairs.

The main use for a dictionary is to look up the value associated with a particular key. This is done through indexing notation.

```
>>> passwd["guido"]
'superprogrammer'
>>> passwd["bill"]
'monopoly'
```

In general,

```
<dictionary>[<key>]
```

returns the object associated with the given key.

Dictionaries are mutable; the value associated with a key can be changed through assignment.

```
>>> passwd["bill"] = "bluescreen"
>>> passwd
{'turing': 'genius', 'bill': 'bluescreen', \
  'guido': 'superprogrammer'}
```

In this example, you can see that the value associated with 'bill' has changed to 'bluescreen'.

Also notice that the dictionary prints out in a different order from how it was originally created. This is not a mistake. Mappings are inherently unordered. Internally, Python stores dictionaries in a way that makes key lookup very efficient. When a dictionary is printed out, the order of keys will look essentially random. If you want to keep a collection of items in a certain order, you need a sequence, not a mapping.

To summarize, dictionaries are mutable collections that implement a mapping from keys to values. Our password example showed a dictionary having strings as both keys and values. In general, keys can be any immutable type, and values can be any type at all, including programmer-defined classes. Python dictionaries are very efficient and can routinely store even hundreds of thousands of items.

11.6.2 Dictionary Operations

Like lists, Python dictionaries support a number of handy built-in operations. You have already seen how dictionaries can be defined by explicitly listing the key-value pairs in curly braces. You can also extend a dictionary by adding new entries. Suppose a new user is added to our password system. We can expand the dictionary by assigning a password for the new username.

```
>>> passwd['newuser'] = 'ImANewbie'
>>> passwd
{'turing': 'genius', 'bill': 'bluescreen', \
 'newuser': 'ImANewbie', 'guido': 'superprogrammer'}
```

In fact, a common method for building dictionaries is to start with an empty collection and add the key-value pairs one at a time. Suppose that usernames and passwords were stored in a file called passwords, where each line of the file contains a username and password with a space between. We could easily create the passwd dictionary from the file.

```
passwd = {}
for line in open('passwords','r'):
    user, pass = line.split()
    passwd[user] = pass
```

To manipulate the contents of a dictionary, Python provides the following methods:

Method	Meaning
`<key> in <dict>`	Returns true if dictionary contains the specified key, false if it doesn't.
`<dict>.keys()`	Returns a sequence keys.
`<dict>.values()`	Returns a sequence of values.
`<dict>.items()`	Returns a sequence of tuples (`key`,`value`) representing the key-value pairs.
`<dict>.get(<key>, <default>)`	If dictionary has `key` returns its value; otherwise returns `default`.
`del <dict>[<key>]`	Deletes the specified entry.
`<dict>.clear()`	Deletes all entries.
`for <var> in <dict>:`	Loop over the keys.

These methods are mostly self-explanatory. For illustration, here is an interactive session using our password dictionary:

```
>>> list(passwd.keys())
['turing', 'bill', 'newuser', 'guido']
>>> list(passwd.values())
['genius', 'bluescreen', 'ImANewbie', 'superprogrammer']
>>> list(passwd.items())
[('turing', 'genius'), ('bill', 'bluescreen'),\
 ('newuser', 'ImANewbie'),('guido', 'superprogrammer')]
>>> "bill" in passwd
True
>>> 'fred' in passwd
False
>>> passwd.get('bill','unknown')
'bluescreen'
>>>  passwd.get('john','unknown')
'unknown'
>>> passwd.clear()
>>> passwd
{}
```

11.6.3   Example Program: Word Frequency

Let's write a program that analyzes text documents and counts how many times each word appears in the document. This kind of analysis is sometimes used as a crude measure of the style similarity between two documents and is also used by automatic indexing and archiving programs (such as Internet search engines).

At the highest level, this is just a multi-accumulator problem. We need a count for each word that appears in the document. We can use a loop that iterates through each word in the document and adds one to the appropriate count. The only catch is that we will need hundreds or thousands of accumulators, one for each unique word in the document. This is where a (Python) dictionary comes in handy.

We will use a dictionary where the keys are strings representing words in the document and the values are ints that count how many times the word appears. Let's call our dictionary counts. To update the count for a particular word, w, we just need a line of code something like this:

```
counts[w] = counts[w] + 1
```

This says to set the count associated with word w to be one more than the current count for w.

There is one small complication with using a dictionary here. The first time we encounter a word, it will not yet be in counts. Attempting to access a non-existent key produces a run-time KeyError. To guard against this, we need a decision in our algorithm.

```
if w is already in counts:
    add one to the count for w
else:
    set count for w to 1
```

This decision ensures that the first time a word is encountered, it will be entered into the dictionary with a count of 1.

One way to implement this decision is to use the in operator.

```
if w in counts:
    counts[w] = counts[w] + 1
else:
    counts[w] = 1
```

A more elegant approach is to use the get method.

```
counts[w] = counts.get(w,0) + 1
```

If w is not already in the dictionary, this get will return 0, and the result is that the entry for w is set to 1.

The dictionary updating code will form the heart of our program. We just need to fill in the parts around it. The first task is to split our text document into a sequence of words. In the process, we will also convert all the text to lowercase (so occurrences of "Foo" match "foo") and eliminate punctuation (so "foo," matches "foo"). Here's the code to do that:

```
fname = input("File to analyze: ")

# read file as one long string
text = open(fname,"r").read()

# convert all letters to lower case
text = text.lower()

# replace each punctuation character with a space
for ch in '!"#$%&()*+,-./:;<=>?@[\\]^_'{|}~':
    text = text.replace(ch, " ")

# split string at whitespace to form a list of words
words = text.split()
```

Now we can easily loop through the words to build the counts dictionary.

```
counts = {}
for w in words:
    counts[w] = counts.get(w,0) + 1
```

Our last step is to print a report that summarizes the contents of counts. One approach might be to print out the list of words and their associated counts in alphabetical order. Here's how that could be done:

```
# get list of words that appear in document
uniqueWords = list(counts.keys())

# put list of words in alphabetical order
```

```
uniqueWords.sort()
```

```
# print words and associated counts
for w in uniqueWords:
    print(w, counts[w])
```

For a large document, however, this is unlikely to be useful. There will be far too many words, most of which only appear a few times. A more interesting analysis is to print out the counts for the n most frequent words in the document. In order to do that, we will need to create a list that is sorted by counts (most to fewest) and then select the first n items in the list.

We can start by getting a list of key-value pairs using the `items` method for dictionaries.

```
items = list(counts.items())
```

Here `items` will be a list of tuples (e.g., `[('foo',5), ('bar',7), ('spam',376), ...]`). If we simply sort this list (`items.sort()`) Python will put them in a standard order. Unfortunately, when Python compares tuples, it orders them by components, left to right. Since the first component of each pair is the word, `items.sort()` will put this list in alphabetical order, which is not what we want.

To sort our list of items according to frequency, we can use the key-function trick again. This time, our function will take a pair as a parameter and return the second item in the pair.

```
def byFreq(pair):
    return pair[1]
```

Notice that tuples, like lists, are indexed starting at 0. So returning `pair[1]` hands back the frequency part of the tuple. With this comparison function, it is now a simple matter to sort our items by frequency.

```
items.sort(key=byFreq)
```

But we're not quite finished yet. When we have multiple words with the same frequency, it would be nice if those words appeared in the list in alphabetical order within their frequency group. That is, we want the list of pairs primarily sorted by frequency, but sorted alphabetically within each level. How can we handle this double-sortedness?

If you look at the documentation for the Python `sort` method (via `help([].sort)`) you'll see that this method performs a "stable sort *IN PLACE*." As you can probably infer, being "in place" means that the method modifies the list that it is applied to rather than producing a new, sorted, version of the list. But the critical point for us here is the word "stable." A sorting algorithm is `stable` if equivalent items (items that have equal keys) stay in the same relative position to each other in the resulting list as they were in the original. Since the Python sorting algorithm is stable, if all the words were in alphabetical order before sorting them by frequency, then words having the same frequency will still be in alphabetical order. To get the result we want, we just need to sort the list twice, first by words and then by frequency.

```
items.sort()                           # orders pairs alphabetically
items.sort(key=byFreq, reverse=True)   # orders by frequency
```

I have added one last wrinkle here. Supplying the keyword parameter `reverse` and setting it to `True` tells Python to sort the list in reverse order. The resulting list will go from highest frequency to lowest.

Now that our items are sorted in order from most to least frequent, we are ready to print a report of the n most frequent words. Here's a loop that does the trick:

```
for i in range(n):
    word, count = items[i]
    print("{0:<15}{1:>5}".format(word, count)
```

The loop index `i` is used to get the next next pair from the list of items, and that item is unpacked into its `word` and `count` components. The word is then printed left-justified in fifteen spaces, followed by the count right-justified in five spaces.[2]

That about does it. Here is the complete program:

```
# wordfreq.py

def byFreq(pair):
    return pair[1]

def main():
    print("This program analyzes word frequency in a file")
```

---

[2]An experienced Python programmer would probably write this loop body as a single line using the tuple unpacking operator `*`: `print("0:<151:>5".format(*items[i])`. The curious should consult the Python documentation to learn more about this handy operator.

```
    print("and prints a report on the n most frequent words.\n")

    # get the sequence of words from the file
    fname = input("File to analyze: ")
    text = open(fname,'r').read()
    text = text.lower()
    for ch in '!"#$%&()*+,-./:;<=>?@[\\]^_`{|}~':
        text = text.replace(ch, ' ')
    words = text.split()

    # construct a dictionary of word counts
    counts = {}
    for w in words:
        counts[w] = counts.get(w,0) + 1

    # output analysis of n most frequent words.
    n = eval(input("Output analysis of how many words? "))
    items = list(counts.items())
    items.sort()
    items.sort(key=byFreq, reverse=True)
    for i in range(n):
        word, count = items[i]
        print("{0:<15}{1:>5}".format(word, count))

if __name__ == '__main__':  main()
```

Just for fun, here's the result of running this program to find the twenty most frequent words in a draft of the book you're reading right now:

```
This program analyzes word frequency in a file
and prints a report on the n most frequent words.

File to analyze: book.txt
Output analysis of how many words? 20

the            6428
a              2845
of             2622
to             2468
```

```
is          1936
that        1332
and         1259
in          1240
we          1030
this         985
for          719
you          702
program      684
be           670
it           618
are          612
as           607
can          583
will         480
an           470
```

11.7 Chapter Summary

This chapter has discussed techniques for handling collections of related information. Here is a summary of some key ideas:

- A list object is a mutable sequence of arbitrary objects. Items can be accessed by indexing and slicing. The items of a list can be changed by assignment.

- Python lists are similar to arrays in other programming languages. Python lists are more flexible because their size can vary and they are heterogeneous. Python lists also support a number of useful methods.

- One particularly important data processing operation is sorting. Python lists have a sort method that can be customized by supplying a suitable key function. This allows programs to sort lists of arbitrary objects.

- Classes can use lists to maintain collections stored as instance variables. Oftentimes using a list is more flexible than using separate instance variables. For example, a GUI application might use a list of buttons instead of an instance variable for each button.

- An entire program can be viewed as a collection of data and a set of operations—an object. This is a common approach to structuring GUI applications.

- A Python dictionary implements an arbitrary mapping from keys into values. It is very useful for representing non-sequential collections.

11.8 Exercises

Review Questions

True/False

1. The median is the average of a set of data.

2. Standard deviation measures how spread out a data set is.

3. Arrays are usually heterogeneous, but lists are homogeneous.

4. A Python list cannot grow and shrink in size.

5. Unlike strings, Python lists are not mutable.

6. A list must contain at least one item.

7. Items can be removed from a list with the `del` operator.

8. A comparison function returns either `True` or `False`.

9. A tuple is similar to a immutable list.

10. A Python dictionary is a kind of sequence.

Multiple Choice

1. Where mathematicians use subscripting, computer programmers use
   a) slicing   b) indexing   c) Python   d) caffeine

2. Which of the following is not a built-in sequence operation in Python?
   a) sorting   b) concatenation   c) slicing   d) repetition

3. The method that adds a single item to the end of a list is
   a) extend   b) add   c) plus   d) append

4. Which of the following is not a Python list method?
   a) `index`   b) `insert`   c) `get`   d) `pop`

5. Which of the following is not a characteristic of a Python list?
   a) It is an object.
   b) It is a sequence.
   c) It can hold objects.
   d) It is immutable.

6. Which of the following expressions correctly tests if x is even?
   a) `x % 2 == 0`   b) `even(x)`   c) `not odd(x)`   d) `x % 2 == x`

7. The parameter `xbar` in `stdDev` is what?
   a) median   b) mode   c) spread   d) mean

8. What keyword parameter is used to send a key-function to the `sort` method?
   a) reverse   b) reversed   c) cmp   d) key

9. Which of the following is *not* a dictionary method?
   a) `get`   b) `keys`   c) `sort`   d) `clear`

10. The `items` dictionary method returns a(n)
    a) int   b) sequence of tuples   c) bool   d) dictionary

Discussion

1. Given the initial statements

   ```
   import string
   s1 = [2,1,4,3]
   s2 = ['c','a','b']
   ```

   show the result of evaluating each of the following sequence expressions:

   (a) `s1 + s2`

   (b) `3 * s1 + 2 * s2`

   (c) `s1[1]`

   (d) `s1[1:3]`

   (e) `s1 + s2[-1]`

2. Given the same initial statements as in the previous problem, show the values of s1 and s2 after executing each of the following statements. Treat each part independently (i.e., assume that s1 and s2 start with their original values each time).

(a) s1.remove(2)

(b) s1.sort()

(c) s1.append([s2.index('b')])

(d) s2.pop(s1.pop(2))

(e) s2.insert(s1[0], 'd')

Programming Exercises

1. Modify the statistics package from the chapter so that client programs have more flexibility in computing the mean and/or standard deviation. Specifically, redesign the library to have the following functions:

   mean(nums) Returns the mean of numbers in nums.

   stdDev(nums) Returns the standard deviation of nums.

   meanStdDev(nums) Returns both the mean and standard deviation of nums.

2. Extend the gpasort program so that it allows the user to sort a file of students based on GPA, name, or credits. Your program should prompt for the input file, the field to sort on, and the output file.

3. Extend your solution to the previous problem by adding an option to sort the list in either ascending or descending order.

4. Give the program from the previous exercise(s) a graphical interface. You should have Entrys for the input and output file names and a button for each sorting order. Bonus: Allow the user to do multiple sorts and add a button for quitting.

5. Most languages do not have the flexible built-in list (array) operations that Python has. Write an algorithm for each of the following Python operations and test your algorithm by writing it up in a suitable function. For example, as a function, reverse(myList) should do the same as myList.reverse(). Obviously, you are not allowed to use the corresponding Python method to implement your function.

    (a) `count(myList, x)` (like `myList.count(x)`)

    (b) `isin(myList, x)` (like `x in myList`))

    (c) `index(myList, x)` (like `myList.index(x)`)

    (d) `reverse(myList)` (like `myList.reverse()`)

    (e) `sort(myList)` (like `myList.sort()`)

6. Write and test a function `shuffle(myList)` that scrambles a list into a random order, like shuffling a deck of cards.

7. Write and test a function `innerProd(x,y)` that computes the inner product of two (same length) lists. The inner product of x and y is computed as:

$$\sum_{i=0}^{n-1} x_i y_i$$

8. Write and test a function `removeDuplicates(somelist)` that removes duplicate values from a list.

9. One disadvantage of passing a function to the list `sort` method is that it makes the sorting slower, since this function is called repeatedly as Python needs to compare various items.

   An alternative to creating a special key function is to create a "decorated" list that will sort in the desired order using the standard Python ordering. For example, to sort `Student` objects by GPA, we could first create a list of tuples `[(gpa0, Student0), (gpa1,Student1), ..]` and then sort this list without passing a key function. These tuples will get sorted into GPA order. The resulting list can then be traversed to rebuild a list of student objects in GPA order. Redo the `gpasort` program using this approach.

10. The Sieve of Eratosthenes is an elegant algorithm for finding all of the prime numbers up to some limit n. The basic idea is to first create a list of numbers from 2 to n. The first number is removed from the list, and announced as a prime number, and all multiples of this number up to n are removed from the list. This process continues until the list is empty.

   For example, if we wished to find all the primes up to 10, the list would originally contain 2, 3, 4, 5, 6, 7, 8, 9, 10. The 2 is removed and announced to be prime. Then 4, 6, 8, and 10 are removed, since they are

multiples of 2. That leaves 3, 5, 7, 9. Repeating the process, 3 is announced as prime and removed, and 9 is removed because it is a multiple
of 3. That leaves 5 and 7. The algorithm continues by announcing that 5 is
prime and removing it from the list. Finally, 7 is announced and removed,
and we're done.

Write a program that prompts a user for n and then uses the sieve algorithm to find all the primes less than or equal to n.

11. Write an automated censor program that reads in the text from a file and
creates a new file where all of the four-letter words have been replaced by
"****". You can ignore punctuation, and you may assume that no words
in the file are split across multiple lines.

12. Extend the program from the previous exercise to accept a file of censored
words as another input. The words in the original file that appear in the
censored words file are replaced by an appropriate number of "*"s.

13. Write a program that creates a list of card objects (see Programming Exercise 11 from Chapter 10) and prints out the cards grouped by suit and in
rank order within suit. Your program should read the list of cards from a
file, where each line in the file represents a single card with the rank and
suit separated by a space. Hint: first sort by rank and then by suit.

14. Extend the previous program to analyze a list of five cards as a poker hand.
After printing the cards, the program categorizes accordingly.

Royal Flush 10, Jack, Queen, King, Ace, all of the same suit.

Straight Flush Five ranks in a row, all of the same suit.

Four of a Kind Four of the same rank.

Full House Three of one rank and two of another.

Flush Five cards of the same suit.

Straight Five ranks in a row.

Three of a kind Three of one rank (but not a full house or four of a kind).

Two pair Two each of two different ranks.

Pair Two of the same rank (but not two pair, three or four of a kind).

X High If none of the previous categories fit, X is the value of the highest
       rank. For example, if the largest rank is 11, the hand is "Jack high."

15. Create a class Deck that represents a deck of cards. Your class should have the following methods:

    constructor Creates a new deck of 52 cards in a standard order.

    shuffle Randomizes the order of the cards.

    dealCard Returns a single card from the top of the deck and removes the card from the deck.

    cardsLeft Returns the number of cards remaining in the deck.

    Test your program by having it deal out a sequence of n cards from a shuffled deck where n is a user input. You could also use your deck object to implement a Blackjack simulation where the pool of cards is finite. See Programming Exercises 8 and 9 in Chapter 9.

16. Create a class called StatSet that can be used to do simple statistical calculations. The methods for the class are:

    __init__(self) Creates a statSet with no data in it.

    addNumber(self,x) x is a number. Adds the value x to the statSet.

    mean(self) Returns the mean of the numbers in this statSet.

    median(self) Returns the median of the numbers in this statSet.

    stdDev(self) Returns the standard deviation of the numbers in this statSet.

    count(self) Returns the count of numbers in this statSet.

    min(self) Returns the smallest value in this statSet.

    max(self) Returns the largest value in this statSet.

    Test your class with a program similar to the simple statistics program from this chapter.

17. In graphics applications, it is often useful to group separate pieces of a drawing together into a single object. For example, a face might be drawn from individual shapes, but then positioned as a whole group. Create a new class GraphicsGroup that can be used for this purpose. A GraphicsGroup will manage a list of graphics objects and have the following methods:

    __init__(self, anchor) anchor is a Point. Creates an empty group with the given anchor point.

`getAnchor(self)` Returns a clone of the anchor point.

`addObject(self, gObject)` `gObject` is a graphics object. Adds `gObject` to the group.

`move(self, dx,dy)` Move all of the objects in the group (including the anchor point).

`draw(self, win)` Draws all the objects in the group into `win`. The anchor point is not drawn.

`undraw(self)` Undraws all the objects in the group.

Use your new class to write a program that draws some simple picture with multiple components and move it to wherever the user clicks.

18. Extend the random walk program from Chapter 9 (Programming Exercise 12) to keep track of how many times each square of the sidewalk is crossed. Start your walker in the middle of a sidewalk of length n where n is a user input, and continue the simulation until it drops off one of the ends. Then print out the counts of how many times each square was landed on.

19. Create and test a `Set` class to represent a classical set. Your sets should support the following methods:

`Set(elements)` Create a set (`elements` is the initial list of items in the set).

`addElement(x)` Adds x to the set.

`deleteElement(x)` Removes x from the set, if present. If x is not in the set, the set is left unchanged.

`member(x)` Returns true if x is in the set and false otherwise.

`intersection(set2)` Returns a new set containing just those elements that are common to this set and `set2`.

`union(set2)` Returns a new set containing all of elements that are in this set, `set2`, or both.

`subtract(set2)` Returns a new set containing all the elements of this set that are not in `set2`.

Chapter 12   Object-Oriented
                           Design

Objectives

- To understand the process of object-oriented design.

- To be able to read and understand object-oriented programs.

- To understand the concepts of encapsulation, polymorphism, and inheritance as they pertain to object-oriented design and programming.

- To be able to design moderately complex software using object-oriented design.

12.1 The Process of OOD

Now that you know some data structuring techniques, it's time to stretch your wings and really put those tools to work. Most modern computer applications are designed using a data-centered view of computing. This so-called object-oriented design (OOD) process is a powerful complement to top-down design for the development of reliable, cost-effective software systems. In this chapter, we will look at the basic principles of OOD and apply them in a couple of case studies.

The essence of design is describing a system in terms of magical black boxes and their interfaces. Each component provides a set of services through its interface. Other components are users or *clients* of the services.

A client only needs to understand the interface of a service; the details of how that service is implemented are not important. In fact, the internal details may change radically and not affect the client at all. Similarly, the component providing the service does not have to consider how the service might be used. The black box just has to make sure that the service is faithfully delivered. This separation of concerns is what makes the design of complex systems possible.

In top-down design, functions serve the role of our magical black boxes. A client program can use a function as long as it understands what the function does. The details of how the task is accomplished are encapsulated in the function definition.

In object-oriented design, the black boxes are objects. The magic behind objects lies in class definitions. Once a suitable class definition has been written, we can completely ignore *how* the class works and just rely on the external interface—the methods. This is what allows you to draw circles in graphics windows without so much as a glance at the code in the `graphics` module. All the nitty-gritty details are encapsulated in the class definitions for `GraphWin` and `Circle`.

If we can break a large problem into a set of cooperating classes, we drastically reduce the complexity that must be considered to understand any given part of the program. Each class stands on its own. Object-oriented design is the process of finding and defining a useful set of classes for a given problem. Like all design, it is part art and part science.

There are many different approaches to OOD, each with its own special techniques, notations, gurus, and textbooks. I can't pretend to teach you all about OOD in one short chapter. On the other hand, I'm not convinced that reading many thick volumes will help much either. The best way to learn about design is to do it. The more you design, the better you will get.

Just to get you started, here are some intuitive guidelines for object-oriented design:

1. *Look for object candidates.* Your goal is to define a set of objects that will be helpful in solving the problem. Start with a careful consideration of the problem statement. Objects are usually described by nouns. You might underline all of the nouns in the problem statement and consider them one by one. Which of them will actually be represented in the program? Which of them have "interesting" behavior? Things that can be represented as primitive data types (numbers or strings) are probably not important candidates for objects. Things that seem to involve a grouping of related data items (e.g., coordinates of a point or personal data about an

employee) probably are.

2. *Identify instance variables.* Once you have uncovered some possible objects, think about the information that each object will need to do its job. What kinds of values will the instance variables have? Some object attributes will have primitive values; others might themselves be complex types that suggest other useful objects/classes. Strive to find good "home" classes for all the data in your program.

3. *Think about interfaces.* When you have identified a potential object/class and some associated data, think about what operations would be required for objects of that class to be useful. You might start by considering the verbs in the problem statement. Verbs are used to describe actions—what must be done. List the methods that the class will require. Remember that all manipulation of the object's data should be done through the methods you provide.

4. *Refine the nontrivial methods.* Some methods will look like they can be accomplished with a couple of lines of code. Other methods will require considerable work to develop an algorithm. Use top-down design and stepwise refinement to flesh out the details of the more difficult methods. As you go along, you may very well discover that some new interactions with other classes are needed, and this might force you to add new methods to other classes. Sometimes you may discover a need for a brand-new kind of object that calls for the definition of another class.

5. *Design iteratively.* As you work through the design, you will bounce back and forth between designing new classes and adding methods to existing classes. Work on whatever seems to be demanding your attention. No one designs a program top to bottom in a linear, systematic fashion. Make progress wherever it seems progress needs to be made.

6. *Try out alternatives.* Don't be afraid to scrap an approach that doesn't seem to be working or to follow an idea and see where it leads. Good design involves a lot of trial and error. When you look at the programs of others, you are seeing finished work, not the process they went through to get there. If a program is well designed, it probably is not the result of a first try. Fred Brooks, a legendary software engineer, coined the maxim: "Plan to throw one away." Often you won't really know how a system should be built until you've already built it the wrong way.

7. *Keep it simple.* At each step in the design, try to find the simplest approach that will solve the problem at hand. Don't design in extra complexity until it is clear that a more complex approach is needed.

The next sections will walk you through a couple of case studies that illustrate aspects of OOD. Once you thoroughly understand these examples, you will be ready to tackle your own programs and refine your design skills.

12.2   Case Study: Racquetball Simulation

For our first case study, let's return to the racquetball simulation from Chapter 9. You might want to go back and review the program that we developed the first time around using top-down design.

The crux of the problem is to simulate multiple games of racquetball where the ability of the two opponents is represented by the probability that they win a point when they are serving. The inputs to the simulation are the probability for player A, the probability for player B, and the number of games to simulate. The output is a nicely formatted summary of the results.

In the original version of the program, we ended a game when one of the players reached a total of 15 points. This time around, let's also consider shutouts. If one player gets to 7 before the other player has scored a point, the game ends. Our simulation should keep track of both the number of wins for each player and the number of wins that are shutouts.

12.2.1   Candidate Objects and Methods

Our first task is to find a set of objects that could be useful in solving this problem. We need to simulate a series of racquetball games between two players and record some statistics about the series of games. This short description already suggests one way of dividing up the work in the program. We need to do two basic things: simulate a game and keep track of some statistics.

Let's tackle simulation of the game first. We can use an object to represent a single game of racquetball. A game will have to keep track of information about two players. When we create a new game, we will specify the skill levels of the players. This suggests a class, let's call it `RBallGame`, with a constructor that requires parameters for the probabilities of the two players.

What does our program need to do with a game? Obviously, it needs to *play* it. Let's give our class a `play` method that simulates the game until it is over. We could create and play a racquetball game with two lines of code:

```
theGame = RBallGame(probA, probB)
theGame.play()
```

To play lots of games, we just need to put a loop around this code. That's all we really need in RBallGame to write the main program. Let's turn our attention to collecting statistics about the games.

Obviously, we will have to keep track of at least four counts in order to print a summary of our simulations: wins for A, wins for B, shutouts for A, and shutouts for B. We will also print out the number of games simulated, but this can be calculated by adding the wins for A and B. Here we have four related pieces of information. Rather than treating them independently, let's group them into a single object. This object will be an instance of a class called SimStats.

A SimStats object will keep track of all the information about a series of games. We have already analyzed the four crucial pieces of information. Now we have to decide what operations will be useful. For starters, we need a constructor that initializes all of the counts to 0.

We also need a way of updating the counts as each new game is simulated. Let's give our object an update method. The update of the statistics will be based on the outcome of a game. We will have to send some information to the statistics object so that the update can be done appropriately. An easy approach would be to just send the entire game and let update extract whatever information it needs.

Finally, when all of the games have been simulated, we need to print out a report of the results. This suggests a printReport method that prints out a nice report of the accumulated statistics.

We have now done enough design that we can actually write the main function for our program. Most of the details have been pushed off into the definition of our two classes.

```
def main():
    printIntro()
    probA, probB, n = getInputs()
    # Play the games
    stats = SimStats()
    for i in range(n):
        theGame = RBallGame(probA, probB) # create a new game
        theGame.play()                    # play it
        stats.update(theGame)             # get info about completed game
    # Print the results
    stats.printReport()
```

I have also used a couple of helper functions to print an introduction and get the inputs. You should have no trouble writing these functions.

Now we have to flesh out the details of our two classes. The SimStats class looks pretty easy—let's tackle that one first.

12.2.2 Implementing SimStats

The constructor for SimStats just needs to initialize the four counts to 0. Here is an obvious approach:

```
class SimStats:
    def __init__(self):
        self.winsA = 0
        self.winsB = 0
        self.shutsA = 0
        self.shutsB = 0
```

Now let's take a look at the update method. It takes a game as a normal parameter and must update the four counts accordingly. The heading of the method will look like this:

```
def update(self, aGame):
```

But how exactly do we know what to do? We need to know the final score of the game, but this information resides inside aGame. Remember, we are not allowed to directly access the instance variables of aGame. We don't even know yet what those instance variables will be.

Our analysis suggests the need for a new method in the RBallGame class. We need to extend the interface so that aGame has a way of reporting the final score. Let's call the new method getScores and have it return the score for player A and the score for player B.

Now the algorithm for update is straightforward.

```
def update(self, aGame):
    a, b = aGame.getScores()
    if a > b:                          # A won the game
        self.winsA = self.winsA + 1
        if b == 0:
            self.shutsA = self.shutsA + 1
    else:                              # B won the game
```

```
        self.winsB = self.winsB + 1
        if a == 0:
            self.shutsB = self.shutsB + 1
```

We can complete the `SimStats` class by writing a method to print out the results. Our `printReport` method will generate a table that shows the wins, win percentage, shutouts, and shutout percentage for each player. Here is a sample output:

```
Summary of 500 games:

             wins (% total)    shutouts (% wins)
------------------------------------------------
Player A:    411  82.2%           60  14.6%
Player B:     89  17.8%            7   7.9%
```

It is easy to print out the headings for this table, but the formatting of the lines takes a little more care. We want to get the columns lined up nicely, and we must avoid division by zero in calculating the shutout percentage for a player who didn't get any wins. Let's write the basic method, but procrastinate a bit and push off the details of formatting the line into another method, `printLine`. The `printLine` method will need the player label (A or B), number of wins and shutouts, and the total number of games (for calculation of percentages).

```
def printReport(self):
    # Print a nicely formatted report
    n = self.winsA + self.winsB
    print("Summary of", n , "games:\n")
    print("          wins (% total)    shutouts (% wins)  ")
    print("--------------------------------------------------")
    self.printLine("A", self.winsA, self.shutsA, n)
    self.printLine("B", self.winsB, self.shutsB, n)
```

To finish out the class, we implement the `printLine` method. This method will make heavy use of string formatting. A good start is to define a template for the information that will appear in each line.

```
def printLine(self, label, wins, shuts, n):
    template = "Player {0}:{1:5}   ({2:5.1%}) {3:11}    ({4})"
    if wins == 0:          # Avoid division by zero!
        shutStr = "-----"
```

```
       else:
           shutStr = "{0:4.1%}".format(float(shuts)/wins)
       print(template.format(label, wins, float(wins)/n, shuts, shutStr))
```

Notice how the shutout percentage is handled. The main template includes it as a fifth slot, and the `if` statement takes care of formatting this piece to prevent division by zero.

12.2.3   Implementing RBallGame

Now that we have wrapped up the `SimStats` class, we need to turn our attention to `RBallGame`. Summarizing what we have decided so far, this class needs a constructor that accepts two probabilities as parameters, a `play` method that plays the game, and a `getScores` method that reports the scores.

What will a racquetball game need to know? To actually play the game, we have to remember the probability for each player, the score for each player, and which player is serving. If you think about this carefully, you will see that probability and score are properties related to particular *players*, while the server is a property of the *game* between the two players. That suggests that we might simply consider that a game needs to know who the players are and which is serving. The players themselves can be objects that know their probability and score. Thinking about the `RBallGame` class this way leads us to design some new objects.

If the players are objects, then we will need another class to define their behavior. Let's name that class `Player`. A `Player` object will keep track of its probability and current score. When a `Player` is first created the probability will be supplied as a parameter, but the score will just start out at 0. We'll flesh out the design of `Player` class methods as we work on `RBallGame`.

We are now in a position to define the constructor for `RBallGame`. The game will need instance variables for the two players and another variable to keep track of which player is serving.

```
class RBallGame:
    def __init__(self, probA, probB):
        self.playerA = Player(probA)
        self.playerB = Player(probB)
        self.server = self.PlayerA  # Player A always serves first
```

Sometimes it helps to draw a picture to see the relationships among the objects that we are creating. Suppose we create an instance of `RBallGame` like this:

```
theGame = RBallGame(.6,.5)
```

Figure 12.1 shows an abstract picture of the objects created by this statement and their inter-relationships.

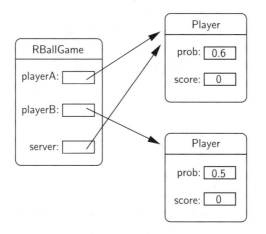

Figure 12.1: Abstract view of RBallGame object

OK, now that we can create an RBallGame, we need to figure out how to play it. Going back to the discussion of racquetball from Chapter 9, we need an algorithm that continues to serve rallies and either award points or change the server as appropriate until the game is over. We can translate this loose algorithm almost directly into our object-based code.

First, we need a loop that continues as long as the game is not over. Obviously, the decision of whether the game has ended can only be made by looking at the game object itself. Let's just assume that an appropriate isOver method can be written. The beginning of our play method can make use of this (yet-to-be-written) method.

```
def play(self):
    while not self.isOver():
```

Inside the loop, we need to have the serving player serve and, based on the result, decide what to do. This suggests that Player objects should have a method that performs a serve. After all, whether the serve is won or not depends on the probability that is stored inside of each player object. We'll just ask the server if the serve is won or lost.

```
if self.server.winsServe():
```

Based on this result, we either award a point or change the server. To award a point, we need to change a player's score. This again requires the player to do something, namely increment the score. Changing servers, on the other hand, is done at the game level, since this information is kept in the `server` instance variable of `RBallGame`.

Putting it all together, here is our `play` method:

```
def play(self):
    while not self.isOver():
        if self.server.winsServe():
            self.server.incScore()
        else:
            self.changeServer()
```

As long as you remember that `self` is an `RBallGame`, this code should be clear. While the game is not over, if the server wins a serve, award a point to the server; otherwise change the server.

Of course, the price we pay for this simple algorithm is that we now have two new methods (`isOver` and `changeServer`) that need to be implemented in the `RBallGame` class and two more (`winsServe` and `incScore`) for the `Player` class.

Before attacking these new methods, let's go back and finish up the other top-level method of the `RBallGame` class, namely `getScores`. This one just returns the scores of the two players. Of course, we run into the same problem again. It is the player objects that actually know the scores, so we will need a method that asks a player to return its score.

```
def getScores(self):
    return self.playerA.getScore(), self.playerB.getScore()
```

This adds one more method to be implemented in the `Player` class. Make sure you put that on our list to complete later.

To finish out the `RBallGame` class, we need to write the `isOver` and `changeServer` methods. Given what we have developed already and our previous version of this program, these methods are straightforward. I'll leave those as an exercise for you at the moment. If you're looking for my solutions, skip to the complete code at the end of this section.

12.2.4 | Implementing Player

In developing the `RBallGame` class, we discovered the need for a `Player` class that encapsulates the service probability and current score for a player. The `Player` class needs a suitable constructor and methods for `winsServe`, `incScore`, and `getScore`.

If you are getting the hang of this object-oriented approach, you should have no trouble coming up with a constructor. We just need to initialize the instance variables. The player's probability will be passed as a parameter, and the score starts at 0.

```python
def __init__(self, prob):
    # Create a player with this probability
    self.prob = prob
    self.score = 0
```

The other methods for our `Player` class are even simpler. To see if a player wins a serve, we compare the probability to a random number between 0 and 1.

```python
def winsServe(self):
    return random() <= self.prob
```

To give a player a point, we simply add one to the score.

```python
def incScore(self):
    self.score = self.score + 1
```

The final method just returns the value of the score.

```python
def getScore(self):
    return self.score
```

Initially, you may think that it's silly to create a class with a bunch of one- or two-line methods. Actually, it's quite common for a well-modularized, objected-oriented program to have lots of trivial methods. The point of design is to break a problem down into simpler pieces. If those pieces are so simple that their implementations are obvious, that gives us confidence that we must have gotten it right.

12.2.5 The Complete Program

That pretty much wraps up our object-oriented version of the racquetball simulation. The complete program follows. You should read through it and make
sure you understand exactly what each class does and how it does it. If you have
questions about any parts, go back to the discussion above to figure it out.

```python
# objrball.py -- Simulation of a racquet game.
#               Illustrates design with objects.

from random import random

class Player:
    # A Player keeps track of service probability and score

    def __init__(self, prob):
        # Create a player with this probability
        self.prob = prob
        self.score = 0

    def winsServe(self):
        # Returns a Boolean that is true with probability self.prob
        return random() <= self.prob

    def incScore(self):
        # Add a point to this player's score
        self.score = self.score + 1

    def getScore(self):
        # Returns this player's current score
        return self.score

class RBallGame:
    # A RBallGame represents a game in progress. A game has two players
    # and keeps track of which one is currently serving.

    def __init__(self, probA, probB):
        # Create a new game having players with the given probs.
        self.playerA = Player(probA)
```

```python
        self.playerB = Player(probB)
        self.server = self.playerA  # Player A always serves first

    def play(self):
        # Play the game to completion
        while not self.isOver():
            if self.server.winsServe():
                self.server.incScore()
            else:
                self.changeServer()

    def isOver(self):
        # Returns game is finished (i.e. one of the players has won).
        a,b = self.getScores()
        return a == 15 or b == 15 or \
               (a == 7 and b == 0) or (b==7 and a == 0)

    def changeServer(self):
        # Switch which player is serving
        if self.server == self.playerA:
            self.server = self.playerB
        else:
            self.server = self.playerA

    def getScores(self):
        # Returns the current scores of player A and player B
        return self.playerA.getScore(), self.playerB.getScore()

class SimStats:
    # SimStats handles accumulation of statistics across multiple
    #   (completed) games. This version tracks the wins and shutouts for
    #   each player.

    def __init__(self):
        # Create a new accumulator for a series of games
        self.winsA = 0
        self.winsB = 0
        self.shutsA = 0
```

```
        self.shutsB = 0

    def update(self, aGame):
        # Determine the outcome of aGame and update statistics
        a, b = aGame.getScores()
        if a > b:                              # A won the game
            self.winsA = self.winsA + 1
            if b == 0:
                self.shutsA = self.shutsA + 1
        else:                                  # B won the game
            self.winsB = self.winsB + 1
            if a == 0:
                self.shutsB = self.shutsB + 1

    def printReport(self):
        # Print a nicely formatted report
        n = self.winsA + self.winsB
        print("Summary of", n , "games:\n")
        print("            wins (% total)    shutouts (% wins)  ")
        print("--------------------------------------------------")
        self.printLine("A", self.winsA, self.shutsA, n)
        self.printLine("B", self.winsB, self.shutsB, n)

    def printLine(self, label, wins, shuts, n):
        template = "Player {0}:{1:5}   ({2:5.1%}) {3:11}    ({4})"
        if wins == 0:            # Avoid division by zero!
            shutStr = "-----"
        else:
            shutStr = "{0:4.1%}".format(float(shuts)/wins)
        print(template.format(label, wins, float(wins)/n, shuts, shutStr))


def printIntro():
    print("This program simulates games of racquetball between two")
    print('players called "A" and "B."  The ability of each player is')
    print("indicated by a probability (a number between 0 and 1) that")
    print("the player wins the point when serving. Player A always")
    print("has the first serve.\n")
```

```
def getInputs():
    # Returns the three simulation parameters
    a = eval(input("What is the prob. player A wins a serve? "))
    b = eval(input("What is the prob. player B wins a serve? "))
    n = eval(input("How many games to simulate? "))
    return a, b, n

def main():
    printIntro()

    probA, probB, n = getInputs()

    # Play the games
    stats = SimStats()
    for i in range(n):
        theGame = RBallGame(probA, probB)  # create a new game
        theGame.play()                     # play it
        stats.update(theGame)              # extract info

    # Print the results
    stats.printReport()

main()
input("\nPress <Enter> to quit")
```

12.3 Case Study: Dice Poker

Back in Chapter 10, I suggested that objects are particularly useful for the design
of graphical user interfaces. I want to finish up this chapter by looking at a
graphical application using some of the widgets that we developed in previous
chapters.

12.3.1 Program Specification

Our goal is to write a game program that allows a user to play video poker using
dice. The program will display a hand consisting of five dice. The basic set of

rules is as follows:

- The player starts with $100.

- Each round costs $10 to play. This amount is subtracted from the player's money at the start of the round.

- The player initially rolls a completely random hand (i.e., all five dice are rolled).

- The player gets two chances to enhance the hand by rerolling some or all of the dice.

- At the end of the hand, the player's money is updated according to the following payout schedule:

Hand	Pay
Two Pairs	5
Three of a Kind	8
Full House (A Pair and a Three of a Kind)	12
Four of a Kind	15
Straight (1–5 or 2–6)	20
Five of a Kind	30

Ultimately, we want this program to present a nice graphical interface. Our interaction will be through mouse clicks. The interface should have the following characteristics:

- The current score (amount of money) is constantly displayed.

- The program automatically terminates if the player goes broke.

- The player may choose to quit at appropriate points during play.

- The interface will present visual cues to indicate what is going on at any given moment and what the valid user responses are.

12.3.2   Identifying Candidate Objects

Our first step is to analyze the program description and identify some objects that will be useful in attacking this problem. This is a game involving dice and money. Are either of these good candidates for objects? Both the money and an individual die can be simply represented as numbers. By themselves, they do not seem to be good object candidates. However, the game uses five dice, and this sounds like a collection. We will need to be able to roll all the dice or a selection of dice as well as analyze the collection to see what it scores.

We can encapsulate the information about the dice in a Dice class. Here are a few obvious operations that this class will have to implement:

constructor Create the initial collection.

rollAll Assign random values to each of the five dice.

roll Assign a random value to some subset of the dice, while maintaining the current value of others.

values Return the current values of the five dice.

score Return the score for the dice.

We can also think of the entire program as an object. Let's call the class PokerApp. A PokerApp object will keep track of the current amount of money, the dice, the number of rolls, etc. It will implement a run method that we use to get things started and also some helper methods that are used to implement run. We won't know exactly what methods are needed until we design the main algorithm.

Up to this point, I have concentrated on the actual game that we are implementing. Another component to this program will be the user interface. One good way to break down the complexity of a more sophisticated program is to separate the user interface from the main guts of the program. This is often called the *model-view* approach. Our program implements some model (in this case, it models a poker game), and the interface is a view of the current state of the model.

One way of separating out the interface is to encapsulate the decisions about the interface in a separate interface object. An advantage of this approach is that we can change the look and feel of the program simply by substituting a different interface object. For example, we might have a text-based version of a program and a graphical version.

Let's assume that our program will make use of an interface object, call it a PokerInterface. It's not clear yet exactly what behaviors we will need from this class, but as we refine the PokerApp class, we will need to get information from the user and also display information about the game. These will correspond to methods implemented by the PokerInterface class.

12.3.3   Implementing the Model

So far, we have a pretty good picture of what the Dice class will do and a starting point for implementing the PokerApp class. We could proceed by working on either of these classes. We won't really be able to try out the PokerApp class until we have dice, so let's start with the lower-level Dice class.

Implementing Dice

The Dice class implements a collection of dice, which are just changing numbers. The obvious representation is to use a list of five ints. Our constructor needs to create a list and assign some initial values.

```
class Dice:
    def __init__(self):
        self.dice = [0]*5
        self.rollAll()
```

This code first creates a list of five zeroes. These need to be set to some random values. Since we are going to implement a rollAll function anyway, calling it here saves duplicating that code.

We need methods to roll selected dice and also to roll all of the dice. Since the latter is a special case of the former, let's turn our attention to the roll function, which rolls a subset. We can specify which dice to roll by passing a list of indexes. For example, roll([0,3,4]) would roll the dice in positions 0, 3 and 4 of the dice list. We just need a loop that goes through the parameter and generates a new random value for each listed position.

```
    def roll(self, which):
        for pos in which:
            self.dice[pos] = randrange(1,7)
```

Next, we can use roll to implement rollAll as follows:

```
    def rollAll(self):
        self.roll(range(5))
```

I used range(5) to generate a sequence of all the indexes.

The values function is used to return the values of the dice so that they can be displayed. Another one-liner suffices.

```
def values(self):
    return self.dice[:]
```

Notice that I created a copy of the dice list by slicing it. That way, if a `Dice` client modifies the list that it gets back from `values`, it will not affect the original copy stored in the `Dice` object. This defensive programming prevents other parts of the code from accidentally messing with our object.

Finally, we come to the `score` method. This is the function that will determine the worth of the current dice. We need to examine the values and determine whether we have any of the patterns that lead to a payoff, namely, Five of a Kind, Four of a Kind, Full House, Three of a Kind, Two Pairs, or Straight. Our function will need some way to indicate what the payoff is. Let's return a string labeling what the hand is and an int that gives the payoff amount.

We can think of this function as a multi-way decision. We simply need to check for each possible hand. If we do so in a sensible order, we can guarantee giving the correct payout. For example, a full house also contains a three of a kind. We need to check for the full house before checking for three of a kind, since the full house is more valuable.

One simple way of checking the hand is to generate a list of the counts of each value. That is, `counts[i]` will be the number of times that the value i occurs in dice. If the dice are: `[3,2,5,2,3]` then the count list would be `[0,0,2,2,0,1,0]`. Notice that `counts[0]` will always be zero, since dice values are in the range 1–6. Checking for various hands can then be done by looking for various values in `counts`. For example, if `counts` contains a 3 and a 2, the hand contains a triple and a pair; hence, it is a full house.

Here's the code:

```
def score(self):
    # Create the counts list
    counts = [0] * 7
    for value in self.dice:
        counts[value] = counts[value] + 1

    # score the hand
    if 5 in counts:
        return "Five of a Kind", 30
    elif 4 in counts:
        return "Four of a Kind", 15
    elif (3 in counts) and (2 in counts):
```

```
            return "Full House", 12
        elif 3 in counts:
            return "Three of a Kind", 8
        elif not (2 in counts) and (counts[1]==0 or counts[6] == 0):
            return "Straight", 20
        elif counts.count(2) == 2:
            return "Two Pairs", 5
        else:
            return "Garbage", 0
```

The only tricky part is the testing for straights. Since we have already checked for 5, 4, and 3 of a kind, checking that there are no pairs—not 2 in counts—guarantees that the dice show five distinct values. If there is no 6, then the values must be 1–5; likewise, no 1 means the values must be 2–6.

At this point, we could try out the Dice class to make sure that it is working correctly. Here is a short interaction showing some of what the class can do:

```
>>> from dice import Dice
>>> d = Dice()
>>> d.values()
[6, 3, 3, 6, 5]
>>> d.score()
('Two Pairs', 5)
>>> d.roll([4])
>>> d.values()
[6, 3, 3, 6, 4]
>>> d.roll([4])
>>> d.values()
[6, 3, 3, 6, 3]
>>> d.score()
('Full House', 12)
```

We would want to be sure that each kind of hand scores properly.

Implementing PokerApp

Now we are ready to turn our attention to the task of actually implementing the poker game. We can use top-down design to flesh out the details and also suggest what methods will have to be implemented in the PokerInterface class.

Initially, we know that the PokerApp will need to keep track of the dice, the amount of money, and some user interface. Let's initialize these values in the constructor.

```
class PokerApp:
    def __init__(self):
        self.dice = Dice()
        self.money = 100
        self.interface = PokerInterface()
```

To run the program, we will create an instance of this class and call its run method. Basically, the program will loop, allowing the user to continue playing hands until he or she is either out of money or chooses to quit. Since it costs $10 to play a hand, we can continue as long as self.money >= 10. Determining whether the user actually wants to play another hand must come from the user interface. Here is one way we might code the run method:

```
def run(self):
    while self.money >= 10 and self.interface.wantToPlay():
        self.playRound()
    self.interface.close()
```

Notice the call to interface.close at the bottom. This will allow us to do any necessary cleaning up such as printing a final message for the user or closing a graphics window.

Most of the work of the program has now been pushed into the playRound method. Let's continue the top-down process by focusing our attention here. Each round will consist of a series of rolls. Based on these rolls, the program will have to adjust the player's score.

```
def playRound(self):
    self.money = self.money - 10
    self.interface.setMoney(self.money)
    self.doRolls()
    result, score = self.dice.score()
    self.interface.showResult(result, score)
    self.money = self.money + score
    self.interface.setMoney(self.money)
```

This code only really handles the scoring aspect of a round. Anytime new information must be shown to the user, a suitable method from interface is invoked.

The $10 fee to play a round is first deducted and the interface is updated with
the new amount of money remaining. The program then processes a series of
rolls (doRolls), shows the user the result, and updates the amount of money
accordingly.

Finally, we are down to the nitty-gritty details of implementing the dice
rolling process. Initially, all of the dice will be rolled. Then we need a loop
that continues rolling user-selected dice until either the user chooses to quit
rolling or the limit of three rolls is reached. Let's use a local variable rolls to
keep track of how many times the dice have been rolled. Obviously, displaying
the dice and getting the list of dice to roll must come from interaction with the
user through interface.

```
def doRolls(self):
    self.dice.rollAll()
    roll = 1
    self.interface.setDice(self.dice.values())
    toRoll = self.interface.chooseDice()
    while roll < 3 and toRoll != []:
        self.dice.roll(toRoll)
        roll = roll + 1
        self.interface.setDice(self.dice.values())
        if roll < 3:
            toRoll = self.interface.chooseDice()
```

At this point, we have completed the basic functions of our interactive poker
program. That is, we have a model of the process for playing poker. We can't
really test out this program yet, however, because we don't have a user interface.

12.3.4 A Text-Based UI

In designing PokerApp we have also developed a specification for a generic
PokerInterface class. Our interface must support the methods for displaying
information: setMoney, setDice, and showResult. It must also have methods
that allow for input from the user: wantToPlay, and chooseDice. These methods can be implemented in many different ways, producing programs that look
quite different even though the underlying model, PokerApp, remains the same.

Usually, graphical interfaces are much more complicated to design and build
than text-based ones. If we are in a hurry to get our application running, we
might first try building a simple text-based interface. We can use this for testing

and debugging of the model without all the extra complication of a full-blown GUI.

First, let's tweak our PokerApp class a bit so that the user interface is supplied as a parameter to the constructor.

```
class PokerApp:
    def __init__(self, interface):
        self.dice = Dice()
        self.money = 100
        self.interface = interface
```

Then we can easily create versions of the poker program using different interfaces.

Now let's consider a bare-bones interface to test out the poker program. Our text-based version will not present a finished application, but rather, it provides a minimalist interface solely to get the program running. Each of the necessary methods can be given a trivial implementation.

Here is a complete TextInterface class using this approach:

```
# textpoker

class TextInterface:

    def __init__(self):
        print("Welcome to video poker.")

    def setMoney(self, amt):
        print("You currently have ${0}.".format(amt))

    def setDice(self, values):
        print("Dice:", values)

    def wantToPlay(self):
        ans = input("Do you wish to try your luck? ")
        return ans[0] in "yY"

    def close(self):
        print("\nThanks for playing!")

    def showResult(self, msg, score):
```

```
        print("{0}. You win ${1}.".format(msg, score))

    def chooseDice(self):
        return eval(input("Enter list of which to change ([] to stop) "))
```

Using this interface, we can test out our `PokerApp` program to see if we have
implemented a correct model. Here is a complete program making use of the
modules that we have developed:

```
# textpoker.py -- video dice poker using a text-based interface.

from pokerapp import PokerApp
from textpoker import TextInterface

inter = TextInterface()
app = PokerApp(inter)
app.run()
```

Basically, all this program does is create a text-based interface and then build a
`PokerApp` using this interface and start it running. Instead of creating a separate
module for this, we could also just add the necessary launching code at the end
of our `textpoker` module.

When running this program, we get a rough but usable interaction.

```
Welcome to video poker.
Do you wish to try your luck? y
You currently have $90.
Dice: [6, 4, 4, 2, 4]
Enter list of which to change ([] to stop) [0,4]
Dice: [1, 4, 4, 2, 2]
Enter list of which to change ([] to stop) [0]
Dice: [2, 4, 4, 2, 2]
Full House. You win $12.
You currently have $102.
Do you wish to try your luck? y
You currently have $92.
Dice: [5, 6, 4, 4, 5]
Enter list of which to change ([] to stop) [1]
Dice: [5, 5, 4, 4, 5]
Enter list of which to change ([] to stop) []
```

```
Full House. You win $12.
You currently have $104.
Do you wish to try your luck? y
You currently have $94.
Dice: [3, 2, 1, 1, 1]
Enter list of which to change ([] to stop) [0,1]
Dice: [5, 6, 1, 1, 1]
Enter list of which to change ([] to stop) [0,1]
Dice: [1, 5, 1, 1, 1]
Four of a Kind. You win $15.
You currently have $109.
Do you wish to try your luck? n

Thanks for playing!
```

You can see how this interface provides just enough so that we can test out the model. In fact, we've got a game that's already quite a bit of fun to play!

12.3.5   Developing a GUI

Now that we have a working program, let's turn our attention to a graphical interface. Our first step must be to decide exactly how we want our interface to look and function. The interface will have to support the various methods found in the text-based version and will also probably have some additional helper methods.

Designing the Interaction

Let's start with the basic methods that must be supported and decide exactly how interaction with the user will occur. Clearly, in a graphical interface, the faces of the dice and the current score should be continuously displayed. The setDice and setMoney methods will be used to change those displays. That leaves one output method, showResult, that we need to accommodate. One common way to handle this sort of transient information is with a message at the bottom of the window. This is sometimes called a *status bar*.

To get information from the user, we will make use of buttons. In wantToPlay, the user will have to decide between either rolling the dice or quitting. We could include "Roll Dice" and "Quit" buttons for this choice. That leaves us with figuring out how the user should choose dice.

To implement `chooseDice`, we could provide a button for each die and have the user click the buttons for the dice they want to roll. When the user is done choosing the dice, they could click the "Roll Dice" button again to roll the selected dice. Elaborating on this idea, it would be nice if we allowed the user to change his or her mind while selecting the dice. Perhaps clicking the button of a currently selected die would cause it to become unselected. The clicking of the button will serve as a sort of toggle that selects/unselects a particular die. The user commits to a certain selection by clicking on "Roll Dice."

Our vision for `chooseDice` suggests a couple of tweaks for the interface. First, we should have some way of showing the user which dice are currently selected. There are lots of ways we could do this. One simple approach would be to change the color of the die. Let's "gray out" the pips on the dice selected for rolling. Second, we need a good way for the user to indicate that they wish to stop rolling. That is, they would like the dice scored just as they stand. We could handle this by having them click the "Roll Dice" button when no dice are selected, hence asking the program to roll no dice. Another approach would be to provide a separate button to click that causes the dice to be scored. The latter approach seems a bit more intuitive/informative. Let's add a "Score" button to the interface.

Now we have a basic idea of how the interface will function. We still need to figure out how it will look. What is the exact layout of the widgets? Figure 12.2 is a sample of how the interface might look. I'm sure those of you with a more artistic eye can come up with a more pleasing interface, but we'll use this one as our working design.

Managing the Widgets

The graphical interface that we are developing makes use of buttons and dice. Our intent is to reuse the `Button` and `DieView` classes for these widgets that were developed in previous chapters. The `Button` class can be used as is, and since we have quite a number of buttons to manage, we can use a list of `Button`s, similar to the approach we used in the calculator program from Chapter 11.

Unlike the buttons in the calculator program, the buttons of our poker interface will not be active all of the time. For example, the dice buttons will only be active when the user is actually in the process of choosing dice. When user input is required, the valid buttons for that interaction will be set active and the others will be inactive. To implement this behavior, we can add a helper method called `choose` to the `PokerInterface` class.

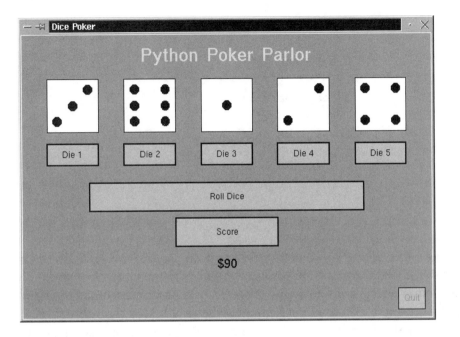

Figure 12.2: GUI interface for video dice poker

The choose method takes a list of button labels as a parameter, activates them, and then waits for the user to click one of them. The return value of the function is the label of the button that was clicked. We can call the choose method whenever we need input from the user. For example, if we are waiting for the user to choose either the "Roll Dice" or "Quit" button, we would use a sequence of code like this:

```
choice = self.choose(["Roll Dice", "Quit"])
if choice == "Roll Dice":
    ...
```

Assuming the buttons are stored in an instance variable called buttons, here is one possible implementation of choose:

```
def choose(self, choices):
    buttons = self.buttons

    # activate choice buttons, deactivate others
```

```
for b in buttons:
    if b.getLabel() in choices:
        b.activate()
    else:
        b.deactivate()

# get mouse clicks until an active button is clicked
while True:
    p = self.win.getMouse()
    for b in buttons:
        if b.clicked(p):
            return b.getLabel()   # function exit here.
```

The other widgets in our interface will be our DieView that we developed in the last two chapters. Basically, we will use the same class as before, but we need to add just a bit of new functionality. As discussed above, we want to change the color of a die to indicate whether it is selected for rerolling.

You might want to go back and review the DieView class. Remember, the class constructor draws a square and seven circles to represent the positions where the pips of various values will appear. The setValue method turns on the appropriate pips to display a given value. To refresh your memory a bit, here is the setValue method as we left it:

```
def setValue(self, value):
    # Turn all the pips off
    for pip in self.pips:
        pip.setFill(self.background)

    # Turn the appropriate pips back on
    for i in self.onTable[value]:
        self.pips[i].setFill(self.foreground)
```

We need to modify the DieView class by adding a setColor method. This method will be used to change the color that is used for drawing the pips. As you can see in the code for setValue, the color of the pips is determined by the value of the instance variable foreground. Of course, changing the value of foreground will not actually change the appearance of the die until it is redrawn using the new color.

The algorithm for setColor seems straightforward. We need two steps:

```
change foreground to the new color
redraw the current value of the die
```

Unfortunately, the second step presents a slight snag. We already have code that draws a value, namely setValue. But setValue requires us to send the value as a parameter, and the current version of DieView does not store this value anywhere. Once the proper pips have been turned on, the actual value is discarded.

In order to implement setColor, we need to tweak setValue so that it remembers the current value. Then setColor can redraw the die using its current value. The change to setValue is easy; we just need to add a single line.

```
self.value = value
```

This line stores the value parameter in an instance variable called value.

With the modified version of setValue, implementing setColor is a breeze.

```
def setColor(self, color):
    self.foreground = color
    self.setValue(self.value)
```

Notice how the last line simply calls setValue to (re)draw the die, passing along the value that was saved from the last time setValue was called.

Creating the Interface

Now that we have our widgets under control, we are ready to actually implement our GUI poker interface. The constructor will create all of our widgets, setting up the interface for later interactions.

```
class GraphicsInterface:
    def __init__(self):
        self.win = GraphWin("Dice Poker", 600, 400)
        self.win.setBackground("green3")
        banner = Text(Point(300,30), "Python  Poker  Parlor")
        banner.setSize(24)
        banner.setFill("yellow2")
        banner.setStyle("bold")
        banner.draw(self.win)
        self.msg = Text(Point(300,380), "Welcome to the Dice Table")
        self.msg.setSize(18)
```

```
self.msg.draw(self.win)
self.createDice(Point(300,100), 75)
self.buttons = []
self.addDiceButtons(Point(300,170), 75, 30)
b = Button(self.win, Point(300, 230), 400, 40, "Roll Dice")
self.buttons.append(b)
b = Button(self.win, Point(300, 280), 150, 40, "Score")
self.buttons.append(b)
b = Button(self.win, Point(570,375), 40, 30, "Quit")
self.buttons.append(b)
self.money = Text(Point(300,325), "$100")
self.money.setSize(18)
self.money.draw(self.win)
```

You should compare this code to Figure 12.2 to make sure you understand how the elements of the interface are created and positioned.

I hope you noticed that I pushed the creation of the dice and their associated buttons into a couple of helper methods. Here are the necessary definitions:

```
def createDice(self, center, size):
    center.move(-3*size,0)
    self.dice = []
    for i in range(5):
        view = DieView(self.win, center, size)
        self.dice.append(view)
        center.move(1.5*size,0)

def addDiceButtons(self, center, width, height):
    center.move(-3*width, 0)
    for i in range(1,6):
        label = "Die {0}".format(i)
        b = Button(self.win, center, width, height, label)
        self.buttons.append(b)
        center.move(1.5*width, 0)
```

These two methods are similar in that they employ a loop to draw five similar widgets. In both cases, a Point variable, center, is used to calculate the correct position of the next widget.

Implementing the Interaction

You might be a little scared at this point that the constructor for our GUI interface was so complex. Even simple graphical interfaces involve many independent components. Getting them all set up and initialized is often the most tedious part of coding the interface. Now that we have that part out of the way, actually writing the code that handles the interaction will not be too hard, provided we attack it one piece at a time.

Let's start with the simple output methods setMoney and showResult. These two methods display some text in our interface window. Since our constructor took care of creating and positioning the relevant Text objects, all our methods have to do is call the setText methods for the appropriate objects.

```python
def setMoney(self, amt):
    self.money.setText("${0}".format(amt))

def showResult(self, msg, score):
    if score > 0:
        text = "{0}! You win ${1}".format(msg, score)
    else:
        text = "You rolled {0}".format(msg)
    self.msg.setText(text)
```

In a similar spirit, the output method setDice must make a call to the setValue method of the appropriate DieView objects in dice. We can do this with a for loop.

```python
def setDice(self, values):
    for i in range(5):
        self.dice[i].setValue(values[i])
```

Take a good look at the line in the loop body. It sets the ith die to show the ith value.

As you can see, once the interface has been constructed, making it functional is not overly difficult. Our output methods are completed with just a few lines of code. The input methods are only slightly more complicated.

The wantToPlay method will wait for the user to click either "Roll Dice" or "Quit." We can use our choose helper method to do this.

```python
def wantToPlay(self):
    ans = self.choose(["Roll Dice", "Quit"])
```

```
self.msg.setText("")
return ans == "Roll Dice"
```

After waiting for the user to click an appropriate button, this method then clears out any message—such as the previous results—by setting the msg text to the empty string. The method then returns a Boolean value by examining the label returned by choose.

That brings us to the chooseDice method. Here we must implement a more extensive user interaction. The chooseDice method returns a list of the indexes of the dice that the user wishes to roll.

In our GUI, the user will choose dice by clicking on corresponding buttons. We need to maintain a list of which dice have been chosen. Each time a die button is clicked, that die is either chosen (its index is appended to the list) or unchosen (its index is removed from the list). In addition, the color of the corresponding DieView reflects the status of the die. The interaction ends when the user clicks either the roll button or the score button. If the roll button is clicked, the method returns the list of currently chosen indexes. If the score button is clicked, the function returns an empty list to signal that the player is done rolling.

Here is one way to implement the choosing of dice. The comments in this code explain the algorithm:

```
def chooseDice(self):
    # choices is a list of the indexes of the selected dice
    choices = []                     # No dice chosen yet
    while True:
        # wait for user to click a valid button
        b = self.choose(["Die 1", "Die 2", "Die 3", "Die 4", "Die 5",
                         "Roll Dice", "Score"])

        if b[0] == "D":                  # User clicked a die button
            i = eval(b[4]) - 1           # Translate label to die index
            if i in choices:             # Currently selected, unselect it
                choices.remove(i)
                self.dice[i].setColor("black")
            else:                        # Currently unselected, select it
                choices.append(i)
                self.dice[i].setColor("gray")
        else:                                # User clicked Roll or Score
```

```
for d in self.dice:      # Revert appearance of all dice
    d.setColor("black")
if b == "Score":         # Score clicked, ignore choices
    return []
elif choices != []:      # Don't accept Roll unless some
    return choices       #   dice are actually selected
```

That about wraps up our program. The only missing piece of our interface class is the close method. To close up the graphical version, we just need to close the graphics window.

```
def close(self):
    self.win.close()
```

Finally, we need a few lines to actually get our graphical poker playing program started. This code is exactly like the start code for the textual version, except that we use a GraphicsInterface in place of the TextInterface.

```
inter = GraphicsInterface()
app = PokerApp(inter)
app.run()
```

We now have a complete, usable video dice poker game. Of course, our game is lacking a lot of bells and whistles such as printing a nice introduction, providing help with the rules, and keeping track of high scores. I have tried to keep this example relatively simple, while still illustrating important issues in the design of GUIs using objects. Improvements are left as exercises for you. Have fun with them!

12.4 OO Concepts

My goal for the racquetball and video poker case studies was to give you a taste for what OOD is all about. Actually, what you've seen is only a distillation of the design process for these two programs. Basically, I have walked you through the algorithms and rationale for two completed designs. I did not document every single decision, false start, and detour along the way. Doing so would have at least tripled the size of this (already long) chapter. You will learn best by making your own decisions and discovering your own mistakes, not by reading about mine.

Still, these smallish examples illustrate much of the power and allure of the object-oriented approach. Hopefully, you can see why OO techniques are becoming standard practice in software development. The bottom line is that the OO approach helps us to produce complex software that is more reliable and cost-effective. However, I still have not defined exactly what counts as objected-oriented development.

Most OO gurus talk about three features that together make development truly object-oriented: *encapsulation*, *polymorphism*, and *inheritance*. I don't want to belabor these concepts too much, but your introduction to object-oriented design and programming would not be complete without at least some understanding of what is meant by these terms.

12.4.1 Encapsulation

I have already mentioned the term *encapsulation* in previous discussion of objects. As you know, objects know stuff and do stuff. They combine data and operations. This process of packaging some data along with the set of operations that can be performed on the data is called encapsulation.

Encapsulation is one of the major attractions of using objects. It provides a convenient way to compose complex solutions that corresponds to our intuitive view of how the world works. We naturally think of the world around us as consisting of interacting objects. Each object has its own identity, and knowing what kind of object it is allows us to understand its nature and capabilities. I look out my window and I see houses, cars, and trees, not a swarming mass of countless molecules or atoms.

From a design standpoint, encapsulation also provides a critical service of separating the concerns of "what" vs. "how." The actual implementation of an object is independent of its use. The implementation can change, but as long as the interface is preserved, other components that rely on the object will not break. Encapsulation allows us to isolate major design decisions, especially ones that are subject to change.

Another advantage of encapsulation is that it supports code reuse. It allows us to package up general components that can be used from one program to the next. The DieView class and Button classes are good examples of reusable components.

Encapsulation is probably the chief benefit of using objects, but alone it only makes a system *object-based*. To be truly objected-*oriented*, the approach must also have the characteristics of *polymorphism* and *inheritance*.

12.4.2 | Polymorphism

Literally, the word *polymorphism* means "many forms." When used in object-oriented literature, this refers to the fact that what an object does in response to a message (a method call) depends on the type or class of the object.

Our poker program illustrated one aspect of polymorphism. The PokerApp class was used both with a TextInterface and a GraphicsInterface. There were two different forms of interface, and the PokerApp class could function quite well with either. When the PokerApp called the showDice method, for example, the TextInterface showed the dice one way and the GraphicsInterface did it another way.

In our poker example, we used either the text interface or the graphics interface. The remarkable thing about polymorphism, however, is that a given line in a program may invoke a completely different method from one moment to the next. As a simple example, suppose you had a list of graphics objects to draw on the screen. The list might contain a mixture of Circle, Rectangle, Polygon, etc. You could draw all the items in a list with this simple code:

```
for obj in objects:
    obj.draw(win)
```

Now ask yourself, what operation does this loop actually execute? When obj is a circle, it executes the draw method from the circle class. When obj is a rectangle, it is the draw method from the rectangle class, etc.

Polymorphism gives object-oriented systems the flexibility for each object to perform an action just the way that it should be performed for that object. Before object orientation, this kind of flexibility was much harder to achieve.

12.4.3 | Inheritance

The third important property for object-oriented approaches, *inheritance*, is one that we have not yet used. The idea behind inheritance is that a new class can be defined to borrow behavior from another class. The new class (the one doing the borrowing) is called a *subclass*, and the existing class (the one being borrowed from) is its *superclass*.

For example, if we are building a system to keep track of employees, we might have a class Employee that contains the general information that is common to all employees. One example attribute would be a homeAddress method that returns the home address of an employee. Within the class of all employees, we might distinguish between SalariedEmployee and HourlyEmployee.

We could make these subclasses of Employee, so they would share methods like
homeAddress. However, each subclass would have its own monthlyPay function,
since pay is computed differently for these different classes of employees.

Inheritance provides two benefits. One is that we can structure the classes of
a system to avoid duplication of operations. We don't have to write a separate
homeAddress method for the HourlyEmployee and SalariedEmployee classes.
A closely related benefit is that new classes can often be based on existing
classes, promoting code reuse.

We could have used inheritance to build our poker program. When we first
wrote the DieView class, it did not provide a way of changing the appearance of
the die. We solved this problem by modifying the original class definition. An
alternative would have been to leave the original class unchanged and create a
new subclass ColorDieView. A ColorDieView is just like a DieView except that
it contains an additional method that allows us to change its color. Here is how
it would look in Python:

```python
class ColorDieView(DieView):

    def setValue(self, value):
        self.value = value
        DieView.setValue(self, value)

    def setColor(self, color):
        self.foreground = color
        self.setValue(self.value)
```

The first line of this definition says that we are defining a new class ColorDieView
that is based on (i.e., a subclass of) DieView. Inside the new class, we define two
methods. The second method, setColor, adds the new operation. Of course, in
order to make setColor work, we also need to modify the setValue operation
slightly.

The setValue method in ColorDieView redefines or *overrides* the definition
of setValue that was provided in the DieView class. The setValue method in
the new class first stores the value and then relies on the setValue method
of the superclass DieView to actually draw the pips. Notice especially how
the call to the method from the superclass is made. The normal approach
self.setValue(value) would refer to the setValue method of the ColorDieView
class, since self is an instance of ColorDieView. In order to call the original
setValue method from the superclass, it is necessary to put the class name
where the object would normally go.

```
DieView.setValue(self, value)
```

The actual object to which the method is applied is then sent as the first parameter.

12.5 Chapter Summary

This chapter has not introduced very much in the way of new technical content. Rather it has illustrated the process of object-oriented design through the racquetball simulation and dice poker case studies. The key ideas of OOD are summarized here:

- Object-oriented design (OOD) is the process of developing a set of classes to solve a problem. It is similar to top-down design in that the goal is to develop a set of black boxes and associated interfaces. Where top-down design looks for functions, OOD looks for objects.

- There are many different ways to do OOD. The best way to learn is by doing it. Some intuitive guidelines can help:

  1. Look for object candidates.
  2. Identify instance variables.
  3. Think about interfaces.
  4. Refine nontrivial methods.
  5. Design iteratively.
  6. Try out alternatives.
  7. Keep it simple.

- In developing programs with sophisticated user interfaces, it's useful to separate the program into model and view components. One advantage of this approach is that it allows the program to sport multiple looks (e.g., text and GUI interfaces).

- There are three fundamental principles that make software object oriented:

  Encapsulation Separating the implementation details of an object from how the object is used. This allows for modular design of complex programs.

Polymorphism Different classes may implement methods with the same signature. This makes programs more flexible, allowing a single line of code to call different methods in different situations.

Inheritance A new class can be derived from an existing class. This supports sharing of methods among classes and code reuse.

12.6 Exercises

Review Questions

True/False

1. Object-oriented design is the process of finding and defining a useful set of functions for solving a problem.

2. Candidate objects can be found by looking at the verbs in a problem description.

3. Typically, the design process involves considerable trial-and-error.

4. GUIs are often built with a model-view architecture.

5. Hiding the details of an object in a class definition is called instantiation.

6. Polymorphism literally means "many changes."

7. A superclass inherits behaviors from its subclasses.

8. GUIs are generally easier to write than text-based interfaces.

Multiple Choice

1. Which of the following was not a class in the racquetball simulation?
   a) `Player`   b) `SimStats`   c) `RBallGame`   d) `Score`

2. What is the data type of `server` in an `RBallGame`?
   a) int   b) `Player`   c) bool   d) `SimStats`

3. The `isOver` method is defined in which class?
   a) `SimStats`   b) `RBallGame`   c) `Player`   d) `PokerApp`

4. Which of the following is not one of the fundamental characteristics of object-oriented design/programming?
   a) inheritance   b) polymorphism
   c) generality   d) encapsulation

5. Separating the user interface from the "guts" of an application is called a(n) ___ approach.
   a) abstract   b) object-oriented
   c) model-theoretic   d) model-view

Discussion

1. In your own words, describe the process of OOD.

2. In your own words, define *encapsulation*, *polymorphism*, and *inheritance*.

Programming Exercises

1. Modify the Dice Poker program from this chapter to include any or all of the following features:

   (a) Splash Screen. When the program first fires up, have it print a short introductory message about the program and buttons for "Let's Play" and "Exit." The main interface shouldn't appear unless the user selects "Let's Play."

   (b) Add a help button that pops up another window displaying the rules of the game (the payoffs table is the most important part).

   (c) Add a high score feature. The program should keep track of the 10 best scores. When a user quits with a good enough score, he/she is invited to type in a name for the list. The list should be printed in the splash screen when the program first runs. The high-scores list will have to be stored in a file so that it persists between program invocations.

2. Using the ideas from this chapter, implement a simulation of another racquet game. See the programming exercises from Chapter 9 for some ideas.

3. Write a program to keep track of conference attendees. For each attendee, your program should keep track of name, company, state, and email address. Your program should allow users to do things such as add a new

attendee, display info on an attendee, delete an attendee, list the name and email addresses of all attendees, and list the name and email address of all attendees from a given state. The attendee list should be stored in a file and loaded when the program starts.

4. Write a program that simulates an Automatic Teller Machine (ATM). Since you probably don't have access to a card reader, have the initial screen ask for user id and a PIN. The user id will be used to look up the info for the user's accounts (including the PIN to see if it matches what the user types). Each user will have access to a checking account and a savings account. The user should able to check balances, withdraw cash, and transfer money between accounts. Design your interface to be similar to what you see on your local ATM. The user account information should be stored in a file when the program terminates. This file is read in again when the program restarts.

5. Find the rules to an interesting dice game and write an interactive program to play it. Some examples are Craps, Yacht, Greed, and Skunk.

6. Write a program that deals four bridge hands, counts how many points they have, and gives opening bids. You will probably need to consult a beginner's guide to bridge to help you out.

7. Find a simple card game that you like and implement an interactive program to play that game. Some possibilities are War, Blackjack, various solitaire games, and Crazy Eights.

8. Write an interactive program for a board game. Some examples are Othello(Reversi), Connect Four, Battleship, Sorry!, and Parcheesi.

Chapter 13   Algorithm Design and Recursion

![separator bar]

Objectives

- To understand basic techniques for analyzing the efficiency of algorithms.

- To know what searching is and understand the algorithms for linear and binary search.

- To understand the basic principles of recursive definitions and functions and be able to write simple recursive functions.

- To understand sorting in depth and know the algorithms for selection sort and merge sort.

- To appreciate how the analysis of algorithms can demonstrate that some problems are intractable and others are unsolvable.

If you have worked your way through to this point in the book, you are well on the way to becoming a programmer. Way back in Chapter 1, I discussed the relationship between programming and the study of computer science. Now that you have some programming skills, you are ready to start considering some broader issues in the field. Here we will take up one of the central issues, namely the design and analysis of algorithms. Along the way, you'll get a glimpse of recursion, a particularly powerful way of thinking about algorithms.

13.1   Searching

Let's begin by considering a very common and well-studied programming problem: *searching*. Searching is the process of looking for a particular value in a collection. For example, a program that maintains the membership list for a club might need to look up the information about a particular member. This involves some form of search process.

13.1.1   A Simple Searching Problem

To make the discussion of searching algorithms as simple as possible, let's boil the problem down to its essence. Here is the specification of a simple searching function:

```
def search(x, nums):
    # nums is a list of numbers and x is a number
    # Returns the position in the list where x occurs or -1 if
    #     x is not in the list.
```

Here are a couple of interactive examples that illustrate its behavior:

```
>>> search(4, [3, 1, 4, 2, 5])
2
>>> search(7, [3, 1, 4, 2, 5])
-1
```

In the first example, the function returns the index where 4 appears in the list. In the second example, the return value -1 indicates that 7 is not in the list.

You may recall from our discussion of list operations that Python actually provides a number of built-in search-related methods. For example, we can test to see if a value appears in a sequence using in.

```
if x in nums:
    # do something
```

If we want to know the position of x in a list, the index method fills the bill nicely.

```
>>> nums = [3,1,4,2,5]
>>> nums.index(4)
2
```

In fact, the only difference between our `search` function and `index` is that the latter raises an exception if the target value does not appear in the list. We could implement `search` using `index` by simply catching the exception and returning -1 for that case.

```
def search(x, nums):
    try:
        return nums.index(x)
    except:
        return -1
```

This approach avoids the question, however. The real issue is how does Python actually search the list? What is the algorithm?

13.1.2 Strategy 1: Linear Search

Let's try our hand at developing a search algorithm using a simple "be the computer" strategy. Suppose that I gave you a page full of numbers in no particular order and asked whether the number 13 is in the list. How would you solve this problem? If you are like most people, you would simply scan down the list comparing each value to 13. When you see 13 in the list, you quit and tell me that you found it. If you get to the very end of the list without seeing 13, then you tell me it's not there.

This strategy is called a *linear search*. You are searching through the list of items one by one until the target value is found. This algorithm translates directly into simple code.

```
def search(x, nums):
    for i in range(len(nums)):
        if nums[i] == x:    # item found, return the index value
            return i
    return -1               # loop finished, item was not in list
```

This algorithm was not hard to develop, and it will work very nicely for modest-sized lists. For an unordered list, this algorithm is as good as any. The Python `in` and `index` operations both implement linear searching algorithms.

If we have a very large collection of data, we might want to organize it in some way so that we don't have to look at every single item to determine where, or if, a particular value appears in the list. Suppose that the list is stored in sorted order (lowest to highest). As soon as we encounter a value that is greater than the target value, we can quit the linear search without looking at the rest of the list. On average, that saves us about half of the work. But, if the list is sorted, we can do even better than this.

13.1.3 Strategy 2: Binary Search

When a list is ordered, there is a much better searching strategy, one that you probably already know. Have you ever played the number guessing game? I pick a number between 1 and 100, and you try to guess what it is. Each time you guess, I will tell you if your guess is correct, too high, or too low. What is your strategy?

If you play this game with a very young child, they might well adopt a strategy of simply guessing numbers at random. An older child might employ a systematic approach corresponding to linear search, guessing $1, 2, 3, 4, \ldots$ until the mystery value is found.

Of course, virtually any adult will first guess 50. If told that the number is higher, then the range of possible values is 50–100. The next logical guess is 75. Each time we guess the middle of the remaining numbers to try to narrow down the possible range. This strategy is called a *binary search*. Binary means two, and at each step, we are dividing the remaining numbers into two parts.

We can employ a binary search strategy to look through a sorted list. The basic idea is that we use two variables to keep track of the endpoints of the range in the list where the item could be. Initially, the target could be anywhere in the list, so we start with variables low and high set to the first and last positions of the list, respectively.

The heart of the algorithm is a loop that looks at the item in the middle of the remaining range to compare it to x. If x is smaller than the middle item, then we move high, so that the search is narrowed to the lower half. If x is larger, then we move low, and the search is narrowed to the upper half. The loop terminates when x is found or there are no longer any more places to look (i.e., low > high). Here is the code:

```
def search(x, nums):
    low = 0
    high = len(nums) - 1
    while low <= high:              # There is still a range to search
        mid = (low + high)//2       # position of middle item
        item = nums[mid]
        if x == item :              # Found it! Return the index
```

```
        return mid
    elif x < item:            # x is in lower half of range
        high = mid - 1        #    move top marker down
    else:                     # x is in upper half
        low = mid + 1         #    move bottom marker up
return -1                     # no range left to search,
                              # x is not there
```

This algorithm is quite a bit more sophisticated than the simple linear search. You might want to trace through a couple of example searches to convince yourself that it actually works.

13.1.4 Comparing Algorithms

So far, we have developed two solutions to our simple searching problem. Which one is better? Well, that depends on what exactly we mean by better. The linear search algorithm is much easier to understand and implement. On the other hand, we expect that the binary search is more efficient, because it doesn't have to look at every value in the list. Intuitively, then, we might expect the linear search to be a better choice for small lists and binary search a better choice for larger lists. How could we actually confirm such intuitions?

One approach would be to do an empirical test. We could simply code up both algorithms and try them out on various sized lists to see how long the search takes. These algorithms are both quite short, so it would not be difficult to run a few experiments. When I tested the algorithms on my particular computer (a somewhat dated laptop), linear search was faster for lists of length 10 or less, and there was not much noticeable difference in the range of length 10–1000. After that, binary search was a clear winner. For a list of a million elements, linear search averaged 2.5 seconds to find a random value, whereas binary search averaged only 0.0003 seconds.

The empirical analysis has confirmed our intuition, but these are results from one particular machine under specific circumstances (amount of memory, processor speed, current load, etc.). How can we be sure that the results will always be the same?

Another approach is to analyze our algorithms abstractly to see how efficient they are. Other factors being equal, we expect the algorithm with the fewest number of "steps" to be the more efficient. But how do we count the number of steps? For example, the number of times that either algorithm goes through its main loop will depend on the particular inputs. We have already guessed that the advantage of binary search increases as the size of the list increases.

Computer scientists attack these problems by analyzing the number of steps that an algorithm will take relative to the size or difficulty of the specific problem instance being solved. For searching, the difficulty is determined by the size of the collection. Obviously, it takes more steps to find a number in a collection of a million than it does in a collection of ten. The pertinent question is *how many steps are needed to find a value in a list of size n*. We are particularly interested in what happens as n gets very large.

Let's consider the linear search first. If we have a list of ten items, the most work our algorithm might have to do is to look at each item in turn. The loop will iterate at most ten times. Suppose the list is twice as big. Then we might have to look at twice as many items. If the list is three times as large, it will take three times as long, etc. In general, the amount of time required is linearly related to the size of the list n. This is what computer scientists call a *linear time* algorithm. Now you really know why it's called a linear search.

What about the binary search? Let's start by considering a concrete example. Suppose the list contains sixteen items. Each time through the loop, the remaining range is cut in half. After one pass, there are eight items left to consider. The next time through there will be four, then two, and finally one. How many times will the loop execute? It depends on how many times we can halve the range before running out of data. This table might help you to sort things out:

List size	Halvings
1	0
2	1
4	2
8	3
16	4

Can you see the pattern here? Each extra iteration of the loop doubles the size of the list. If the binary search loops i times, it can find a single value in a list of size 2^i. Each time through the loop, it looks at one value (the middle) in the list. To see how many items are examined in a list of size n, we need to solve this relationship: $n = 2^i$ for i. In this formula, i is just an exponent with a base of 2. Using the appropriate logarithm gives us this relationship: $i = \log_2 n$. If you are not entirely comfortable with logarithms, just remember that this value is the number of times that a collection of size n can be cut in half.

OK, so what does this bit of math tell us? Binary search is an example of a *log time* algorithm. The amount of time it takes to solve a given problem grows as the log of the problem size. In the case of binary search, each additional iteration doubles the size of the problem that we can solve.

You might not appreciate just how efficient binary search really is. Let me try to put it in perspective. Suppose you have a New York City phone book with, say, twelve million names listed in alphabetical order. You walk up to a typical New Yorker on the street and make the following proposition (assuming their number is listed): "I'm going to try guessing your name. Each time I guess a name, you tell me if your name comes alphabetically before or after the name I guess." How many guesses will you need?

Our analysis above shows the answer to this question is $log_2 12,000,000$. If you don't have a calculator handy, here is a quick way to estimate the result. $2^{10} = 1024$ or roughly 1000, and $1000 \times 1000 = 1,000,000$. That means that $2^{10} \times 2^{10} = 2^{20} \approx 1,000,000$. That is, 2^{20} is approximately one million. So, searching a million items requires only 20 guesses. Continuing on, we need 21 guesses for two million, 22 for four million, 23 for eight million, and 24 guesses to search among sixteen million names. We can figure out the name of a total stranger in New York City using only 24 guesses! By comparison, a linear search would require (on average) 6 million guesses. Binary search is a phenomenally good algorithm!

I said earlier that Python uses a linear search algorithm to implement its built-in searching methods. If a binary search is so much better, why doesn't Python use it? The reason is that the binary search is less general; in order to work, the list must be in order. If you want to use binary search on an unordered list, the first thing you have to do is put it in order or *sort* it. This is another well-studied problem in computer science, and one that we should look at. Before we turn to sorting, however, we need to generalize the algorithm design technique that we used to develop the binary search.

13.2   Recursive Problem-solving

Remember, the basic idea behind the binary search algorithm was to successively divide the problem in half. This is sometimes referred to as a "divide and conquer" approach to algorithm design, and it often leads to very efficient algorithms.

One interesting aspect of divide and conquer algorithms is that the original problem divides into subproblems that are just smaller versions of the original.

To see what I mean, think about the binary search again. Initially, the range to search is the entire list. Our first step is to look at the middle item in the list. Should the middle item turn out to be the target, then we are finished. If it is not the target, we continue *by performing binary search on either the top-half or the bottom half of the list.*

Using this insight, we might express the binary search algorithm in another way.

```
Algorithm: binarySearch -- search for x in nums[low]...nums[high]

mid = (low + high) // 2
if low > high
    x is not in nums
elif x < nums[mid]
    perform binary search for x in nums[low]...nums[mid-1]
else
    perform binary search for x in nums[mid+1]...nums[high]
```

Rather than using a loop, this definition of the binary search seems to refer to itself. What is going on here? Can we actually make sense of such a thing?

13.2.1 Recursive Definitions

A description of something that refers to itself is called a *recursive* definition. In our last formulation, the binary search algorithm makes use of its own description. A "call" to binary search "recurs" inside of the definition—hence, the label "recursive definition."

At first glance, you might think recursive definitions are just nonsense. Surely you have had a teacher who insisted that you can't use a word inside its own definition? That's called a circular definition and is usually not worth much credit on an exam.

In mathematics, however, certain recursive definitions are used all the time. As long as we exercise some care in the formulation and use of recursive definitions, they can be quite handy and surprisingly powerful. The classic recursive example in mathematics is the definition of factorial.

Back in Chapter 3, we defined the factorial of a value like this:

$$n! = n(n-1)(n-2)\ldots(1)$$

For example, we can compute

$$5! = 5(4)(3)(2)(1)$$

Recall that we implemented a program to compute factorials using a simple loop that accumulates the factorial product.

Looking at the calculation of $5!$, you will notice something interesting. If we remove the 5 from the front, what remains is a calculation of $4!$. In general, $n! = n(n-1)!$. In fact, this relation gives us another way of expressing what is meant by factorial in general. Here is a recursive definition:

$$n! = \begin{cases} 1 & \text{if } n = 0 \\ n(n-1)! & \text{otherwise} \end{cases}$$

This definition says that the factorial of 0 is, by definition, 1, while the factorial of any other number is defined to be that number times the factorial of one less than that number.

Even though this definition is recursive, it is not circular. In fact, it provides a very simple method of calculating a factorial. Consider the value of $4!$. By definition we have

$$4! = 4(4-1)! = 4(3!)$$

But what is $3!$? To find out, we apply the definition again.

$$4! = 4(3!) = 4[(3)(3-1)!] = 4(3)(2!)$$

Now, of course, we have to expand $2!$, which requires $1!$, which requires $0!$. Since $0!$ is simply 1, that's the end of it.

$$4! = 4(3!) = 4(3)(2!) = 4(3)(2)(1!) = 4(3)(2)(1)(0!) = 4(3)(2)(1)(1) = 24$$

You can see that the recursive definition is not circular because each application causes us to request the factorial of a smaller number. Eventually we get down to 0, which doesn't require another application of the definition. This is called a *base case* for the recursion. When the recursion bottoms out, we get a closed expression that can be directly computed. All good recursive definitions have these key characteristics:

1. There are one or more base cases for which no recursion is required.

2. All chains of recursion eventually end up at one of the base cases.

The simplest way to guarantee that these two conditions are met is to make sure that each recursion always occurs on a *smaller* version of the original problem. A very small version of the problem that can be solved without recursion then becomes the base case. This is exactly how the factorial definition works.

13.2.2   Recursive Functions

You already know that the factorial can be computed using a loop with an accumulator. That implementation has a natural correspondence to the original
definition of factorial. Can we also implement a version of factorial that follows
the recursive definition?

   If we write factorial as a separate function, the recursive definition translates
directly into code.

```
def fact(n):
    if n == 0:
        return 1
    else:
        return n * fact(n-1)
```

Do you see how the definition that refers to itself turns into a function that calls
itself? This is called a *recursive function*. The function first checks to see if we
are at the base case n == 0 and, if so, returns 1. If we are not yet at the base
case, the function returns the result of multiplying n by the factorial of n-1. The
latter is calculated by a recursive call to `fact(n-1)`.

   I think you will agree that this is a reasonable translation of the recursive
definition. The really cool part is that it actually works! We can use this recursive
function to compute factorial values.

```
>>> from recfact import fact
>>> fact(4)
24
>>> fact(10)
3628800
```

   Some beginning programmers are surprised by this result, but it follows naturally from the semantics for functions that we discussed way back in Chapter 6.
Remember that each call to a function starts that function anew. That means it
has its own copy of any local values, including the values of the parameters.
Figure 13.1 shows the sequence of recursive calls that computes 5!. Note especially how each return value is multiplied by a value of n appropriate for each
function invocation. The values of n are stored on the way down the chain and
then used on the way back up as the function calls return.

   There are many problems for which recursion can yield an elegant and efficient solution. The next few sections present examples of recursive problem
solving.

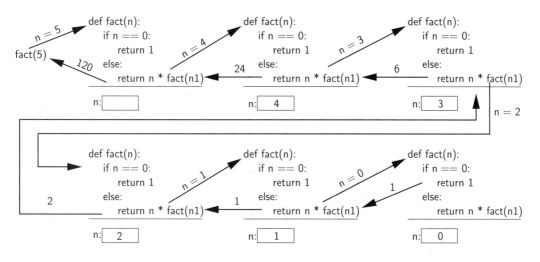

Figure 13.1: Recursive computation of 5!

13.2.3 Example: String Reversal

Python lists have a built-in method that can be used to reverse the list. Suppose that you want to compute the reverse of a string. One way to handle this problem effectively would be to convert the string into a list of characters, reverse the list, and turn the list back into a string. Using recursion, however, we can easily write a function that computes the reverse directly, without having to detour through a list representation.

The basic idea is to think of a string as a recursive object; a large string is composed out of smaller objects, which are also strings. In fact, one very handy way to divide up virtually any sequence is to think of it as a single first item that just happens to be followed by another sequence. In the case of a string, we can divide it up into its first character and "all the rest." If we reverse the rest of the string and then put the first character on the end of that, we'll have the reverse of the whole string.

Let's code up that algorithm and see what happens.

```
def reverse(s):
    return reverse(s[1:]) + s[0]
```

Notice how this function works. The slice s[1:] gives all but the first character of the string. We reverse the slice (recursively) and then concatenate the first character (s[0]) onto the end of the result. It might be helpful to think in terms of a specific example. If s is the string "abc", then s[1:] is the string "bc". Reversing this yields "cb" and tacking on s[0] yields "cba". That's just what we want.

Unfortunately, this function doesn't quite work. Here's what happens when I try it out:

```
>>> reverse("Hello")
Traceback (most recent call last):
  File "<stdin>", line 1, in ?
  File "<stdin>", line 2, in reverse
  File "<stdin>", line 2, in reverse
...
  File "<stdin>", line 2, in reverse
RuntimeError: maximum recursion depth exceeded
```

I've only shown a portion of the output, it actually consisted of 1000 lines! What's happened here?

Remember, to build a correct recursive function we need a base case for which no recursion is required, otherwise the recursion is circular. In our haste to code up the function, we forgot to include a base case. What we have written is actually an *infinite recursion*. Every call to reverse contains another call to reverse, so none of them ever return. Of course, each time a function is called it takes up some memory (to store the parameters and local variables), so this process can't go on forever. Python puts a stop to it after 1000 calls, the default "maximum recursion depth."

Let's go back and put in a suitable base case. When performing recursion on sequences, the base case is often an empty sequence or a sequence containing just one item. For our reversing problem we can use an empty string as the base case, since an empty string is its own reverse. The recursive calls to reverse are always on a string that is one character shorter than the original, so we'll eventually end up at an empty string. Here's a correct version of reverse:

```
def reverse(s):
    if s == "":
        return s
    else:
        return reverse(s[1:]) + s[0]
```

This version works as advertised.

```
>>> reverse("Hello")
'olleH'
```

13.2.4 Example: Anagrams

An anagram is formed by rearranging the letters of a word. Anagrams are often used in word games, and forming anagrams is a special case of generating the possible permutations (rearrangements) of a sequence, a problem that pops up frequently in many areas of computing and mathematics.

Let's try our hand at writing a function that generates a list of all the possible anagrams of a string. We'll apply the same approach that we used in the previous example by slicing the first character off of the string. Suppose the original string is "abc", then the tail of the string is "bc". Generating the list of all the anagrams of the tail gives us ["bc", "cb"], as there are only two possible arrangements of two characters. To add back the first letter, we need to place it in all possible positions in each of these two smaller anagrams: ["abc", "bac", "bca", "acb", "cab", "cba"]. The first three anagrams come from placing "a" in every possible place in "bc", and the second three come from inserting "a" into "cb".

Just as in our previous example, we can use an empty string as the base case for the recursion. The only possible arrangement of characters in an empty string is the empty string itself. Here is the completed recursive function:

```
def anagrams(s):
    if s == "":
        return [s]
    else:
        ans = []
        for w in anagrams(s[1:]):
            for pos in range(len(w)+1):
                ans.append(w[:pos]+s[0]+w[pos:])
        return ans
```

Notice in the else I have used a list to accumulate the final results. In the nested for loops, the outer loop iterates through each anagram of the tail of s, and the inner loop goes through each position in the anagram and creates a new string with the original first character inserted into that position. The expression w[:pos]+s[0]+w[pos:] looks a bit tricky, but it's not too hard to decipher. Taking w[:pos] gives the portion of w up to (but not including) pos, and w[pos:]

yields everything from pos through the end. Sticking s[0] between these two effectively inserts it into w at pos. The inner loop goes up to len(w)+1 so that the new character can be added to the very end of the anagram.

Here is our function in action:

```
>>> anagrams("abc")
['abc', 'bac', 'bca', 'acb', 'cab', 'cba']
```

I didn't use "Hello" for this example because that generates more anagrams than I wanted to print. The number of anagrams of a word is the factorial of the length of the word.

13.2.5 Example: Fast Exponentiation

Another good example of recursion is a clever algorithm for raising values to an integer power. The naive way to compute a^n for an integer n is simply to multiply a by itself n times $a^n = a * a * a * \ldots * a$. We can easily implement this using a simple accumulator loop.

```
def loopPower(a, n):
    ans = 1
    for i in range(n):
        ans = ans * a
    return ans
```

Divide and conquer suggests another way to perform this calculation. Suppose we want to calculate 2^8. By the laws of exponents, we know that $2^8 = 2^4(2^4)$. So if we first calculate 2^4, we can just do one more multiply to get 2^8. To compute 2^4, we can use the fact that $2^4 = 2^2(2^2)$. And, of course, $2^2 = 2(2)$. Putting the calculation together we start with $2(2) = 4$ and $4(4) = 16$ and $16(16) = 256$. We have calculated the value of 2^8 using just three multiplications. The basic insight is to use the relationship $a^n = a^{n/2}(a^{n/2})$.

In the example I gave, the exponents were all even. In order to turn this idea into a general algorithm, we also have to handle odd values of n. This can be done with one more multiplication. For example, $2^9 = 2^4(2^4)(2)$. Here is the general relationship:

$$a^n = \begin{cases} a^{n//2}(a^{n//2}) & \text{if } n \text{ is even} \\ a^{n//2}(a^{n//2})(a) & \text{if } n \text{ is odd} \end{cases}$$

In this formula I am exploiting integer division; if n is 9 then $n//2$ is 4.

We can use this relationship as the basis of a recursive function, we just need to find a suitable base case. Notice that computing the nth power requires computing two smaller powers ($n//2$). If we keep using smaller and smaller values of n, it will eventually get to 0 ($1//2 = 0$ in integer division). As you know from math class, $a^0 = 1$ for any value of a (except 0). There's our base case.

If you've followed all the math, the implementation of the function is straight-forward.

```
def recPower(a, n):
    # raises a to the int power n
    if n == 0:
        return 1
    else:
        factor = recPower(a, n//2)
        if n%2 == 0: # n is even
            return factor * factor
        else:           # n is odd
            return factor * factor * a
```

One thing to notice is that I used an intermediate variable `factor` so that $a^{n//2}$ only needs to be calculated once. This makes the function more efficient.

13.2.6 Example: Binary Search

Now that you know how to implement recursive functions, we are ready to go back and look again at binary search recursively. Remember, the basic idea was to look at the middle value and then recursively search either the lower half or the upper half of the array.

The base cases for the recursion are the conditions when we can stop; namely, when the target value is found or we run out of places to look. The recursive calls will cut the size of the problem in half each time. In order to do this, we need to specify the range of locations in the list that are still "in play" for each recursive call. We can do this by passing the values of `low` and `high` as parameters along with the list. Each invocation will search the list between the low and high indexes.

Here is a direct implementation of the recursive algorithm using these ideas:

```
def recBinSearch(x, nums, low, high):
    if low > high:              # No place left to look, return -1
        return -1
    mid = (low + high) // 2
    item = nums[mid]
    if item == x:               # Found it! Return the index
        return mid
    elif x < item:              # Look in lower half
        return recBinSearch(x, nums, low, mid-1)
    else:                       # Look in upper half
        return recBinSearch(x, nums, mid+1, high)
```

We can then implement our original search function using a suitable call to the recursive binary search, telling it to start the search between 0 and len(nums)-1.

```
def search(x, nums):
    return recBinSearch(x, nums, 0, len(nums)-1)
```

Of course, our original looping version is probably a bit faster than this recursive version because calling functions is generally slower than iterating a loop. The recursive version, however, makes the divide-and-conquer structure of binary search much more obvious. Below we will see examples where recursive divide-and-conquer approaches provide a natural solution to some problems where loops are awkward.

13.2.7   Recursion vs. Iteration

I'm sure by now you've noticed that there are some similarities between iteration (looping) and recursion. In fact, recursive functions are a generalization of loops. Anything that can be done with a loop can also be done by a simple kind of recursive function. In fact, there are programming languages that use recursion exclusively. On the other hand, some things that can be done very simply using recursion are quite difficult to do with loops.

For a number of the problems we've looked at so far, we have had both iterative and recursive solutions. In the case of factorial and binary search, the loop version and the recursive version do basically the same calculations, and they will have roughly the same efficiency. The looping versions are probably a bit faster because calling functions is generally slower than iterating a loop, but in a modern language the recursive algorithms are probably fast enough.

In the case of the exponentiation algorithm, the recursive version and the looping version actually implement very different algorithms. If you think about it a bit, you will see that the looping version is linear and the recursive version executes in log time. The difference between these two is similar to the difference between linear search and binary search, so the recursive algorithm is clearly superior. In the next section, you'll be introduced to a recursive sorting algorithm that is also very efficient.

As you have seen, recursion can be a very useful problem-solving technique that can lead to efficient and effective algorithms. But you have to be careful. It's also possible to write some very inefficient recursive algorithms. One classic example is calculating the nth Fibonacci number.

The Fibonacci sequence is the sequence of numbers $1, 1, 2, 3, 5, 8, \ldots$ It starts with two 1s and successive numbers are the sum of the previous two. One way to compute the nth Fibonacci value is to use a loop that produces successive terms of the sequence.

In order to compute the next Fibonacci number, we always need to keep track of the previous two. We can use two variables, `curr` and `prev`, to keep track these values. Then we just need a loop that adds these together to get the next value. At that point, the old value of `curr` becomes the new value of `prev`. Here is one way to do it in Python:

```python
def loopfib(n):
    # returns the nth Fibonacci number

    curr = 1
    prev = 1
    for i in range(n-2):
        curr, prev = curr+prev, curr
    return curr
```

I used simultaneous assignment to compute the next values of `curr` and `prev` in a single step. Notice that the loop only goes around $n - 2$ times, because the first two values have already been assigned and do not require an addition.

The Fibonacci sequence also has an elegant recursive definition.

$$fib(n) = \begin{cases} 1 & \text{if } n < 3 \\ fib(n-1) + fib(n-2) & \text{otherwise} \end{cases}$$

We can turn this recursive definition directly into a recursive function.

```
def fib(n):
    if n < 3:
        return 1
    else:
        return fib(n-1) + fib(n-2)
```

This function obeys the rules that we've set out. The recursion is always on smaller values, and we have identified some non-recursive base cases. There-fore, this function will work, sort of. It turns out that this is a horribly inefficient algorithm. While our looping version can easily compute results for very large values of n (loopFib(50000) is almost instantaneous on my computer), the recursive version is useful only up to around 30.

The problem with this recursive formulation of the Fibonacci function is that it performs lots of duplicate computations. Figure 13.2 shows a diagram of the computations that are performed to compute fib(6). Notice that fib(4) is calculated twice, fib(3) is calculated three times, fib(2) four times, etc. If you start with a larger number, you can see how this redundancy really piles up!

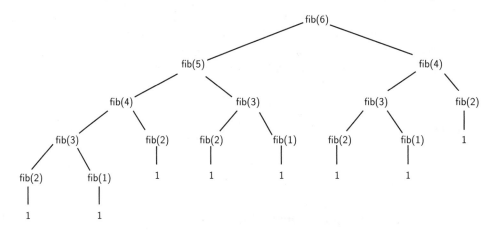

Figure 13.2: Computations performed for fib(6)

So what does this tell us? Recursion is just one more tool in your problem-solving arsenal. Sometimes a recursive solution is a good one, either because it is more elegant or more efficient than a looping version; in that case use recursion. Often, the looping and recursive versions are quite similar; in that case, the edge probably goes to the loop, as it will be slightly faster. Sometimes the recursive version is terribly inefficient. In that case, avoid it; unless, of course, you can't come up with an iterative algorithm. As you'll see later in the chapter, sometimes there just isn't a good solution.

13.3 Sorting Algorithms

The sorting problem provides a nice test bed for the algorithm design techniques we have been discussing. Remember, the basic sorting problem is to take a list and rearrange it so that the values are in increasing (actually, nondecreasing) order.

13.3.1 Naive Sorting: Selection Sort

Let's start with a simple "be the computer" approach to sorting. Suppose you have a stack of index cards, each with a number on it. The stack has been shuffled, and you need to put the cards back in order. How would you accomplish this task?

There are any number of good systematic approaches. One simple method is to look through the deck to find the smallest value and then place that value at the front of the stack (or perhaps in a separate stack). Then you could go through and find the smallest of the remaining cards and put it next in line, etc. Of course, this means that you'll also need an algorithm for finding the smallest remaining value. You can use the same approach we used for finding the max of a list (see Chapter 7). As you go through, you keep track of the smallest value seen so far, updating that value whenever you find a smaller one.

The algorithm I just described is called *selection sort*. Basically, the algorithm consists of a loop and each time through the loop, we select the smallest of the remaining elements and move it into its proper position. Applying this idea to a list of n elements, we proceed by finding the smallest value in the list and putting it into the 0th position. Then we find the smallest remaining value (from positions 1–(n-1)) and put it in position 1. Next, the smallest value from positions 2–(n-1) goes into position 2, etc. When we get to the end of the list, everything will be in its proper place.

There is one subtlety in implementing this algorithm. When we place a value into its proper position, we need to make sure that we do not accidentally lose the value that was originally stored in that position. For example, if the smallest item is in position 10, moving it into position 0 involves an assignment.

```
nums[0] = nums[10]
```

But this wipes out the value currently in nums[0]; it really needs to be moved to another location in the list. A simple way to save the value is to swap it with the one that we are moving. Using simultaneous assignment, the statement

```
nums[0], nums[10] = nums[10], nums[0]
```

places the value from position 10 at the front of the list, but preserves the original first value by stashing it into location 10.

Using this idea, it is a simple matter to write a selection sort in Python. I will use a variable called bottom to keep track of which position in the list we are currently filling, and the variable mp will be used to track the location of the smallest remaining value. The comments in this code explain this implementation of selection sort:

```
def selSort(nums):
    # sort nums into ascending order

    n = len(nums)

    # For each position in the list (except the very last)
    for bottom in range(n-1):
        # find the smallest item in nums[bottom]..nums[n-1]

        mp = bottom                      # bottom is smallest initially
        for i in range(bottom+1,n):      # look at each position
            if nums[i] < nums[mp]:       # this one is smaller
                mp = i                   #     remember its index

        # swap smallest item to the bottom
        nums[bottom], nums[mp] = nums[mp], nums[bottom]
```

One thing to notice about this algorithm is the accumulator for finding the minimum value. Rather than actually storing the minimum seen so far, mp just remembers the position of the minimum. A new value is tested by comparing the item in position i to the item in position mp. You should also notice that bottom stops at the second to last item in the list. Once all of the items up to the last have been put in the proper place, the last item has to be the largest, so there is no need to bother looking at it.

The selection sort algorithm is easy to write and works well for moderate-sized lists, but it is not a very efficient sorting algorithm. We'll come back and analyze it after we've developed another algorithm.

13.3.2 Divide and Conquer: Merge Sort

As discussed above, one technique that often works for developing efficient algorithms is the divide-and-conquer approach. Suppose a friend and I were working together trying to put our deck of cards in order. We could divide the problem up by splitting the deck of cards in half with one of us sorting each of the halves. Then we just need to figure out a way of combining the two sorted stacks.

The process of combining two sorted lists into a single sorted result is called *merging*. The basic outline of our divide and conquer algorithm, called *merge-Sort* looks like this:

```
Algorithm: mergeSort nums

split nums into two halves
sort the first half
sort the second half
merge the two sorted halves back into nums
```

The first step in the algorithm is simple, we can just use list slicing to handle that. The last step is to merge the lists together. If you think about it, merging is pretty simple. Let's go back to our card stack example to flesh out the details. Since our two stacks are sorted, each has its smallest value on top. Whichever of the top values is the smallest will be the first item in the merged list. Once the smaller value is removed, we can look at the tops of the stacks again, and whichever top card is smaller will be the next item in the list. We just continue this process of placing the smaller of the two top values into the big list until one of the stacks runs out. At that point, we finish out the list with the cards from the remaining stack.

Here is a Python implementation of the merge process. In this code, lst1 and lst2 are the smaller lists and lst3 is the larger list where the results are placed. In order for the merging process to work, the length of lst3 must be equal to the sum of the lengths of lst1 and lst2. You should be able to follow this code by studying the accompanying comments:

```python
def merge(lst1, lst2, lst3):
    # merge sorted lists lst1 and lst2 into lst3

    # these indexes keep track of current position in each list
    i1, i2, i3 = 0, 0, 0   # all start at the front
```

```
    n1, n2 = len(lst1), len(lst2)

    # Loop while both lst1 and lst2 have more items
    while i1 < n1 and i2 < n2:
        if lst1[i1] < lst2[i2]:   # top of lst1 is smaller
            lst3[i3] = lst1[i1]   #   copy it into current spot in lst3
            i1 = i1 + 1
        else:                     # top of lst2 is smaller
            lst3[i3] = lst2[i2]   #   copy it into current spot in lst3
            i2 = i2 + 1
        i3 = i3 + 1               # item added to lst3, update position

    # Here either lst1 or lst2 is done. One of the following loops will
    # execute to finish up the merge.

    # Copy remaining items (if any) from lst1
    while i1 < n1:
        lst3[i3] = lst1[i1]
        i1 = i1 + 1
        i3 = i3 + 1
    # Copy remaining items (if any) from lst2
    while i2 < n2:
        lst3[i3] = lst2[i2]
        i2 = i2 + 1
        i3 = i3 + 1
```

OK, now we can slice a list into two, and if those lists are sorted, we know how to merge them back into a single list. But how are we going to sort the smaller lists? Well, let's think about it. We are trying to sort a list, and our algorithm requires us to sort two smaller lists. This sounds like a perfect place to use recursion. Maybe we can use mergeSort itself to sort the two lists. Let's go back to our recursion guidelines to develop a proper recursive algorithm.

In order for recursion to work, we need to find at least one base case that does not require a recursive call, and we also have to make sure that recursive calls are always made on smaller versions of the original problem. The recursion in our mergeSort will always occur on a list that is half as large as the original, so the latter property is automatically met. Eventually, our lists will be very small, containing only a single item. Fortunately, a list with just one item is already sorted! Voilá, we have a base case. When the length of the list is less than 2, we do nothing, leaving the list unchanged.

Given our analysis, we can update the mergeSort algorithm to make it properly recursive.

```
if len(nums) > 1:
    split nums into two halves
    mergeSort the first half
    mergeSort the second half
    merge the two sorted halves back into nums
```

We can translate this algorithm directly into Python code.

```python
def mergeSort(nums):
    # Put items of nums in ascending order
    n = len(nums)
    # Do nothing if nums contains 0 or 1 items
    if n > 1:
        # split into two sublists
        m = n // 2
        nums1, nums2 = nums[:m], nums[m:]
        # recursively sort each piece
        mergeSort(nums1)
        mergeSort(nums2)
        # merge the sorted pieces back into original list
        merge(nums1, nums2, nums)
```

You might try tracing this algorithm with a small list (say eight elements), just to convince yourself that it really works. In general, though, tracing through recursive algorithms can be tedious and often not very enlightening.

Recursion is closely related to mathematical induction, and it requires practice before it becomes comfortable. As long as you follow the rules and make sure that every recursive chain of calls eventually reaches a base case, your algorithms *will* work. You just have to trust and let go of the grungy details. Let Python worry about that for you!

13.3.3 Comparing Sorts

Now that we have developed two sorting algorithms, which one should we use? Before we actually try them out, let's do some analysis. As in the searching problem, the difficulty of sorting a list depends on the size of the list. We need to figure out how many steps each of our sorting algorithms requires as a function of the size of the list to be sorted.

Take a look back at the algorithm for selection sort. Remember, this algorithm works by first finding the smallest item, then finding the smallest of the remaining items, and so on. Suppose we start with a list of size n. In order to find the smallest value, the algorithm has to inspect each of the n items. The next time around the outer loop, it has to find the smallest of the remaining $n - 1$ items. The third time around, there are $n - 2$ items of interest. This process continues until there is only one item left to place. Thus, the total number of iterations of the inner loop for the selection sort can be computed as the sum of a decreasing sequence.

$$n + (n - 1) + (n - 2) + (n - 3) + \cdots + 1$$

In other words, the time required by selection sort to sort a list of n items is proportional to the sum of the first n whole numbers. There is a well-known formula for this sum, but even if you do not know the formula, it is easy to derive. If you add the first and last numbers in the series you get $n + 1$. Adding the second and second to last values gives $(n - 1) + 2 = n + 1$. If you keep pairing up the values working from the outside in, all of the pairs add to $n + 1$. Since there are n numbers, there must be $\frac{n}{2}$ pairs. That means the sum of all the pairs is $\frac{n(n+1)}{2}$.

You can see that the final formula contains an n^2 term. That means that the number of steps in the algorithm is proportional to the square of the size of the list. If the size of the list doubles, the number of steps quadruples. If the size triples, it will take nine times as long to finish. Computer scientists call this a *quadratic* or n^2 algorithm.

Let's see how that compares to the merge sort algorithm. In the case of merge sort, we divided a list into two pieces and sorted the individual pieces before merging them together. The real work is done during the merge process when the values in the sublists are copied back into the original list.

Figure 13.3 depicts the merging process to sort the list [3, 1, 4, 1, 5, 9, 2, 6]. The dashed lines show how the original list is continually halved until each item is its own list with the values shown at the bottom. The single-item lists are then merged back up into the two item lists to produce the values shown in the second level. The merging process continues up the diagram to produce the final sorted version of the list shown at the top.

The diagram makes analysis of the merge sort easy. Starting at the bottom level, we have to copy the n values into the second level. From the second to

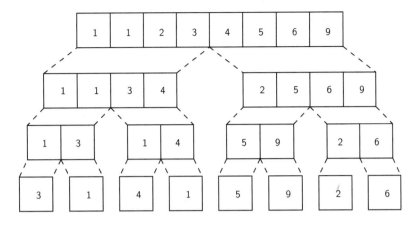

Figure 13.3: Merges required to sort [3, 1, 4, 1, 5, 9, 2, 6]

third level, the n values need to be copied again. Each level of merging involves copying n values. The only question left to answer is how many levels are there? This boils down to how many times a list of size n can be split in half. You already know from the analysis of binary search that this is just $\log_2 n$. Therefore, the total work required to sort n items is $n \log_2 n$. Computer scientists call this an *n log n* algorithm.

So which is going to be better, the n^2 selection sort or the $n \log n$ merge sort? If the input size is small, the selection sort might be a little faster because the code is simpler and there is less overhead. What happens, though as n gets larger? We saw in the analysis of binary search that the log function grows *very* slowly ($\log_2 16,000,000 \approx 24$) so $n(\log_2 n)$ will grow much more slowly than $n(n)$.

Empirical testing of these two algorithms confirms this analysis. On my computer, selection sort beats merge sort on lists up to size about 50, which takes around 0.008 seconds. On larger lists, the merge sort dominates. Figure 13.4 shows a comparison of the time required to sort lists up to size 3000. You can see that the curve for selection sort veers rapidly upward (forming half of a parabola), while the merge sort curve looks almost straight (look at the bottom). For 3000 items, selection sort requires over 30 seconds while merge sort completes the task in about $\frac{3}{4}$ of a second. Merge sort can sort a list of 20,000 items in less than six seconds; selection sort takes around 20 minutes. That's quite a difference!

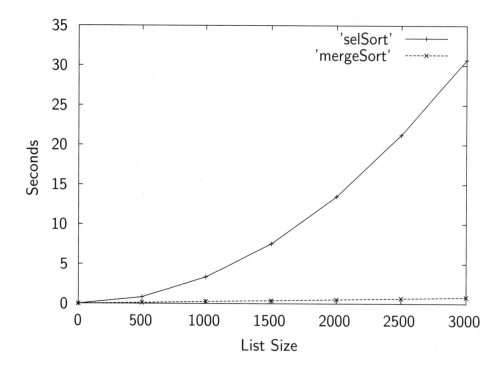

Figure 13.4: Experimental comparison of selection sort and merge sort

13.4 Hard Problems

Using our divide-and-conquer approach we were able to design good algorithms for the searching and sorting problems. Divide and conquer and recursion are very powerful techniques for algorithm design. However, not all problems have efficient solutions.

13.4.1 Towers of Hanoi

One very elegant application of recursive problem solving is the solution to a mathematical puzzle usually called the Tower of Hanoi or Tower of Brahma. This puzzle is generally attributed to the French mathematician Édouard Lucas, who published an article about it in 1883. The legend surrounding the puzzle goes something like this:

Somewhere in a remote region of the world is a monastery of a very devout religious order. The monks have been charged with a sacred task that keeps time for the universe. At the beginning of all things, the monks were given a table that supports three vertical posts. On one of the posts was a stack of 64 concentric golden disks. The disks are of varying radii and stacked in the shape of a beautiful pyramid. The monks were charged with the task of moving the disks from the first post to the third post. When the monks have completed their task, all things will crumble to dust and the universe will end.

Of course, if that's all there were to the problem, the universe would have ended long ago. To maintain divine order, the monks must abide by certain rules.

1. Only one disk may be moved at a time.

2. A disk may not be "set aside." It may only be stacked on one of the three posts.

3. A larger disk may never be placed on top of a smaller one.

Versions of this puzzle were quite popular at one time, and you can still find variations on this theme in toy and puzzle stores. Figure 13.5 depicts a small version containing only eight disks. The task is to move the tower from the first post to the third post using the center post as sort of a temporary resting place during the process. Of course, you have to follow the three sacred rules given above.

We want to develop an algorithm for this puzzle. You can think of our algorithm either as a set of steps that the monks need to carry out, or as a program that generates a set of instructions. For example, if we label the three posts A, B, and C. The instructions might start out like this:

```
Move disk from A to C.
Move disk from A to B.
Move disk from C to B.
...
```

This is a difficult puzzle for most people to solve. Of course, that is not surprising, since most people are not trained in algorithm design. The solution process is actually quite simple—*if* you know about recursion.

Let's start by considering some really easy cases. Suppose we have a version of the puzzle with only one disk. Moving a tower consisting of a single disk is simple enough; we just remove it from A and put it on C. Problem solved. OK, what if there are two disks? I need to get the larger of the two disks over to post

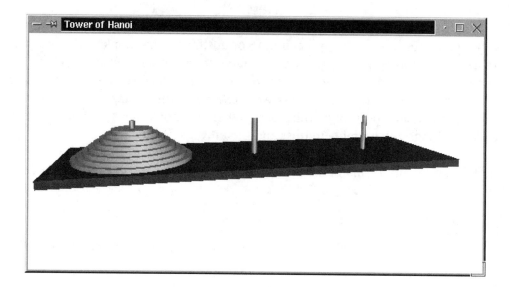

Figure 13.5: Tower of Hanoi puzzle with eight disks

C, but the smaller one is sitting on top of it. I need to move the smaller disk out of the way, and I can do this by moving it to post B. Now the large disk on A is clear; I can move it to C and then move the smaller disk from post B onto post C.

Now let's think about a tower of size three. In order to move the largest disk to post C, I first have to move the two smaller disks out of the way. The two smaller disks form a tower of size two. Using the process I outlined above, I could move this tower of two onto post B, and that would free up the largest disk so that I can move it to post C. Then I just have to move the tower of two disks from post B onto post C. Solving the three disk case boils down to three steps:

1. Move a tower of two from A to B.

2. Move one disk from A to C.

3. Move a tower of two from B to C.

The first and third steps involve moving a tower of size two. Fortunately, we have already figured out how to do this. It's just like solving the puzzle with two disks, except that we move the tower from A to B using C as the temporary resting place, and then from B to C using A as the temporary.

We have just developed the outline of a simple recursive algorithm for the general process of moving a tower of any size from one post to another.

```
Algorithm: move n-disk tower from source to destination via resting place

move n-1 disk tower from source to resting place
move 1 disk tower from source to destination
move n-1 disk tower from resting place to destination
```

What is the base case for this recursive process? Notice how a move of n disks results in two recursive moves of $n-1$ disks. Since we are reducing n by one each time, the size of the tower will eventually be 1. A tower of size 1 can be moved directly by just moving a single disk; we don't need any recursive calls to remove disks above it.

Fixing up our general algorithm to include the base case gives us a working moveTower algorithm. Let's code it up in Python. Our moveTower function will need parameters to represent the size of the tower, n; the source post, source; the destination post, dest; and the temporary resting post, temp. We can use an int for n and the strings "A," "B," and "C" to represent the posts. Here is the code for moveTower:

```python
def moveTower(n, source, dest, temp):
    if n == 1:
        print("Move disk from", source, "to", dest+".")
    else:
        moveTower(n-1, source, temp, dest)
        moveTower(1, source, dest, temp)
        moveTower(n-1, temp, dest, source)
```

See how easy that was? Sometimes using recursion can make otherwise difficult problems almost trivial.

To get things started, we just need to supply values for our four parameters. Let's write a little function that prints out instructions for moving a tower of size n from post A to post C.

```python
def hanoi(n):
    moveTower(n, "A", "C", "B")
```

Now we're ready to try it out. Here are solutions to the three- and four-disk puzzles. You might want to trace through these solutions to convince yourself that they work.

```
>>> hanoi(3)
Move disk from A to C.
Move disk from A to B.
Move disk from C to B.
Move disk from A to C.
Move disk from B to A.
Move disk from B to C.
Move disk from A to C.

>>> hanoi(4)
Move disk from A to B.
Move disk from A to C.
Move disk from B to C.
Move disk from A to B.
Move disk from C to A.
Move disk from C to B.
Move disk from A to B.
Move disk from A to C.
Move disk from B to C.
Move disk from B to A.
Move disk from C to A.
Move disk from B to C.
Move disk from A to B.
Move disk from A to C.
Move disk from B to C.
```

So, our solution to the Tower of Hanoi is a "trivial" algorithm requiring only nine lines of code. What is this problem doing in a section labeled *hard problems*? To answer that question, we have to look at the efficiency of our solution. Remember, when I talk about the efficiency of an algorithm I mean how many steps it requires to solve a given size problem. In this case, the difficulty is determined by the number of disks in the tower. The question we want to answer is *how many steps does it take to move a tower of size n?*

Just looking at the structure of our algorithm, you can see that moving a tower of size n requires us to move a tower of size $n - 1$ twice, once to move it off the largest disk, and again to put it back on top. If we add another disk to the tower, we essentially double the number of steps required to solve it. The relationship becomes clear if you simply try out the program on increasing puzzle sizes.

Number of Disks	Steps in Solution
1	1
2	3
3	7
4	15
5	31

In general, solving a puzzle of size n will require $2^n - 1$ steps.

Computer scientists call this an *exponential time* algorithm, since the measure of the size of the problem, n, appears in the exponent of this formula. Exponential algorithms blow up very quickly and can only be practically solved for relatively small sizes, even on the fastest computers. Just to illustrate the point, if our monks really started with a tower of just 64 disks and moved one disk every second, 24 hours a day, every day, without making a mistake, it would still take them over 580 *billion* years to complete their task. Considering that the universe is roughly 15 billion years old now, I'm not too worried about turning to dust just yet.

Even though the algorithm for Towers of Hanoi is easy to express, it belongs to a class known as *intractable* problems. These are problems that require too much computing power (either time or memory) to be solved in practice, except for the simplest cases. And in this sense, our toy-store puzzle does indeed represent a hard problem. But some problems are even harder than intractable, and we'll meet one of those in the next section.

13.4.2 The Halting Problem

Let's just imagine for a moment that this book has inspired you to pursue a career as a computer professional. It's now six years later, and you are a well-established software developer. One day, your boss comes to you with an important new project, and you are supposed to drop everything and get right on it.

It seems that your boss has had a sudden inspiration on how your company can double its productivity. You've recently hired a number of rather inexperienced programmers, and debugging their code is taking an inordinate amount of time. Apparently, these wet-behind-the-ears newbies tend to accidentally write a lot of programs with infinite loops (you've been there, right?). They spend half the day waiting for their computers to reboot so they can track down the bugs. Your boss wants you to design a program that can analyze source code and detect whether it contains an infinite loop before actually running it on test data. This sounds like an interesting problem, so you decide to give it a try.

As usual, you start by carefully considering the specifications. Basically, you want a program that can read other programs and determine whether they contain an infinite loop. Of course, the behavior of a program is determined not just by its code, but also by the input it is given when it runs. In order to determine if there is an infinite loop, you will have to know what the input will be. You decide on the following specification:

Program: Halting Analyzer

Inputs: A Python program file.
The input for the program.

Outputs: "OK" if the program will eventually stop.
"FAULTY" if the program has an infinite loop.

Right away you notice something interesting about this program. This is a program that examines other programs. You may not have written many of these before, but you know that it's not a problem in principle. After all, compilers and interpreters are common examples of programs that analyze other programs. You can represent both the program that is being analyzed and the proposed input to the program as Python strings.

There is something else very interesting about this assignment. You are being asked to solve a very famous puzzle known as the *Halting Problem*, and it's unsolvable. There is no possible algorithm that can meet this specification! Notice, I'm not just saying that no one has been able to do this before; I'm saying that this problem can never be solved, in principle.

How do I know that there is no solution to this problem? This is a question that all the design skills in the world will not answer. Design can show that problems are solvable, but it can never prove that a problem is not solvable. To do that, we need to use our analytical skills.

One way to prove that something is impossible is to first assume that it is possible and show that this leads to a contradiction. Mathematicians call this proof by contradiction. We'll use this technique to show that the halting problem cannot be solved.

We begin by assuming that there is some algorithm that can determine if any program terminates when executed on a particular input. If such an algorithm could be written, we could package it up in a function.

```
def terminates(program, inputData):
    # program and inputData are both strings
    # Returns true if program would halt when run with inputData
    #    as its input.
```

Of course, I can't actually write the function, but let's just assume that this function exists.

Using the terminates function, we can write an interesting program.

```
# turing.py

def terminates(program, inputData):
    # program and inputData are both strings
    # Returns true if program would halt when run with inputData
    #    as its input.

def main():
    # Read a program from standard input
    lines = []
    print("Type in a program (type 'done' to quit).")
    line = input("")
    while line != "done":
        lines.append(line)
        line = input("")
    testProg = "\n".join(lines)

    # If program halts on itself as input, go into an infinite loop
    if terminates(testProg, testProg):
        while True:
            pass    # a pass statement does nothing

main()
```

I have called this program turing in honor of Alan Turing, the British mathematician considered by many to be the "Father of Computer Science." He was the one who first proved that the halting problem could not be solved.

The first thing `turing.py` does is read in a program typed by the user. This is accomplished with a sentinel loop that accumulates lines in a list one at a time. The `join` method then concatenates the lines together using a newline character (`"\n"`) between them. This effectively creates a multi-line string representing the program that was typed.

`Turing.py` then calls the `terminates` function and sends the input program as both the program to test and the input data for the program. Essentially, this is a test to see if the program read from the input terminates when given itself as input. The `pass` statement actually does nothing; if the `terminates` function returns true, `turing.py` will go into an infinite loop.

OK, this seems like a silly program, but there is nothing in principle that keeps us from writing it, provided that the `terminates` function exists. `Turing.py` is constructed in this peculiar way simply to illustrate a point. Here's the million dollar question: What happens if we run `turing.py` and, when prompted to type in a program, type in the contents of `turing.py` itself? Put more specifically, does `turing.py` halt when given itself as its input?

Let's think it through. We are running `turing.py` and providing `turing.py` as its input. In the call to `terminates`, both the program and the data will be a copy of `turing.py`, so if `turing.py` halts when given itself as input, `terminates` will return true. But if `terminates` returns true, `turing.py` then goes into an infinite loop, so it *doesn't* halt! That's a contradiction; `turing.py` can't both halt and not halt. It's got to be one or the other.

Let's try it the other way around. Suppose that `terminates` returns a false value. That means that `turing.py`, when given itself as input goes into an infinite loop. But as soon as `terminates` returns false, `turing.py` quits, so it does halt! It's still a contradiction.

If you've gotten your head around the previous two paragraphs, you should be convinced that `turing.py` represents an impossible program. The existence of a function meeting the specification for `terminates` leads to a logical impossibility. Therefore, we can safely conclude that no such function exists. That means that there cannot be an algorithm for solving the halting problem.

There you have it. Your boss has assigned you an impossible task. Fortunately, your knowledge of computer science is sufficient to recognize this. You can explain to your boss why the problem can't be solved and then move on to more productive pursuits.

13.4.3 Conclusion

I hope this chapter has given you a taste of what computer science is all about. As the examples in this chapter have shown, computer science is much more than "just" programming. The most important computer for any computing professional is still the one between the ears.

Hopefully this book has helped you along the road to becoming a computer programmer. Along the way, I have tried to pique your curiosity about the science of computing. If you have mastered the concepts in this text, you can already write interesting and useful programs. You should also have a firm foundation of the fundamental ideas of computer science and software engineering. Should you be interested in studying these fields in more depth, I can only say "go for it." Perhaps one day you will also consider yourself a computer scientist; I would be delighted if my book played even a very small part in that process.

13.5 Chapter Summary

This chapter has introduced you to a number of important concepts in computer science that go beyond just programming. Here are the key ideas:

- One core subfield of computer science is analysis of algorithms. Computer scientists analyze the time efficiency of an algorithm by considering how many steps the algorithm requires as a function of the input size.

- Searching is the process of finding a particular item among a collection. Linear search scans the collection from start to end and requires time linearly proportional to the size of the collection. If the collection is sorted, it can be searched using the binary search algorithm. Binary search only requires time proportional to the log of the collection size.

- Binary search is an example of a divide and conquer approach to algorithm development. Divide and conquer often yields efficient solutions.

- A definition or function is recursive if it refers to itself. To be well-founded, a recursive definition must meet two properties:

  1. There must be one or more base cases that require no recursion.

  2. All chains of recursion must eventually reach a base case.

A simple way to guarantee these conditions is for recursive calls to always be made on smaller versions of the problem. The base cases are then simple versions that can be solved directly.

- Sequences can be considered recursive structures containing a first item followed by a sequence. Recursive functions can be written following this approach.

- Recursion is more general than iteration. Choosing between recursion and looping involves the considerations of efficiency and elegance.

- Sorting is the process of placing a collection in order. A selection sort requires time proportional to the square of the size of the collection. Merge sort is a divide and conquer algorithm that can sort a collection in $n \log n$ time.

- Problems that are solvable in theory but not in practice are called intractable. The solution to the famous Towers of Hanoi can be expressed as a simple recursive algorithm, but the algorithm is intractable.

- Some problems are in principle unsolvable. The Halting problem is one example of an unsolvable problem.

- You should consider becoming a computer scientist.

13.6   Exercises

Review Questions

True/False

1. Linear search requires a number of steps proportional to the size of the list being searched.

2. The Python operator `in` performs a binary search.

3. Binary search is an $n \log n$ algorithm.

4. The number of times n can be divided by 2 is $exp(n)$.

5. All proper recursive definitions must have exactly one non-recursive base case.

6. A sequence can be viewed as a recursive data collection.

7. A word of length n has $n!$ anagrams.

8. Loops are more general than recursion.

9. Merge sort is an example of an $n \log n$ algorithm.

10. Exponential algorithms are generally considered intractable.

Multiple Choice

1. Which algorithm requires time directly proportional to the size of the input?
   a) linear search   b) binary search
   c) merge sort   d) selection sort

2. Approximately how many iterations will binary search need to find a value in a list of 512 items?
   a) 512   b) 256   c) 9   d) 3

3. Recursions on sequences often use this as a base case:
   a) 0   b) 1   c) an empty sequence   d) None

4. An infinite recursion will result in
   a) a program that "hangs"
   b) a broken computer
   c) a reboot
   d) a run-time exception

5. The recursive Fibonacci function is inefficient because
   a) it does many repeated computations
   b) recursion is inherently inefficient compared to iteration
   c) calculating Fibonacci numbers is intractable
   d) fibbing is morally wrong

6. Which is a quadratic time algorithm?
   a) linear search   b) binary search
   c) tower of Hanoi   d) selection sort

7. The process of combining two sorted sequences is called
   a) sorting   b) shuffling   c) dovetailing   d) merging

8. Recursion is related to the mathematical technique called
   a) looping   b) sequencing   c) induction   d) contradiction

9. How many steps would be needed to solve the Towers of Hanoi for a tower of size 5?
   a) 5   b) 10   c) 25   d) 31

10. Which of the following is *not* true of the Halting Problem?
    a) It was studied by Alan Turing.
    b) It is harder than intractable.
    c) Someday a clever algorithm may be found to solve it.
    d) It involves a program that analyzes other programs.

Discussion

1. Place these algorithm classes in order from fastest to slowest: $n \log n$, n, n^2, $\log n$, 2^n

2. In your own words, explain the two rules that a proper recursive definition or function must follow.

3. What is the exact result of anagram("foo")?

4. Trace recPower(3,6) and figure out exactly how many multiplications it performs.

5. Why are divide-and-conquer algorithms often very efficient?

Programming Exercises

1. Modify the recursive Fibonacci program given in the chapter so that it prints tracing information. Specifically, have the function print a message when it is called and when it returns. For example, the output should contain lines like these:

```
Computing fib(4)
. . .
Leaving fib(4) returning 3
```

Use your modified version of fib to compute fib(10) and count how many times fib(3) is computed in the process.

2. This exercise is another variation on "instrumenting" the recursive Fibonacci program to better understand its behavior. Write a program that counts how many times the fib function is called to compute fib(n) where n is a user input.

   Hint: To solve this problem, you need an accumulator variable whose value "persists" between calls to fib. You can do this by making the count an instance variable of an object. Create a FibCounter class with the following methods:

   __init__(self) Creates a new FibCounter setting its count instance variable to 0.

   getCount(self) Returns the value of count.

   fib(self,n) Recursive function to compute the nth Fibonacci number. It increments the count each time it is called.

   resetCount(self) Set the count back to 0

3. A palindrome is a sentence that contains the same sequence of letters reading it either forwards or backwards. A classic example is: "Able was I, ere I saw Elba." Write a recursive function that detects whether a string is a palindrome. The basic idea is to check that the first and last letters of the string are the same letter; if they are, then the entire string is a palindrome if everything between those letters is a palindrome. There are a couple of special cases to check for. If either the first or last character of the string is not a letter, you can check to see if the rest of the string is a palindrome with that character removed. Also, when you compare letters, make sure that you do it in a case-insensitive way.

   Use your function in a program that prompts a user for a phrase and then tells whether or not it is a palindrome. Here's another classic for testing: "A man, a plan, a canal, Panama!"

4. Write and test a recursive function max to find the largest number in a list. The max is the larger of the first item and the max of all the other items.

5. Computer scientists and mathematicians often use numbering systems other than base 10. Write a program that allows a user to enter a number and a base and then prints out the digits of the number in the new base. Use a recursive function baseConversion(num,base) to print the digits.

   Hint: Consider base 10. To get the rightmost digit of a base 10 number, simply look at the remainder after dividing by 10. For example, $153\%10$ is

3. To get the remaining digits, you repeat the process on 15, which is just 153/10. This same process works for any base. The only problem is that we get the digits in reverse order (right to left).

Write a recursive function that first prints the digits of $num//base$ and then prints the last digit, namely $num\%base$. You should put a space between successive digits, since bases greater than 10 will print out with multi-character digits. For example, baseConversion(245, 16) should print 15 5.

6. Write a recursive function to print out the digits of a number in English. For example, if the number is 153, the output should be "One Five Three." See the hint from the previous problem for help on how this might be done.

7. In mathematics, C_k^n denotes the number of different ways that k things can be selected from among n different choices. For example, if you are choosing among six desserts and are allowed to take two, the number of different combinations you could choose is C_2^6. Here's one formula to compute this value:

$$C_k^n = \frac{n!}{k!(n-k)!}$$

This value also gives rise to an interesting recursion:

$$C_k^n = C_{k-1}^{n-1} + C_k^{n-1}$$

Write both an iterative and a recursive function to compute combinations and compare the efficiency of your two solutions. Hints: when $k = 1$, $C_k^n = n$ and when $n < k$, $C_k^n = 0$.

8. Some interesting geometric curves can be described recursively. One famous example is the Koch curve. It is a curve that can be infinitely long in a finite amount of space. It can also be used to generate pretty pictures.

The Koch curve is described in terms of "levels" or "degrees." The Koch curve of degree 0 is just a straight line segment. A first degree curve is formed by placing a "bump" in the middle of the line segment (see Figure 13.6). The original segment has been divided into four, each of which is 1/3 the length of the original. The bump rises at 60 degrees, so it forms two sides of an equilateral triangle. To get a second degree curve, you put a bump in each of the line segments of the first degree curve.

Successive curves are constructed by placing bumps on each segment of
the previous curve.

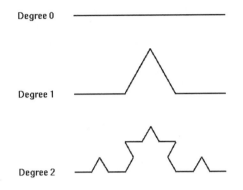

Figure 13.6: Koch curves of degree 0 to 2

You can draw interesting pictures by "Kochizing" the sides of a polygon.
Figure 13.7 shows the result of applying a fourth degree curve to the sides
of an equilateral triangle. This is often called a "Koch snowflake." You are
to write a program to draw a snowflake.

Hints: Think of drawing a Koch curve as if you were giving instructions to
a turtle. The turtle always knows where it currently sits and what direction
it is facing. To draw a Koch curve of a given length and degree, you might
use an algorithm like this:

```
Algorithm Koch(Turtle, length, degree):
    if degree == 0:
        Tell the turtle to draw for length steps
    else:
        length1 = length/3
        degree1 = degree-1
        Koch(Turtle, length1, degree1)
        Tell the turtle to turn left 60 degrees
        Koch(Turtle, length1, degree1)
        Tell the turtle to turn right 120 degrees
        Koch(Turtle, length1, degree1)
```

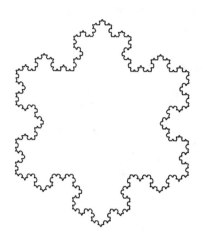

Figure 13.7: Koch snowflake

```
Tell the turtle to turn left 60 degrees
Koch(Turtle, length1, degree1)
```

Implement this algorithm with a Turtle class that contains instance variables location (a Point) and Direction (a float) and methods such as moveTo(somePoint), draw(length), and turn(degrees). If you maintain direction as an angle in radians, the point you are going to can easily be computed from your current location. Just use dx = length * cos(direction) and dy = length * sin(direction).

9. Another interesting recursive curve (see previous problem) is the C-curve. It is formed similarly to the Koch curve except whereas the Koch curve breaks a segment into four pieces of $length/3$, the C-curve replaces each segment with just two segments of $length/\sqrt{2}$ that form a 90 degree elbow. Figure 13.8 shows a degree 12 C-curve.

Using an approach similar to the previous exercise, write a program that draws a C-curve. Hint: your turtle will do the following:

```
turn left 45 degrees
draw a c-curve of size length/sqrt(2)
```

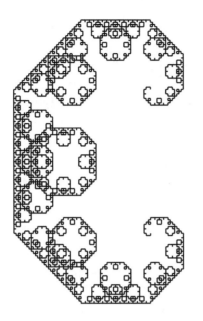

Figure 13.8: C-curve of degree 12

```
turn right 90 degrees
draw a c-curve of size length/sqrt(2)
turn left 45 degrees
```

10. Automated spell checkers are used to analyze documents and locate words that might be misspelled. These programs work by comparing each word in the document to a large dictionary (in the non-Python sense) of words. If the word is not found in the dictionary, it is flagged as potentially incorrect.

    Write a program to perform spell-checking on a text file. To do this, you will need to get a large file of English words in alphabetical order. If you have a Unix or Linux system available, you might poke around for a file called words, usually located in /usr/dict or /usr/share/dict. Otherwise, a quick search on the Internet should turn up something usable.

    Your program should prompt for a file to analyze and then try to look up every word in the file using binary search. If a word is not found in the dictionary, print it on the screen as potentially incorrect.

11. Write a program that solves word jumble problems. You will need a large
dictionary of English words (see previous problem). The user types in a
scrambled word, and your program generates all anagrams of the word
and then checks which (if any) are in the dictionary. The anagrams appearing in the dictionary are printed as solutions to the puzzle.

Appendix A

Python Quick Reference

Chapter 2: Writing Simple Programs

Reserved Words

```
False     class     finally   is        return
None      continue  for       lambda    try
True      def       from      nonlocal  while
and       del       global    not       with
as        elif      if        or        yield
assert    else      import    pass
break     except    in        raise
```

Print Function

```
print(<expr>, <expr>, ..., <expr>)
print()
print(<expr>, <expr>, ..., <expr>, end="\n")

<variable> = <expr>
<variable1>, <variable2>, ..., <variableN> = <expr1>,<expr2>, ..., <exprN>
```

Input (numeric)

```
<variable> = eval(input(<prompt>))
<variable1>, <variable2>, ..., <variableN> = eval(input(<prompt>))
```

Definite Loop

```
for <var> in <sequence>:
```

```
<body>
```

Chapter 3: Computing with Numbers

Numeric Operators

operator	operation
+	addition
−	subtraction
*	multiplication
/	float division
**	exponentiation
abs()	absolute value
//	integer division
%	remainder

Module Import

```
import <module_name>
```

Math Library Functions

Python	Mathematics	English
pi	π	An approximation of pi.
e	e	An approximation of e.
sqrt(x)	$\sqrt{x}$	The square root of x.
sin(x)	$\sin x$	The sine of x.
cos(x)	$\cos x$	The cosine of x.
tan(x)	$\tan x$	The tangent of x.
asin(x)	$\arcsin x$	The inverse of sine x.
acos(x)	$\arccos x$	The inverse of cosine x.
atan(x)	$\arctan x$	The inverse of tangent x.
log(x)	$\ln x$	The natural (base e) logarithm of x
log10(x)	$\log_{10} x$	The common (base 10) logarithm of x.
exp(x)	e^x	The exponential of x.
ceil(x)	$\lceil x \rceil$	The smallest whole number $>= x$
floor(x)	$\lfloor x \rfloor$	The largest whole number $<= x$

Built-in Functions

Function	Description
range(stop)	Returns list of ints from 0 to stop-1.
range(start, stop)	Returns list of ints from start to stop-1.
range(start, stop, step)	Returns a list of ints from start to stop counting by step.
type(x)	Returns the Python data type of x.
int(x)	Returns value of x converted to int. x may be either numeric or string.
float(x)	Returns value of x converted to a float. x may be either numeric or string.
round(x)	Returns nearest whole value of x (as a float).

Chapter 4: Objects and Graphics

Direct Import from Module

```
from <module> import <name1>, <name2>, ...
from <module> import *
```

Object Constructor

```
<class-name>(<param1>, <param2>, ... )
```

Object Method Call

```
<object>.<method-name>(<param1>, <param2>, ... )
```

For a summary of the objects and methods contained in the graphics module included with the book, see Section 4.8.

Chapter 5: Sequences: Strings, Lists, and Files

Input (string)

```
<variable> = input(<prompt>)
```

Sequence Operations (strings and lists)

Operator	Meaning
<sequence>+<sequence>	Returns concatenation of sequences. Sequences must be of same type.
<sequence>*<n>	Returns sequence concatenated with itself n times. n must be int.
<sequence>[<n>]	Returns item at n (0 based from left). n must be int.
<sequence>[<n>] where $n < 0$	Returns item at n (1 based from right). n must be int.
len(<sequence>)	Returns the length of the sequence.
<sequence>[<start>:<end>]	Returns subsequence from start up to (not including) end.
for <var> in <sequence>:	Iterates through items in sequence.

String Methods

Function	Meaning
s.capitalize()	Copy of s with only the first character capitalized.
s.center(width)	Copy of s centered in a field of given width.
s.count(sub)	Count the number of occurrences of sub in s.
s.find(sub)	Find the first position where sub occurs in s.
s.join(list)	Concatenate list into a string, using s as separator.
s.ljust(width)	Like center, but s is left-justified.
s.lower()	Copy of s in all lowercase characters.
s.lstrip()	Copy of s with leading white space removed.
s.replace(oldsub,newsub)	Replace all occurrences of oldsub in s with newsub.
s.rfind(sub)	Like find, but returns the rightmost position.
s.rjust(width)	Like center, but s is right-justified.
s.rstrip()	Copy of s with trailing white space removed.
s.split()	Split s into a list of substrings (see text).
s.title()	Copy of s with first character of each word capitalized.
s.upper()	Copy of s with all characters converted to upper case.

Appending to a List

<list>.append(<item>)

Type Conversion Functions

Function	Meaning
float(<expr>)	Convert expr to a floating point value.
int(<expr>)	Convert expr to an integer value.
str(<expr>)	Return a string representation of expr.
eval(<string>)	Evaluate string as an expression.

String Formatting

Expression Syntax

```
<template-string>.format(<value0>, <value1>, <value2>, ...)
```

Specifier Syntax

```
{<index>}
{<index>:<width>}
{<index>:<width>.<precision>}
{<index>:<width>.<places>f}
```

Notes:

- The last form is for a fixed number of decimal places.

- Width of 0 means use whatever space is required.

- Width with leading zero means pad as necessary with 0 (space is default).

- Width may be preceded by < for left-justify, > for right-justify, or ^ for center.

File Processing

Opening and Closing Files

```
<variable> = open(<name>, <mode>)
```

Mode is "r" for reading, "w" for writing, "a" for appending.

```
<fileobj>.close()
```

Reading a File

`<file>.read()` Returns the entire remaining contents of the file as a single (potentially large, multi-line) string.

`<file>.readline()` Returns the next line of the file. That is all text up to *and including* the next newline character.

`<file>.readlines()` Returns a list of the remaining lines in the file. Each list item is a single line including the newline character at the end.

Note: The file object may also be used in a `for` loop where it is treated as a sequence of lines.

Writing to a File

```
print(..., file=<outputFile>)
```

Chapter 6: Defining Functions

Function Definition

```
def <name>(<formal-param1>, <formal-param2>, ... )
    <body>
```

Function Call

```
<name>(<actual-param1>, <actual-param2>, ... )
```

Return Statement

```
return <value1>, <value2>, ...
```

Chapter 7: Decision Structures

Simple Conditions

```
<expr><relop><expr>
```

Relational Operators

Python	Mathematics	Meaning
<	$<$	Less than.
<=	$\leq$	Less than or equal to.
==	$=$	Equal to.
>=	$\geq$	Greater than or equal to.
>	$>$	Greater than.
!=	$\neq$	Not equal to.

Note: These operators return a bool value (`True`/`False`)

If Statement

```
if <condition>:
    <statements>
```

```
if <condition>:
    <statements1>
else:
    <statements2>
```

```
if <condition1>:
    <case1 statements>
elif <condition2>:
    <case2 statements>
...
else:
    <default statements>
```

Note: `else` clause is optional in `elif` form.

Preventing Execution on Import

```
if __name__ == "__main__":
    main()
```

Exception Handling

```
try:
    <statements>
except <ExceptionType>:
    <handler1>
except <ExceptionType>:
    <handler2>
```

```
...d
except:
    <default handler>
```

Chapter 8: Loop Structures

For Loop

```
for <var> in <sequence>:
    <body>
```

While Loop

```
while <condition>:
    <body>
```

Break Statement

```
while True:
    ...
    if <cond>: break
    ....
```

Boolean Expressions

Literals: True, False
Operators: and, or, not

operator	operational definition
x and y	If x is false, return x. Otherwise, return y.
x or y	If x is true, return x. Otherwise, return y.
not x	If x is false, return True. Otherwise, return False.

Type conversion function: bool

Chapter 9: Simulation and Design

Random Library

random() Returns a uniformly distributed pseudorandom value in the range [0,1).

randrange(<params>) Returns a uniformly distributed pseudorandom from range(<params>).

Chapter 10: Defining Classes

Class Definition

```
class <class-name>:
    <method-definitions>
```

Notes:

- A method definition is a function with a special first parameter, self, that refers to the object to which the method is being applied.

- The constructor is a method named __init__.

Documentation Strings

A string at the beginning of a module, class, function, or method can be used for documentation. Docstrings are carried along at runtime and are used for interactive help and the PyDoc utility.

Chapter 11: Data Collections

Sequence Operations (List and Strings)

Operator	Meaning
<seq> + <seq>	Concatenation
<seq> * <int-expr>	Repetition
<seq>[ ]	Indexing
len(<seq>)	Length
<seq>[:]	Slicing
for <var> in <seq>:	Iteration
<expr> in <seq>	Membership check (returns a Boolean)

List Methods

Method	Meaning
<list>.append(x)	Add element x to end of list.
<list>.sort()	Sort (order) the list. Keyword parameters: key, reverse.
<list>.reverse()	Reverse the list.
<list>.index(x)	Returns index of first occurrence of x.
<list>.insert(i,x)	Insert x into list at index i.
<list>.count(x)	Returns the number of occurrences of x in list.
<list>.remove(x)	Deletes the first occurrence of x in list.
<list>.pop(i)	Deletes the ith element of the list and returns its value.

Dictionaries

Dictionary Literal: {<key1>:<value1>, <key2>:<value2>, ...}

Method	Meaning
<key> in <dict>	Returns true if dictionary contains the specified key, false if it doesn't.
<dict>.keys()	Returns a sequence keys.
<dict>.values()	Returns a sequence of values.
<dict>.items()	Returns a sequence of tuples (key,value) representing the key-value pairs.
<dict>.get(<key>, <default>)	If dictionary has key returns its value; otherwise returns default.
del <dict>[<key>]	Deletes the specified entry.
<dict>.clear()	Deletes all entries.
for <var> in <dict>:	Loop over the keys.

Appendix B　　　Using Python and IDLE

Python is an exceptionally easy language to start programming with. Nevertheless, you still might have to do a bit of initial setup to get Python and other textbook resources up and running on your computer. This appendix contains step-by-step instructions for setting up Python on a Windows-based computer and also gives some pointers on running Python on other platforms.

Preliminaries

Locating Resources

The place to go for all things Pythonic is the Python web site: `http://www.python.org`. There you can download the latest version of Python, browse documentation, find information on Python books, and get pointers to lots of interesting Python-related applications and projects.

Resources specifically related to this textbook, including the graphics module, source code for all of the example programs, and supplementary materials are available from the author's web site:

`http://mcsp.wartburg.edu/zelle/python`.

About Python Versions

This textbook is written for Python 3. The code here should be compatible with versions of Python from 3.0 on. Because Python 3 is not backwards compatible with Python 2.x, the Python developers are currently maintaining two versions of the language. As this book is going to press, the current versions are 2.6.4 for the "old" Python and 3.1.1 for "new" Python. *To run the programs in this edition, you will need to use Python 3.0 or later.* If you are still using Python 2.6 or earlier, you might try locating a first edition of this text.

Python on Windows

Installing Python

Information on downloading and installing Python can be found on the Python web site. For Windows users, installation is simply a matter of downloading the Windows installer program (it will be called something like Python-3.1.1.msi) to a temporary location on your hard drive (the desktop is fine), running the installer, and following the instructions. You can probably accept all of the offered default settings (keep clicking "Next").

Once the installation wizard has finished you should see a program group for Python on your programs menu. If you accepted the default values, this group will be labeled something like "Python 3.1" and contain the following items:

IDLE (Python GUI) Starts IDLE, a program development environment for Python. I'll walk you through using this below.

Module Docs Starts PyDoc, a utility for browsing the internal documentation of modules in the Python library.

Python (command line) Starts an interactive session with the Python interpreter.

Python Manuals Opens the standard Python HTML manual set inside your default web browser. This should probably be your starting place for answering Python-specific questions. The "Library Reference Manual" is particularly helpful.

Uninstall Python For removing Python from your computer.

Interactive Python

Now that you've got Python installed, it's time to try it out. First, fire up the command-line interpreter. Selecting the Python (command line) option will pop up a console window running Python. At this point, you are ready to try out some of the interactive examples that are discussed in Chapter 1. For example, give this a try:

```
Python 3.1.1 ...
Type "help", "copyright", "credits" or "license" for more information.
>>> print "Hello, World"
Hello, World
>>> print 2 + 3
5
>>> print "2 + 3 =", 2 + 3
2 + 3 = 5
>>>
```

After you've played around a bit, you can quit the interactive session by typing Ctrl-Z (holding the Ctrl key and pressing "Z") or by typing exit() at the Python prompt.

Writing a Program

The next step is to try your hand at writing and running a small Python program. You will want to create a folder on your computer in which to store your Python programs. Usually, you would create a folder somewhere inside My Documents. If you plan to use multiple machines, you might want to put the folder on a USB memory stick or some other mobile media. For this walkthrough, I created a folder called Python Programs inside of My Documents.

In order to create a program, you will have to use a text editor. IMPORTANT: Do not type your programs into the interactive Python shell; the shell is for experimenting with Python, not program creation. For now, you can just use Window's Notepad to create a program file. Start Notepad (it's under Accesories on the Programs menu) and type in the following lines exactly as shown here. *Do not indent at the beginnings of the lines!*

```
print("Hello, World!")
input("Press <Enter>")
```

Figure B.1 shows how your Notepad window will look. Double check your typing, and

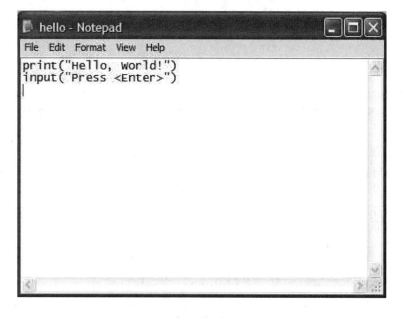

Figure B.1: Notepad with short Python program

then save this file into your new Python Programs folder with the name "hello.py." Don't forget the .py extension—that tells windows this is a Python module file.

Once you have saved the file, go ahead and quit Notepad; you are ready to try running your file. Go to your `Python Programs` folder; it should now have the `hello.py` file in it with Python icon (see Figure B.2). Double-click on your program to run it. This

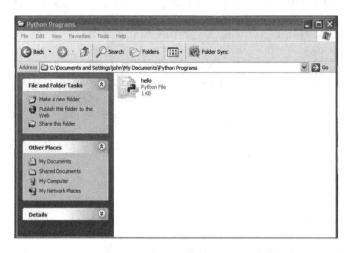

Figure B.2: Python program file: hello.py

will pop up a console window with the output from your program. Pressing the `<Enter>` key will cause the window to vanish again. Congratulations, you have just run your first Python program.

Another way to run Python programs is to import them into an interactive Python session. In order to do this, you need to start a Python command line session inside the folder where your program file is. Probably the easiest way to do this is to create a shortcut to Python inside your `Python Programs` folder. Here's one way to do it:

1. Go to the Python group on the Start menu, then right-click on the `Python (command line)` entry and select `Copy`.

2. Go to your `Python Programs` folder and do a right-click `Paste Shortcut`.

3. Right-click on the new shortcut icon and select `Properties`.

4. In the dialog box, delete the "Start in:" entry. The properties should look similar to Figure B.3.

5. Click OK.

Now you should be able to double-click on the Python (command line) shortcut and type `import hello` to run your program inside the interactive session (see Figure B.4).

Figure B.3: Properties for Python command line shortcut

By the way, after importing your `hello` program, you will notice a new file in your Python programs directory called `hello.pyc` (Compiled Python File) . This is the byte-code intermediate file that is described in Chapter 1.

That's all it takes to create and run your own Python programs. If you are going to do a lot of programming, however, you will want a text editor that is Python aware. There are many good freely available programming editors that include a Python mode; I personally use Emacs for most of my Python development. Another option is to use an integrated development environment, and that is where IDLE comes in.

Figure B.4: Interactive session running `hello.py`

Using IDLE

IDLE combines an interactive Python interpreter and editor into a single package. To use IDLE effectively, *you must start it in your* `Python Programs` *folder.* You can make a copy of the `IDLE (Python GUI)` shortcut from the Start Menu, the same way you created the command line shortcut above. Don't forget to blank out the `Start in:` property of the shortcut. Your Python Programs folder should now look something like Figure B.5.

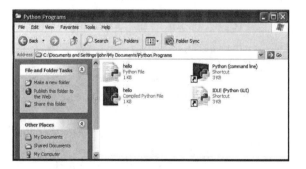

Figure B.5: Python Program folder with IDLE shortcut

Now run IDLE using this shortcut. IDLE may take a little while to start up, and then you will be greeted with a Python shell window (see Figure B.6). This is an interactive Python session that can be used much the same way as the Python command line.

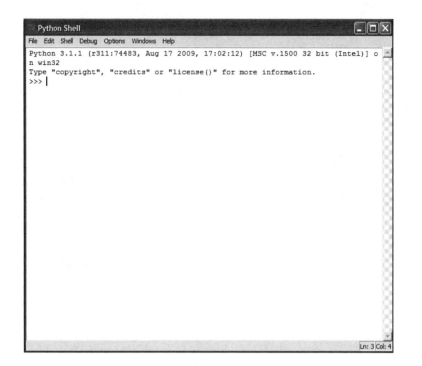

Figure B.6: IDLE Python shell window

IDLE can be used to edit Python programs, but this is done in an editor window, not the shell window. Let's take a look at the `hello` program file using IDLE. Use the `File/Open...` menu to open the file `hello.py`. You will get an editing window that looks like Figure B.7.

Notice that the IDLE editor provides color highlighting of your code; this is just one of many nice features that you'll uncover if you spend some time playing with the editor. IDLE allows you to do things you'd expect of any editor such as opening, saving, and printing files; cutting, pasting, and searching for text; and undoing and redoing commands. In addition, the `format` menu gives you many Python-specific options such as indenting, dedenting (de-indenting), commenting, and uncommenting regions of code.

IDLE is called an "integrated" environment because it also allows you to directly test out the program that you're editing. To give it a try, you can go to the `Run` menu and select `Run Module`, or you can just hit the <F5> key. Doing so will bring the Python shell window to the top and run your program in it.

Let's finish up by creating another program. Try the following steps:

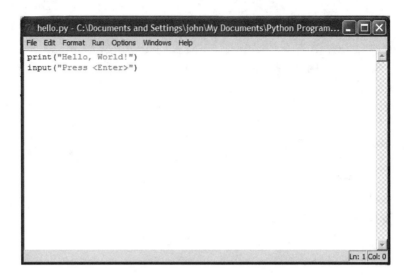

Figure B.7: IDLE editing window

1. Close the `hello.py` window (using `File/Close`).

2. Create a new editor window by selecting `File/New Window`.

3. Give your file a name by saving it (`File/Save`) with the name `chaos.py`. You need to give the file a name right away so that IDLE knows that this is a Python file, not just regular text. That way you get the Python-specific editing features such as color highlighting and automatic indentation.

4. Type in the `chaos` program from Chapter 1. I've duplicated it here for your convenience:

```python
# File: chaos.py
# A simple program illustrating chaotic behavior.

def main():
    print("This program illustrates a chaotic function")
    x = eval(input("Enter a number between 0 and 1: "))
    for i in range(10):
        x = 3.9 * x * (1 - x)
        print(x)

main()
```

Be sure to make the file look exactly like this. You'll notice that IDLE indents lines for you. To unindent again, just use the backspace key.

5. Run the program (use <F5>). If there are error messages, go back and try to fix the file and then run it again.

That should be enough to get you going with IDLE. You can consult the documentation to learn more.

Other Platforms

Installation

If you are a Linux or Unix user, chances are your distribution includes a version of Python. Unfortunately, the default Python is likely to be some flavor of Python 2 (likely 2.6). You will probably need to install a package (or packages) for Python 3. For example, on Ubuntu or other Debian based systems, you might use a command like:

```
sudo aptitude install python3 idle3
```

This will install the necessary packages for python 3 and IDLE.

If you can't find an appropriate Linux/Unix binary package, Python can easily be built from source by downloading the complete tarball (called something like `Python-3.1.1.tgz`) and performing the usual `tar`, `./configure`, `make` ritual. Consult the documentation files included in the tarball for details. By default, Python will install into the /usr/local directory, so it won't clobber any existing Python that your distribution might be using.

Apple users running OSX will also have a default Python install that is almost certainly not compatible with the programs in this text. You should update your Python by downloading and running the latest Python 3.x Mac installer disk image from the Python web site.

Running Python Programs

In a Linux/Unix/Mac OSX environment, you can run a program from a command line by typing something like `python3 hello.py`. This assumes that the Python interpreter is in your command path. If not, you'll have to type the entire path to the Python interpreter (or change your startup files to put Python on your path).

If you are running an integrated desktop such as KDE or Gnome, you should also be able to configure your desktop manager to run Python programs at a mouse click. For example, in KDE you can right-click on any .py file and select `Other...` from the `Open With` menu. In the pop-up dialog, type "python3" (or browse around to find the Python interpreter), click the `Run in Terminal` and `Remember application association...` boxes, and then `OK`. Other desktops will have a similar process for associating Python files with the Python interpreter.

If you want to use the Python interpreter interactively to `import` and experiment with code (as demonstrated throughout the book), you need to be sure to start Python in the directory/folder where your programs are. For command-line based systems, you can just open a console in the appropriate directory and type "python3" to start the interpreter.

Program Development

You can use the text editor of your choice for writing Python programs. Emacs and Vi are obvious choices in any Unix-like environment. Chances are your distribution already has a Python mode for your favorite editor. If not, look around; there is sure to be one available.

Provided your platform supports TKinter, you can also use IDLE as an interactive shell and programming environment. You should be able to start IDLE by typing `idle3` on a command line. If that doesn't work, you'll have to poke around your Python installation to find out where the tools directory was installed. It will probably be under the /usr/lib/python or /usr/local/lib/python directories. Since IDLE is just a Python application, you can also try a "locate" on idle.py. Once you've found it, try invoking Python on the IDLE file explicitly: `python idle.py`.

Installing Graphics

To use the graphics module (`graphics.py`), you need to place this file where Python can locate it. One simple approach is to put it in the same folder where you keep your Python programs. Starting Python in this folder will also let you import the graphics library to experiment interactively.

Alternatively, you can place the `graphics.py` file in a system-wide directory so that it is available for import no matter what directory Python starts in. The standard directory for placing local additions to Python is the `site-packages` directory. On my Windows installation, the complete path to the folder is:

`C:\Python31\Lib\site-packages`

On a Debian/Ubuntu Linux system, the file can go in:

`/usr/lib/python3.1/dist-packages`

On OSX, look for the folder:

`/Library/Frameworks/Python.framework/Versions/3.1/lib/python3.1/site-packages/`

You should be able to locate a similar folder on whatever system you are using. Simply copy `graphics.py` to that folder, and the graphics module will be available in any Python 3 session.

To test out your graphics installation, simply open up an interactive session of Python and try to import the module.

```
>>> import graphics
>>>
```

If you just get the prompt back, that means everything is fine. If you get the message ImportError: No module named graphics, that means Python was unable to find the file graphics.py. Double check to make sure that you named the file correctly (it *must* have the extension .py) and placed it in the proper directory.

If importing the graphics module produces an error message about Tkinter, it probably means that your Python installation is not set up with the Tkinter standard library module. You'll have to consult the Python documentation for your platform to figure how to install Tkinter.

One last note on the graphics package. Since it uses Tkinter, some strange things can happen when trying to use the graphics library interactively in a Python shell that is also using Tkinter (e.g., the IDLE shell window). When experimenting interactively with the graphics commands, it's safest to use a plain-vanilla Python command line rather than a graphical shell such as IDLE.

Appendix C   Glossary

---

abstraction The purposeful hiding or ignoring of some details in order to concentrate on those that are relevant.

accessor method A method that returns the value of one of more of an object's instance variable(s), but does not modify the object.

accumulator pattern A common programming pattern in which a final answer is built a piece at a time in a loop.

accumulator variable A variable that is used to hold the result in the accumulator programming pattern.

actual parameter A value that is passed to a function when it is called.

algorithm A detailed sequence of steps for carrying out some process. A recipe.

aliasing The situation in which two or more variables refer to exactly the same object. If the object is mutable, then changes made through one variable will be seen by the others.

analysis 1) In the context of the software development lifecycle, this refers to the process of studying a problem and figuring out what a computer program might do to solve it. 2) Studying a problem or algorithm mathematically to determine some of its properties, such as time efficiency.

and Binary Boolean operator that returns true when both of its subexpressions are true.

application programming interface (API) A specification of the functionality provided by a library module. A programmer needs to understand the API to be able to use a module.

argument Actual parameter.

array A collection of similar objects that can be accessed through indexing. Usually arrays are fixed-size and homogeneous (all elements are of the same type). Compare to list.

ASCII American Standard Code for Information Interchange. A standard for encoding text where each character is represented by a number 0–127.

assignment The process of giving a value to a variable.

associative array A collection where values are associated with keys. Called a *dictionary* in Python.

attributes The instance variables and methods of an object.

base case In a recursive function or definition, a situation in which recursion is not required. All proper recursions must have one or more base cases.

batch A mode of processing in which input and output is done through files rather than interactively.

binary Base two numbering system in which the only digits are 0 and 1.

binary search A very efficient searching algorithm for finding items in a sorted collection. Requires time proportional to $\log_2 n$ where n is the size of the collection.

bit Binary digit. Fundamental unit of information. Usually represented using 0 and 1.

body Generic term for the block of statements inside a control structure such as a loop or decision.

Boolean algebra The rules that govern simplification and rewriting of Boolean expressions.

Boolean expression A truth statement. A Boolean expression evaluates to either true or false.

Boolean logic *See* Boolean algebra.

Boolean operations Connectives for constructing Boolean expressions. In Python, and, or, and not.

bug An error in a program.

butterfly effect Classic example of dynamical systems in nature (chaos). Supposedly, an event as small as the flapping of a butterfly's wing can significantly influence subsequent large-scale weather patterns.

byte code An intermediate form of computer language. High-level languages are sometimes compiled into byte code, which is then interpreted. In Python, files with a pyc extension are byte code.

call The process of invoking a function's definition.

central processing unit The "brain" of the computer where numeric and logical operations are carried out.

cipher alphabet The symbols that are used to encrypt a message.

ciphertext The encrypted form of a message.

class A class describes a set of related objects. The `class` mechanism in Python is used as a "factory" to produce objects.

client In programming, a module that interfaces with another component is called a client for the component.

coding The process of turning an algorithm into a computer program.

comment Text placed in a program for the benefit of human readers. Comments are ignored by the computer.

compiler A complex program that translates a program written in a high-level language into the machine language that can be executed by a particular computer.

computer A machine that stores and manipulates information under the control of a changeable program.

computer science The study of what can be computed.

conditional Another term for a decision control structure.

constructor A function that creates a new object. In a Python class, it is the `__init__` method.

control codes Special characters that do not print, but are used in the interchange of information.

control structure Programming language statement that controls the execution of other statements (e.g., `if` and `while`).

coordinate transformation In graphical programming, the mathematics of changing a point or set of points from one coordinate system to a related one.

counted loop A loop written to iterate a specific number of times.

CPU *See* central processing unit.

cryptography The study of techniques for encoding information to keep it secure.

data The information that a computer program manipulates.

data type A particular way of representing data. The data type of an item determines what values it can have and what operations it supports.

debugging The process of finding and eliminating errors in a program.

decision structure A control structure that allows different parts of a program to execute depending on the exact situation. Usually decisions are controlled by Boolean expressions.

decision tree A complex decision structure in which an initial decision branches into more decisions, which branch into more decisions in a cascading fashion.

definite loop A kind of loop where the number of iterations is known at the time the loop begins executing.

design The process of developing a system that can solve some problem. Also the product of that process.

dictionary An unordered Python collection object that allows values to be associated with arbitrary keys.

docstring A documentation technique in Python that associates a string with a program component.

empty string An object that has the data type string, but does not contain any characters ("").

encapsulation Hiding the details of something. Usually this is the term used to describe the distinction between the implementation and use of an object or function. Details are encapsulated in the definition.

encryption The process of encoding information to keep it private.

end-of-file loop A programming pattern used to read a file line-by-line.

event In GUI programming, an outside action such a mouse click that causes something to happen in a program. Also used to describe the object that is created to encapsulate the information about the event.

event-driven A style of programming in which the program waits for events to happen and responds accordingly.

exception handling A programming language mechanism that allows the programmer to gracefully deal with errors that the language detects when a program is running.

execute To run a program or segment of a program.

exponential time An algorithm that requires a number of steps proportional to a function having a measure of the size of the problem in an exponent. Such algorithms are generally considered intractable.

expression Part of a program that produces data.

fetch-execute cycle The process a computer carries out to execute a machine code program.

float A data type for representing numbers with fractional values. Short for "floating point."

flowchart A graphical depiction of the flow of control in a program or algorithm.

function A subprogram within a program. Functions take parameters as input and can return values.

functional decomposition *See* top-down design.

garbage collection A process carried out by dynamic programming languages (e.g., Python, Lisp, Java) in which memory locations that contain values that are no longer in use are freed up so that they can store new values.

graphical user interface A style of interaction with a computer application that involves heavy use of graphical components such as windows, menus, and buttons.

graphics window A window on screen where graphics can be drawn.

GUI *See* graphical user interface.

halting problem A famous unsolvable problem. A program that determines if another program will halt on a given input.

hardware The physical components of a computing system. If it goes "crash" when you toss it out the window, then it's hardware.

hash Another term for *associative array* or *dictionary*.

hello, world The ubiquitous first computer program.

heterogeneous Capable of containing more than a single data type at one time. Python lists, for example.

homogeneous Capable of holding values of only a single type.

identifiers The names that are given to program entities.

if statement Control structure for implementing decisions in a program.

import statement Makes an external library module available for use within a program.

indefinite loop A loop for which the number of iterations required is not necessarily known at the time the loop begins to execute.

indexing Selecting a single item from a sequence based on its relative position in the sequence.

infinite loop A loop that does not terminate. *See* loop, infinite.

inheritance Defining a new class as a specialization of another class.

input, process, output A common programming pattern. The program prompts for input, processes it, and outputs a response.

input validation The process of checking the values supplied by a user to make sure that they are legitimate before performing a computation with those values.

instance A particular object of some class.

instance variable A piece of data stored inside an object.

int A data type for representing numbers with no fractional component. Int is short for Integer and represents a number with a fixed number of bits (commonly 32).

integer Positive or negative whole number. *See* int.

interactive loop A loop that allows part of a program to repeat according to the wishes of the user.

interface The connection between two components. For a function or method, the interface consists of the name of the function, its parameters and return values. For an object, it is the set of methods (and their interfaces) that are used to manipulate the object. The term "user interface" is used to describe how a person interacts with a computer application.

interpreter A computer program that simulates the behavior of a computer that understands a high-level language. It executes the lines of source one-by-one and carries out the operations.

intractable Too difficult to be solved in practice, usually because it would take too long.

invoke Making use of a function.

iterate To do multiple times. Each execution of a loop body is called an iteration.

key 1) In encryption, it is a special value that must be known to either encode or decode a message. 2) In the context of data collections, it is a way to look up a value in a dictionary. Values are associated with keys for future access.

lexicographic Having to do with string ordering. Lexicographic order is like alphabetical order, but based on the underlying numeric codes of the string's characters.

library An external collection of useful functions or classes that can be imported and used in a program. For example, the Python `math` and `string` modules.

linear search A search process that examines items in a collection sequentially.

linear time algorithm An algorithm that requires a number of steps proportional to the size of the input problem.

local variable A variable defined inside a function. It may only be referred to within the function definition. *See* scope.

log time algorithm An algorithm that requires a number of steps proportional to the log of the size of the input problem.

loop and a half A loop structure that has an exit somewhere in the midst of the loop body. In Python this is accomplished via a `while True:`/`break` combination.

list A general Python data type for representing sequential collections. List are heterogeneous and can grow and shrink as needed. Items are accessed through subscripting.

literal A way of writing a specific value in a programming language. For example, 3 is an int literal and "Hello" is a string literal.

loop A control construct for executing portions of a program multiple times.

loop index A variable that is used to control a loop. In the statement: for i in range(n), i is being used as a loop index.

loop, infinite *See* infinite loop.

machine code A program in machine language.

machine language The low-level (binary) instructions that a given CPU can execute.

main memory The place where all data and program instructions that the CPU is currently working on resides. Also known as random access memory (RAM).

mapping A general association between keys and values. Python dictionaries implement a mapping.

merge The process of combining two sorted lists into a single sorted list.

merge sort An efficient divide-and-conquer sorting algorithm.

meta-language A notation used to describe the syntax of a computer language.

method A function that lives inside an object. Objects are manipulated by calling their methods.

mixed-typed Expression An expression involving more than one data type. Usually used in the context of combining ints and floats in numeric computations.

model-view architecture Dividing up a GUI program by separating the problem (model) from the user interface (view).

modular Consisting of multiple relatively independent pieces that work together.

module Generally, any relatively independent part of a program. In Python, the term is also used to mean a file containing code that can be imported and executed.

module hierarchy chart A diagram showing the functional decomposition structure of a program. A line between two components shows that the one above uses the one below to accomplish its task.

Monte Carlo A simulation technique that involves probabilistic (random or pseudorandom) elements.

mutable Changeable. An object whose state can be changed is said to be mutable. Python ints and strings are not mutable, but lists are.

mutator method A method that changes the state of an object (i.e., modifies one or more of the instance variables).

n log n algorithm An algorithm that requires a number of steps that is proportional to the size of the input times the log of the size of the input.

n-squared algorithm An algorithm that requires a number of steps that is proportional to the square of the size of the input.

name error An exception that occurs when Python is asked to produce a value for a variable that has not been assigned a value.

namespace An association between identifiers and the things that they represent in a program. In Python modules, classes, and objects act as namespaces.

nesting The process of placing one control structure inside of another. Loops and decisions may be arbitrarily nested.

newline A special character that marks the division between lines in a file or a multi-line string. In Python, it is denoted "\n".

not Unary Boolean operator to negate an expression.

object A program entity that has some data and a set of operations to manipulate that data.

object-based Design and programming that uses objects as the principle form of abstraction.

object-oriented Object-based design or programming that includes characteristics of polymorphism and inheritance.

open The process of associating a file in secondary memory with a variable in a program through which the file can be manipulated.

operator A function for combining expressions into more complex expressions.

or Binary Boolean operator that returns true when either or both subexpressions are true.

override The term applied to a situation when a subclass changes the behavior of an inherited method.

parameters Special variables in a function that are initialized at the time of call with information passed from the caller.

pass by value Parameter passing technique used in Python. The formal parameters are assigned the values from the actual parameters. The function cannot change which object an actual parameter variable refers to.

pass by reference Parameter passing technique used in some computer languages that allows the value of a variable used as an actual parameter to be changed by the called function.

pixel Short for picture element. A single dot on a graphical display.

plaintext In encryption, this is the term used for an unencoded message.

polymorphism Literally "many forms." In object-oriented programming, the ability for a particular line of code to be implemented by different methods depending on the data type of the object involved.

portability The ability to run a program unmodified on various different systems.

post-test loop A loop construct where the loop condition is not tested until after the loop body has been executed.

pre-test loop A loop construct where the loop condition is tested before executing the body of the loop.

precision The number of digits of accuracy in a number.

priming read In a sentinel loop, a read before the loop condition is tested.

private key A kind of encryption where the same key is used to both encrypt and decrypt and must therefore be kept secret.

program A detailed set of instructions for a computer to carry out.

programming The process of creating a computer program to solve some problem.

programming environment A special computer program that provides facilities to make programming easier. IDLE (in the standard Python distribution) is an example of a simple programming environment.

programming language A notation for writing computer programs. Usually used to refer to high-level languages such as Python, Java, C++, etc.

prompt A printed message that signals to the user of a program that input is expected.

prototype An initial simplified version of a program.

pseudocode Notation for writing algorithms using precise natural language, instead of a computer language.

pseudorandom Sequences of numbers generated by computer algorithms and used to simulate random events.

public key A form of encryption that uses two different keys. A message encoded with a public key can only be decoded using a separate private key.

random access memory (RAM) *See* main memory.

random walk A simulation process in which movement of some object is determined probabilistically.

read A term used to describe computer input. A program is said to read information from the keyboard or a file.

record A collection of information about a single individual or object. For example, a personnel record contains information about an employee.

recursive A function or definition that refers to itself. See recursive.

recursive function A function that calls itself, either directly or indirectly.

relational operator A comparison between values that returns true or false (e.g., $<$, $<=, ==, >=, >, !=$).

reserved words Identifiers that are part of the built-in syntax of a language.

resolution The number of pixels on a graphics screen. Usually expressed as horizontal by vertical (e.g., 640x480).

scope The area of a program where a given variable may be referenced. For example, variables defined in functions are said to have local scope.

script Another name for a program. Usually used to refer to a relatively simple program written in an interpreted language.

search The process of finding a particular item in a collection.

secondary memory Generic term referring to nonvolatile storage devices such as hard disks, floppy disks, magentic tapes, CD-ROMs, DVDs, etc.

seed The value used to start generation of a pseudorandom sequence.

selection sort An n squared time sorting algorithm.

self parameter In Python, the first parameter of a method. It is a reference to the object to which the method is being applied.

semantics The meaning of a construct.

sentinel A special value used to signal the end of a series of inputs.

sentinel loop A loop that continues until a special value is encountered.

short-circuit evaluation An evaluation process that returns an answer as soon as the result is known, without necessarily evaluating all of its subexpressions. In the expression (True or isover()) the isover() function will not be called.

signature Another term for the interface of a function. The signature includes the name, parameter(s), and return value(s).

simulation A program designed to abstractly mimic some real-world process.

simultaneous assignment A statement that allows multiple variables to be assigned in a single step. For example, x,y = y,x swaps two variables.

slicing Extracting a subsequence of a string, list, or other sequence object.

software Computer programs.

sorting The process of arranging the items in a sequence into a pre-determined ordering.

source code The text of a program in a high-level language.

spiral design Creating a system by first designing a simplified prototype and then gradually adding features.

statement A single command in a programming language.

step-wise refinement The process of designing a system by starting with a very high-level, abstract description and gradually adding in details.

string A data type for representing a sequence of characters (text).

structure chart *See* module hierarchy chart.

subclass When one class inherits from another, the inheriting class is called a subclass of the class from which it inherits.

substring A sequence of contiguous characters inside a string. *See* slicing.

superclass A class which is being inherited from.

syntax The form of a language.

Tkinter The Standard GUI framework that comes with Python. The graphics.py module used in this book is built on Tkinter.

top-down design The process of building a system by starting with a very high-level algorithm that describes a solution in terms of subprograms. Each subprogram is then designed in turn. Also called step-wise refinement or functional decomposition.

truth table A table showing the value of a Boolean expression for all possible combinations of values of its subexpressions.

tuple A Python sequence type that acts like an immutable list.

unary An operator that acts on a single operand.

unicode An alternative to ASCII that encodes characters from virtually all of the world's written languages. Unicode is designed to be ASCII-compatible.

unit testing Trying out a component of a program independent of other pieces.

unpack In Python, the assignment of items in a sequence into independent variables. For example, a list or tuple of two values can be unpacked into the variables like this: x,y = myList.

variable An identifier that labels a value for future reference. The value of a variable can be changed through assignment.

widget A user interface component in a GUI.

write The process of outputting information. For example, data is said to be written to a file.

Index